SAVING *the* WHITE LIONS

Also by Linda Tucker

Mystery of the White Lions: Children of the Sun God

Praise for *Mystery of the White Lions*

"Linda Tucker has done a great job of chronicling the whole story and mythology of these sacred animals. . . . Through understanding the White Lion we will understand ourselves and our great role in the chain of being."

—Deepak Chopra

"An entrancing story, told by a rare individual . . . a phenomenal book that comes at a critical time in environmental history."

—Dr. Ian Player, internationally renowned conservationist

SAVING *the* WHITE LIONS

One Woman's Battle for Africa's Most Sacred Animal

LINDA TUCKER

Foreword by Andrew Harvey

North Atlantic Books
Berkeley, California

Published by
North Atlantic Books
P.O. Box 12327
Berkeley, California 94712

Cover image: still from video clip, by Rijk Keyser, of Linda Tucker with Marah at nine months
Cover design by Jasmine Hromjak and Suzanne Albertson
Book design by Suzanne Albertson

Printed in the United States of America

Saving the White Lions: One Woman's Battle for Africa's Most Sacred Animal is sponsored by the Society for the Study of Native Arts and Sciences, a nonprofit educational corporation whose goals are to develop an educational and cross-cultural perspective linking various scientific, social, and artistic fields; to nurture a holistic view of arts, sciences, humanities, and healing; and to publish and distribute literature on the relationship of mind, body, and nature.

North Atlantic Books publications are available through most bookstores. For further information, visit our website at www.northatlanticbooks.com or call 800-733-3000.

Library of Congress Cataloging-in-Publication Data

Tucker, Linda, 1963–
Saving the white lions : one woman's battle to save Africa's most sacred animal / Linda Tucker ; foreword by Andrew Harvey.
pages cm
Summary: "White lion conservationist Linda Tucker describes her perilous struggle to protect the sacred white lion from the merciless trophy-hunting industry"— Provided by publisher.
ISBN 978-1-58394-605-3
1. Lion—Conservation—South Africa. 2. Lion—Conservation—Africa, Southern. 3. South Africa—Social life and customs—20th century. I. Title.
QL737.C23T757 2013
599.7570968—dc23

2012043019

1 2 3 4 5 6 7 8 9 VERSA 18 17 16 15 14 13

Printed on recycled paper

For Marah

Author's Note

WHEREVER POSSIBLE, this is my most accurate account of events, allowing for the occasional adjustment in date or fact to assist the flow of the narrative. In certain cases, names have been changed to protect the individuals involved, and occasionally, identities have been combined, as in the case of Zeus, whose identity is a composite of two lions.

A percentage of the proceeds of this book is donated to the Global White Lion Protection Trust to ensure the White Lions' survival in their natural endemic habitat.

Acknowledgments

My heartfelt thanks to the many lionhearted people who have made this book possible. First and foremost, Jason A. Turner, my partner, the lion ecologist who dedicated his life and expertise to protecting the White Lions through groundbreaking scientific research and by ensuring this rare animal's reintroduction into its endemic habitat. Jen and Pat Turner for their unconditional support at all times. My sister Mae and my family for their unwavering enthusiasm and support for my cause throughout the years.

Sheryl Leach and Mireille Vince, my godmother, for supporting the foundation of the White Lion sanctuary and heritage lands, while also providing the "ransom money" to free the most sacred animals on Earth. Ray and Liz Vince for assisting me to build on these foundations. Udo and Angela Neumann, generous benefactors who have helped me secure more sacred White Lion heritage lands. Jane McGregor and Ileen Maisel, Hollywood experts who read the earliest draft of this book and helped me translate my life's story into a motion picture.

Organizations and individuals such as Howard Rosenfield, Martin Bornman, Brad Laughlin, Leslie-Temple Thurston (Corelight), Maurice Fernandez, Ruth Underwood, Jen Gardy, Mike Booth (Aurasoma), Gillian Keane (Dandelion Trust), Vance Martin (Wild Foundation), Stephen Pomeroy (Remarkable Group), Stephen Leigh (Leigh Group), Diane Berke (OneSpirit), Jim and Claire Morrison

(Wisdom University), Robert Powell, Karen Rivers (Sophia Foundation), Jeremy Ball, Kari Noren-Hoshal, Dorothy Shields, Jill Angelo, and Carol Pepper—leading lights among the many who have supported this book and its principles in establishing a safe haven for the White Lions in their natural and spiritual homelands.

There are many people who have selflessly assisted my conservation and community upliftment work. Among them, my particular thanks goes to the advisors of the Global White Lion Protection Trust, Dr. Ian Player, Philippa Hankinson, Don MacRobert, Paul Saayman, Harold Posnik, Marianne van Wyk, Coenraad Jonker, Princess Irene of the Netherlands, Advocate Nkosi Phathekile Holomisa, member of parliament Mninwa Mahlangu, Hosi Solly Sekhororo, Prince Jan and Princess Kabelo Chiloane, and other traditional leaders in South Africa. I would like to acknowledge with eternal gratitude, among the many indigenous elders from other continents who have given their approval to the content of these pages: Dr. Apela Colerado (Oneida people, Hawaii) retired High Chief Francois Paulette (Dene people, Canada), Dr. E. Richard Atleo (Nuu-chah-nul people, Canada), Mother Moon (Chippewa people, Ojibwa Nation, Native America), Jan Si Ku (Ku Koi San people, southern Africa), Angaangaq Lyberth (Inuit people, Greenland), and Ilarion lmerculieff (Aleut people, Alaska). I will always be indebted to the many shamans, primarily Maria Khosa, Credo Vusamazula Mutwa, Baba Mathaba, Selby Gumbi, Mathabi Nyedi, Wilberforce Maringa, and others, who have lent an authentic voice to the protection of the White Lions as a sacred animal of global importance. Wynter Worsthorne, Anna Breytenbach, Amelia Kinkade, Jackie Freemantle, Hazel Jeannes, and others who have supported this project and its principles by upholding and practicing responsible and loving animal communication techniques on White Lion territories. Yolandi van Jaarsveld, Karen-Jane Dudley, Connie Neubold, Berit Brusletto, Alison Effting, Jane Bell, Steffie Betts, Wendy Hardie, Linda Hall, Kathy Pierce, Mary Selby,

Lianne Cox, Sharon Brett, Michelle Stewart, Stella Horgan, and the extended pride of dedicated lioness-like ladies who support this project from different corners of the globe. Nelson Mathebula, Nelias and Winnah Ntete, Amon Mashile, and Patrick Mkansi, the security officers, and our whole team and staff who serve the protection of the White Lions on the ground. Rob Thompson, Chris Job, Lindie Serrurier, Leander Gaum, Peter Rutsche, and the many dedicated envirolawyers who have generously given their time and expertise to the White Lion cause. A battle-weary thank you to the many individuals and organizations who have united over many years in campaigning for the abolishment of canned hunting, primary among them Greg Mitchell, Gareth Patterson, Karen Trendler, Paul Hart, Greg McKewen, and Mike Cadman.

Of all the zoos around the world holding White Lions in captivity, I wish to thank Ouwehans Zoological Foundation in Holland for following ethical principles and putting significant funds back into the conservation of this critically endangered animal in the wild.

As you will note, this is no longer "one woman's battle." There are many more who have played an important part, made a donation, written a letter of support—and still remain unnamed.

Finally, my very special thanks to Andrew Harvey, a dear friend and fellow Sacred Activist, who introduced this book to my publishers, and to Douglas Reil, Wendy Taylor, Elizabeth Kennedy, and the whole team at North Atlantic Books and Random House for seeing the true value of the White Lions, and for taking my message to the world.

Contents

Foreword

DURING THE LAST THREE DECADES, more and more of us have begun to understand that unless the human race listens to the voices of the first world—the voices, that is, of those original indigenous cultures that live in naked and reverent intimacy with nature—it will continue in its suicidal and matricidal path of destruction and die out. These voices still speak to us in those tribal cultures that have weathered tragic odds to survive into the modern era—in, for example, the Achuar of Ecuador, the Kogi of Columbia, the Aborigines of Australia, the Hopi and Navaho, the Eskimo of the Arctic Circle, and the Tsonga and Sepedi of South Africa, which venerate the White Lions as "Star-Beings," radiating by their presence a power of love and wisdom that keep alive the soul of Africa and the world.

What do these voices have to tell us that we so deeply need to hear? They tell us of our essential, primordial, interbeing with nature; they tell us of the mystery of the creation of which we are part, which they know to be everywhere sustained by and saturated with divine presence; they tell us of the laws of profound respect for all life that should govern our relationship with all sentient beings at all times; they tell us of a great all enveloping peace that is the birthright of those who obey this law; they tell us of the urgency of humility before the majesty of the universe; they tell us, again and again, of the depth of our responsibility as human beings to be wise guardians, and not stonehearted destroyers, of the natural world.

When Oren Lyons, Chief of the Onondaga, was invited to address the United Nations in 1977, he said, speaking on behalf of all the indigenous traditions:

> Power is not manifested in the human being. True power is in the Creator. If we continue to ignore the message by which we exist and we continue to destroy the source of our lives, then our children will suffer. . . . I must warn you that the Creator made us all equal with one another. And not only human beings, but all life is equal. The equality of our life is what you must understand and the principle by which you must continue on behalf of the future of this world.

Oren Lyons then paused, scanned row after row of suited diplomats before him, and continued:

> I do not see a delegation for the four-footed. I see no seat for the eagles. We forget and we consider ourselves superior, but we are after all a mere part of the Creation. And we must continue to understand where we are. And we stand between the mountain and the ant, somewhere and there only, as part and parcel of the Creation. It is our responsibility, since we have been given the minds to take care of these things. The elements and the animals, and the birds, they live in a state of grace. They are absolute; they can do no wrong. It is only we, the two-legged, that can do this. And when we do this to our brothers, to our own brothers, then we do the worst in the eyes of the Creator.

It is this message of the "voices of the first world" that echoes throughout Linda Tucker's heroic and magnificent book and radiates from the divine presence of the White Lions who Linda has risked her life, again and again, to protect. I know of no other book in which the poignant and devastating urgency of this message for our survival is more clearly and vividly embodied. As a sophisticated and Cambridge-trained white woman, chosen by the African shamanic tradition to be the guardian of the White Lions and instructed by many of its greatest luminaries, such as Credo Mutwa, Linda is, in her being and witness, a unique bridge between the "first world" and ours—one whose testimony and vision we ignore at our peril.

As any reading of this tremendous book will make clear, however, getting this message through to a world paralyzed by denial and addicted to corporate bottom-line fundamentalism is an exhausting and often dangerous business, because it challenges not only the arrogance of modern materialism, but also the anthropocentric hubris of the mystical and religious systems by which we largely live, and the lucrative systems of destruction of nature that our whole way of life corruptly thrives on. To give your life, as Linda Tucker has done, to be a champion of the divine reality of nature and the rights of all animals to live in security and peace at a moment of such genocidal rape of nature is to put yourself directly in the firing line of the darkest forces on Earth, with often very little to rely on except your own deepest convictions and the mysterious power of a divine grace that continues to will the birth of a new humanity out of a growing, and exploding, global dark night.

I have known Linda Tucker now for five years, visited her and her beloved partner Jason Turner many times in Timbavati, taught with Linda both in South Africa and the United States, and have been humbled and permanently amazed by the force and splendor of the message of unity and love that the White Lions, by the grandeur of their presence and the divine transmission embodied in them, are giving the world. Linda's passion, dedication, total commitment to her cause, and humble wise heroism inspire me at the deepest level and show me what sacred activism in practice looks and feels like, and demands. Linda is destined, I am convinced, to be a figure on the world stage such as Jane Goodall, or Desmond Tutu—someone whose eloquence and sheer force of lived conviction can move millions to see the creation with fresh eyes and act on its behalf.

The wonder of this book—Linda's first volume of autobiography—is that it can be read on many interlinked levels: as a thrilling adventure story, as an account of radical sacred activism in grueling and dangerous practice, and as a profound and deeply moving unfolding of a sometimes brutal but finally revelatory shamanic initiation into the glory of the cosmos. In her telling of her story, Linda is fiercely honest about her own struggles and mistakes, the agonies and disappointments she has had continually to face in the pursuit of her mission, and about the vicious ruthlessness of the powers that have to be confronted without illusion if the human race is to have a chance of surviving our current world crisis. And yet, for all Linda knows and has endured and suffered, no one reading this book could fail to be galvanized by the diamantine hope that shines from its pages, and the noble, passionate love of the creation in general and the White Lions in particular that inform everything that Linda does.

This is a great, blazing, lionhearted book by a great warrior woman of our times, and anyone who comes to it with an open heart and humble mind will be not only deeply inspired but also challenged to wake up to the immensity of what now confronts the creation, and to do whatever possible to put love into action—calmly, persistently, urgently, before it is too late—to birth a new world.

As Rumi wrote, "You have been weak as milk, now become jungle lions. The greatest adventure of all awaits you."

—Andrew Harvey
January 2013

CHAPTER 1

Survival in the Bushveld

IN NOVEMBER 1991, A BRUSH WITH DEATH changed the course of my life.

On a moonless night in the African springtime, my husband John and I found ourselves back in Timbavati, a regular haunt of my childhood. A group of us—eight friends and family members including John and myself—had driven out into the night from a remote tented camp in the middle of the bushveld wilderness, hoping to find a lioness who had just given birth. A rare genetic code in the golden prides in this area occasionally produces a cub with pure white coloring, and we hoped we might have a chance to see such a rarity.

Nothing could be more different from the world I had been inhabiting—the fashion jungles of Paris, Milan, and London, where the only lions I knew were frozen in marble and bronze in city squares, woven in fashionable designer clothing, or live but caged and roaring plaintively from the zoological gardens in city centers.

In my years in the European glamour industry, Africa always haunted my dreams. Now, back for a holiday, my African dream—or nightmare, rather—was about to come true. As our low, open-backed Land Rover crossed the reserve in the pitch dark, we suddenly hit a tree stump. The steering column was busted, and we were stranded in the black of night, with a nonfunctional radio and a fast-fading spotlight attached to the vehicle's battery. We had no means of attracting help, but we did manage to attract the attention of the nearby pride of agitated lions.

Lions are nocturnal predators: they are programmed to hunt and kill at night; so my intrepid ranger friend Leonard, who'd gotten us into this predicament, assessed the gravity of the situation. The pride comprised as many as twenty-four members, including a coalition of five males who were notorious in the region—particularly a large and irritable individual known as Stompie. This male lion's tail had been ripped off in a territorial fight; gangrene was steadily making its way up his stump and would eventually be agonizing and fatal. So he was known for his aggression toward humans and vehicles. I'm still not sure how many of the five dominant males were present that night; it was impossible to tell, but male and female lions were all around us—snarling. A flash of our spotlight seemed to pick out the imposing figure of either Stompie or the largest of the five males, Ngwazi.

Either way, our situation was precarious. This was in the days before game lodges had been established in that wilderness region, so lions were neither familiar with nor habituated to humans. Today, many tourists in open safari vehicles mistakenly think lions are placid, especially during daylight hours when they're fast sleep. In most of Africa's wildlife reserves nowadays, lions are accustomed to daily visits by guided guests in open vehicles, and the big cats tend to cast a lazy if watchful eye. But make no mistake, they are fully aware of the presence of each and every one of these tourists—and if humans do something unusual, such as suddenly stand up or dismount from their vehicles, lions may instantly revert to their predatory instincts. Consequently, there have been a number of grisly incidents in safari parks, in large part due to human ignorance.

Surrounded by sinister, prowling felines in the undergrowth, we knew that if we remained cool-headed and sat calmly—possibly for days on end, or until such time as the lions dispersed—we'd probably be safe. But in the darkened confusion, we couldn't tell which lion was where. And while everyone knows what it feels like to be alone and scared of the dark, group hysteria is something different—more primal and archetypal, something infinitely harder to manage than private terror. For our desperate group, it was almost more than we could do to stay in our seats. The smell of fear in that open vehicle was overwhelming. And indeed, just then, the woman next to me began calling out for help, a pitiful sound in the African wilderness. The camp was only a few kilometers away, but between our captive place in the middle of the African bushveld and that safe haven lay near-certain death. In our shared panic, we humans were now behaving like prey, meat in an open butcher's shop.

Unable to handle the fear, Rosie, the plump Swiss woman in the seat behind our driver, started screaming—what a fatally flawed move. I remember the instant response of snarls and low growls that issued back from the bushes. Leonard snapped at Rosie to sit down, to keep calm, but he had lost command of the group. His own nerves were shot. As he shouted, the growls came closer. There was a shuffle in the bushes on one side of the vehicle, and the spotlight's beam picked out a pair of fiery eyes. Then Mae, my sister, gave a cry on the other side of the vehicle, and the swinging spotlight picked out another pair of angry eyes, then another pair, and another. The predators were everywhere! It was terrifying beyond my worst imaginings. We only had twenty minutes of battery life left before darkness swallowed us whole. I realized then that the only thing worse than seeing man-eaters crouched in predatory mode, ready to spring, was the creeping thought that the spotlight was about to die. I'd see nothing at all. Nothing. Just pitch blackness, knowing nocturnal predators, with their perfect night vision, were watching me.

We had no way out. One or more of us was destined to die that night, devoured in front of everyone else's terrified eyes. Looking back, I realize we should have known better. We had invaded their sacred space; but at the time all we could think of was *they* were attacking *us!* Even if I were destined to be a survivor, I couldn't imagine living with this ghoulish memory for the rest of my life . . . horror of all horrors.

But then something happened that no one could ever have anticipated.

A woman appeared. She was walking on foot, in the dark night without a flashlight, through the bush, right into the pride of lions. Unbelievably, she was carrying a small baby on her back. She was an indigenous woman draped in tribal fabric, and she walked very slowly, as if in a trance. Hearing our cries of panic in the bushveld, she had come to our rescue.

The eight of us sat spellbound in the Land Rover, watching this woman make her way with mesmerizing, slow steps toward us. With the infant on her back, she was accompanied by a small boy and girl, whom she was leading through the jaws of death. But a calm had descended upon the lions. The snarling and growls ended abruptly, replaced with a deathly silence.

She carried no lantern to light her passage, but it was as if she held a burning flame. Instantly, that flame transformed fear into courage, and the entire scenario changed in a flash. Once she reached us, she climbed into the vehicle without a word. Then she turned her face to give me a stare I'll never forget, sitting in silence in the seat in front of me. She may have said something in Tsonga, which was incomprehensible to me. Then she passed on this flame of courage. I was numb with confusion, but I watched it ignite the man in front of me, who just moments before had been stricken with fear, like the rest of us.

Suddenly heroic, this man, a dark and silent Afrikaner, my sister's boyfriend at the time, climbed down from the open jeep, leaving the only gun behind with us. Clutching a wheel spanner in one hand, Theuns returned on the route that the woman herself had taken, walking right through the lion-infested bushveld. Miraculously, he arrived safely back at the camp, where he managed to start up a spare vehicle; he then came to retrieve us from our dreadful circumstances.

After the events that night, my sister said she'd marry him, and they are still happily married today. Theuns had saved us. We owed our lives to him, and to the other true heroine of the story—that amazing woman who risked not only her life, but also the lives of her grandchildren, to come to our rescue.

CHAPTER 2

Accepting My Destiny

After that night, I returned to my superficial world of marketing and advertising in Europe's fashion centers, but every step I took felt like walking in someone else's shoes. I'd been drifting through life, but now my former existence had been reduced to trappings, to exterior casing. My disillusionment mounted day after day, every day, intensifying the emptiness I felt under the facade I showed to the outside world. When it came to my profession, I no longer enjoyed the thrill of leading trends, playing with people's minds, manipulating them into buying products they didn't need or really want. And personally, in my own everyday existence, I could no longer endure the hollow sense of barely living, all the while consuming—eating, buying, spending, utilizing, wasting—and giving nothing back.

Despite my disenchantment, I continued to resist my true calling—I was wrestling with the challenges and implications of leaving my old, familiar, apparently safe world. While I tried to suppress my fear of the unknown, my life looked more and more meaningless.

Like a slow-burning fuse lit by the mysterious woman on that dark night, a quantum shift was waiting, and finally—three years later—it exploded. By this time, I was suicidally depressed. Nothing in my previous life made sense any longer. In a state of physical and mental burnout, I was forced to face the revelation that my glamorous existence was a farce. I was living a lie. Utterly despairing, I came to the revelation that to follow my own truth, I had to leave everything behind—without any guarantees.

It had been three years of confusion and resistance since my dramatic rescue when I finally made an overnight decision to give up everything: my career, my city life, my house and all its paraphernalia, and my marriage and all its failings. Finally, I was prepared to return to the Timbavati wilderness of my childhood to find that heroic woman who had saved my life. This—at last—was my destiny.

After tracking Leonard down again, and then going from one local Tsonga person to the next, I finally found her. Her name, I learned, was Maria Khosa, but she had another title: Lion Queen of Timbavati. People traveled great distances in rickety public buses and on foot on long dusty roads in order to seek her healing. When I finally found her, Maria spoke wryly in her native Tsonga tongue.

"Huh! It took *you* a long time to wake up!" she said through a translator.

Maria was a beautiful woman, with a powerful physique, draped in colored beads. Her eyes were piercing, but one was murky blue in color, since a cobra had spat into it, activating her shamanic inner sight. She was somewhere between sixty and seventy, yet seemed ageless. I soon realized that she didn't view time the way I did, and didn't count her years.

She was a *sangoma,* a medicine woman or traditional healer, and a queen of lion warriors. She hailed from an ancient lineage of lion shamans or high priests who were initiated in the knowledge and the way of the lion, and she herself regarded these kings and queens of animals as her beloved family. Indigenous people throughout the region revered her for her wisdom and healing abilities, yet I discovered her in living conditions that were humble to the point of poverty. I found her in staff barracks of sorts, without easy access to water or ablution facilities, her only income derived from working as a house cleaner and not from her healing arts, which she practiced without charge. In bygone times, she would have been advisor to the king. The reduced circumstances in which I found her were a consequence of the colonization of Africa, where traditional structures and belief systems were systematically broken down, and where the original leadership was forcibly eroded as Western values were instated. Still, when she took me back to her village, she was honored and respected by her people—she slept on the floor on a grass mat in the traditional way, and she was proud of it.

I knew I was forever indebted to her for saving my life in the wilds of Timbavati. With time, I came to realize I was indebted to her for so much more: for continuing the lions' work of awakening me from a life in which I was barely alive, for helping me find true purpose and direction.

I had to know what had motivated her heroic action that dark night. How was she able to walk through that angry pride of lions without harm? It had haunted me over the years. When I put this question to her, her face showed a quizzical expression, as if my question were nonsensical, and the answer obvious. She explained there are only two rules in relating to Nature: the first is love and the second, respect. If you follow those two golden rules, you will never be harmed.

Maria Khosa was courage personified, a lioness in human form. Before she came to us out in the darkened bushveld, she had spoken to her ancestors—once-heroic lion-warrior figures themselves—and they had sanctioned her passage through the angry pride of lions. She was granted safe passage, and she knew she was protected. The presence of the baby and children was a token of her faith. No one takes their infant grandchild into the jaws of death unless they're absolutely sure the baby won't come to harm.

This kind of certainty was something completely foreign to me. Never in my life had I felt sure of anything. But my emerging awareness did not come without growing pains. To gain entry into this new life, I'd given up everything I knew. And being academic and overly rational, I still doubted what I heard. I was overawed, confused by the enormity of everything being shared with me. Deep down in my soul, I knew it was a profoundly fated transition. And day by day, as I shed my old life, my growing eco-consciousness had to develop, fast. I realized that by unconsciously following daily principles of consumerism and exploitation, I had been harming Mother Earth. And as I worked more closely with Maria, I came to learn that there was nothing unnatural about what she'd done under the darkened African skies, walking into the lions' realm to come to our rescue. In fact, it was entirely natural, given the loving and respectful relationship between the Lion Queen and Nature's kings and queens, the lions of Timbavati. With time, I came to the conclusion that this harmonious condition between humans and apex predators is the balance of power intended from the beginning of creation, before we humans mistakenly started believing we're superior, dominant, and unaccountable for our actions, no matter how brutal and disrespectful these actions may be.

Through Maria, I came to learn that Nature is magical and magic natural. And that we live in a meaningful universe, where everything happens for a reason. A universe in which Nature continually provides lessons of growth and awareness, and the only appropriate attitude to this great loving, nurturing, healing, creative force is one of absolute love and utter reverence.

As Lion Queen of Timbavati, Maria taught me that the White Lions are the holiest animals on the African continent, and consequently, that to harm a White Lion is to harm the land, to kill a White Lion is to kill the soul of Africa.

Maria and I spent the next few years together, and I learned the ways of lion shamanism from my lionhearted teacher. In uncovering layer upon layer of the mystery behind these rare, elusive creatures, I came to learn that the ancient Tsonga name of Timbavati means "the place where something angelic came down to Earth from the heavens." Furthermore, *tsimba* means "lion," and *vati* means "to come down," so *timbavati* could be translated as "place where the angelic lions came down," or "place where the starlions came down." By the time I met up with Maria, the tragedy was that Africa's most holy animals, the White Lions, had disappeared into the realms of myth and mystery. None now roamed the bushveld plains of Timbavati. In fact, unbeknownst to our terrified group stranded on that dark night in 1991, we had been in the presence of the last sacred White Lion cub, born that very night in the wilds of its ancestral homelands. But sadly, after investigating further, I learned this cub disappeared a couple of years later, and no White Lions had been sighted since.

This haunted me. The White Lions, the most sacred animals on the African continent, no longer roamed the bushveld plains of Timbavati. Here I was, alive and present in their ancestral lands, recovering and reclaiming ancient secrets about them, coming to understand their critical importance, yet these magnificent beasts were no more.

While working with Maria, I started receiving messages through my dreams and in moments of quiet meditation. Maria explained that these messages came directly from my ancestors, whom she sometimes referred to as the Lion People. She told me to record it all, because these messages might one day change the world.

For the first time in my life, I felt that my Cambridge training in interpreting ancient symbolism could finally be put to good use. So I started committing the secrets I was uncovering to a book—a book I might one day share with the world.

Nonetheless, coming from the prejudices of modern Western conditioning, I also found that reading Nature's signs wasn't always so simple. It was all so foreign—yet strangely familiar, as if I were retrieving this wisdom from long-forgotten ancestral experiences.

After returning to Timbavati to find Maria, I gradually came to accept that occurrences around this leonine woman and the rare White Lions of Timbavati had deeper meaning than first appeared. I learned from her, an indigenous shaman, that everything in Nature carries significance; one simply has to know how to read the signs.

CHAPTER 3

Ingwavuma, My Spirit Lion

OUR FIRST INTRODUCTION CAME THROUGH A DREAM—or rather the same recurring nightmare that had been terrifying me since childhood. A huge male lion with a golden mane was staring down at me while I was sleeping. Sometimes his massive visage was so close he was literally upon me, open-jawed, breathing into my own face—and roaring! Time and again, this lurid vision recurred, jerking me out of sleep—I found myself sitting upright, screaming with deep-rooted terror.

The dream had become so persistent I could no longer ignore it. However, when I shared it with Maria, she smiled knowingly and explained that of course my lion was roaring at me—because I was screaming at him. Once I embraced him lovingly—as my Lion Guardian—only then could he and I work as one. She also informed me that my Lion Guardian would now make an appearance—in physical form. What's more, she said mysteriously that I would recognize my special lion without any doubt in my heart.

"How?" I asked.

"Because he has wings," she said.

From what I'd learned of the elevated spiritual overtones of the White Lions, it didn't surprise me that these legendary beasts may be associated with the angelic lion—symbolic bearers of spiritual enlightenment, such as the winged lion of Saint Mark. At Cambridge University, I'd studied heraldic gryphon-type emblems and taken them to be symbols merely—part lion, part eagle—but Maria suggested that this mythical creature would soon make an appearance in the flesh. Not only was this ancestral lion my spiritual guide and guardian, but he was also, in fact, a pride male ruling over the Timbavati region. Furthermore, she explained my lion had long since known of my presence in Timbavati but was awaiting my recognition of him. She also informed me that he carried the secret code and would be progenitor of the future White Lions, bringing the royal lineage back to the wild after many years of extinction.

Ignited by an excitement deep within my soul, I determined to venture out into the bushveld and look for him, as soon as possible. That night, after Maria's prediction of an impending meeting between my Lion Guardian and me, I stayed awake all night. Through the long hours, I lay in the reed hut listening to the roars of the territory's dominant male. Was this the Lion King who would, according to Maria, shortly declare himself to me? The next morning, I cautiously joined the Tsonga trackers who had picked up his paw prints, which led directly past my rondavel and into the bushveld. We followed the huge paw prints, but after a distance, his tracks suddenly disappeared. We picked up the pugmarks again, only for them to dematerialize a few paces later. Losing tracks is not unusual in the bushveld, but afterward, thinking back with a smile, I realized the experience was like following a lion who kept taking wing, then landing again a little further on, before taking off again!

Hours later, we finally found my Lion Guardian in the middle of the bushveld wilderness on a gravel landing strip, where the occasional light aircraft might land, carrying a warden or veterinarian. He was a monumental male, truly magnificent, in his prime, standing proudly—with the aviation windsock fluttering orange and white behind him like a heraldic flag. My Lion had landed! Even upon my first sighting of this great lion, I felt an instant connection, a soul bond. His laser-sharp eye contact stirred a deep familiarity in my consciousness. He had a Maltese cross on his forehead, formed by a double band of dark fur from his mane. Maria referred to such beings as Lions of God, and said that they naturally carry sacred encodings in their physiological makeup, which I have since witnessed for myself. There could be no better symbol of the winged lion of Timbavati. I wanted to laugh out loud and couldn't wait to return to Maria, with joy in my heart. In that instant, I remembered the ancient Tsonga meaning of the name Timbavati: "the place where angelic lions came down." And that landing strip, it turned out, was one of the main locales for rare White Lions sightings in previous decades when these luminous winged lions were spotted in Timbavati.

Declaring himself to me in this way seemed to corroborate Maria's information that he was the bearer of the white gene, and held the genetic master code that would return the White Lion lineage to Timbavati. As the dominant male of the region, he had pride of place in mating with many females from different prides—this meant that if he was the last surviving gene bearer, he had a good chance of passing on his rare genes. Genetic laws of inheritence would suggest the materialization of White Lions not in the next generation, but the following one.

From this moment on, I had to accept the amazing fact that this lion, Ingwavuma, was simultaneously alive as a physical lion in Timbavati, as well as a wise and elevated guide in my dreams. A luminous presence in both. I had no option but to take him with the seriousness he demanded of me. Whenever this magnificent beast appeared in my dreams, I felt the ancient connection all over again.

Ingwavuma was the name given to him by the rangers in that region, but when I returned, Maria informed me of another name, one she called his secret spirit name. The meaning of this secret name was "wise one of great knowledge." Maria took my encounter with the wise one as the sign she'd been waiting for. The dream messages I'd shared with her and the sudden manifestation of this dream lion in the flesh—both served to validate my authenticity for her.

It was shortly after this real-life meeting with Ingwavuma that Maria revealed the ancient title the ancestors had bestowed on me: *Mulangutezu wa Ngala yo Basa* (Keeper of the White Lions), a mantle of great responsibility and gravity, the full seriousness of which I was yet to comprehend.

CHAPTER 4

Taking On the Mantle

BY CONVEYING THE MESSAGE OF MY ANCIENT TITLE as Keeper of the White Lions, Maria implied I was in line to take over her own mantle one day. This was an impossible thought. My first reaction was to resist, but Maria conveyed an urgency to hand over her title. I couldn't understand why she should be preparing to relinquish this responsibility when she herself held it with such force and magnitude. I was not of her tribe, her culture, her bloodline, yet it seemed there was a task to be undertaken, one of great seriousness and danger, which somehow only I was equipped to manage. She told me I was her "star-daughter," beyond color or race.

Overawed by Maria's suggestions, I fell back on my academic training and retreated to the city in order to research this fascinating lion-human bond that, in the real world, Maria Khosa lived to the full. Strangely, I was able to locate information, however obscure, much more easily than in my university days. My Lion Guardian, Ingwavuma, was present in the libraries with me, guiding me effortlessly to this esoteric information, as if we had no time to waste.

In the late eighteenth and early nineteenth century, European travelers to Africa had documented how certain indigenous high priests were capable of entering into a contract with the dominant lion of a pride, offering ceremonial beer at harvest time in exchange for meat from the lions' kill. These explorers expressed disbelief, but recorded it nevertheless. In my time with Maria, I had discovered that she was still practicing this ancient tradition, which I now recognized as a soul-contract between the Lion Queen and the King of animals. She would leave an offering of beer or *mieliepap* at a ceremonial stone in thanksgiving to the lions of Timbavati, which she regarded as her kith and kin. Then she would return a day or so later when they made their next kill, and walk into their midst, where, unharmed, she was allowed to carve off chunks of their feast. Unfortunately, through ignorance and possibly fear, this time-honored priestly practice was prohibited by the Timbavati authorities, who dubbed it "carcass robbing." Maria, the Lion Queen, must have been one of the last practitioners of this time-honored exchange, a last survivor of her lineage.

In precolonial Africa, Maria Khosa's wisdom would have guided the decisions of royalty. She would have been advisor to the most respected governing monarchs. In fact, kingship and lions have always been synonymous throughout old Africa, giving rise to the prevailing belief that the noblest of kings were able to reach the condition of what one can only call lionhood—then, being so enlightened, they were able to return to the stars when they died.

Between periods of intensive research in libraries in Johannesburg, London, and Cambridge, I returned many times to Timbavati, the place of the starlions, in order to be with Maria, and with Ingwavuma, who roamed the bushveld. I could now connect with him in dream as well as in physical form. When I closed my eyes, he'd sometimes come to welcome me—and roar his hot greeting directly into my face. He was no longer threatening—Maria's explanation had effectively changed that—and in these reveries, he often seemed to walk by my side, or sit sphinx-like at the entrance of my hut while I was taking an afternoon nap. In the city, there were moments when I felt him standing guard beside the chair in which I sat reading or typing up my research, so physically present I could almost see him. There were other moments when I became aware of his presence padding beside me on the pavement, like an invisible bodyguard. On one occasion when I gave a public talk, a member of the audience approached me afterward and described the presence of a huge lion standing beside me, as if on guard. But it was the real physical encounters with Ingwavuma in the bushveld wilderness that were the most spine-tingling of all.

On one occasion, I returned to the Timbavati region after seeing on the news that devastating floods had occurred in the neighboring country of Mozambique, killing thousands of people. It was around the turn of the millennium, almost a year after my initial sighting of Ingwavuma, and I'd heard the Timbavati Private Nature Reserve itself was badly affected. I was desperately anxious for reassurance that my lion hadn't been harmed. The rangers who traversed this vast wilderness area daily said they hadn't seen the territorial male for months, which added to my concerns about his welfare. But when I joined Maria at her village in the bushveld and expressed my concern, she told me that my Lion Guardian would make his appearance within the next day or so of my arrival if I called him in my mind—that is, telepathically. Through Maria's methods, I'd learned that the way to connect telepathically is by opening your heart and soul to another and allowing the flow of information to pass between you. The person or creature with whom you communicate doesn't need to be nearby. Even if you are separated by distance, the connection is instantaneous once the channel opens between you.

Eager to connect, I headed out that dark night in 1999 in search of Ingwavuma in an old 4x4 vehicle with a flashlight, armed only with this ancient shamanic technique. Significantly, I was also accompanied by two trackers and my young niece, Margo, a highly intuitive little girl who loved hearing my stories of the lions. Although it was getting dark, I asked the trackers to direct me to that same landing strip where Ingwavuma had made his debut appearance a couple of years before. Once there, on instinct, we got out of the vehicle and stood on the landing strip. While the trackers sat quietly talking to each other in the truck, Margo and I stood on the gravel, visualizing Ingwavuma's magnificent face in our mind's eyes, calling him to us telepathically.

Moments later, we heard a roar. We stared in the direction from where it came—then a moment later, a massive lion came padding out of the darkness toward us. *It was Ingwavuma.* In a flash, he revealed himself—a golden gleam in our spotlight, huge and muscular, his golden mane more majestic than ever. Margo and I were thrilled beyond words, while the trackers were totally speechless. Still on the runway, we didn't even try to move. We simply stood respectfully staring at him. Not too far away from us, a comfortable distance, he lay down, totally relaxed, on the landing strip. I was overjoyed he was alive, and he certainly looked very well indeed. Bearing in mind that Timbavati Private Nature Reserve is no less than 150,000 acres of wilderness, which borders the greater Kruger reserve of some 4,500,000 acres (without fences), my lion's sudden appearance out of nowhere seemed nothing short of miraculous to everyone present, including myself. But I appreciated that he responded to our heartfelt prayers and visualizations.

In that moment, I quietly committed my heart and soul more fully to my new path as Keeper of the White Lions, however strange and challenging it seemed to be. Of course, it no longer surprised me that telepathic communication should be employed by lions, since, fearsome as these great cats may be, I'd come to know them as heart-beings capable of great acts of love and tenderness. What took me by surprise was that I was able to apply these powerful shamanic techniques, which Maria assured me had been lying latent for much too long.

After this thrilling reunion with Ingwavuma, I actively started refining the shamanic techniques shown to me by Maria in communicating with Ingwavuma and other wild animals I met in Timbavati. Being with Maria, and having access to her wisdom, reawoke an unquenchable thirst for knowledge. And the overwhelming need to know more took me down many avenues of academic pursuit, straight to the answers my heart was seeking for so long. These were no longer theoretical or rhetorical research projects; they were all too real. Rather than being stuck in stuffy libraries, I mostly brought my library books with me to Timbavati, where I would share my mornings with Maria, learning her ancient ways, and then spend the afternoons reading in my reed hut, trying to make sense of Maria's compelling teachings.

Maria seldom wore shoes, which made following in her footsteps all the more challenging. It was becoming clear to me that only by reviving my connection with Mother Earth, and becoming lionlike myself, could I hope to honor the legacy she was imparting to me. For the first time in my life, the path I was treading felt profoundly and urgently *real.* In order to find the answers that had been plaguing me for years, I had to reconnect with the Earth, the stars, and the causal connection behind all things.

In my meditations, I started uncovering the most astounding connections between the present day White Lions and the Ancient Egyptian mysteries. Primary among these connections was the fact that the birthplace of the White Lions in the Timbavati region geographically aligns exactly with the Great Sphinx of Giza, humankind's greatest lion riddle. Exploring this further led me to delve into Ancient Egyptian belief systems, where I discovered that the concept of starlions *(neteru)* was intrinsic to the understanding of the very origins of life on Earth. In my efforts to comprehend where this concept of stellar or angelic lions originated, I immersed myself in the study of ancient astrology. I uncovered an ever-deepening mystery, which went some way in explaining why so many lions are depicted with wings. And as I went deeper, I found similar references in the mythology of virtually every ancient culture on our planet. Not only did the White Lions have godlike attributes, but also, many of the luminous leaders of humankind—the so-called avatars, including Buddha, Vishnu, Muhammad, and indeed Christ, Lion of Judah—are associated with lions and are themselves lionlike. I came to the conclusion that the mystery behind the White Lions was a profound Book of Truth that links humankind not only with our origins, but also our destiny.

The more I learned, the more I began to understand the urgency. As my spiritual consciousness began to reawaken through Maria's teachings, and as my own self-awareness grew and expanded in relationship to Ingwavuma and the sacred lands I was now inhabiting, I simultaneously came to see the terrible risks these holy animals face in the world today.

Tragically, due to poaching and other forced removals from their original homelands into captivity, White Lions were extinct in the wild. Yet commercial trophy hunting and blood sport continued to be common practice and were condoned by many echelons of modern society, including the upper-crust British society in which I myself had been schooled.

Awakening to the ancient magic, while simultaneously discovering the shameful and shocking events in my present day, was agonizing for me. I finally accepted that I had an urgent mission to protect these critically endangered animals. And with this realization, at last, I began systematically formulating my action plan. But I also knew that the intellectual questionings and self-doubt of my past approach to life had no place any longer. Only through following my heart, not my head, would I succeed.

By saving the King of kings, I would assist in the protection of all the other kingdoms, animals, plants, and ecosystems on Earth. And in making a commitment to pledge my life to redress the plight of

CHAPTER 5

Burden of the Lion Priest

For years, these rarest of animals, sacred messengers from God, had been mercilessly removed from their natural birthplace in the wilds of Timbavati, by the international trophy-hunting industry headquartered in South Africa. Because of this practice, White Lions were now technically extinct in the wild.

Despite this catastrophe, Maria's prophecy envisioned a future in which Ingwavuma brought the White Lions back to these lands through the secret code he carried in his genes. Over time, Maria introduced me to other shamans who carried the Great Knowledge of the White Lions, African astronomer-priest elders from different cultures who were custodians of hidden historical records, passed down from one initiate to the next in a time-honored oral tradition. Humbled by the closely guarded secrets that were handed over to me, I was beginning to comprehend the enormity of my appointed role as guardian of the holiest animals on Earth. From wiseman and cosmologist Dr. Mathole Matseho, I learned that the connections I'd been uncovering in my research between Ancient Egypt and the White Lions were corroborated within the teachings of Africa's priestly initiates.

From Dr. Koka, the wise elder and cofounder of the Kara Institute, I learned that the White Lions are bringers of light to the darkest corners of the Earth, the "capstone of the hierarchy of light" through which we can commune directly with the divine.

From the San Bushman elder Jan Si Ku, I learned that there were still some surviving practitioners of the art of lion shamanism among his people, carriers of the oldest genetics on Earth. And he himself was one such lion shaman.

Selby Gumbi, a medicine man serving the Zulu monarch King Goodwill Zwelithini, embraced me as a long-lost sister. Confirming the view that the White Lions were the "First Born of God's creatures," this commanding high shaman told me my name, Linda Tucker, means "Guardian of the Sacred Knowledge" *(Lion-Da Tu-Ka)*. In the ancient Ngoni language, *to linda* means "to stand guard like a lion," while *tu-ka* means "the spirit of wisdom." My destiny was not only to protect the White Lions but also to guard over their sacred spiritual wisdom. My soul plan was written in my very name, at birth.

Baba Mathaba, initiate of the Swazi tradition, had long foreseen my arrival in his life. *Baba* in African culture means "father" and when I first met this distinguished elder, seated in his apothecary of rare medicinal roots and herbs in his village close to the Swaziland border, he announced that I was late in coming forward to do my life's task. With bright eyes shining and a gray beard framing his dark face, he told me that the White Lions were his brothers and sisters, his grandmothers and grandfathers. I thought about my own family; how I had been raised a white child entrenched in Apartheid times, with all public spaces divided by race. I had felt trapped within this unjust system. I knew it was cruel and unfair, but I was simply one cog in its grinding mechanism. I imagined I was helpless and inconsequential, and couldn't make any difference even if I tried. Baba Mathaba changed that feeling of meaningless completely. The fact that I was a white woman did not hold Baba Mathaba back from embracing me as an equal and a trusted family member from the very moment I stepped across the threshold of his healing hut. He told me that a couple of years before, he had been very ill, in fact passing into spirit, when he saw a premonition of me, together with the great lion walking by my side. In this visionary state beyond the physical realms, he said, the lion and I supported him, each taking one of his arms around our shoulders, and bringing him back to life on Earth—with the firm instruction that he had work to do.

In following the mysterious trail left in the mists of time by the legendary White Lions, I was introduced to other esteemed elders from an ancient cast of African priesthood, now almost an extinct breed themselves. But, above all, it was Credo Vusamuzula Mutwa, the most eminent of Africa's lion shamans, who shared his great knowledge with me and helped me appreciate the almost overwhelming responsibility bestowed on me by Maria.

I traveled together with Maria in an old bus from Timbavati to the foothills of the Magaliesberg Mountains to visit this great man. He was a monumental presence, emanating a female and male consciousness simultaneously, as if his wisdom could not be contained in a single gender. I had learned from Maria that it was Credo Mutwa, the greatest living elder historian of Africa, who had broken the oath of silence held throughout the ages by the priestly initiates, in order to deliver critical information to humanity at a time of crisis on Earth. Unfortunately, in breaking this oath, Credo believed he had brought a curse upon himself, his children, and his children's children. And sadly, his life's story corroborated this tragic belief.

Credo Mutwa is a *sanusi*, the highest rank among the African medicine people. But I soon realized that this extraordinary man had earned his enlightenment through indescribably relentless suffering, and nothing, apparently, could break that tragic pattern. Credo also grew up in the Apartheid regime. As a boy, he witnessed his uncle beaten to death in a vicious racially motivated assault by a white farmer. Credo experienced equally brutal treatment from his own people. Like many other young Zulu warriors, he went to work in the mines, but there he was brutally gang-raped by his fellow workers. This was the ultimate humiliation in Zulu culture, intended to destroy self-respect, pride, and any vestiges of manhood. He was in desperate need of support, but instead of receiving sympathy for his acute suffering, Credo was rejected by his direct family, and then his community, which had recently taken to Christianity and regarded Credo's rape as his own sin. Even the Christian priest expelled him with the same reasoning. He barely survived the shame and humiliation. Clinging to life, Credo lapsed into a three-year illness that kept him bedridden, during which time his first shamanic extrasensory experiences and healing abilities started to manifest in earnest.

Things seemed to turn around when he finally found love. He was ready to commit to marriage. But then his beloved was gunned down in the streets during the infamous 1976 Sharpville Massacre by the Apartheid police. Bereft, Credo continued with his work as an indigenous healer and medicine man, misunderstood, scorned, and persecuted.

He was never a political figure. As a prophet and initiate under many African wisdom keepers, he upheld ancient knowledge ahead of his times. But higher wisdom was not good enough for the political saber rattling of the times. In the midst of South Africa's violent struggle for independence, Credo's private house and sacred temples were burned to the ground by a crowd of angry black youths demanding that Credo take sides in the political uprisings. Most devastating of all, his dearly beloved son, Innocent Mutwa, was murdered. Innocent was to be Credo's successor, and he'd been lovingly initiated into the ways of lion shamanism by his father. His merciless slaying was a deliberate premeditated attempt to destroy Credo's shamanic lion lineage. Credo's first daughter died young, then his second. I was with him at the time he received the news that his wife, Cecilia, had been murdered while in the hospital. He showed me a shocking X-ray showing the knitting needle that had been driven into her gut and womb. But he refused to agree that any further action should be taken against the perpetrators. He seemed resigned to the continuation of a cursed existence that would affect not only him but also his loved ones. Credo himself was beaten and tortured by an incensed mob of his own people—some five hundred strong—and to save his life against all odds, the *sanusi* had to summon starforce—the blinding power of White Lion light—to dispel the hordes. Now in his eighties, Credo still bore scars of human brutality on his body. He had survived countless assassination attempts on his life, and it was little wonder that he continued to prophecy his own death, since it was now clear to me he wished for nothing more than to be relieved from a lifetime of suffering. The gods simply wouldn't let him go.

Credo was also misled by people acting as agents, bodyguards, even publishers. He once signed with someone posing as a literary agent, giving away the right of ownership to all his written and spoken words, whether historical, current, or future. Though this crass deception wouldn't stand up in any court, it revealed Credo's vulnerability to such manipulation and his continued relentless victimization through similar acts. He informed me that much of his material had been taken by other parties and deliberately buried, as if they had vested interests in preventing truth and salvation from coming to light.

Over the years, the feelings I had on first meeting Credo—that somehow I'd known him for many lifetimes—grew to deep love and respect. But there was never a moment when I didn't ache for him and the pain he'd had to endure without relief in order to fulfill his mission for humanity. It seemed to me he carried the karma of Africa on his shoulders. But when I came to know him and understand him better, I realized there were aspects of his own personal karma with which he apparently still had to deal. Understandably, he was a deeply troubled man, a man who no longer appeared to know friend from foe. It seemed to me this great prophet was more comfortable with dark, depraved, and dishonest treatment than loving kindness. He allowed the dishonest agents to control his work, the vultures to pick his brains, the assassination attempts on his life to go unchallenged. The greatest tragedy of all was that he recoiled from unconditional love because he feared it would evaporate before his eyes, and all he could trust was his repeated firsthand experience of interminable suffering. He was more comfortable in the presence of evil because it was familiar. Consequently, there were many times in visiting Credo when I had to share his space with dark entities, hosting intangible evil, because he wouldn't expel them.

I spent several years studying with this great luminary, and returned time and time again from Timbavati, first to Soweto to receive his tutelage, and then to the base of the Magaliesberg Mountains in the Valley of the Kings, where he relocated. Historically, wherever he had set up camp and tried to establish his healing centers, decorated with colossal artworks that he himself had constructed of car parts, monumental pieces of wood, and glass-inlay concrete, Credo had been hunted down and forced to relocate. Repeatedly, his temples had been vandalized. But, for this period in his life, in the shadow of this great mountain, he seemed settled.

Very possibly because I had Maria Khosa's blessing, Credo felt safe in sharing with me his knowledge of the White Lions. Perhaps too he felt he could trust my heart, where others had failed him. Over time, and through many return visits, Credo confirmed Maria's belief that the White Lions hold a secret that could save humanity in this time of crisis. They are the guardians of the human soul, and they invite us to reawaken our own souls in order to protect our planet—and ourselves along with it. The question that haunted him most, as it did me, is why people were killing these rare and holy animals.

He said he himself had visited the Timbavati Private Nature Reserve, eager to witness with his own eyes a legendary White Lion in the flesh, but he learned to his grief that they were no more. He said he had demanded of the landowners, "Where are your lions? Where are the holy children of the sun god?" But he never received a straight answer. He quaked to think of the consequences to humanity if we continued to destroy God's most sacred creatures.

As Credo and I worked together, day by day, this great man entrusted me with the secret knowledge about the stellar origins of the White Lions, with the instruction that I was to be the carrier of this knowledge to the world: the "enlightenment bearer." His information from the oral records corroborated the findings to which I'd been led by Ingwavuma, my own spiritual lion guide, in my many excursions into national libraries. These revelations had to do with a great celestial master plan unfolding at this time—one of profound consequence for our precious planet and all life upon it. And more and more I came to see not only how important this knowledge was, but also how urgent.

It had been indicated to me through my searchings that the White Lion origins date back to a "creation moment" that took place on this planet, which coincided with specific stellar alignments. Credo corroborated this. He said that the White Lions originated from the star Sirius, and the Orion constellation (the lion-hero formation known as *Matsieng*), most specifically the central star of the belt of Orion known as *Mbube,* meaning "lion." Most significant of all in the starmap on Earth was the red heart-star of the Leo constellation, Regulus, the epicenter of the mystery of the White Lions' origins on Earth. Mind-boggling as these concepts were, I knew in my heart they stemmed from a profound truth, and my heart, along with my God-given instinct, was the only barometer I was prepared to trust now that I had committed to my true calling of White Lion Guardian.

Credo came to recognize me as the Warrior Lioness Queen, his own counterpart, as if from some distant past life in which he and I were wed and united in one mission. It was deeply compelling but profoundly disconcerting when he summoned me to take up my spiritual armament once again.

He said, poignantly, that he was history while I was the future. And he called on me to sharpen my sword and *assegaai* (spear) of the spirit . . . to sharpen the gifts God gave me—that I might help liberate mankind from mental imprisonment. He also urged me to "sharpen my natural powers of prophecy," that innate power I shared with the animals I so loved. According to Credo, the present day is the most important time for humanity—the "time of catastrophes and miracles." I could feel his bitter frustration and loneliness at having been branded a fool despite his lifetime's service to the truth. Yet underneath all the agony, I was relieved to make out a glimmer of hope when he reminded me that "a prophecy does not have to be fulfilled. It only comes about if we are blinded into believing that we can do nothing about these warnings."

Upon receiving this wisdom, I asked humankind's oldest, most soul-searching question: "Can we humans control our destinies?"

And he replied, "Of course we can."

Before long, I came to agree. This is the truth that the White Lion messengers bring us. We should not forget that we as individuals and as humankind can make a positive difference and thereby determine our future.

Credo had been subjected to deeply awe-inspiring initiations, in the time-honored tradition of lion shamanism. Buried up to his neck in sand and left out in the open bushveld, he was left vulnerable, with lions and other predators free to come to sniff at his exposed head. Had he shown fear, he would not have survived the ordeal. He held his faith, though, and the predators left him be. This was the same story as the tales of Daniel and the lion, and Androcles and the lion. The role of the lion shaman is to trust his lion-heart and befriend the lion, thereby gaining the support of Nature's most powerful creature.

It was the same lesson I'd come to learn through integrating my terrifying dream experience into real life. Clearly, this lifetime was not the first time I'd been required to shoulder the lionhearted responsibility of being the White Lion's guardian. Many of Credo's initiations seemed familiar to me as I started to access my own residual memories dating back to Egyptian times, and even further back to what seemed the earliest times on Earth. For this reason, Maria informed me that I would not be required to undertake all the same techniques as Credo's in my present life. According to her, I had passed these initiations in previous lives.

Still, there were other initiations that Maria shared with me, which were less onerous than Credo's and more celebratory, but dangerous nonetheless. One ritual entailed laying out stone crystals she and I found embedded in the Timbavati soil so as to create a circle formation, with four axes pointing to the cardinal points: north, south, east, and west. I was required to spend the whole night lying in the center of this circle, alone, under the stars, with the elephants silently passing by, like massive shadowy presences, and a male leopard rasping in the near undergrowth. Somehow, in the middle of that sacred circle, in the middle of the bushveld, under the limitless African skies, I felt completely and utterly protected. I feared for nothing. I knew that I was on the side of Nature, and Nature was on my side. Maria's two simple rules—love and respect—held sway. I had no reason to doubt this timeless wisdom for a moment. It was these gentle, loving initiations from ancestral times that would equip me for the most challenging obstacles that lay ahead, not with regard to Nature, but to humans.

During my apprenticeship, there was one unforgettable occasion when I traveled from Timbavati together with Maria in order to spend the whole day and evening with Credo. It was his eightieth birthday, and we laid out eighty candles in sandbags in his healing garden among his monolithic stone sculptures and lit these lights to glimmer under the stars. Being with Credo, the occasion was more somber than festive. I observed it was important for him and Maria to have time together, and much was shared between them of an intensely private nature that I took care not to impose on. I had no way of knowing that this would be the last time they would see each other. Later that night, Credo summoned me and took the opportunity to forewarn me that my long-term battle to save the White Lions would see casualties along the way, and I shuddered, knowing that he was unlikely to be wrong.

The next day, I returned with Maria to Timbavati, feeling burdened rather than uplifted by Credo's wisdom. One evening, shortly afterward, I was delighted to be invited out on a game drive by a friend who owned a guest lodge in the region, only to overhear game rangers say that Ingwavuma had been marked as the next trophy. Apparently, a photographic identikit had already been made up on him, as if he were a bandit to be hunted down for bounty. Immediately, Credo's words about casualties came back to haunt me. In my newly appointed vocation of White Lion Guardian, I found myself at odds with Timbavati's mercenary trophy-hunting policies like never before. Knowing Ingwavuma to be a winged lion of God returned to Earth to protect humankind at a time of ecological and psychological crisis, and to guard the higher plan of humanity at this time, I agonized over my impossible task.

If the White Lions are the guardians of the human soul, as Maria and other great lion shamans of Africa had taught me, then to kill the father of the future White Lions for money is contemptuously disrespectful not only of Mother Nature, but also of our own destiny. The only appropriate response to Mother Nature, with all her miracles of creation and wonderment, is one of loving awe. Instead, the ignorance and crude materialism of placing a price on the head of her most precious creature is a grim index of just how degraded our value system and consumer culture has become. It was clear to me that devaluing Mother Nature in this way could bring about the most serious consequences.

Of all the lions in Timbavati, why my lion? Why any lion?

Horrified, my first approach was to assess any immediate practical action I could take. I had the option of approaching Timbavati's executive committee and making a plea for my lion's life, but I knew they'd never accept my rationale about the spiritual importance of the White Lions, let alone my belief that Ingwavuma was carrying the secret code. What proof did I have? As to my unlikely claim that Ingwavuma was my own spirit guide and guardian, they would dismiss me as insane and show me the door. What other measures could I take? It struck me that I could have an urgent court interdict served to prohibit the hunt. But trophy hunting in Timbavati Private Nature Reserve is legal in South Africa, so I had no case. My best strategy would be to approach the landowners directly, singly and one on one, appealing to their hearts and conscience. Timbavati Private Nature Reserve was owned by some fifty-nine private titleholders who had combined their properties into one centrally managed conservancy, almost all of whom lived elsewhere in South Africa and abroad, not on site. Those individuals whom I knew stayed permanently on the reserve were vehemently pro-hunting, so it would have been detrimental to ask them to intervene. I had no doubt there were other landowners who were morally upstanding citizens, and who would have been appalled to learn of a hunt of the proud male who commanded the females of several prides in these territories—a lion that these very landowners must have enjoyed viewing in all his majesty many times over the years. And why? To raise money for the reserve that could equally be raised through the many wealthy landowners reaching into their own pockets for a joint contribution. These were the people to whom I would appeal. It was imperative that I access their names and addresses, even if timing and resources made it impossible to travel and meet with them in person.

Without explaining my reasons, I immediately made a courtesy call to the warden, requesting the landowners' names and addresses, but despite my desperate pleas, he was absolutely not divulging. After this failed attempt, and with a sense of rising panic, I was left weighing my options on a scale that was tipping dangerously toward disaster.

Among the techniques of lion shamanism that Credo had shared with me during my apprenticeship was his method of protecting lions from being hunted. He told me that while visiting the Timbavati Private Nature Reserve some years back, he'd been angered to discover that the dominant lion was due to be trophy-hunted. In order to protect this magnificent beast from being shot as a trophy, Credo had cast a very powerful spell. He then publicly announced that he'd placed a curse not only on the trophy hunter but the trophy hunter's entire bloodline: proclaiming that "anyone who shoots this lion would be killed by his own bullet—and his family blighted unto the sixteenth generation."

Despite all attempts to discredit him, Credo Mutwa still commanded such suspicion and awe in South Africa's white and black communities that word soon got around the bush telegraph, and the hunt was immediately called off. In recalling his success, Credo informed me with some amusement how the gung-ho trophy hunter packed himself off back to the States with his tail between his legs. It was a brilliant scheme, and I might even have remembered Credo's account with humor if my present situation weren't so critically serious.

Could I summon the ways of the wizard to sabotage this plan? True, Credo's method had worked successfully. But what if the trophy hunter had failed to take Credo's curse seriously? What if he'd gone ahead and shot his prize, only to meet with some indescribably gory death when his own gun was turned against himself—by accident, or through murder? Much as I detested the actions of such an uncouth individual, could I live with myself for bringing about his bloody end, as well as the demise of his whole progeny? My answer was that I couldn't.

I decided to track down Maria to seek her urgent intervention. Returning to her village, I felt sickened, as if I'd unearthed a plot to murder my own father. I felt desperate and powerless, having failed to identify any further practical steps toward a solution. But now that I had returned to Timbavati's Lion Queen, there was one last recourse open to me: to apply the enlightened principles that Maria herself had taught me in order to place a prayer of protection on my dearly beloved lion.

Through shamanic principles of love and light technology, I knew that it was possible to activate a forcefield around Ingwavuma, an energetic shield that would protect him against malign intention. This protective forcefield would, in effect, render him invisible to the brutal outside world.

Maria and my prayers must have worked. That day passed. Then another, and another. Timbavati reported that the trophy hunters had experienced the greatest difficulty and inconvenience trying to locate Ingwavuma. Mysteriously, he seemed to have disappeared from the territory, as if instinctively sensing danger.

For a period of time, Ingwavuma remained invisible. Trying to track him down, the trophy hunters spent days plowing through the bushveld in their high-powered vehicles, aided and abetted by the warden and paid trackers, but Ingwavuma was nowhere to be found. Eventually, a couple of weeks later, the posse intercepted another hapless lion roaming through Ingwavuma's kingdom and decided to take out this unfortunate beast instead. So the life of my beloved guardian was spared. The exco had fulfilled its annual trophy-hunting quota, and everyone was satisfied.

For a month following the trophy hunt, I attempted to get on with my life as normal, spending my days with Maria, and my evenings writing up my research on the White Lions. The days went by, and still there was no sign of Ingwavuma. Having prayed with all my heart that he'd vanished out of harm's way, I could only believe he was safely wandering the remote wilderness somewhere.

Eventually, after about forty days, Ingwavuma returned. Hearing word that he'd been sighted again, I breathed the greatest sigh of relief. However, the Timbavati authorities decided to get themselves another trophy-hunting permit. A couple of days later, they shot him anyway.

Appallingly, my guardian lion died on August 22, 2000, on the last day of the month of Leo, as the sun set over the Timbavati wilderness.

CHAPTER 6

Death of a King

Months of loss and mourning passed. My lion was dead and my heart was broken.

Ancient lion shamanism teaches, "When you kill a lion, you kill the sun." It also warns, "For every lion killed, a human soul will be lost." There's something eternally damning about this concept. It isn't the rough justice of the human variety: tooth for a tooth, life for a life. The balance of scales is a soul for a life (human soul for a lion's life), which signifies divine justice.

As for the coward who butchered my king, *I knew his name.* The wealthy American hunter paid $25,000 for the pleasure of killing Ingwavuma. I was in no state to track down this brute and gun him down in the streets of Chicago to die in a pool of his own blood, but time and again this gruesome wish filled my mind. I felt mortally wounded by Ingwavuma's futile slaying, incensed with anger and outrage. And I wondered what deep psychological problem had led this weak man to commit such a heinous act. His decision to obliterate the life of the King of beasts was a conscious decision, presumably, but made without consciousness, without conscience. I knew he would carry the blood of my lion on his soul, whether he was capable of knowing it or not.

With a burning, aching, weeping heart at Ingwavuma's senseless murder, I submerged my sorrows in astrology books and sacred texts, trying to etch out meaning for my loss. It was then that I discovered the timing of this tragic event was profoundly poignant.

The particular day of his death—that day only, and at that very time—the setting sun was in perfect alignment with Regulus, the heartstar of the Leo constellation. I knew from my studies of Ancient Egypt that the moment when the sun passes through Regulus is the pinnacle of cosmic events. In old Africa, as in Ancient Egypt, this moment symbolizes the birth, or death, of a Lion King or kingdom on Earth. The ancient mysteries of Egypt also indicate that this cosmic occurrence is the moment when the Pharaoh, or Lion King, becomes immortal and returns to the stars.

Astounded, I now realized that my Lion Guardian's departure aligned with a stellar plan in the heavens, which gave me greater insight into Ingwavuma's sacrificial death. Myth had become real, and reality mythical.

Realizing there was meaning behind the timing of Ingwavuma's assassination, I now saw that while the preposterous trophy hunter, with his inflated ego and high-caliber weapon, may have slaughtered my Lion King for a stuffed trophy on his wall, he couldn't undo Ingwavuma's holy power.

As an attempt to divert my sorrow in the midst of mourning, I dragged myself to Johannesburg to see the newly released screening of Disney's *The Lion King,* only to find the parallels played out in the cartoon version. I couldn't help but identify with the orphaned lion cub Simba when he stared sadly at the stars reflected in a dark pool searching for his murdered father, Mafasa.

The omnipotent ancestral voice speaks from the heavens:

> Look at the stars. The Lion Kings of the past look down on us from those stars. So, whenever you feel alone, remember those kings will always be there to guide you.

In the darkness of that crowded cinema, I sat and wept in isolation. The same was true of my own story. Only it was real.

In the wake of Ingwavuma's killing, like never before in my life, I began to question the nature of justice on Earth. It helped me to remember that two justice systems exist: man-made law and higher law. The former is known as *lex,* while original law is derived from Nature and is known as *logos.* Originating from divine rules embedded and encoded in Mother Nature's higher workings, the word *logos* is Greek for "the word," as in "the word of God" (John 1:1). Furthermore, I understood from my in-depth studies on the lion symbol that this first-born of God's creatures is the bearer of *Solar Logos,* the law of God and God's creation, just as the Lion of Judah brought enlightened principles to Earth.

Having myself emerged from the unjust Apartheid system, I knew only too well that human laws may be oppressive, unfair, and totally inadequate. There may even be times when true-hearted individuals and communities are compelled to rise up against them, as in the struggle against Apartheid and the uprisings against the Third Reich. But while man-made justice systems should be opposed if unjust, it is the *Solar Logos* that we humans transgress at our peril.

The *Solar Logos* originates from a primordial time on Earth when everything was in perfect balance, a creative moment referred to by the ancient Greek scholars as "The Golden Age." If we honestly consider humankind's history, we will recognize that the process of so-called development and progress—as we modern-day humans would like to think of our successive civilizations—has not altogether been a constructive and beneficial one. In fact, since this time of harmonious creation, it would appear that humankind has gone through various epochs in an escalating decline and dissociation from Nature and God, which has been likened by some scholars to a degeneration from the Golden Age, to the Silver Age, Bronze, and so on until the age of the basest metal, which is our current industrial age of leaden pollution and corruption.

In fact, this ever-declining process of dissociation has taken us so far down the path of destruction of our Earth's precious resources that we humans are on the brink of self-destructing. It is precisely at this time of imminent catastrophe, forecast in so many sacred texts and prophecies of many different cultures around the globe, that the enlightenment bearers return to Earth in order to protect and guide humanity through the difficult transitions ahead. These luminous ones are the leonine avatars, the children of the sun god. While Christ himself appeared at the brink of the turning point in astrological history, two thousand years ago (at the commence of the Age of Pisces–Virgo), the times we live in now are infinitely more challenging and, conversely, potentially more enlightening.

The difference is that in a previous epoch, the Son of God died for our sins, while in our current epoch of imminent cataclysm—the last in a series of epochs leading to the prophetic times of Revelation—we are required to take responsibility for our own actions (and our own sins) and thereby secure a positive future for humanity on this blessed Earth of ours.

So it was that my personal tragedy, and the loss of my Lion, gave me insight into the greater workings of our time, and the scales of justice that exist above human folly. I continued to put my thoughts down into the book I was compiling, and although my writing did little to ease the heartache, it helped clarify my mind.

Shortly after Ingwavuma's sacrificial departure, while still in this desperate low point in my new life of service to the White Lion cause, I was introduced to Jason A. Turner, a former game ranger and the resident lion ecologist working in the Timbavati region. He was a good-looking, six-foot-four lion man with a friendly personality and the warmest heart. It should have been easy to fall in love with Jason, but my heart was broken.

Were it not for Jason, I'd never have uncovered the factual details behind Ingwavuma's trophy hunting. The Timbavati Exco controlled any information leaking out to the public and was highly circumspect about revealing anything regarding their trophy-hunting policies. No doubt they'd long since recognized I might be problematic and had put up impenetrable screens against me, so I had very little access to information. But, as a scientist specializing in the study of the lions of the region, Jason had free rein and traversing rights to the entire greater area of some 150,000 hectares. Contracted for a three-year research program with the private reserve and its direct neighbors, Jason had been brought in specifically to determine the impact of lion predation on the prey in the region, since the reserve had an intention to increase their lion-trophy quotas. Given that I was intensively researching the lions of the same region, it was inevitable that our paths would cross.

Although I'd been requesting information and researching any material pertaining to the lions of the Timbavati region for the past few years, no one had informed me that a lion ecologist was also researching them and could therefore be of assistance to me. One day, however, a family with kids and an auntie decided to rent a camp in Timbavati Private Nature Reserve for a long weekend, requiring that a game ranger take them out on game drives. For some unlikely reason, there weren't any game rangers available for that weekend, so the resident scientist, Jason, who also had extensive game-ranger training, was called upon to help out as an emergency measure. It turned out that family was *my* family, and *I* was the aunt.

Jason and I immediately started talking about lions, a discussion that continued throughout the game drive, then around the fire after dinner, until the sun rose the following morning.

Jason was a strong-minded and genuinely committed conservationist, and he believed everyone had a right to know the truth. Since he himself was eyewitness to Ingwavuma's bloodied body being carted into Timbavati HQ, he sympathized deeply with my loss. In this case, the truth was something neither of us could easily live with.

Shortly after the weekend meeting with Jason, I returned to Maria's village to continue my shamanic work. Maria seemed to think I had met my match. She told me that my predestined meeting with Jason was written in the stars, and that once our minds and hearts united in a single-minded conservation mission, nothing could separate us. Back to back, we would fight for the same cause. I wasn't ready to hear this. Ingwavuma, now a guiding light from unseen realms, indicated clearly that this bloody incident would not be the last time an ignorant butcher would take the life of a just monarch through ego and vainglory. My only concern was to equip myself with all the shamanic techniques I might require to be effective in protecting the future White Lions. I became a Warrior of Light and took up the spiritual weaponry that Credo and Maria had set aside for me: the sword of truth, the bow and arrow of love, and the shield of lightforce. Ingwavuma's assassination sealed my commitment to protect the lions of this region. If any White Lion cubs were ever born again in the natural and spiritual kingdom of Timbavati, these future kings and queens would have an unfaltering gladiator to ensure their survival.

Approximately two months after Ingwavuma's death, Maria made an astonishing forecast. She reminded me that "no matter how humans try to destroy sacredness in Nature, they cannot! God is supreme. Nature belongs to the Creator."

She threw the bones of divination and observed with a deep knowing expression as the lion bone rolled off the mat and came to rest directly in front of me. I will never forget the glimmer in her eye as she predicted that a lioness would soon be born, outside the borders of Timbavati Private Nature Reserve, but in a place of great symbolic significance to humanity. She warned me that I must take special care not to overlook the signs. Seemingly, my Lion King had had to depart to make way for the arrival of a Lion Queen.

As the Keeper of the White Lions, I was called to return this new Sacred One to the land of her origins, Timbavati, the place of the angelic starlions, no matter the obstacles.

CHAPTER 7

The Queen Is Born

HOLDING THIS TINY NEWBORN WHITE LION CUB against my chest, I'm moved by an overwhelming maternal sense of love and protectiveness. It is December 26, 2000, the first day after Christmas, in Bethlehem, South Africa.

I cup my palm around her rounded little belly, so soft and downy, and the pinkness of her tender paws. I breathe the exquisite milky, talcum scent of baby lion. She's so vulnerable, she can't keep her head from lolling if I don't support her. The bond between us is so exquisitely close, it seems she's trying to suckle.

It feels like a revelation, the most overwhelming moment of my life. Absolutely nothing will ever be the same again. I'm filled with love, but at the same time torn in confusion. She isn't *my* newborn baby. This little lion-lamb was ripped from her own lioness mother only hours ago and will now be bottle-fed by callous humans in preparation for her future as a trophy animal.

This softest, gentlest creature is so full of latent fire. Holding her in a loving embrace, I see her blue eyes connect with mine. Soul to soul. Flame to flame.

From deep within a timeless place, from now to eternity, I make a pledge to this lion baby, future Queen of Lionesses. *I promise you I will never rest, not for a single day, not until I've returned you to your ancestral kingdom of Timbavati. No matter the cost.*

It's the end of a long, excruciating day. 6:30 p.m. I'm sitting on one of the deckchairs on the veranda of the trophy hunter's fortress-like house, sipping the cocktail he's just offered me, numb and bewildered, watching the dying sun burn the horizon. All around me are caged animals, in a concentration camp of suffering and misery.

I've been invited to dine with this grim hunting operator and his wife. The owner of the farm is a self-styled Rambo and a publicly confirmed PH (professional hunter). He was friendly to begin with but left me a moment ago to fetch his rifle from behind the bar counter; something in the distance had annoyed him. His appearance was affable, beneath which I detected a powder keg of barely contained rage.

From our preliminary discussions, I've determined he has no qualms about taking cubs from their mothers at birth, hand-rearing them to frolic about the house with his own daughters, until such time as they grow unmanageable a couple of months later, put them in enclosures to grow up, and sell them to be shot as trophies. In fact, earlier today he produced an advertisement in the local papers that pictures one of these subadult cubs dining at the dinner table with his family, under the headline:

Shoot This Lion for $25,000

I dared not ask the canned hunter, but a staff member has since informed me that the tawny-colored lion in the ad—which was bottle-fed by his wife, slept in the beds of his daughters, and sat incongruously eating dinner out of a bowl together with the family—was duly shot as a trophy.

As his guest, I'm struggling with a surging range of confused emotions. Beside me on the coffee table is a brochure of this man's pretty daughters, smiling as they hold up lion cubs, with the caption:

> Trophy hunting is conducted in season
> with excellent slaughtering facilities.

Beneath me on the floor is a spread-eagled skin of a lion as a rug, the head intact.

This is madness. Where am I?

Sitting on the veranda of the trophy hunter's farmhouse, I'm hemmed in on all sides by cages housing rare endangered animals, looking desperate and demented and awaiting their fate. There are so many cages that they extend all the way from the back of the house to the front, where they form our view.

In 1997, the hard-nosed British investigative television program *The Cook Report* first exposed the atrocities taking place in these commercial hunting operations and gave them a name: "canned lion hunting." The term "canned hunting" refers to the malpractice of raising endangered wild animals in cages to be shot as trophies. But while the concept of "lions in a can" does convey the grim notion of sensitive living creatures being turned into commodities, it conveys little of the real horror: Newborn cubs are wrenched from their mothers by the use of mechanical weed eaters. They are then hand-reared, bottle-fed, and made to be dependent upon and trusting of humans. Many are parceled out to be petted and cuddled by the public for money before finally being caged, baited, and mercilessly slain in their confined spaces.

I made a pilgrimage to this God-forsaken little town, acting on inside information that a magnificent White Lion is illegally being held captive here. Once I arrived, I discovered that Bethlehem, South Africa, is the black heart of this notorious canned-hunting industry.

Having traveled during Christmas Day, I arrived in Bethlehem early this morning: Boxing Day. I then met up with Greg Mitchell, the game ranger running this place. Greg told me he signed up for this job thinking it was a genuine scientific breeding program, only to discover he was running a factory-farm-cum-killing-camp.

First Greg showed me the massive White Lion male, housed here illegally. I met this great presence face to face through a diamond-mesh fence—a monarch-in-hostage—and, in an instant, I recognized him: King of kings, a presence of majesty and high consciousness beyond anything I've ever experienced before. His authoritative presence seemed to maintain sanity for all the stricken animals in this merciless prison. Not surprisingly, the canned hunter had named him Rambo, but Greg renamed him Aslan, after the Christ-like lion in the Narnia series. This was a fitting name, particularly as I knew from ancestral guidance that *as-lan* means "starlion."

Greg told me this magnificent White Lion was one of twenty-two cubs born in this breeding program, all tawny or golden in color. But, then yesterday, another cub suddenly appeared: snow white.

A baby lioness born in Bethlehem on Christmas Day! When Greg gave me this news on arrival, I suddenly realized: this sacred birth is the fulfillment of Maria's prophecy!

Sacredness is present in Nature, no matter how humans try to destroy it. And now, for one rash moment as I sit in this ghoulish place surrounded by living animals waiting to become stuffed trophies, I consider sharing with this trophy hunter the knowledge I've gained about the White Lions—their role as angelic beings of pure light sent to save humanity at a time of crisis. If he could only see the signs Nature is gifting him, might he relent—and redeem himself?

From my deck chair, I observe this man, marching on his stout rugby-playing legs down to his fishpond on his front lawn—rifle in hand, raised skyward. He points it and lets off a couple of resounding shots. A flutter of brightly colored feathers, and two kingfishers drop from the skies. The symbology of the kingfisher is of Christ consciousness (the Fisher King) in Nature. Watching this senseless act reminds me that the task ahead is monumental.

Is this man the mastermind behind this horror, I wonder, or is there someone or something else controlling him? I feel shaken to the marrow of my bones—and lift my eyes again to find the trophy hunter's wife, prancing toward me, past her cages of innocents, with a young cheetah cub on a black leather harness. The sensitive creature is shaking uncontrollably in shock and fear.

Greg Mitchell informed me earlier that this cheetah cub and its mother were removed from the wild just days ago. The mother died last night in her cage from shock. The thought of what will become of this cheetah cub in the grip of this pitiless animal-laundering industry wracks my body with helpless distress. I'm shaking like she is, and I need to muster every ounce of strength to control my emotions.

The hunter's wife comes closer. She's in a country-girl floral frock, with a broad-rimmed hat (Christmas being summer in South Africa), but her eyes are metallic and her grip of greeting is viselike. Having heard I'm doing an article on White Lions, she introduces herself, boasting:

"We got lucky over Christmas. You know how much that thing's worth?"

She's referring to the little downy cub I held in my arms only a few hours ago: the love of my life, the child I will fiercely protect like a mother lioness, come what may.

Gold, frankincense, and myrrh I will give to this little one, leaving them hidden under the straw of her box. But I will not make the naive error of sharing my belief with the robotic woman, staring me in the face at this moment, unblinking. She may have dollar signs in her eyes, but she must never ever know how much this little cub is worth to me.

TWO MONTHS SINCE MY VISIT TO BETHLEHEM. It gives me strength to remember Credo Mutwa's first words when I informed him of this baby cub's miraculous arrival on December 25, 2000. He announced, "Ah! *She* has come. The one for whom the African elders have been waiting: Marah, mother of Ra, the sun god."

Maria Khosa celebrated the news of Marah's birth in a secret shamanic ceremony, the details of which I was not to share with others. However, she was insistent that I speak out about the White Lions and their urgent meaning for humanity at this time. Ever since Ingwavuma's death, she's been urging me that the secret knowledge I've uncovered in my studies over the past six years is ready to be published. Now she's emphatic. According to her, it's time the world knows the truth.

Credo Mutwa issued the same imperative. He said it is "critically urgent" to get the White Lions' message out to the world, now, without delay. In one of my earliest meetings with Credo, I remember how he indicated that long stories hidden in the oral tradition of the mandated storytellers have no ending. Like a scroll from his memory bank, he then unrolled the story of the White Lions for me as it was recorded in oral records from the distant past right up to the present day, where it lay poised, ready to unroll into the future. Now more than ever, it feels that I am part of the scroll of the living White Lion legend.

After nearly a decade, my book, *Mystery of the White Lions,* is complete and finally going to press. But the story isn't over. It's just begun.

And there's an imperative now, like never before. Once she knew of Marah's arrival, Maria warned me that saving the Sacred One will seem an impossible task, but I may not falter. Like a hungry lioness on a hunting mission for her young, I may never lose sight of my goal, however many opponents stand in the way of my reaching it.

Accordingly, my focus has been unwavering, but over the past two months since my meeting with baby Marah, I've been wondering how to take the next steps. I don't have the authority to intervene in practices that are legalized in our country, but I can't live with myself if I do nothing about them.

Since I returned to Africa nearly seven years ago, Maria Khosa's training has been illuminating and liberating, but now I feel caged and suffocated, pacing back and forth, back and forth, like those lions behind bars who've haunted my memories since childhood.

And I know now that the pledge I made with all my heart to Marah—to release this sacred lioness from brutal imprisonment and return her to her rightful birthplace in the wild—is essentially the same pledge I have made to my own spirit: to resist confinement and entrapment, always, and remain forever free.

CHAPTER 8

Marah's Star Rising

THREE MONTHS AFTER MARAH'S BIRTH. MARCH 21, 2001. I now have a clear plan of action.

In the intervening period, I was busy establishing, and formally registering, a nonprofit organization called the Global White Lion Protection Trust, with the objective of protecting the critically endangered White Lions as a global heritage, as well as preserving the cultural knowledge that upholds them as sacred. The objective of the trust is to secure Marah's freedom and return this iconic lioness to the land that is her birthright. In order to embark on such a mission, however, I need a credible organization behind me.

I determined from Greg Mitchell that Marah and Aslan are half siblings, since they share the same father but have different mothers. Their mothers were both golden lionesses who originated from the Timbavati Private Nature Reserve after having been tragically stolen from the wild bushveld there.

Their father, Zeus, was also acquired in an illegal deal, not directly from the wild but from a well-known South African zoo, which was keeping him as a stud. They suspected the tawny male was carrying the white gene after he was brought to their premises with a bullet lodged in his body, following a failed trophy hunt in the Timbavati region.

It's not impossible that Zeus is directly related to my own lion, Ingwavuma. According to Maria Khosa, although Ingwavuma was the dominant male in the region, he originally had a brother. Significantly, his sibling disappeared from the wild at around the same time Zeus appeared at the zoo with gunshot wounds in him. It's likely that the zoo's second-tier personnel were colluding with the canned hunters, because an under-the-counter deal resulted in Zeus being removed from the institution one night, to an unknown destination. Having since met with the head of the institution, I determined that the director and his colleagues were persuaded by their staff that Zeus had died. When I informed him otherwise, the director expressed total surprise that the zoo's lion was, in fact, being held by third parties from the canned-hunting industry, alive, for speed-breeding purposes.

It has become clear to me that I need to gain the support of these governing authorities if I am to succeed in my strategy. The director of the zoo is a large, meticulously groomed man of Zulu descent, without any formal background or qualifications in animal husbandry. When I first met him in his offices, I noticed from the framed certificates that lined the walls that he directs many emerging black-empowerment businesses, and he's clearly collecting more. For him, the zoo seems to be just another commercial enterprise.

At each of our several meetings, the director was dressed in a different Armani or Lagerfeld silk suit, with crocodile-skin shoes, a conspicuous gold watch on his wrist, large gold chains around his neck, and gold rings on several fingers. I would have thought he'd surround himself with advisors from his own people, but instead his henchmen all seem to be Afrikaners of the staunch militaristic variety, as if having these relics from the past on his staff somehow raises his status and power.

It wasn't an easy negotiation. At first I thought I'd have a lot in common with the director, given his Zulu background. Several of the medicine people with whom I've studied are Zulu, including Credo Mutwa and Selby Gumbi, and their cultural beliefs with respect to the White Lions are profound and illuminating. As soon as I started sharing the rich cultural material surrounding these legendary animals with the zoo director, however, he cut me short with a sarcastic smirk. I imagined he might object to my knowing more about his own culture than he. That would have been understandable. I now appreciate that he neither knows nor cares about such things.

During the anti-Apartheid struggle, a generation's education was disrupted not only by violent upheavals in the police-occupied townships, but also by the dictum "freedom now, education later." The youth's freedom struggle, combined with migrant labor and a litany of Apartheid devastation, delivered a crushingly negative impact on traditional culture, a loss that will take decades of dedication to recover. This man, however, is no ex-cadre of the freedom movement. He is simply a capitalist skimming the benefits of postcolonialism.

Nevertheless, over several intensive meetings, I finally managed to secure a written agreement from the designer-clad director and his colleagues to ensure Marah's protection. The zoo plans to execute a police raid into the canned-hunting camp to seize Zeus and his offspring. Where compassion failed, their monetary stakes finally swayed them to take action. In the event of their police raid being successful, and on the basis of my having provided them with the inside information, the director has agreed to grant me first rights of adoption over Marah. He also agreed to a price fix for Marah, in accordance with current international trading rates for White Lions. It's creepy to think the most sacred animal on Earth is regarded as having a kind of stock market value. And it's somehow even creepier that her trading price is astronomical, due to White Lions being so rare and only found in hunting/breeding camps and in a few zoos across the globe, including Siegfried and Roy's Mirage Gardens in Las Vegas. Naturally, I agreed to the price. I would have agreed to anything. Maria Khosa—whose information comes directly from ancestral guidance, not materialistic considerations—predicted that the international trading value of White Lions would skyrocket once my book was published. So her instruction was to secure the sacred lioness's safety at all costs and tie up the deal without delay.

I am pleased with the progress but also saddened by my failure to secure a further deal for Zeus's other offspring—in particular Aslan. All my efforts were stonewalled by the zoo authorities; so I have to accept the limits of my hard-earned victory and retreat to fight another day for Marah's siblings.

My action plan for Marah's rescue was clear in my mind, but the zoological institution is the party taking the next steps, so I have to rely on their nail-bitingly slow process to run its course and pray for the best outcome.

April 22, 2001. Almost exactly four months after Marah's birth, and I am housesitting a friend's trendy upmarket apartment in Johannesburg, more than seven hours' drive from Maria's bushveld village.

It's midafternoon. The pages of my book are finally rolling through the press and my head is reeling. I've held my manuscript of *Mystery of the White Lions* back from publication for so long, questioning and doubting what the world would make of this unusual material. Now, at last, I've committed to the idea of disseminating it publicly, after being urged to do so by Maria and Credo, following Ingwavuma's death. Over the period of almost a year, I approached one publisher after another, only to find that the material had no proper place. Some publishers told me the information was ahead of its time. Others instructed me to remove the secret shamanic material since it was incomprehensible to the modern mind. They told me to cut the material by half. By contrast, Maria and Credo urged me to get it out to the world as if my life—and many others'—depended on it. Finally, after dozens of publishers' rejections, I decided I'd raise the funds to publish it myself, if necessary. At that moment, I got the green light from a publisher called Earthyear, who offered to publish it pretty much on my own terms. To me, what is important is the opportunity to disseminate a message in Maria's honor, the woman whose lionhearted actions saved my life and whose Earth wisdom changed my consciousness.

I know that delivering the book into the public domain will be another turning point. I will be required to defend every word I have written, however intimate the truths are to my own life.

My cell phone rings with an undisclosed number, and I imagine it's my PR agent, newly appointed by my publisher. Turns out it's a family member of Maria Khosa's, and my first response is to ask how my teacher is doing. Stunned, I drop the telephone and crumple, weak and defeated, into a chair. I've just received the worst news: Maria Khosa is dead.

I dedicated my book to Maria and Ingwavuma, my two most powerful teachers, the Lion King in the ancestral realms and the Lion Queen in human form. Now both were gone.

With my city friend away for a two-week business trip, I'm alone in this empty apartment. Just as I've achieved the immovable goal my teacher placed before me, she's shifted the playing field. Weeping furiously, I remember that old saying: the teacher always leaves before the student is ready. I stare out of the window at the once-familiar city scene of Johannesburg's high life, gasping for breath, knowing that somewhere in the industrial center, my book's pages are being churned through the printing presses in preparation for being bound, covered, stacked, and delivered to the world. Maria's name will live on through them, but I'm not ready for my beloved teacher's sudden departure. I want to flee and hide. *I'm not ready. I'm simply not ready!*

Following the Lion Queen's death, the unbearable months have been filled with agonizing doubts. How can *I* take over her mantle? A white woman from a Western background? So today, May 15, 2001, I am meeting with Maria Khosa's family. From the glances among her family members, I feel painfully self-conscious being her successor, without any direct bloodline or cultural link—and most of all, without Maria Khosa present to explain her unlikely decision in identifying me as her inheritor, her star daughter.

The family tolerates my presence. I've come over to pay my respects numerous times, but I feel painfully self-conscious being her successor at the closing ceremony in honor of Maria. I look around me. Not all the family members allow eye contact, and my instincts, all the more exposed and raw at this time of grieving, pick up what I detect is racial antagonism. I imagine them thinking: *What is this strange woman doing here? Who does she think she is?* Among the Khosa family are three women in traditional *sangoma* attire, swathed in bright fabrics with ostrich-plume headdresses and strings of beads around their wrists and ankles. As we gather around Maria's grave, the drummers begin to strike up a familiar drumbeat. It is the pulse I know so well from Maria's own shamanic trance rhythms, and for a moment I feel myself transported back into her presence.

The drumbeats rise to a crescendo, echoing and pounding against the earth, pounding in my head. The three medicine women's heads are rocking as, one after the other, they go into a state of trance, shivering and quivering as the ancestral spirit enter them. When the pounding of the drums suddenly subsides, the imposing voices of the ancestors come through, with greetings and blessings for kith and kin. Gathered around the grave, everyone is in hushed silence, pressing in as the three medicine women's bodies become channels for the ancestor's message. I can't understand the words being pronounced in the ancient Tsonga language, but Maria's nephew, Axon Khosa, a princely man with generous features, translates what's being said for me.

Suddenly the frequency alters, and an upgrade and surge of urgent energy comes through the voice of the lead *sangoma*. It is a new ancestral voice, one I've never previously heard, yet one of highest authority and strangely familiar. The message is so forceful and commanding it seems everyone present cowers under its fierce instruction. I wait for Axon to translate for me, but he doesn't attempt to do so. Glancing in his direction, I note he's hanging his head, as if chastened. I realize with a primal jolt that the message is coming from Queen Maria herself. None of the family looks me in the eye, and it is only after the ancestral authority recedes that Axon speaks again.

"Mother Maria, our ancestor, has said the family must support you and protect you, because . . . ," he pauses momentarily, casting his gaze around his people, "you are her daughter and you are Queen Maria's titleholder."

I STAND BEFORE THE MICROPHONE, in front of about 150 people. My book launch, barely five months after the gut-wrenching news of Maria's death, marks a turning point in my life. The Zulu medicine man Selby Gumbi, dressed in a priestly snow-white caftan with sunray golden braiding in celebration of the White Lions, has just introduced me in glowing terms. I'm humbled, dazed, but I fall back on my former modeling training to keep my composure, as I walk up to the microphone and hold it to my trembling lips.

There's a long pause.

"It seems Maria required no acknowledgment during her lifetime," I hear myself speaking boldly and purposefully, inadvertently casting my eyes to the ceiling, with its many recessed electric spotlights, as if searching for the stars. "I hope she can hear me now when I say: I owe her my life."

As I describe how much this inspirational motherly person means to me, it's all I can do to stop myself from breaking down. I feel the full responsibility of Maria's royal mantle now on my shoulders, invisible yet so weighty. The past few years of quietly working in secret with this great woman and other shamanic teachers are over. Maria warned me once my book was disseminated, my private life would be altered forever. But she also indicated there was no alternative. To do the work required of me by the White Lions, I had to take their message to the world. Now, with the family's sanction and acknowledgment, my responsibility feels all the more heavy.

Immediately after Maria's unexpected death, I had to focus on strategizing for Marah's release. I knew that once material I'd guarded so fiercely finally went public through my book, the battle lines for the White Lions would be irreversibly drawn. Already, with my work hot off the press and available in the public domain for but a matter of days, I've come to see how my published words can be twisted and deliberately misrepresented, or how my mission can be both misunderstood and exploited even by my supporters. Earlier today, my publicist, who said she'd wanted to surprise me, carted several newborn cubs to this venue, to be touted as live exhibits. I was furious. The thought of those little creatures being passed around the crowded auditorium for hundreds of guests to handle and gawk at, as a promotion for my work, totally sickened me. I intervened immediately—and no doubt made some enemies for my pains.

As for the canned-hunting operators who generously coughed up these cubs, I've just cost them a commercial opportunity. No doubt, they won't forgive or forget easily. Over this past decade, I've been lying low. Now, for the first time, as I've stepped out into the public arena, they must be gauging exactly what kind of opponent they've spawned in me. With a shudder, I think of those poor little cubs being carted back to the captive camps by angered breeders who feel cheated and obstructed.

Still, while some allies may have been lost, others are stepping up in support. Dr. Ian Player, the octogenarian world-conservation gladiator, has been a heroic figure of mine since childhood. When he agreed to give the keynote address at my book launch, I couldn't believe my good fortune. Right now, I'm listening spellbound as he delivers an impassioned speech in support of my work. His wisdom from a lifetime of conservation battles and victories gives me context as I stand on the threshold of this public life. I realize with a sense of profound relief that I'm not alone. This path has been trodden by lionhearted generals before me.

EQUINOX, MARCH 18, 2002. I'm in a procession of tribal elders circling a crystal stone circle that was arranged by Maria Khosa while she was still alive. Four months ago, I received a message from Maria Khosa from the ancestral realms. She indicated that I was to summon a gathering of eighty-eight shamans from around the globe to witness "and celebrate the birth of the Blue Star," which she prophesized would take place in the heavens on this very day.

Although the Blue Star pertains directly to the birth of Marah and is allied to the Star of Bethlehem, she said it also signifies my initiation into the role as Marah's mother, Keeper of the White Lions. Transmitted through the lead medicine woman of her family while in a state of shamanic trance, Maria's instructions for this undertaking seemed so monumental when I first heard them, and the objective so far-fetched, that my logical course of action should have been to decline. But caution was never Maria's philosophy, and if she could walk among an unruly pride of lions when they were justifiably angered and dangerously aggressive, with only the star-spangled skies to guide her way, I felt I had little choice but to follow in her footsteps in the sacred lands of Timbavati, looking to the heavens for the sign she prophesized.

As usual, given my cautionary academic background, I tried to do my homework. With my uncle being South Africa's chief astronomer, my first step was to contact the astronomical associations and observatories around South Africa, but no one had any inkling of a new star in the making. My inquiries on the matter to NASA revealed that they have no method or technology to predict the birth of a heavenly body, only its death by witnessing and measuring its process of decline. There has been no way of hedging my bets that this event prophesized by the ancestral realms was actually going to happen in our world. So, like Maria on that fateful night of my rescue, I have simply had to go on faith.

Today, after several months of preparation, I have gathered shamans from around the world, along with midwives from the animal kingdom, who Maria had informed me would come forward, both seen and unseen, to honor this moment in celebration of the birth of the Blue Star and my initiation as her successor.

Maria wanted this event to take place on the White Lions' ancestral territories, but the governing bodies of the Timbavati Private Nature Reserve run the wildlife reserve like a military outfit, with entrenched protocols and prohibitions. They do not welcome indigenous peoples, nor their "strange" shamanic practices. Fortunately, Jason has joined my efforts in putting the event together and helped me find ways to quietly bend Timbavati's rigid regulations. There's no way on earth I'd have gained access to sacred soil without his assistance.

A few days after my initial call, the NASA contact reported that gamma ray impulses had been detected in the area around Sirius. I was flabbergasted! It was from Sirius that my ancestral source told me the Blue Star would be born. This was monumental news—an occasion fit for celebration and homage—linking the African legends with Egypt, and corroborating the secret knowledge shared by Maria and Credo about the White Lions' origin in the Sirian star system.

It didn't pass my notice that Maria's message also referenced the Star of Bethlehem, which was born and observed by the three wise men an entire astrological age ago—approximately two thousand years prior—and which represents the birth of the new era. Astrologically speaking, the Southern Hemisphere is on the brink of the Age of Leo, while the Northern Hemisphere is on the brink of the Age of Aquarius.

So at this most auspicious moment, on this sacred site of great power and White Lion guardianship, a small group of *sangomas* and environmentalists have gathered to join me in the heartlands of Timbavati to pay homage to South Africa's unique living treasure: the starlions of Timbavati, and their Queen Marah, whose messianic birth coincides with the turning of ages.

Most have traveled from foreign lands to participate, not knowing what to expect. I feel profoundly humbled. Three kings from the local tribes have joined the occasion: King Solly Sekhoro, King Thobejane, and Axon Khosa, Maria's nephew and King Kapama's grandson. There are no donkeys, and we are not gathering around a manger, but I am acutely aware too of the animals that have assembled for this occasion, just as Maria indicated.

A couple of hours ago, as we trudged down Timbavati's white river sands, we passed the tracks of a leopard (Maria's totem), an antbear, an eland, and a cheetah, and just before we arrived at the site, an elephant matriarch appeared from behind a huge marula tree, majestic and calm, as if overseeing the procession. Maria said that any of the eighty-eight places not taken by human pilgrims during the ceremony would be filled by a representative animal, and sure enough, the presence of animals was all around us.

By the time we reached the site, darkness was falling, so we are all carrying lanterns, creating a glittering, serpentine procession encircling and then settling down around the medicine wheel. Now the darkness is complete. I step into the center of the stone circle, to hold the axle point, as Maria instructed me. The intense silence is broken as the characteristic drumming of the medicine women starts up. The darkness deepens. Then silence again, tremoring, as animal sounds echo on all horizons. We hold this space for an immeasurable term, suspended in time.

Then suddenly, there's a flash of green-blue light across the heavens!

It's much brighter than a falling or shooting star, and its illumination lingers several seconds spanning the heavens, then flashes again.

Marah's star is rising in the heavens. The next step is her freedom on Earth.

TODAY, THREE MONTHS AFTER MY BOOK LAUNCH, I am one dramatic step closer to freeing Marah. I'm sitting with Dr. Ian Player in the lounge of Johannesburg's sumptuous Saxon Hotel, where he is being hosted as a guest speaker. Ian has become my mentor and close advisor in conservation strategy and strike tactics, and our relationship has strengthened into a deeply entrenched support base.

Since that first sighting of the blue flashes across the heavens, the same dramatic pyrotechnics have been seen again and again in the Timbavati heavens—fifteen times in all, by seven different eyewitnesses who reported the times of the sightings to Jason. He himself was one of the main eyewitnesses, as his tracking of lions night after night under the starry Timbavati skies means he's ideally located to spot these dramatic occurrences. They took place over the period of several successive days, protracted birth pangs, it seemed, until all of a sudden they stopped, and the star itself was visible flickering blue in the skies. The unusual stellar event was then reported in astronomical journals. The miracle of this cosmic blessing, and its unlikely prediction months before the event, should have given me a moment to pause, but I've been fully focused on an action plan to save Marah.

Every day since Christmas in Bethlehem has been one day closer to achieving my strategic goal. I've only had one further encounter with my little lioness. On September 21, 2001, when Marah was nine months old, I visited her in a grasslands field while the canned-hunting camp owners were away at a game auction. Released from her cage by Greg Mitchell, Marah ran, bounded, frolicked, and played with me; we romped and tumbled over each other, again and again.

It was so exquisitely joyous; nothing in my life will ever compare with that experience of love and freedom. We knew each other from lifetimes ago: my daughter, my sister, my mother. But I remember equally the pain when I had to return her to her cage. So brief our joy, one afternoon's escape. After that life-changing experience, I returned to my Johannesburg hotel and wept, reaffirming my commitment to Marah's best chances of rewilding, to her wildness. To ensure I did not contribute to her dependency on humans, I could never again play or frolic with my little lioness.

I've shared the story of the Blue Star with Ian. He's a deeply spiritual man, but he's also a military-style tactician and pragmatist. In the lead-up to this week's landmark events in the strategy for Marah's freedom, he has advised me well. He and I did not accompany the police on their raid into Bethlehem to free Zeus and Marah, but we set it in motion through pressure on the zoo. Sitting here in the Saxon Hotel, we are anxiously awaiting news of the outcome, but there's been a stony silence ever since, with the zoo answering neither Ian's nor my calls.

Unfolding the national Sunday paper, now, I discover with a shock its headlines announcing this police raid:

Rip-Roaring Custody Battle

"Hmm," Ian observes me closely. "I've stopped trying to warn you off making bold and risky decisions. You're a living example of the heroine-savior archetype. You have to save. You don't even expect people to thank you for your sacrifices—you'll make them regardless. It's your nature. So my best bet is to support you."

"I'll do anything for Marah. *Anything,*" I respond, glancing at my watch, as my imagination ranges over the dramatic events that took place in Bethlehem, to which the papers only allude.

My cell phone is ringing. It's Saaywitz, the zoo's attorney, who was present at the time of the police raid. He describes how the canned hunter was "apoplectic with rage" and proceeded to release his lions from their cages in a frenzied attempt to stave off the zoo officials. He admits he's never been in such a bizarre situation in his life, and he recounts more soberly how he himself was "almost beaten to a pulp" by the canned hunter and was only saved after shifty-eyed exchanges with members of the local police force, who, rather than arresting the canned hunter, only warned the incensed man to back off for his own good. Saaywitz tells me he smells collusion between the canned hunter and the local police force.

Whatever the allegiances the outcome is a mess. The good news: Zeus was seized and confiscated, and his noble head was saved from ending up a stuffed trophy. However, in all other respects, the zoo has botched the raid and failed to retrieve Zeus's cubs. Both Marah and Aslan, as well as all their golden siblings, remain in the clutches of one of the most disreputable and mercenary industries on Earth.

With a sinking heart, I realize that yet another follow-up strike of sorts will have to be launched. This time, the accompanying police officers will have to come from another province, so as to avoid the close affiliations becoming apparent between the mafia-like canned-hunting operators and sectors of South Africa's national police force itself.

CHAPTER 9

Adversaries

THERE'S BEEN A BREAKTHROUGH, BUT NOW a new opponent has raised its ugly head. Earlier this month of May 2002, a second zoo raid into Bethlehem took place, following information that the canned hunter was parceling out Zeus's cubs to his canned-hunting buddies in order to disguise their whereabouts. The raid succeeded in confiscating Marah and Aslan, as well as a handful of Zeus's golden cubs. However, in a shocking betrayal, the zoo has since made yet another under-the-counter deal with the canned hunters, and traded Aslan, as well as all his golden siblings, back into the notorious canned-hunting industry. Only Marah was excluded from this mercenary deal, because of my preexisting contract with the zoo.

Marah's rescue represents the first of many impossible missions accomplished, but the future of Marah's family, and most particularly, her half brother, Aslan, trapped in the Bethlehem killing camps, remains desperately bleak.

Along with this brutal twist of fate, I have unexpectedly found myself face to face with a lethal new adversary, the zoo veterinarian. In contrast to other vets I know, who tend to be gentle people and who treat animals like extended family, Dr. Cloete is a specialist in taxidermy and animal trade. What's more, this stocky taxidermist holds a dubious position in veterinary services, whereby he is allowed to trade animals without recourse to permits or accountability, an ideal platform for animal laundering, in which he appears to have had unfettered engagement.

From that first day of introduction, when Dr. Cloete marched over in combat fatigues tucked into tiny pork trotter cowboy boots and vigorously shook my hand, I intuited it was not going to be a happy partnership. To serve his own ends, Cloete has exposed my identity to the canned hunters, targeting me as the leak responsible for the raids into their stronghold. The climate has become explosive and unpredictable, with the canned hunters incensed.

My close ally, Greg Mitchell, warned me that, by taking on this corrupt vet, I am pitting myself against an entire industry—one that kills for a living. Now that the perpetrators have identified me, I need to watch my back.

But my friends are in greater trouble than I am. Since the second police raid on Bethlehem, which freed up Marah, Greg himself has had to appear in court to give evidence on the trial. In the lead-up to the first court hearing, his house and vehicle were trashed, and sinister messages were left on his phone. Then a helicopter repeatedly started circling, lower and lower, over his house. During the last years of Apartheid, Greg was conscripted and trained in a special unit of the South African defense force (the fabled "101 Battalion," known for its black ops into hostile territories led by Khoisan indigenous trackers), so his approach to the intimidations of the chopper was to go outside and point his rifle directly at it. But he wasn't as prepared for the next steps. Shortly after his court hearings, Greg himself made a daring escape out of the Bethlehem canned-hunting camp, together with eight of Marah's golden siblings. His motives were sound, but unfortunately his plan went horribly wrong. Despite the fact that he had purchased the lions, as well as a sanctuary of some five thousand hectares to ensure their well-being, he was denied a permit to relocate them to this land.

He then spent nine months repeatedly applying for permission, in vain, with the rescued lions cooped up in miserable captive conditions, awaiting transfer. Finally, out of patience, and desperately concerned for their welfare, he relocated them to his wildlife sanctuary. Since then, tragically, on the grounds that Greg didn't have formal permission to transfer the cubs, they were seized by Nature Conservation officials and returned to canned-hunting holding pens, using aircrafts owned by none other than the operators from whom Greg had rescued the lions in the first place.

Greg is not alone. My activist friend Gareth Patterson, the well-known lion conservationist who took over some of George Adamson's famous lions after George's assassination, also had his life threatened after he published a grim exposé of the canned-hunting industry, entitled *Dying to Be Free.*

Another lion custodian, Simon Tricky, who approached me after he rescued some golden lions carrying the rare White Lion gene, and who had courageously provided some of the names in Gareth Patterson's exposé, was rewarded for his pains by having his prize lion shot with a crossbow, and disemboweled, in retaliation.

A few weeks ago, I myself started to receive sinister phone calls from unidentified parties telling me to back down or "someone might get hurt." They forget that a mother's love will stop at nothing to save her young.

MONTHS AND MONTHS OF PATIENT NEGOTIATION with the zoo have led nowhere. Today, in my effort to free Marah, I've been sitting in the zoo conference room for seven hours, in tense negotiations with Dr. Cloete and the zoo director in his Pierre Cardin suit and snakeskin shoes, with our respective hard-core lawyers on either side of the table.

At the end of another year of fighting for Marah's freedom, I have assembled a war council for today's zoo meeting. Along with my trusted attorney, I called in my most seasoned of gladiators, Dr. Ian Player, to provide conservation clout; the straight-talking ecologist Jason Turner, to provide scientific expertise; and Selby Gumbi, to represent the spiritual beliefs behind the White Lions.

My team begins in a conciliatory fashion. Ian keeps the forum spellbound by retelling tales of his successful battles to save South Africa's white rhino from extinction, going on to make the same case for the White Lions. Jason Turner follows with a detailed outline of the critical importance of protecting the White Lion gene pool for the biodiversity of its endemic habitat, effectively producing data to warn the zoo against any premature breeding with Marah or the use of fertility-inducing drugs.

I summarize the cultural importance of the White Lions, not only for the indigenous people of our country, but also for other First Nations around the globe, whose knowledge of the Earth is profoundly consistent. And Selby Gumbi concludes with a prayer in Zulu.

One might have expected that a heartfelt prayer in any language would have softened the atmosphere and united our purpose, but it's as cold and hard as a vivisectionist's laboratory in here.

It's four months since I first met Dr. Cloete, in which time he has set up an Animal Disposal Unit and declared Marah to be the zoo's highest genetic specimen. It's clear that nothing short of a ten-phase battle plan will extract Dr. Cloete's prize hostage from his viselike grip.

For him, my signed agreement with the zoo was a meaningless scrap of waste paper. First he blocked any prospects of returning Marah to the wild by claiming the captive lioness would never survive and that I was intent on "killing her." Then he began genetic tests on Marah. Furthermore, in the eventuality that I might actually succeed in winning my claim for Marah's adoption, he's embarked on an aggressive speed-breeding program to retain Marah's genetics by mating her underage. The earliest breeding age for lionesses in the wild is four years. But that hasn't stopped the mercenary vet from putting plans in place to impregnate Marah prematurely—under two years of age—without regard for the young female's health or welfare.

With Marah held prisoner in the zoo, which has now reneged on their contract after Cloete identified her as their prize specimen, the situation has become fraught and dangerous. I urgently have to restrategize. My emotions are in turmoil. Lives depend on my trusting my instincts and following my innate sense of higher justice, above and beyond the man-made status quo.

Furthermore, there is a celebrity aspect to all this, which makes the situation all the more complicated. The famous illusionists Siegfried and Roy are playing a central role in this chess game, having signed an existing contract with the zoo that gives them (the celebrities) equal ownership rights of all White Lions in the zoo's possession. Since I met with them in Las Vegas in the '90s while writing *Mystery of the White Lions,* I imagined they would assist my cause, particularly as I found Roy to be a genuine animal lover under his showman's facade. I imagined that he and Siegfried would be horrified to hear that the magnificent White Lion Thor, whose kingly image they had splashed over their billboards and publicity material to pull in crowds to their show at the Mirage Hotel, had been appropriated by Riccardo Ghiazza, one of South Africa's most notorious animal-cruelty figures, recently found guilty on two counts. I also imagined they would wish to support any genuine attempts to reestablish White Lions in their natural endemic territories, given that these regal animals had so significantly contributed to their fame and fortune. However, all my attempts at collaboration have been stonewalled by their agents. I went so far as booking a flight to Las Vegas, flying all the way from South Africa to meet with them again to ask their approval for me to adopt Marah (which, apparently, as half owners, they need to provide), but even after my arrival, their agents refused my calls.

As Maria predicted, the trading value for White Lions has skyrocketed since the publication of my book. But having advance notice hadn't helped me. A moment ago, I offered the zoo a figure for Marah, double the trading rates of White Lions at the time of my book launch. However, with glinting retinas, Cloete has just dismissed this figure as "paltry."

I feel ill. If there is justification for the existence of zoos, it can only be for educational purposes (educating children and adults on the critical importance of nature and species) or conservation purposes (raising funds to protect species at risk in their natural habitat). By contrast, a zoo run solely as a commercial enterprise to make money from innocent animals trapped in cages is not very different from the child-slave trade.

We've been in tough, hard, clinical negotiations all day and have gotten nowhere. What next? Only through Maria Khosa's powerful example can I take each uncharted step. Her loving maternal presence continues to guide my actions from the ancestral realms, but I miss her down-to-earth practical wisdom. What would she have advised? Aware that Marah's future hangs in the balance, I summoned not only my lawyers but also my council of advisors. With Maria Khosa gone, I've had to draw on the wisdom of Credo Mutwa, Selby Gumbi, Dr. Koka, and other indigenous wise men and women from around the globe. Now that my book has reached foreign shores, I've also been invited to present at a number of international environmental congresses, where I was introduced to indigenous leaders of different continents and various tribes. It's been a tremendous honor and privilege. Many of these First Nations leaders have lent their names in support of my cause, identifying the similarities between the prophecies of their indigenous people and the mystery of the White Lions.

Among them are High Chief Francois Paulette of Canada's Dene Nation, Mother Moon of the Chippewa Ojibwa Nation of Native America, Dr. E. Richard Atleo of Canada's Nuu-chah-nul people, and

Dr. Apela Colerado of Hawaii's Oneida people—all indigenous leaders of great standing and ancestral wisdom. From Kitasu elders of British Columbia, I learned of the fabled "Spirit Bear": snow-white bears born from the Black Bear species, as a long-prophesized sign of climate change. On June 21 of this year, I was fortunate enough to join Chief Arvol Looking Horse of America's Sioux Nation in leading a crowd of some ten thousand people marching for peace. We were on horseback, with the Native American leader in full-feathered regalia. This date has been declared World Peace and Prayer Day, and Chief Arvol himself holds the title of nineteenth-generation Keeper of the White Buffalo prophecies, while the wisdom of his people corroborate my own beliefs about the White Lions' spiritual importance.

Meeting with representatives of such deep Earth knowledge and standing was extremely humbling for me, but it also strengthened my heart. It provided profound support of my cause for the protection of the White Lions as sacred harbingers of climate change on Earth. All the white animals—the White Raven of Canadian First Nations, the White Reindeer of the Sami people, the White Whale of the Icelandic people, and the White Buffalo of the fourteen nations—they are sacred signs from Nature and the fulfillment of ancient prophecy.

My own beliefs were further corroborated by two indigenous leaders from the Inuit people: Ilarion Imerculieff (of the ancient Aleut people of Alaska) and Angaangaq Lyberth, of Greenland, who pointed out the parallels between the White Lion mysteries and the prophesies of their own people, which speak of the coming of the fabled Black Polar Bear. At a time when the Earth is in ecological crisis, it is said the Black Polar Bear will appear on the ice, which will signal great change but also great hope. It is Nature's sign that humanity should unite spiritually, or great devastation will ensue. Angaangaq—a short man with a long, twisted gray beard and intense blue eyes that belied his advanced years—spoke about his people's belief in polar reversal. Polar regions that were once icy and snow-bound would melt, and other places that had been clement could suddenly become frozen wastes. With a deep knowing, he simply asked me, "Why should snow lions appear in a sunny landscape in Africa? Mother Nature doesn't make mistakes. What is she telling us?"

Far from being freaks of nature, out of time and place, the profound wisdom from indigenous wisdom keepers confirmed for me that the White Lions are not an isolated phenomenon but a global one, impeccably related to our present time and age.

Recently, I received a message from Angaangaq through a third party, which gave me much encouragement. He wrote, "Tell [Linda] that my heart truly belongs to her and that I am wishing her my very best and that I am in support of her and all she does for the Great Cat—Qitsussuaq Qaqurtaq, or the Great White Lion—whose importance the world over will become known in spiritual significance."

Here, now, I need that encouragement. In a context where spiritual significance is at risk of dissolving in Cloete's callous test tube laboratory, I imagine Ingwavuma, my Spirit Guardian, standing by my side. I remind myself that I am not alone: in the midst of all my trials for Marah's freedom, the convergence of wise men and women from all over the world in support of the White Lion as a holy animal has been wondrous and confirmed what Maria herself forecast: "The White Lions will bring the rainbow nations together."

From these many esteemed First Nations advisors, I have now established an official advisory council of indigenous elders, whose sage guidance the Global White Lion Protection Trust takes very seriously. All in all, the united wisdom of these various indigenous elders combines in one clear message, which links the White Lions with peace on Earth.

Yet, in my efforts toward achieving this noble goal, it seems I have to be prepared to go to war.

Following my official offer of payment for Marah, which was rudely dismissed, I now hand over to Dr. Cloete the file with letters from many of these esteemed indigenous leaders, who committed in writing their support of the global importance of the White Lions and demanded the return of Marah to her sacred ancestral lands. Whether or not the director is interested in local or global culture is not the issue; the weight of opinion from esteemed First Nations leaders around the globe should have significant sway. Or so I thought. Instead, I see that any mention of indigenous people's beliefs has fallen on stony ears.

Cloete snaps my file closed, unread, and flicks a glance at the zoo director, as if waiting for his next tactical instruction.

Apartheid South Africa was a good training ground in resisting institutionalized injustice, and one would have hoped that since the collapse of the previous regime, people in power would be more open to appreciating the rights of all stakeholders. Clearly, however, as far as the zoological institution is concerned, rights don't extend to animals, or native peoples. In this chilling moment, I stare into the unblinking, reptilian eyes of Dr. Cloete. With glinting retinas, he's snapping my file closed, unread, and flicks a glance at the zoo director, as if waiting for his next tactical instruction.

"Excuse me, sir," he says to the director, who gives him the nod. "I need to get back to the lab."

The director concludes, looking exasperated, as if we've taken up too much of his precious time already: "We're a serious institution. We don't have time for primitive people and their childish theories."

Glancing conspicuously at the clock on his wall, he adds: "Thank you for your presentations, but my staff and I need to get back to work."

Work? War! I know my campaign is far from over.

I am reminded how contemptuously my shamanic indigenous teacher, Credo Mutwa, was treated for his prophetic warnings, so much so that when he was compelled to finish an oil painting of the dreaded 9/11 events before these events happened, no one even took notice.

Selby Gumbi and our attorney have gone home, while Jason, Ian, and I sit at the zoo restaurant late in the afternoon having a post-mortem on the failed meeting. I'd like to follow Ian's example and down a stiff Scotch, but I know it won't help. I suppose it was naive of me to imagine the confrontation was over after that second police raid into Bethlehem. I think back to the short-lived sense of relief I first felt after rescuing Marah from the Bethlehem killing camp. I had no way of anticipating that the institution itself would have its own reasons for incarcerating Marah. First the zoo refused to honor the agreement we'd made prior to the police raid on Bethlehem. Then the haggling over genetics and threats of artificial insemination began. How much better are her new confines in the zoo than those razor-wire fences of the hunting camp?

From our position at the restaurant, we are no more than five hundred meters from Marah. Not taking into account how many walls, man-made moats, electrified fences, fast-moving traffic lanes, and other barriers stand between us. Perhaps most formidable of all, there's the stone wall of Dr. Cloete himself. Of my opponents in the canned-hunting industry, Dr. Cloete has to be counted among the most recalcitrant.

Jason answers his cell phone. By the time he gets off the call, he looks ashen. It was Greg Mitchell relaying terrible news: the canned hunter has offered Aslan as a trophy on the Internet. A rare White Lion is worth more dead than alive, and Greg just learned that a Dubai sheik was prepared to pay *more than triple* the current trading value for Aslan's head on a platter.

This dreadful intel has caught me off-guard. We had emerged from the deadlock at the zoo feeling three-quarters defeated but ready to up our offensive. Poised in strategic battle mode, I feel my resistance failing.

"Keep focused *and* keep your gunpowder dry," Ian instructs me, taking careful stock. I hear his words but barely comprehend their meaning.

Sympathetic, but battle-scarred by a half century of tough environmental campaigns, he advises me to accept that Aslan would be but one of the inevitable casualties in my lifelong efforts to save the White Lions. Having himself won many crusades on behalf of Nature, including a campaign against the world's biggest mining company that would have destroyed the greatest wetlands in the Southern Hemisphere, Ian cautions me to approach this as guerilla warfare that will demand every possible resource available to me for the rest of my life.

Sound as his advice is, I'm simply not prepared to accept any inevitable casualties. Having lost Ingwavuma to the hunter's bullet, I cannot count Aslan among the dead.

It's October 3, 2003, and I've just had the most shocking news from Las Vegas. An accident occurred that has stunned the world. During a Siegfried and Roy show on Roy's sixtieth birthday, today, in the midst of a magic act, while he was instructing his white tiger Montecore to lie down, the big cat refused; then, when Roy insisted, he took Roy's head in his jaws and carried the performer off stage like a ragdoll.

Montecore is no novice. He is, in fact, Roy's favorite male tiger, who has been meticulously trained from the time he was a little cub. He was just a few days old when Roy removed him from his mother. This magnificent beast went on to perform for many years on stage prior to the incident, helping to establish Siegfried and Roy's stardom. In fact, Montecore was the brightest star of the highest income-earning show in Las Vegas, a spectacle that has drawn crowds for thirty years and more than thirty thousand showings.

Shocked, like everyone else, I've sent several messages of condolence and heartfelt sympathy to Roy Horn, whose love for animals I know to be genuine under his showman's makeup and glitter. But while I feel deep compassion for Roy, I can't help formulating the obvious question over and over again: What was Montecore's message for Roy? And perhaps more importantly, what was Montecore's message for humanity at this time?

I know through my shamanic training that nothing in Nature happens by accident. Everything has an impeccable meaning and karmic significance, if we humans are only prepared to open our eyes and hearts to the truth. The spectacle of Roy taken by his white tiger was seen live by thousands of people at the show itself, while the story is being aired to millions through news channels around the globe. So, what is Nature's message to the world?

Certainly, the unfortunate incident has raised considerable awareness. Figures are emerging in the press. There are more than fifteen thousand tigers in the United States, all bred in captivity—a distressing statistic, given that this equates to one-third of the existing wild population. According to authorities, there are more big cats in the backyards of Texas than in all the jungles of Asia. In the United States, the sale of tigers and other exotic animals to be kept as pets, or for meat, fur, or medicinal uses, is a multibillion-dollar industry. Many of the transactions are illegal, but many more are legal and equally unjust. Even those wild animals kept as pets end up euthanized for convenience, or living out their lives in inadequate sanctuary camps. Exotic animals raised by humans in captivity can never be returned to the wild, because they are dependent on humans—they can't fend for themselves and are regarded as a danger. So they are doomed to cages for the rest of their miserable lives.

Siegfried and Roy's publicity protests that they are saving the White Lions and White Tigers from extinction. But even the American Zoo and Aquarium Association doesn't buy that stunt. The AZAA has published numerous articles educating the public about the fact that breeding white tigers in captivity is not conservation. They're emphatic: "It would be different if [Siegfried and Roy] took all their profits and gave them to conservation in the wild. Because the only way to contribute to conservation is with money. Breeding just to breed is not conservation. Especially if you are breeding a genetic rarity."

As for mass-producing rare animals in captivity for commercial purposes, investigations have now made it clear that while South Africa is the canned-hunting capital of the world, Texas is the breeding ground of the world's worst canned hunters, subhuman humans whose idea of fun is a South African trophy-hunting holiday to massacre White Lions in cages.

With Siegfried and Roy sadly out of the picture, I only have the local zoo to deal with.

NOVEMBER 16, 2003. After an incredibly difficult three and a half months of urgent and focused press exposure, we have managed to stave off the planned trophy hunt of Aslan. Through some well-placed calls to trusted members of the media, the story was splashed over the front page of leading South African and international newspapers. Even with his vast ego and budget to match, the sheik shied away from the spectacle of his misdemeanor being open to public. Few people like to commit murder under that level of scrutiny. No doubt, tomorrow will bring new challenges, but for the moment, the Lion King's life has been spared.

All my focus has returned to extracting Marah from the zoo. Not yet three years old, she's just produced a litter of tiny cubs. Cloete went ahead and force-bred my young lioness prematurely so as to reproduce her rare genes for the zoo's benefit.

The situation is fraught with all that I hold dear at stake. It's not only Marah I'm fighting for, but also for the lives of her three little ones, whose genetics the zoo so rapaciously covets. A legal skirmish is raging, with lawyers' letters flying back and forth, like cross fire. However, frustratingly, I know that tactically I cannot risk taking this feud all the way to court, since court battles often last years, and for a lioness locked in solitary confinement, that's a life sentence.

Meanwhile, Greg Mitchell has been in litigation mode too, appealing against the seizure of his lions, through all possible legislative structures in South Africa, from High Court to Supreme Court—at huge emotional and financial cost. Tragically, his best efforts have failed. This travesty of justice sets the grim scene for my own relentless challenges. The law is not on our side, nor the lions'. But on the path of White Lion protector prophesized by Maria, there's no going back.

CHAPTER 10

Royalty in the Dungeon

DOWN A LONG, CONCRETE CORRIDOR illuminated by a dull, blue light, I pass rows of high-security cells housing prisoners behind bars. The strong smell of disinfectant rises from the floor. The man just ahead of me has his bunch of keys attached to his belt, jingling like a jailor as he walks. My heart's thumping and I feel a churning sickness in the pit of my stomach. In the inside pocket of my jacket, I have the secret parcel for the imprisoned hostage. One of the inmates I've just passed is pacing to and fro, to and fro, to and fro. Like fire behind a grate, there's huge energy transmitted through him, an energy that cannot be contained behind prison walls. I try to recall how the legend goes: fire—was it a gift from the Gods, or did humanity steal it? But I know for sure that these incarcerated lions, like flames burning in the hearth, cannot be owned or bought. They belong to a higher order. They might be held captive for a period of time, confined behind bars, burning and flickering, until they die. But they do not belong to us humans. The concrete has recently been washed down, and my boots leave imprints on the sodden floor. I pass cell after cell housing lion prisoners, some lying listless in the far corner of their bare rooms like coals barely glowing, and others, in dire frustration, pressing their noses up against the bars. I'm not sure I can go through with this. The disinfectant in my nostrils is sickening.

Then I see her. *Marah!* The still point at the center of the turning world. She's a vision, a goddess, watching me, wide eyed, serene, and noble behind the bars. Ma-rah. Mother of Ra, the sun goddess!

There's a buzzing tone, which prompts the lion keeper walking just ahead of me to answer his cell phone. He cannot get reception down here in the dungeon, so he excuses himself for a moment. It's the moment I've been waiting for! I count his departing footsteps as they ascend the staircase toward the viewing tower, from where the public views the lions in an open camp, unaware that the big cats spend most of their time in darkened concrete dungeons down below.

As soon as the sound of his footsteps fades, I settle down, cross-legged on the wet concrete floor, directly in front of Marah. Behind her, on a pile of straw in the corner, are her three small cubs, huddled together for warmth, peeping out with tiny polar bear–like faces. Marah is lying in a sphinx position in front of them, looking directly at me, an open expression of quiet endurance on her majestic face. I remove the crystal from its leather pouch and hold the stone up to her, as instructed. She stares at it with wide, innocent eyes as it gleams even in the dull light. Unbelievably, she slips her paw under the low grate as far as it can reach—the left paw! Trembling, I place the sand, mixed with my saliva, under this velvety paw she offers me. She takes the sand without extending her claws, drawing her paw back into the cell.

December 21, 2003. Mission accomplished!

Maria Khosa's imperative—the mission of freedom for the Lion Queen—had felt no less than Herculean. Before she passed on, Maria had called upon me to enact a powerful shamanic ceremony, requiring that I relocate soil from the White Lions' sacred homelands to the queen-in-hostage, so that the true monarch might place her paw on the sands of her kingdom once more, thereby reclaiming her birthright. Furthermore, I was required to place my own signature—saliva—as proof of my undying commitment to Marah's freedom.

And now the task is complete. Effortlessly. As if Marah knew what was required and has been waiting patiently to receive it. Marah will spend her birthday, Christmas Day, in the dungeon. But at least her prospects look brighter.

Footsteps sound down the concrete steps again. Urgently, I whisper parting words to this beloved lioness: "Not long now, Queen, not long."

The lion keeper appears at the far end of the concrete corridor and beckons to me, indicating he's needed elsewhere in the zoo.

Still shaking, I retrace my steps past the other lions, burning behind the grates. I reach out to shake the lion keeper's hand, thanking him warmly for his time and for bringing me to see Marah. He has agreed to do so without permission from his superiors, as I am now officially persona non grata. In the best of all worlds, this courageous man would himself have been the director of the zoo; instead he had to go under the radar in defiance of his superiors to let me catch a glimpse of my lioness.

As I head down the central pathway to the main entrance, I force myself not to look into the polar bear's white-painted concrete compound simulating snow in Africa's searing summer, and although I heard their whoops, I avoid making eye contact with the chimpanzees dangling in their cramped enclosure. I want to ensure that nothing dampens the unfamiliar sense of achievement rising through my body. I keep walking, picking up speed, and by the time I reach the double metal grill gates to the outside world, I'm shaking uncontrollably but totally elated. I burst through the gateway into the streets and pause to catch my breath. At long last, Marah's freedom is in sight! Not only hers, but—against all odds—that of her sacred lineage, her cubs! This counts as an achievement beyond everyone's prayers and dreams. I pause on the curb outside as cars in the four-laned traffic race by. I don't care what the drivers think; I can't stop myself from doing a tap dance along the pavement, waiting for the lights to turn green.

Sitting at the nearby coffee shop in a small park overlooking a lake, with waiters bustling around in blue turbans and leather sandals, I try to integrate what I've learned from this morning's experience at the zoo. I've washed my hands, but the smell of disinfectant clings to my clothes.

I order a salad from the elegant waiter in his African ethnic print pantsuit, standing over me with his tray. It's late afternoon, and as he disappears to the kitchen, there's no one else around in the restaurant's courtyard section, populated with empty plastic garden furniture. I'm alone.

It's probably the quietest spot in the city, but all around I hear the human sounds and sirens and horns. If this noise pollution bothers me, what must all the exotic and rare creatures at the zoo experience? Recently, a gold mining company donated over a million dollars toward the lion enclosure, hence the newly constructed parapets and viewing walkways and even the conference center overlooking the big cats. But minimal consideration was given to the animals themselves, on show from all angles in a small camp, or worse, locked up in that dungeon below the human walkway, for days or even months at a time, without the city dwellers caring, or even knowing. From birth a month ago, Marah's cubs have experienced nothing else—darkness punctured by electric lights, concrete floor softened only by a heap of dry straw.

Soaking in the last sun of the day, I tilt my face up to the source of light, trying to savor this fragile moment. Sunlight! The source of all life on Earth. I remember my great teacher, Credo Mutwa, describing the White Lions as the children of the sun god and Marah as the chosen one. Her cubs too have been given names by ancestral spirit sources: Regeus, Letaba, and Zihra. Their names mean "first ray of sunlight" in three root languages: Latin, African, and Hebraic. Mother of the Sun and her blessed children, the first rays of sunlight on Earth—still under lock and key in the darkened dungeons below the city.

With the shamanic ceremony complete, I believe my battles with Dr. Cloete will soon be a thing of the past. After two years of holding my breath at the very thought of this automaton claiming the world's most sacred lioness as a breeding machine, I finally allow myself a deep sigh of relief. After this morning's coup, victory is in sight! It's the conclusion of a carefully implemented strategy that has the ancestors on its side.

Perhaps I can at last erase the invasive presence of the taxidermist, with his spiky pineapple-colored hairdo and lecherous grin, from my sleepless nights and my worst nightmares.

Though I cannot help wondering how many surplus specimens have been dumped by the zoo's disposal unit into the canned-hunting industry, I dare not let my thoughts wander too far, in case I lose this hard-fought sense of fragile achievement.

Seeing Marah was such an overwhelmingly powerful experience. And what I'd first thought impossible now looks attainable: the Queen's return to her sacred homelands—together with her all-important genetic lineage, those adorably precious cubs. Inevitably, I know in my bones there will be more clashes to come.

My personal battle is directly linked with a greater battle for the Earth. Since I committed to this conservation work, I've become acutely aware of the urgency with which we need to take up arms to fight for what it right, and so protect what is necessary for our survival.

When my salad arrives, I decide to order a coffee to follow—but what kind? Café latte, café crème, café au lait, espresso, filter coffee, cappuccino, café mocha. I've always loved variety, but today this man-made paradox hits me hard. Our consumer society keeps giving us more and more and yet more choices, so that we live with the delusion of abundance—at the very time when our options are dying out, as we incrementally destroy the infinite wealth of our last natural resources. It's all part of this dangerous illusion, or virtual world, we humans have created for ourselves. A bubble that we all know, in our darkest moments, is about to burst.

"A rooibos tea, thanks," I say.

I savor my fresh salad as a gift from Nature, but I'm battling confused feelings. We, as consumers, have been so effective in creating choices for ourselves. Yet what option have we allowed the other inhabitants of our planet? I bleakly wonder what choice my friends at the zoo really have. To accept food, or not to accept food. To live, or to die. Come to think of it, they do have another choice: to remain compliant, or to bite the hand that feeds them. But would Marah ever turn against her human jailors or brutal canned hunters? I don't believe so. She would rather turn the other cheek. And thinking about that now, it occurred to me how few zookeepers and circus handlers are actually harmed by the animals they keep captive. With all the damage and cruelty that humans continually perpetrate on Mother Earth and her creatures, how much retaliation have we humans witnessed? The answer, of course, is virtually none. So why, I wonder, is Nature so patient with us?

More than ever, I'm struggling with these issues and the role that the African elders foresaw for the White Lions as guardians of the Earth at a time of crisis. Try as I might to hold onto the exhilaration I felt earlier, inevitably I start focusing on urgent issues involved in the battle to save Marah. My entire objective has been to open the way to relocate Timbavati's fair Lion Queen back to her land of origins. Now that it's becoming a reality, the real threats and challenges that await her are also becoming clear.

Setting my plate aside, I know these anxious thoughts will keep me awake again. Having defied all obstacles in order to secure Marah's release papers from the zoo, am I really prepared for the dangers confronting her in her homelands? Am I being realistic? I pull back to the present and scan the faces of the people dining around me. The restaurant has suddenly filled up. How many of these fellow South Africans have heard of the White Lions, unique to our country? How many of them know that these animals once roamed freely in the wilderness lands of their origins but are now extinct in the wild?

More than a decade has passed since the last White Lion was born in Timbavati, the same day I was rescued by Maria: November 10, 1991. The unexplained disappearance of that last White Lion cub follows four decades of merciless artificial removals: hunting and stealing of White Lions, as well as large-scale lion culling programs in neighboring Kruger Park between 1975 and 1980, at a time when twelve White Lions were recorded in nine different prides in the region. Once, these magnificent creatures were multiplying. Now none are left. It's desperate. Whenever I visit Timbavati Private Nature Reserve, I feel a ghostly presence of sadness shrouding the place. Yet even in the place of their origins, people don't seem to notice. Trophy hunting of lions in this wilderness reserve continues even today—long after the White Lions tragically departed these ancestral homelands, effectively eradicating potential gene carriers of the unique White Lion genetic marker from the region's population of golden lions. If Maria's guidance is correct, Ingwavuma was the last gene bearer and progenitor of the future White Lions in the region. As the reserve's most recent casuality, he took with him the last surviving White Lion genes into obscurity.

What's the solution? Since Timbavati's wilderness area is the only place on Earth where White Lions were born by natural occurrence, my commitment has always been to ensure Marah's return to the land of her birthright. But in reintroducing Marah to her ancestral homelands, I need to find out exactly what I'm getting myself into, and more importantly, what I'm getting Marah into. Because of my necessary step-by-step process, I haven't been able to give the threats and challenges of Timbavati my full attention. Now they are staring me in the face: Timbavati Private Nature Reserve hunts lions commercially. What was I thinking? From a captive killing camp into the dungeons of a zoological institution, then from the zoo to a commercial trophy hunting reserve—am I totally insane trying to return Marah and her family home?

My tea's cold, but I sip it nonetheless. In the crammed coffee shop in the park in the middle of the Johannesburg traffic, I visualize the vast expanses of Timbavati bushveld where this rare creature should be protected by law. I've committed my life to ensuring the survival of Marah and her kind. But what is the point of returning this most sacred animal to her natural and spiritual homelands where, once again, she'll be at risk of being hunted?

Ever since Christmas Day 2000, I've been driven by one single overriding imperative: to get the newborn lioness of Bethlehem back to her land of origin. But for the first time I realize this pledge is simply not good enough: Marah's freedom is paramount. Not only do I have to ensure she returns safely home; once there, I have to find a way of guaranteeing her survival.

I pay and leave abruptly, driven by clear intent: First secure the great escape from the zoological dungeons; then cross the hurdles waiting for us at Timbavati once we get there.

I'M ENGRAVING THE DATE: FEBRUARY 4, 2004. Against all odds, I've achieved the impossible. I've managed to extract a mandate, not only for the freedom of Marah, but also for her three adorable cubs! At last I can lay down my weary weaponry, the sword of truth, bow and arrow of love, and shield of lightforce.

The breakthrough with the zoo finally came when I threatened to take Marah's story to the press, my only means of exposing the truth. Shrinking from the public exposure, the institution reluctantly conceded to releasing Marah, but only on condition their name was never mentioned in public.

This is nothing short of a military coup! Having so readily signed the contract, I was about to rest my battle-weary bones, until I had a closer look at the fine print. First they've conceded to my price for adopting Marah and cubs: itself an astronomical figure, more than double the previously agreed-upon price prior to my book launch. In a further sleight of hand, knowing I do not possess sufficient funds at the present time, the institution has conveniently stipulated that the deal will be annulled within two weeks if the money is not transferred into their account within the stipulated deadline. They must know, as I do, only a miracle can raise the ransom money at such short notice. My life's savings are tied up in a divorce settlement still being resolved, so my hands are tied. Just when I was about to lay my armaments to rest, I have to gear up for battle all over again. But deep-down inner guidance tells me not to fret. Help is at hand.

THE ELEVENTH HOUR. FEBRUARY 14, 2004. Without the required sum to free Marah, all my efforts would have been in vain. However, one phone call changed everything. An unknown British woman tracked me down yesterday morning after seeing Marah's picture in Britain's *Daily Mail* newspaper.

"Is that Linda Tucker?" she inquired assertively.

I said it was.

"Good morning, young lady. My name is Mrs. Mireille Vince. I'm phoning to let you know that I have the funds to save Marah. And I'm serious."

Naturally, I responded: "How serious are you, Mrs. Vince? Because Marah also has three cubs."

"See you tomorrow," she replied. "I'm catching a plane from Leeds tonight."

What a miracle! Indeed, Mireille is my initiation into the law of miracles. Her unconditional offer of provision of funds to liberate Marah and her cubs at the *moment critique* has changed my life. Of course, that inner knowing, which Maria Khosa taught me to trust, always signaled that help would arrive. So when this amazing silver-haired lady swooped out of the blue at Johannesburg airport this morning and informed me that her name means "sunshine" or "miracle" in French, there was a strange familiarity about it.

And she is deadly serious. Having verified the authenticity of my project, her subsequent declaration on arrival that she is my "long-lost godmother"—mother sent from God—didn't surprise me, either. In reality, Mireille is nothing less.

But what made her do it? At sixty-something, this matriarch tells me she was adopted as a baby by a stern aristocratic couple who were unable to have children of their own. They spirited her out to Africa as a two-year-old baby for a period of time before finally returning to Europe, and for the rest of her life, Mireille longed for Africa, for the African animals she loved, and for the African people who raised her. Now, finally, through an instant lionhearted decision made over a cup of coffee and a morning newspaper, this amazing matriarchal lady has come to my rescue, and the rescue of Africa's most sacred animal. The executioner's axe is suspended, and the exiled queen has been spared. Mireille Vince has saved the day.

CHAPTER 11

Under the Camel Thorn

June 7, 2004. I will remember this day for the rest of my life. Six months after my delivery of the secret parcel to Marah, I've finally managed to secure my lioness's freedom!

I'm standing outside the zoo's caged dungeons once again. The difference is we are about to relocate Marah and the cubs to a temporary retreat in the Karoo mountain lands—all the difference in the world! It's a triumph beyond my darkest hours and wildest imaginings.

I made sure I arrived at the zoo this morning more than an hour before the prearranged time, only to find myself accosted by Cloete's officials. The zoo gave me their express agreement that I could be present in person to oversee the tranquilizing of my cats. It's a highly sensitive procedure, using Schedule 7 drugs, and I've been independently advised that an overdose or miscalculation could prove fatal.

Finally, after an argument lasting almost an hour, Cloete's officials have let me through. I hasten to the scene, where I find Marah and her precious little ones lying outside, comatose on the cold concrete slab. All four lions are laid out in front of me, totally knocked out by anesthesia, their tongues lolling out. I want to retch. What a kick in the gut. Cloete is nowhere in sight, but I've managed to extract information from my friendly official, who informs me Cloete darted the family more than forty-five minutes prior. My mind's spinning, and I think back to the last time I saw Marah—the only other zoo access I was granted after signing the mandate.

On that occasion, I introduced my godmother, Mireille, to Marah. We could see Marah somehow knew she was about to be freed. As my godmother and I approached, Marah had risen up to greet us. Her eyes were wide and burning brightly behind the bars, like an angel. Then one of the male cubs—Letaba—hurled his little body forward, snarling in a baby voice in an effort to protect his mother—so deeply touching. But Marah brushed him aside gently, using her sweeping paw, like a cloak or downy wing. She was giving my godmother her undivided attention, conveying a message of gratitude and love—as if she somehow knew that Mireille was her benefactor, and benefactor of her cubs. She looked at me with the dignity and majesty of a high queen, about to take up her true title. Awe-inspiring.

What a contrast to this body on the cold, stone slab.

It feels like the stuffing's been knocked out of me, and I'm faint with nausea. Will Marah survive the journey? Through a haze of biliousness, I hear a voice that brings hope back to my heart. Jason Turner. He arranged to meet me here at 7:00 a.m. this morning. I glance at my watch—it's exactly 7:00 a.m. Jason's walking toward me, with his friend Tindall, a dedicated vet, clean-cut, with impeccable professionalism and a deep love for animals. Help at last.

Jason gives me a hug, and I just manage to stop myself bursting into tears.

"Don't worry. We'll take over," Jason says.

He steps forward to test Marah's pupils and covers her face with toweling, explaining this will protect her unblinking eyes from the dry atmosphere. I watch Tindall fit a syringe into a vein on Marah's soft furry foreleg and set up a drip for hydration. He'll do the same for all four lions.

There's a scuffling sound as the officials make way, and that armored tank Cloete comes thundering in, officious and shouting orders. Jason stands up and says, "Step aside. Your jurisdiction is officially terminated."

I watch Cloete grind to a halt, then retreat, grim-faced. "That's not the last you'll hear of me!"—his final salvo.

We had planned so carefully, but everything feels like a whirl of events. Jason helps me wrap the lions in blankets so that their body temperatures don't plunge. We lift the cubs, one by one, onto stretchers. Only nine months old, yet so heavy. And moving Marah requires the lion keeper and two burly assistants to help Jason, Tindall, and me. The six of us carry her out to the paneled van, a large black vehicle we've hired for the day, with all the windows blacked out and a sliding door. Jason and Tindall clamber into its interior, dragging the two front rods of the stretcher along with them, while the four of us help to hold Marah's body stable. We heave her up gently and settle her on the van floor beside her sleeping cubs. Inside, I tuck the blankets around them.

We start moving the van slowly, finally exiting the zoo premises. I scrutinize the police escort ahead of us and catch a flash of silver hair. Mireille is sitting in a stately fashion at the rear of the police vehicle. In a slow-motion convoy, we travel through the streets of Johannesburg. The police car siren sounds, and ahead of us vehicles in the crowded streets pull aside for the cavalcade, no doubt imagining it's transporting another group of self-important politicians in black suits. I can see out, but the crowds can't see in. If only they knew what precious cargo is actually being transported to freedom!

I see the road sign indicating the private airport. We are still driving very slowly. Finally, we cross the tarmac and come to a halt. Jason swings the sliding door open, and a cloud of hot air and jet fumes fill the interior. The airport staff must have been tipped off because people on foot are crowding in now—as if for royalty. We finally come to a halt—and all around us the crowd is closing in.

With Jason and Tindall's help, I carry the cubs one by one, forcing our way through a heated phalanx of people and on toward the hull of the aircraft. Having settled them, we return to lift Marah, while everyone wants to help carry or just hold onto the stretcher.

"Make way! Make way!" I hear Mireille's voice on the bullhorn. But they can't help crowding in—pilots, flight attendants, airport staff, cleaning staff—all wanting to touch the beautiful pink paws of these great kitties, sleeping like angels . . . and I really can't blame them.

What a relief to be in the back of the jet at last. The doors have closed. Speeding down the runway and taking off, what a top-of-the-clouds feeling. I'm dizzy with exhaustion and relief. It will be another nine hours before we reach our destination.

We've arranged a convoy of Land Rovers to be ready when we touch down on the runway. Timing is critical. We don't want to keep the cats tranquilized any longer than absolutely necessary. So far, so good; I'm praying next steps go according to plan.

Dawn, in a spartan Karoo landscape. June 8, 2004. It's been a long night: first the seemingly endless plane flight, then the slow drive in the Land Rovers along endless dusty roads, then the careful settling of the lions lying covered with blankets under a camel thorn tree on the dry earth at sunset, where they've been lying all night, drugged and unmoving. It's been a tense, worrisome night.

Mireille and I stand in the open back of the Land Rover outside the pride's enclosure; Jason and Tindall are in the cabin interior, holding up binoculars. It's a subzero desert morning.

This isn't paradise. Marah's new home is a two-hectare electrified camp, no bigger than a football field. And it's not her natural habitat but a harsh semidesert with rocky outcrops, occasional scrub brush, dust eddies, and no significant dense-leaved tree in sight, apart from one camel thorn tree, around which we specifically built the lions' camp. Nevertheless, until I can safely secure the next step to Timbavati, this dry land is a merciful safe haven. It's all we have.

All night long there's been no movement from Marah and her cubs. I'm deeply worried. But as the sun begins to rise, finally the lions start to rouse. First the cubs. The little female is just strong enough to balance on her unsteady legs, and she staggers over to her sleeping mother, looking visibly anxious and confused because Marah is still totally knocked out.

Breathless, I'm watching the scene unfold in the morning light. At last, Marah opens her eyes—the first time since she left the zoo. Thank heavens she's emerging from her drugged sleep, although drowsy and confused. Seeing her daughter, she's regaining her strength fast. She gathers her little ones around her, the boys still teetering on unsteady paws. Ah! I breathe easily for the first time in more than twenty-four hours.

All four are in a tight huddle, staring out into the dawn—through the mesh of their new enclosure. It's the very first time the cubs have seen the sun. They're huddled tightly together in a tableau of grace and beauty. For me, watching them, it's the most beautiful sight in the world—Madonna and cubs! They're staring back at us; and then at the open, rolling plains; then at the mountains; and then at the rising red disc of the sun beyond.

Even though they are not free to roam yet, horizon after horizon is opening up for them. And my heart feels like singing. Mireille and I are both so emotional; we're clinging onto each other, weak at the knees. If I didn't have my godmother for moral support at this moment, I'd be sobbing.

It's not only the first time the cubs have seen the sun, it's also the first time they've felt the earth beneath their pads. Confined to a concrete floor until this moment, because the zoo didn't want them on public display due to the sensitive negotiations taking place behind the scenes, the cubs have known nothing else. I watch the tots cautiously testing the sand with their little paws. For such bravehearts, they seem a little frightened. Absolutely everything is new: the grass, the birdsong—one cub tilts his head this way and that, trying to identify where the bird's voice is coming from. A twig cracks under the weight of his little sister, Zihra, and she's so startled she darts to her mother. Tucked under Marah for protection, they stare into the sunlight that should have been their birthright. Such vivid images of the lions, etched into my heart forever. Such a triumphant day!

"This changes everything," I murmur to Mireille.

On this crisp winter's morning, she has sensibly brought with her a flask of hot chocolate, which she pours out into two mugs.

"A cuppa, gentlemen?"

Behind the wheel of our vehicle, Jason and Tindall take mugs for themselves, grateful for the warmth.

"What a long wait through the night for them to wake up," Mireille chirps. "And, hey presto, here they are!"

She's gazing appreciatively into the fenced enclosure, and Marah and cubs gaze back.

"A little disoriented, true, but bright as buttons!" she announces, proudly. "Joy of joys!"

I stare back at Marah and her young ones, radiant in the golden morning light. The miracle of their first day of sunshine, far away from the horns and sirens and madding crowds of the city! Here the only sign of traffic is a distant dust eddy, which I've been watching for the past fifteen minutes, approaching from behind a series of hillocks. The semidesert is so sparse that we picked it out in the far distance, some ten kilometers away. After noticing Marah pricking up her ears and staring in that direction, Jason first pointed it out to us. The dust eddy is coming closer now, and Marah turns her head to stare—then all three cubs adopt the same posture in unison.

As it approaches from a distance, Marah springs up and ushers her cubs to cover under the nearby tree. Disoriented, they follow her. They've never seen a tree before, and Marah had only known the dry logs and constructed stone dens of the zoo. Prior to that, in the canned-hunting camp, there was one spiny cactus and a concrete floor in her cage. In this dry semidesert landscape, the camel thorn under which the lions are lying is one of the few trees in sight. They peep out from behind its leaves, peering at the vehicle approaching now some five hundred meters away.

"Wildlife manager JJ," Jason comments, "Scheduled to drive us back to camp."

"Your opportunity to get some good rest at last, Mireille!" I prompt.

"Come to think of it, we've been in transit since predawn yesterday!" Mireille replies, "And we were in prep for the transit the night before! Nearly thirty-six hours without sleep. Better recharge batteries, everyone!"

The vehicle finally joins us, ushering in a cloud of Karoo dust. JJ behind the wheel, arm out the window. Mireille sensibly opts to return to the nearest camp with him.

"I'll join you too," Tindall says. "They've all safely recovered from the drugs. Need to get back home by day's end."

But Jason and I are going nowhere.

"Sure you don't want to get back?" JJ prompts me. "It'll be a long day in the desert heat—and Jason can handle it on his own."

"Absolutely sure," I respond.

"Nothing will separate Linda from her lions now!" retorts Mireille.

"Well, here're your sandwiches, packed in the cooler, with cartons of fruit juice—just as your godmother instructed," JJ comments, passing the crate over to me.

I watch Jason and Tindall exchange careful instructions. For safety reasons, Jason makes sure he'll be in radio contact with Tindall over the next few hours, should there be any unexpected cause for concern.

JJ's vehicle departs, with a last view of Mireille sitting regally at the back, waving enthusiastically. She must be one of the proudest grandmamas on earth!

Raising my binoculars to my eyes, I watch the 4x4 disappear over the nearby hills, then shift focus to the nearby camel thorn, where, from its deep shade, I can just discern four sets of cats' eyes peering anxiously. What a brave new world it is for my precious ones. Jason climbs out of the driver's seat and joins me in the back of the monitoring vehicle, watching closely. The dust eddy behind JJ's vehicle passes over the next crest of hills now, and the heat slowly starts to break through the morning chill. Looking back to the camel thorn, I see Marah emerge. She tentatively puts her head out of the fringe of leaves and steps into clear view, steady on all fours as the drug has worn off, and instructs the cubs to follow. They are wide awake and looking around them as they pad into the rising sun.

Is it possible Marah knows the importance of her new environment? All those messages I've been sending her in my daily prayers over these many months—is it possible they've reached her? Maria's training primed me for this very moment. I know how Marah is feeling, and she can read my thoughts. Marah and I are as one.

As if confirming this, she turns her gaze to me—my heart feels like bursting! Her eyes so direct, yet so loving and all-knowing. The cubs are cuddled up together in full sunlight, sleepy lids closed. I imagine she's about to drop off to sleep, together with them. But she stands up and heads over to test the electric fence. It's a terrible moment. I know Jason checked the charge earlier, but I can tell from a sharp intake of breath that he's also concerned.

"Should I worry she might get out?" I ask him. "Try to escape?"

"Don't think so. Reckon she's assessing her boundaries," Jason observes, "gauging the dangers of the electrics for her offspring."

I feel totally helpless as Marah steps forward and puts out her soft, velvety paw. Oh no! I try to warn her by conveying a telepathic message, but she's too quick. She's touching the charged trip wire. Now springing back from the electrical charge, recoiling in shock. I watch her tail flicking, serpentine with irritation. She shoots me a fiery glance—and I feel utterly wretched with guilt. I try to apologize, but she turns her head away with an angry expression. She pads back to her agitated youngsters, gathering them around her protectively again. I notice lots of affectionate cheek-rubbing between the four cats. Watching her closely, I decide this must be a deliberate effort to get a warning message to them. Finally, Marah glances up at me again—and I'm so relieved to see her eyes warm and maternal again. All is forgiven, but hopefully the lesson is not forgotten.

"I deliberately kept the electric charge low," Jason explains, "in anticipation that *that* might happen."

The cubs are up and off again, adventuring and exploring their new environment, toddling through the dust and the dry grass. Jason and I notice them heading straight toward the electric fence—just as Marah did moments before.

"Oh, no! Here we go again!" Jason mutters.

We are bracing ourselves a second time. Another heart-stopping moment.

The thought of the cubs shocking their little bodies on the fence is totally mortifying! Or worse, their damp little noses. I expect Marah to intervene—to bound forward and use a mother's paw to cuff them out of harm's way. But instead, she stands intensely gazing after them, as if she knows what she's doing. At the very same moment, all three juveniles turn to look at their mother, as if she's called them—without making a sound.

"Could it be she's communicating the dangers of the electrified boundaries to them?" Jason asks under his breath.

"Telepathically? Yes! That's exactly what she's doing," I watch with pride. Marah must have conveyed her unpleasant experience of being shocked to them. Having turned to look back at their mother, as if acknowledging her concerns, the tots change direction, all three avoiding the fence completely. They return and settle down comfortably with their mother, one big cuddly heap.

"Well done!" Jason says turning to me with a warm hug of congratulations. "Great job getting them to freedom!"

He's one of the few people with any idea of the long and treacherous uphill path I've been treading. So I hug him back.

What a roller coaster it's been: challenges, breakthroughs, and then even greater challenges. First the police raids and successful seizing of Marah from the iron fist of the trophy-hunting operations—a narrow escape! But then the totally unexpected foe in Dr. Cloete. I didn't have a chance to savor the hard-fought success of that first rescue mission before the fraught custody battles began with the zoo. Instead, I had to secure Marah's release all over again, this time from the clutches of a seemingly legitimate institution and its mercantile genetic speed-breeding programs. From the start, I understood the canned-hunting industry as a shadowy underworld of animal laundering, but to find reputable zoological bodies with direct links with these nefarious, underground syndicates was my worst setback.

"It's not over yet," I say to Jason.

"Sure. But this temporary safe haven's a huge step forward," he says encouragingly. "Agreed, it's an arid wilderness and it isn't the White Lions' indigenous range. So our objective remains to return them to their endemic habitat of Timbavati."

I nod. "But the question that's haunting me is: To what fate?"

Jason picks up my tacit reference to the trophy-hunting policies in the Timbavati Private Nature Reserve. I wonder whether he and I would have established the same deep bond if it weren't for these tragic circumstances.

"Still feel terrible about Ingwavuma," Jason comments kindly, picking up my own thoughts. "So unnecessary."

As always, I am moved by his reference to the lion Maria Khosa called my Spirit Guardian, the lion I loved with all my heart, whose assassination I was unable to prevent. I find myself fighting back tears all over again.

"I don't think I'll ever get over Ingwavuma's death," I observe.

"Understandably," Jason responds with compassion. As a conservationist with a deep love of his subject matter, Jason is also appalled by such irresponsible hunting activities.

I hesitate, then verbalize the words in my heart. "And I don't think I could live with myself if the same happened to Marah."

"We've gotta ensure it doesn't," he responds.

"How?"

"By getting our facts straight. And fighting for them."

Ensuring Marah's safety remains my primary worry, and ever since committing to her return to Timbavati, I've been proactively researching the facts, but nothing I uncovered put my mind at rest. In fact, my investigations into Timbavati and its trophy-hunting policies have largely been stonewalled. Everything's shrouded in secrecy and intrigue. Jason's the only person who's prepared to talk openly and transparently with me, while virtually everyone else acts as if they've something to hide. It came as a total surprise to find such a sympathetic hearing from a scientist—a profession that, in my experience, tends to detach from its subject matter. But I've come to see there's a passion guiding Jason's scientific thinking, unusual for the conventional scientific mindset. This distinguishes him from many other scientists whose intellectual indifference often leaves them without heart or soul—even to the point that it allows them to commit terrible atrocities on laboratory animals "in the name of science."

"Done some more research for you," Jason comments, producing a document from a file he'd stashed at the back of the vehicle. "I remembered you saying that 1993 was the year a fully grown White Lion male suddenly appeared at the commercial hunting operation bordering Timbavati, right?"

"Right!" I confirm.

"Well, I found this affidavit," he explains, "in which the warden from Kruger National Park recorded that a huge White Lion male was sighted south of Timbavati in 1993—in Tshokwane. It was the only White Lion recorded at that time, and fully grown. But the warden notes that this White Lion male suddenly disappeared and was never seen again. Then I remembered you telling me you have an account of a fully grown, drugged White Lion male being transported in the back of an open pickup truck to the commercial hunting operation that same year, 1993."

My whole body freezes. A chilling coincidence. Another grim piece in the puzzle.

Jason verbalizes what I'm thinking. "Probabilities are this is the same male that ended up in the canned-hunting camp."

I reach for the notebook I always keep in my back pocket, in order to show Jason an entry. I have documented an eyewitness account from a game ranger who sighted the incident in 1993. He said he was outside a gate of a captive breeding operation bordering Timbavati when a man arrived in a pickup truck. The man stopped and opened up the back of his truck to gloatingly show what he was transporting: a huge, drugged White Lion male. The game ranger said this man openly bragged about his newly acquired prize. He learned later that this very man was the godfather of the canned-hunting industry.

I hand the entry over to Jason and comment, "That White Lion skin hanging in the curio shop in 1985, which shocked me at the time, is just the tip of the iceberg. Where'll it end?"

I know these shadowy beginnings have spawned a notorious burgeoning industry that knows no restraint. Investigating the current situation has uncovered a crisis worse than I could ever imagine. Each small piece of this disturbing puzzle is clearly testimony of a much greater entrenched and merciless strategy that targets the King of animals as its most prized commodity. Trophy hunts, White Lions baited and snared, clandestine deals struck by people in positions of power. And on the borders of the Timbavati Private Nature Reserve, commercial hunting operations where the lions, poached from the wild, are bred to be shot in cages.

By contrast with the killing camps, the Timbavati Private Nature Reserve itself is a reputable conservancy area. It's collectively owned by some seventy private landowners in a patchwork of title deeds. Many owners are high-flying city dwellers who purchased this land during Apartheid times for purposes of occasional retreat and hunting holidays. It was then organized into a well-run reserve, directed by an executive committee and centrally managed by a warden and his staff. But the problem is these landowners take no responsibility for the custodianship of ancestral territories, which ultimately in my view don't belong to them but to the White Lions themselves, the true guardians of the land.

"The situation's worse than I ever imagined," I admit.

Jason responds, "The owners probably aren't aware of all the disreputable activities taking place."

"Either they're not informed or they're not interested," I comment.

Jason himself was an eyewitness to a lioness being stolen from Timbavati by a canned-hunting operator. He reported it to the warden, but nothing was done.

Having looked into the situation more deeply, it seems to me the warden's hands were tied. Having met with him several times over the years, I've developed a great respect for this tough talker. He's a macho man with a warm heart—ex-Special Forces. He runs the reserve with integrity and passion in a firm, orderly, militaristic fashion. He's dedicated and structured, having instituted a systematic antipoaching protocol that has been detecting illicit activities on all borders. When I questioned him, he admitted he'd found bait on fence lines and fences cranked up to lure lions under. There was at least one incident uncovered when a vehicle entered Timbavati's land, only to exit again with drugged lions under tarpaulins in the back. But again, nothing was done about this. Why?

I think back to my discussions with the warden. Clearly, he's a fearless and unstoppable kind of man, but when we spoke about these issues, he was on the brink of tears, describing how he was forced into a defensive position, and how the local police themselves had warned him off with a sinister threat that if he stuck his nose into other people's business, his wife and kids could get hurt.

"If the landowners knew what's going on," I ask, "could they stop it?"

"Seems they're more concerned about bad publicity than the issue itself," Jason comments.

Seeing as we are on this controversial issue, I decide to ask Jason for his professional opinion. "Jase, I know you were personally appalled when Ingwavuma was killed, but, as a scientist, what's your view on trophy hunting?"

"As a scientist?" Jason ponders. "People try make a case for sustainable utilization, sure. But my problem is trophy hunters always go for the prize specimens—the antelope with the biggest horns; the elephant with the largest tusks; the lion with the thickest mane. It's not ethical, and it's not environmentally sound. By taking out the dominant specimens, they're not only killing the individual, they're damaging the species."

I nod slowly.

"And frankly, my personal view is it's a despicable sport for modern-day men to get their kicks."

"Wonder what they're trying to prove," I mutter. "Something's missing."

The desert heat is building up and a warm wind blows dried tumbleweeds across the dust road in front of us. All four cats have settled down together under their camel thorn in a heap of entangled white furry paws, limbs, and tails to sleep off the midday sun. For the first time, they look content.

"They should be asleep for a while now," Jason observes, "even if they're a little jittery."

Apart from the lions' camel thorn, the only tree in sight is a desiccated, spindly-looking species, a desert willow casting minimal shade. But I notice Jason eyeing it.

"We should catch some sleep under that tree for a couple of hours ourselves, if you're intending doing the night shift with me," he says.

"Good idea!" I reply, weak with fatigue.

The desert willow is only some three hundred meters away, so I am about to open the vehicle door and walk over to it.

"Lindz—we've gotta talk this through," Jason cautions me, somewhat firmly. "I appreciate you'd love more than anything to be one with Marah and her cubs. And knowing your relationship with her, I've no doubt she'd accept you as one of the family."

"I'd love nothing more in the world than to be cuddled up with them right now," I admit, knowing only too well what he's about to say.

"Problem is, if you truly value Marah's freedom, you need to immediately stop all forms of human imprinting."

"Yeah, I know," I respond with an aching heart.

"Like walking past them on foot, or getting out and going up to their fence."

"Yeah, I know," I repeat the explanation he's given me previously. "This could prejudice their chances in the wild and make them dependent on humans."

He nods sympathetically.

"But it's such a wrench!" I confess. "For me, it's the most natural thing in the world to be with them."

"It's in her best interests. If your intention is for her to spend her life in captivity or in a circus, well, it'd be another matter."

"A circus! God, no!"

I appreciate Jason's sound argument, but it goes against all my greatest longings. Having just saved her, but never being able to approach her on foot again, or cuddle her, or hug her as I did when she was nine months old, that's my greatest sacrifice! I know in my aching heart that each of these painful steps of separation is vital in undoing the unnatural dependencies that hold this great cat in bondage to humans. In putting the necessary steps in place for Marah's freedom, I know I have to resist my yearning heart and withdraw all contact with my beloved lioness to allow her primal umbilical cord with Mother Nature to revive once more.

So, rather than walk past the lions, we drive the vehicle over to the nearest tree some three hundred meters away and climb out. The gentle shade beckons.

Jason rolls out an army-style sleeping bag on the warm earth and unzips it to double-size. Given the slightest encouragement, I can see us making love in the dappled shadows under the desert willow, with our lions nestled nearby, peacefully sleeping away the midday heat. But we've both been awake and vigilant for more than forty hours, and before I even realize it, Jason is sound asleep, a contented figure in the half shade, head resting comfortably on his right arm.

The tranquility of the moment is sublime. I am with my lion family for the first time in my life! For a long, lingering moment, I savor the sweet sensation of victory.

CHAPTER 12

Reclaiming the White Lion Kingdom

SIX WEEKS AFTER MY SUCCESSFUL RESCUE of Marah and cubs, and their relocation to the sanctuary in the Karoo, I stand in the minuscule bathroom of the tiny apartment I rented in Pretoria, trying to shut my mind down for the night. August 1, 2004. I need rest in order to focus and find a way to secure land in Timbavati for Marah's protection—whatever the cost.

There's a specific piece of privately owned property, in the middle of the greater Timbavati region that was identified years back by Maria Khosa—at the very heart of the original sacred lands of the White Lions. This highly strategic property is on the market. In fact, I was informed it's been on the market for quite some time, but now is at risk of being snapped up.

In order to return Marah to her natural habitat, there is only one way forward. Since Timbavati hunts lions, releasing Marah directly into the danger zone is unthinkable. Until there's a genuine revision in the hardened pro-hunting attitude of the current landowners and their wildlife management, my only option is to somehow purchase my own property. What a huge, life-changing decision. This strategy hadn't occurred to me before. But how else can I ensure Marah's safety and the future of her kind in their endemic habitat? Of course, it seems an impossible dream. Lion prides ideally require thousands and thousands of acres upon which to roam. So if I am to get real about this decision, my looming challenge is not only to identify large tracts of wilderness that once belonged to the White Lions as their natural endemic kingdom, but, most intimidatingly, to find the funds to purchase them.

That's why I've rented this one-room apartment in the city. I call it The Cupboard due to its size. It's even smaller than some of the diminutive Paris apartments I shared with other fashion models in the early '90s, crammed with several beds, dirty dishes, and expensive cosmetics. At least The Cupboard is clean and central—which wasn't the case in those modeling days. Shower unit, minute kitchenette, and little bedroom with a fold-up bureau and double-size futon, which takes up almost all the floor space. I remember reading somewhere that rats in confinement start killing each other, so it's no surprise the crime rate in the cities is so appallingly high. If it weren't for my commitment to conservation, I'd never consider being cooped up here. But The Cupboard is a refuge, a convenient place in the city center, and it's all I need from a practical perspective to focus on fundraising as my most urgent next step. My divorce settlement has finally come through, so I'm in a position to at least put a down payment on the property, but I'll need much more money to purchase it outright.

I was heading to bed early, but my cell phone's ringing. It's Ian. Dear Ian! I know he's worried, but I can't face his interrogation. So I let it ring. Unusually, my mentor doesn't leave a voice message.

But I hear my cell phone peep insistently. It's a follow-up text message. "Where r u??"

I text back: "Call you in the morning."

After a lifetime in conservation, Ian's advice is worth more than anyone's in the conservation world, but ultimately, I know this is a decision only I can make. Come to think of it, looking back at how far I've come, there have never been any real decisions. My deliberation always turns on what's best for Marah, and I simply act accordingly. So in facing this critical action step now—one of a series of difficult strategic choices I've had to make since Marah's birth four years ago—I simply need to follow the same principle of ensuring her best interests. First and foremost, I have to secure a critical piece of ancestral land and return the Lion Queen home.

My space has one superlative difference to those cramped Paris quarters: the magnificent White Lions! One entire wall is taken up with a truly spectacular oil portrait of Aslan, King of kings. His image creates infinity. He stares through laser-blue eyes into my world, as if into my soul. After the police raids into the canned-hunting camp that finally led to Marah's rescue, I've never been able to forget the king I left behind. After I helped save her life, my great pain remains that I'm in no position financially or legally to rescue him or even to negotiate his freedom. But not a single day has since passed without a silent prayer for Aslan, monarch-in-waiting—a prayer to ensure that an unjust regime does not execute him.

Agitated, I get ready for bed, but can't settle down. The decision I've made to purchase the property can float or sink my life's project. I know what's at stake, but I have to follow through. I'm wrapped up in a warm, long-sleeved T-shirt and thick woolen socks and heading for bed. But my cell phone rings again. Ian didn't save the world's wilderness regions by being a wilting wallflower, waiting for morning. He's the most persistent man I've ever met. This time, I answer the phone.

"So you're going through with it?" he demands in his gruffest voice.

"Hi Ian. How're ya doing?"

"Hope you know what *you're* doing, sweetheart!" he retorts.

He's alluding to the property purchase: invading my pipe dream of securing land for Marah and forcing a reality principle. When we discussed this earlier, he didn't hesitate to point out I'd be moving onto territory surrounded by hunting activity on all borders and, furthermore, purchasing this besieged land with my last existing funds.

True, it doesn't sound smart. But this isn't just any property. It's the heartland of the animal kingdom on Earth. It's the sacred land Maria herself prophesized.

"Yes, Ian. Might seem impossible," I explain. "But it's the logical next step."

"Hope you appreciate you're venturing where angels fear to tread."

"I hear you, Ian. But if the White Lions are angelic messengers, there's nothing to fear, right?"

Ian's accustomed to my symbolic way of thinking. "Sincerely hope you're right," he grunts.

"Where's your fighting spirit, Ian?" I ask.

I'm not forgetting this is the man who galloped bare-chested on horseback through the African wilderness, chasing after the world's critically endangered white rhinos in an attempt to relocate them to safety. When I last visited him at his farm in Howick, he and I dug up old black-and-white movie footage that records Ian Player as a kind of bushveld Rhett Butler figure, performing macho feats, like leaping onto rhino's backs in order to dart these great prehistoric beasts with a tranquilizer and wrestle them down to the ground. As Ian nears his eightieth birthday, his mind has never been sharper, but he's suffering spinal injuries dating back to those rhino-capture days in his youth. And the walk he and I took through his grounds was painfully slow, for an ecowarrior who once ranged the bushveld. But his spirit remains indomitable.

"My spirit, huh?" he snorts in response. "In the old days, when I talked about Spirit in Nature, the men in khaki told me: what spirit are you going on about now, Ian: gin, brandy, *witblits?* Don't expect them to understand what you're doing, sweetheart. Remember, men are terrified of a woman with balls."

I chuckle.

"Think it's funny?" he continues gruffly. "That's what makes these men dangerous. They feel emasculated by you."

"Well, maybe they aren't real men, Ian. Someone's gotta protect the lions."

"True. And we both know you can't do anything other than what you're doing. But I do worry about you."

"You'd have done the same in my position, Ian."

I know I've struck a sympathetic chord, although he won't necessarily admit it. My dear friend is the legend who stood up to the world's biggest mining company in a David and Goliath conservation battle over critically important natural wetlands that were targeted for titanium mining—and, what's more, he won! Through large-scale battles and long-term paramilitary tactics, he's sustained a lifetime of injuries on behalf of conservation. Need I remind my mentor how his own risky decisions paid off?

"The white rhino saga, St. Lucia Wetlands, iMfolozi wilderness—these were all life and death for you, Ian, so why are you cautioning *me?*" I comment defensively, padding around and around my tiny apartment.

"Understood, you're fighting to protect an animal from extinction," he concedes. "And you've won some skirmishes with those canned-hunting brutes and now the zoo. But, Linda, may I remind you: this isn't a battle waged with an end in sight; it's lifelong guerilla warfare."

I take a deep breath. It's not the first time Ian's made this point, and besides, I know he's right.

"Right now, time's of the essence, Ian. We've managed to save Marah's life, sure, but if she and her offspring are gonna return to the wild, we need to move fast."

He huffs again. "So you're sinking your life savings into this land—that's the idea?"

"Wouldn't you?"

"No, sweetheart. No. How many times've I cautioned you not to put your personal savings into your work? Anything goes wrong, you'll sink—and take your project down with you."

Ian's right; but then, I know his heart has always ruled his head and won many great battles on behalf of conservation.

"You're asking me to apply cold, calculated logic to a project I believe in with every fiber of my heart and soul," I challenge him after hearing him out. "Sorry, no can do. You know what I'm talking about."

Another huff. "I appreciate your commitment to White Lion conservation, sure. You've funded not only yourself, but also Global White Lion Protection Trust, for the past ten years. Without a salary. And if you had a shirt on your back, girl, you'd probably contribute that to the cause too."

"That's where the modeling and advertising savings can finally be put to good use," I butt in. "I'm gonna find a way to buy this property if it's the last thing I do."

It is such a relief to finally do something meaningful with the modeling spoils. But these funds aren't limitless, and what is required of me will all but empty my coffers. Of course it's nerve-wracking, but I'm insistent.

"Well, what can I say? If anyone can do it . . ." he concedes. "How much are we looking at?"

"Let's put it this way. If I put down my existing savings as a deposit, the sellers have agreed to a five-month option on the property."

"Wouldn't be surprised if that's your entire life's savings."

"Pretty much."

He pauses, as if moving into a new gear. "Okay. So, what're we saying here?"

"The option buys me five months to raise the funds."

"What proportion you putting down?"

"About 7 percent."

"Ahem!" his tone is less than impressed, but I suspect the old Trojan is secretly warming to the challenge, and I can picture him pondering at the other end of the line, brow furrowed with strategic thinking. When it comes to saving wilderness areas, this is a man prepared to stand in front of the bulldozer. He won't take anything lying down, but he's also ruthlessly tactical in his strategy.

"So those are the odds. You mean after putting down 7 percent of the purchase price, you've got the next five months to raise the balance—literally millions of rands?" Although I know I've finally won him over, he's snorting through my cell phone again like an old rhino bull. "And if you don't manage to raise the funds, you'll lose everything?"

"Yup. That's the bottom line."

"Well, I can hear that tone in your voice," he concedes, finally. "Nobody's gonna change your mind—and I'm afraid that includes me!"

"Stakes are high, Ian, but I'm prepared to dedicate every minute of the next five months to raising the money for the property."

Another momentary silence, then a slight softening. "In that case, sweetheart, you'd better get some rest. May I wish you sweet dreams."

"Night, Ian. Thanks for taking this all so seriously on my behalf."

"Just don't want you to get hurt. Believe me, if I was a couple of years younger, I'd be out there fighting the cause for you!"

Earlier I was preparing to sleep on this matter, but after Ian's call, my head's buzzing again. I need to do some serious thinking.

From my studies with Maria Khosa, Credo Mutwa, and other African elders, I've learned that the present-day borders of Timbavati Private Nature Reserve do not constitute the full extent of the original sacred lands of the White Lions. In fact, the White Lions' original kingdom was many times larger than the existing private reserve of some 150,000 acres. And it once comprised a magnificent ecosystem, teeming with biodiversity. The original kingdom spanned both sides of a river originally called the Tsau River (today known as the Klaserie). This great river is a primordial artery that, significantly, flows in direct geographic alignment with the Nile in the north. Furthermore, it's an intrinsic part of the mystery I uncovered—the mystery that links the White Lions to the Ancient Egyptian deities.

Wide awake, I open my bureau. I remove the large Timbavati district map from its tube and roll it out to study the area bordering the Kruger National Park of five million acres, which has now been incorporated into the Transfrontier Park of some fifteen million acres. A larger acreage than the countries of Holland and Belgium combined. This year, this bushveld region was declared the world's third-largest "biosphere region" by the United Nations.

I try to focus. Acquiring land on the scale I'm planning seems a superhuman challenge. But I remind myself that some years before her sudden departure, Maria Khosa gave me the seed of a long-term solution, which I've never forgotten. She informed me that my starting point was to be a specific piece of property through which the Tsau River runs. She illustrated this by casting the bones of divination out onto the grass mat in front of me. Arranged in a specific order of clustered relics, they resembled a symbolic map of the region, and she pointed to the particular property in question, which was identifiable in the center of this symbolic map. The ancestral spirits of the White Lions who spoke directly to Maria communicated information of great significance—and in this case, the piece of land (bisected by the Tsau River) is truly the heartland of the natural kingdom on Earth, and the core of the White Lions' ancestral homeland. The United Nations accreditation came years after Maria's message, but scrutinizing the map of this great body of land, I observe that the property Maria identified is in fact at the epicenter of this biosphere region.

Like everything else about Maria's mysterious ways, this can be no coincidence.

At the time, Maria's guidance seemed strikingly similar to a mythical story I studied in Egyptology. According to Ancient Egyptian legend, there was once a great and noble king named Osiris who was dethroned and murdered by his power-hungry brother, Seth. His body was then carved up into many pieces, which were scattered to various corners of the globe in an attempt to prevent the success of the Plan of Light: the great plan of enlightenment, which was God's intention for humanity, rather than abysmal destruction. So it was the task of his brave queen, Isis, to find the parts of the dismembered monarch and bring them together again, to ensure the success of the Plan of Light.

Remembering this gives me such spine tingles I feel the hair stand up on the back of my neck, as if the remnants of mane fur still exist there. Maria's instruction that my reclaiming this piece of land would revive the heart of an ancient kingdom was also her call for me "to remember who I am." She informed me that by putting all the pieces of the severed kingdom together, I would be reinstating true kingship on Earth, and the White Lions themselves would usher in the plan of light. She reminded me that each of the vital organs had to be reclaimed until this great body of sacred lands was brought together again, piece by piece.

But the very first step was to reclaim the heart of the severed kingdom—in doing so, my courage could not fail me. I heave the large hard-covered book onto the desk's surface and open it to a full page of Africa. As I've done several times before, using maps in my research into the White Lion mystery, I now redraft the golden line with a ruler all the way down the continent of Africa, from Giza in the north, due south along the same meridian to Timbavati. This geographic alignment was a revelation shown to me through guidance from my own ancestral sources and was corroborated in my shamanic studies with Maria Khosa and Credo Mutwa: the birthplace of the White Lions aligns exactly with the resting place of humankind's greatest lion monument, illustrating that the mystery of the White Lions is directly linked to the riddle of the Sphinx. I think back on how this profound alignment set me on a journey of discovery, which has led me into the very nucleus of ancient knowledge. Although this knowledge originates from the ancient past, I believe it offers urgently applicable solutions to our modern-day ecological and psychological crisis. But rather than sit and ponder over the meaning of this astounding correspondence, as I've done so many times before, I know I need to act on this knowledge—immediately.

I take a deep breath and survey the land before me. When I first visited Timbavati as a child, I couldn't deny a creeping sense of destiny. Having set foot on this land as a prospective landowner earlier this week, I felt the sense of providence all the more strongly. I loved the feel of this ancient ancestral land. I knew it in my bones, and I wanted to save the land, just as I want to save Marah! The present owners, a hunter-farmer and his wife, were not home at the time of my visit, but fortunately one of their laborers, a striking elderly Sotho man in his seventies, showed me around. He'd worked on this land for the past half century and gave the distinct impression he was showing me some of his favorite sites. I loved them too: a wild forest of ancient sycamore fig trees reaching up high over the floodplains of the Tsau River, a massive baobab some fifteen hundred years old rising out of a dry ravine, and a particular favorite of mine—a precipitous rocky promontory like Pride Rock from the famous opening scene of Disney's *The Lion King*. I could already envisage Marah padding over to the cliff's edge and overlooking the vast bushveld savanna stretching far to the distant Drakensberg Mountains. There was also, somehow, a sense of trauma hanging over the property, but this damage seems a more recent occurrence, while the land's real power transmits from the most primordial past.

Acting upon Maria Khosa's original instruction has sharpened my perception. In a modern context, this land she identified before she died is highly strategic because it borders directly on the western fence line of Timbavati Private Nature Reserve. It is, in fact, located alongside the reserve's headquarters. It shares a fence with the Timbavati Reserve, but being outside its borders, it doesn't fall under the governing constitution. This is vitally important. It means I won't have to follow the reserve's existing constitution of Timbavati, which advocates trophy hunting of the so-called Big Five: rhino, elephant, buffalo, leopard, and the most sought-after, the King of the beasts, the lion. In purchasing this land bordering the private reserve, I'm in a position to redraft the constitution and to ensure the urgent protection of the White Lions in their endemic habitat.

But there is an additional challenge. Timbavati is not alone in trophy hunting lions. On all other frontiers, Maria's Heartland is bordered by specialized trophy hunting outfits, with the headquarters of the godfather of the canned-hunting industry on the southern frontier. This is the same individual who bragged about stealing a White Lion from the Kruger National Park, the selfsame individual whom Jason witnessed stealing a Timbavati lioness. A staunch member of the Afrikaner right-wing neo-Nazi movement known as the AWB, this treacherous man lives with his three middle-aged, gun-toting sons, barricaded in a stronghold rumored to house his impressive arsenal and vast collection of animal trophies, while outside his family farmhouse, word has it, are numerous dejected lions in cages waiting to be trophy-hunted.

Ian's right. It does seem foolhardy trying to establish myself right in the middle of this antagonistic region. On the other hand, purchasing land here is the obvious—and only—next step.

I sigh with exhaustion as I fold up the atlas, and then the desk and then the chair. I am about to switch off my cell phone when it rings again. It's Mireille. I note from the missed calls that she's tried me several times during my conversation with Ian, so she knows I'm still awake.

"How's my darling daughter doing?" That cheery Swiss-Yorkshire accent always encourages me. Mireille's one of the most enthusiastic personalities I've ever known.

"Better for hearing your voice," I reply before going on to briefly explain the new looming challenge. Her instant response is to get practical. "What're you eating, darling? It's very late in South Africa, isn't it? Worried your line was still busy. You had supper? Remember: if you collapse, this entire project crumbles."

"I'll have some soup before bed."

"With lots of fresh vegetables, presumably? Sounds good," she instructs encouragingly. "Okay. Bedtime now—off you go!"

"Will try. But this decision's keeping me awake."

"Take heart, darling daughter. Remember their first day of freedom? All will work out. Now you make sure you record everything you've achieved so far! Stop and smell the roses."

"You're so right," I admit. "The challenges are so relentless; I tend to forget the achievements."

"Absolutely! List and write down all those things you should be grateful for. Puts it all in perspective," she advises. "And don't worry about next steps. You know in your heart of hearts what needs to be done, when. The night brings good council. Sleep tight, darling. Love you."

"Night, Mum. Love you too."

I had no appetite earlier, but I now I'm yearning for comfort food. I boil water in the kettle and try to settle down with some warm soup, reminded of those steaming mugs of hot chocolate from the flask Mireille and I shared on that unforgettable crystal morning: The day Queen Marah and her cubs awoke after their rescue from the zoo. I relive my last view of Mireille—disappearing, proud, and waving like a queenly grandmother in the back of a 4x4—in a cloud of desert dust, while I stayed on with Jason to monitor the newly arrived lion family. She returned to Leeds directly afterward, but she's been in regular contact since, to offer moral support.

In bed, I take out my notepad and follow Mireille's sound advice, reminding myself of progress so far and giving thanks for all that's been achieved. Sounds simple enough.

Point 1: Marah rescued—and her cubs!

Point 2: Book published. It's reached a fair number of people over the past three years.

Point 3: Radio and TV interviews. This and other media has helped raise awareness.

Point 4: Nonprofit organization. All the effort that went into establishing the Global White Lion Protection Trust is now beginning to prove worthwhile.

Point 5: Foot in the door.

Crossing out foot and changing it to paw, I can't help a little smile. I now have a paw in the door of parliament!

This, at least, is a massive step forward. Look on the positive side, I tell myself. I've presented in parliament, but will the new proposed regulations come through in time to save Marah and her kin? Almost certainly not. If Marah is to be safely returned to her natural habitat, this strategic piece of land has to be secured immediately.

Will I succeed in raising funds for the property? And if not, must I face the reality that Marah may never be free?

Feeling cold sweat break out on my forehead, I try to settle down for the night and switch off the lamp. My head's throbbing. Reviewing my progress so far has focused my mind on just how urgent my next step is. I'm not anywhere near tired. The neighbor opposite has left his porchlight on again, and hard beams of light are cracking through my blinds onto the wall behind me, carving slats into Aslan's face. I would have gotten up again and closed the blinds, but it's some comfort having Aslan's presence visible above me.

I force my eyes closed. Maria Khosa often appears in my dreams. If she were alive, I know what she'd say: "Just walk, lioness! You can do it!"

I creep deeper under the duvet, less for sleep than comfort. The room temperature in my little apartment is chilly, but I'm overheated and bothered, and the thought of falling asleep is completely remote.

It's after 3:00 a.m. I switch on the bedside lamp again and get up to make myself another mug of soup. It's simply a distraction, even less palatable than before. I drink it standing up rather than trying to settle back into bed. I wish I could pace, but there isn't room in these cramped quarters.

I open the front door and step out into the chilly night. Most of the city sounds are hushed at this hour, and there are no bird sounds from the darkened trees. It would be lunatic walking the abandoned streets or the nearby parklands, so I close the door against the cold night and return to the futon with its rumpled duvet.

Come morning, I feel ready. I didn't get much sleep, but I woke with a radiantly clear resolution: however difficult it is to raise the funds, the money has to be unconditional.

Simply put, those are the terms. Admittedly, I've had minimal experience in fundraising, but it's clear to me that no strings can be attached. Hard experience in childhood with my dearly loved but highly manipulative father taught me that most gifts come with a price tag—which is sometimes more costly than the gift is worth. So the burden of receiving can be greater than the deprivation of doing without. But Mireille's extraordinary gift of freedom to Marah and her cubs illustrated that it's not always the case. Her motto: "Give liberally, without counting the cost." Expect nothing in return, she told me, and you'll find your rewards are greater than anything imaginable. I know these are the only terms by which I will represent the White Lions and their rights. As the true kings of the wilderness, no self-respecting lion should be expected to beg, borrow, or steal what's rightfully theirs. Nor should I on their behalf, desperate as I may be to secure financial help.

CHAPTER 13

Where the Starlions Came Down

DAWN IS BREAKING. IT'S BEEN A LONG, BREEZY NIGHT under the stars. September 29, 2004. I've been invited back to my favorite place on Earth by Jason: the Timbavati bushveld. Nearly three months since pledging my life's savings and signing the option the morning directly after Ian and Mireille's respective pep talks.

From day one of the option, I began systematically working toward a successful outcome. Generally, the office hours of every day were dedicated to contacting business associates. Then, after hours, I sorted through my contact lists, phoning private individuals who might assist. Once it got too late to phone, I started listing positive leads so I could start again the following day. I made lists overnight, waking up several times in the early hours. Sleep became sporadic, and every day was progressively more fraught. As to the elusive sponsorship, I have no doubt it's on its way. I simply have to find it! I've managed to stay positive, but recently I was hit by waves of tension. Day by day, I feel the tensions mounting. I am having increasing trouble sleeping.

Admittedly, my track record for the property deal is dismal. I've been looking everywhere for assistance, without success. Despite what seems a superhuman effort over the past three months, I haven't succeeded in sourcing any significant additional funding. Seems I've pursued every possible avenue: institutions, charities, corporations, private individuals, sponsorships, and business associates, as well as friends and family. I began by tracking down everyone I know for leads, even old university and school colleagues. My appeal was always the same: the White Lions are not just a rare animal whose existence is relevant to a few local landowners; these rarities are a global treasure whose survival is critical to us all. Mostly, I've been shrugged off with stony, polite—and sometimes impolite—rebuffs. Why hasn't my approach worked?

I haven't wanted to face it, but over these past three months, I've been forced to look long and hard at my own relationship with money and try to identify where the blockage is, and why the funds simply aren't coming in. It's true, gifts in childhood always seemed to come at a price, and I developed a suspicion and aversion to receiving. Perhaps I am harboring that same fear, dreading the hidden costs associated with accepting funds. By necessity, I've had to start analyzing my upbringing and the role money played. It isn't something I relish owning up to, but I've come to the conclusion that on both sides of my family, there's an unhealthy relationship to money. My mother's Calvinistic family had a negative association with material assets as the root of all evil. Of course, this poverty consciousness contrasted directly with my father's materialistic attachment to money. Neither approach is wholesome. I have to somehow move beyond my confused childhood relationship with money if I am to succeed in pulling in the funds I urgently need for the White Lion property.

With the benefit of hindsight, I've realized that those constant pendulum swings between poverty and affluence actually prepared me for both extremes in life. I feel equally comfortable meeting an indigenous elder in a remote wilderness area as I do a senior advocate or merchant banker in a high-rise. Growing up, I slept in caves and shantytowns in Turkey, Israel, and Greece; I also slept in some of the most expensive hotels in the world—the Creole in Paris, the Ritz in London, and Central Park Hotel in New York. Despite these contrary experiences, I can't say I feel at home in either. Only Nature feels like home to me.

So Jason's invitation to join him on his lion-monitoring sessions in the Timbavati Private Nature Reserve was a breath of fresh air. That said, it couldn't have come at a worse time: I have a back-to-back lineup of meetings with bank managers and corporate marketing managers, scheduled in two days' time. But I took the leap, headed for the wilderness, and haven't looked back.

In the middle of the dense Timbavati bushveld, I look around me at a very different landscape from the arid Karoo: thick, tall, silvery grasses, shady umbrella acacia thorn trees, the lush thick-trunked marula trees favored by the elephants, and those characteristic ancient leadwoods that attract vultures into their high branches to roost. This place, without the people politics, is paradise. I'm sitting in the passenger seat of Jason's monitoring vehicle, and he's standing on the roof, holding up the telemetry antennae, trying to pick up a signal on the radio collar of a territorial male, one of two spectacular governing lions called the Sohebele brothers. From what Jason has observed, these magnificent brothers might in fact be the sons of Ingwavuma, so they have even more personal interest for me.

Jason's master's study involves tracking a number of different prides through the night in order to determine the frequency of predation, and he undertakes this sustained monitoring method for as many as ten nights in succession to ensure continuity of data. Then he recuperates for a couple of days and starts again. This grueling regime is indicative of an unfailing commitment to conservation, and I can see he loves his work with a passion. We haven't had a chance to catch up on news yet, because we've been tracking all night, and this Sohebele male has been on the move, territorially patrolling without much of a break.

On the roof above me, Jason tries the telemetry again now.

"No signal," he reports.

Ideal moment to untwist the lid of a flask of hot coffee and pour us both a mug. I pass Jason's coffee up to him and he crouches down and touches my fingers briefly in reaching for the hot mug. The warmth of the first sun illuminates the dawn, and his touch is quite electric.

"So, let's hear your news," Jason prompts.

Shifting his weight off the roof, Jason indicates that the male lion we've been tracking overnight must have settled down in a ravine some distance away, so it's safe for me to climb out from the passenger seat. I do so to find him standing with his arm outstretched, holding the telemetry receiver, taking another scan to make doubly sure this male hasn't come to join us for breakfast. He puts down the telemetry equipment and reaches out a bronzed arm to offer me a hand up.

I'm beside him on the back of the vehicle. There's a large metal trunk, with all the telemetry equipment, datasheets, mechanical implements, and spares as a precaution, should the vehicle break down in a tricky location while tracking the lions. He gestures toward it, and I settle down, cross-legged, using this trunk as a seat, my coffee mug in hand.

As usual, he's wearing casual khaki over suntanned limbs. Despite it's being the end of winter, Jason spends most of his time outdoors, so he's permanently tanned. His baggy khaki trousers have multiple pockets, for convenience, fastened with a canvas belt, on which his radio hangs. He switches off the GPS and drops it into one of these deep pockets, then opens a carton of Ouma's rusks to offer me. They're the Boer version of Italian biscotti—something of a bushveld ritual, great to crunch or dip in morning coffee, particularly on an early spring morning.

"Status on Marah and cubs?" he asks, dunking the muesli rusk in his coffee, enjoying the first rays of sunlight beaming over the distant Drakensberg Mountains. He's a strong comforting figure, athletic and bronzed in the morning light. And the strong coffee has never been more welcome.

"Well, you know I get weekly updates from JJ, which look positive, but I have some serious worries."

"Talk me through them," he says. "Describe your visit to Marah and cubs two weeks ago."

Because of my intensive focus on fundraising, that brief visit to the Karoo was the only time I'd seen my lion family since their relocation there.

"Amazing thing is she recognized me—instantly!" I recount for him. "She lifted her head and stared with that soft, regal face—for what must have been ten minutes!"

"One of *those* stares!"

"Totally. And you know her exquisite blue eyes, rimmed with black eyeliner, like an Egyptian goddess?"

He smiles. "Sure. She's awesome."

"Then she suddenly flopped down again, exposing her underbelly to her cubs, so they could suckle."

Jason grins affectionately at the description. "How's their morale?"

"They looked content, if a little bored. At least there was no anxious pacing the fence line."

"Not much stimulation in a camp that size, without natural bushveld habitat," Jason comments reassuringly. "But the great thing is they have each other."

"True," I respond. "When I was there they spent virtually all their time huddled together under that desiccated camel thorn. But I'm really worried about the scorching summer months ahead."

"Valid concern," Jason concurs, wiping his hand across his suntanned brow even before the heat builds up. "The Karoo desert's not their endemic habitat, so yes, it's gonna be tough for them. Make sure you get regular updates from JJ that their water troughs are filled. They're in the middle of nowhere."

"Absolutely will do. But there're other aspects I'm really anxious about."

"Okay, let's go through them systematically," Jason settles down comfortably on his haunches to listen. "First, how'd it go with the wildebeest carcass?"

"That's what I need to speak to you about, Jase. I have to confess I broke our golden rule."

"No human imprinting?"

"Afraid so. I was desperate."

"Okay, let's hear."

Jason previously advised me the next crucial step in our carefully planned scientific reintroduction program was to make sure Marah fed on wild-game carcasses. So I implemented this, as instructed, but I was disturbed by Marah's lack of response.

"Frankly, the exercise was harrowing," I admit. "I did what you advised. Told JJ Marah should be denied feeding for five days beforehand."

"Remember," Jason encourages me, "lions have the ability to go for up to twelve days at a time without food under duress. So the idea was to sharpen her natural instincts."

He dunks his rusk again in the last of his coffee, looking thoughtful, then adds, "You've gotta bear in mind she's been fed on nothing other than processed chunks of meat until now, so she probably has no idea what to look for in the wild."

"Well, that soon became apparent," I continue. "I don't think I'll ever forget the sequence of events."

Reliving it almost moves me to tears. I recount for Jason how I'd watched their behavior from a distance in the rented 4x4, outside their enclosure. I specifically didn't want to disturb them or impact negatively by getting out and walking to the fence. JJ had managed to put the whole wildebeest carcass in the camp for Marah earlier that same morning without her seeing. But if it was meant to sharpen her appetite, it didn't work. She looked hungry and thin. I observed for hours and hours. But by the end of the day, she still hadn't detected the carcass, which had been lying in the far corner of her camp all along.

"Hmm. Tell me," Jason prompts, running his hand across his brow again with concern. "Didn't she pick up the scent on the wind?"

"No! Probably wasn't much wind," I explain. "But she certainly didn't seem to know how to sniff something out, let alone track it down. She showed no instinct for the game carcass. Just stayed with her cubs all day—suckling them."

"Hmm," he says, his concern showing. "And at eight months old, the cubs should be weaned and joining her to feed on a carcass."

"Well, the most worrying thing is she eventually took a territorial patrol of her borders—but she walked straight past the offering, without noticing!"

"Oh dear," he comments, looking increasingly troubled. "An apex predator, without the natural predatory instincts of her kind—that's sad."

"I felt desperate for her. Hours had passed. I just couldn't sit back and watch the situation any longer," I explain, feeling the emotion rise again. "I had to intervene!"

"So you got out of the vehicle?"

"Yes!"

"Understandable," he says, kindly. "Tell me what happened."

Having to watch, helpless, as a hungry nursing mother fed her demanding eight-month-old cubs without any prospect of finding food for herself nearly broke my heart. Eventually, I couldn't help myself. I clambered out of the vehicle and called to her. Her cubs were well fed on mother's milk and dozing contentedly. But as soon as I called Marah, she lifted her head, then all three of their little heads popped up after her. So I walked over to the far end of Marah's camp—a distance of about one length of a football field—and called.

She stood up and gave an instruction to her cubs, because all three hid behind a scrubby Karoo bush nearby, peeping out. She gave them a stern backward glance, and they darted back behind the bush again. But she came over to me immediately—as if she knew me—as if we're family.

I was so emotional, the tears started to flow. To get this close to her, I had switched off the electrics and she must have known it. She moved so graciously and swiftly that in a flash, she was suddenly right in front of me! She was pressing herself against the fence, asking me to stroke her soft coat through the wires. Her downy fur was so soft behind the metal wires. Stroking her, I called out: Marah! Marah! Marah! There's food for you! Don't you see it, Marah?

But she just stared back at me with the most beautiful, wide eyes and a slight frown on her face. I pointed to the nearby carcass, calling to her, and walking along the fence line toward the offering. It hurt so much—me, a human, having to show her, a predator, what real prey is. I was trying to explain to her: You're a lioness. Can't you pick up the scent on the wind? It's food, Marah, food!

But she just padded beside me, like a sister on the other side of the fence. She seemed to have absolutely no idea what she was meant to be looking for; only that, somehow, I was crying for her. I remember thinking: *Will you ever be able to provide for yourself and your cubs in the wild, beloved Lion Queen?* I despaired for her. And the sheer trust she showed me made me cry all the more.

"She followed me with that curious, gentle, furrowed expression on her face—then she virtually tripped over the carcass, which was lying a couple of meters from the fence line. From that moment, everything changed!" I explain, tears filling my eyes at the memory. "She looked at me, then looked down at the earth again, curiously. Then, suddenly, *she knew who she was!* A lioness! Then she picked up the lifeless wildebeest calf by the throat, dragging it between her four paws like an experienced huntress transporting her prize. What an epic moment!"

"Her instincts suddenly kicked in?" Jason observes, "And the cubs' reaction?"

I describe how all three were peering out of the bushes in the distance, trying to stay put, just as their mother had instructed them. But when they saw their mother returning with the kill she'd hunted for them, the little white teddies started bobbing up and down, like the three little bears in the storybook, waiting for their supper.

"Amazing story!" Jason comments. "Really pleased it worked out. Vitally important next step. Well done."

Marah didn't give me another glance, proudly padding over to her young ones, her powerful neck straining under the weight of her prey. After the cubs started tugging enthusiastically on the carcass their mother had provided, I returned to my vehicle and sat quietly watching them, my lion family, happily feasting. She was a hungry mother now sharing her first taste of wildness with her three fast-growing youngsters—and they were experiencing meat for the first time in preparation for their freedom.

"Bottom line is: they're okay!" Jason encourages me, reaching out and taking my hand in his, with a warm squeeze. His hands are warm and sensitive, but practical and oversized. "What was your last view of them?"

"Under their camel thorn. Light fading," I recall. "I could just make out the cubs, full-bellied and asleep. Only Marah raised her head to watch me leave."

"Great work!" Jason observes.

"Can't say the whole exercise was easy."

"Sure," he concedes, standing up, backlit in the morning light.

The rising sun in the far distance transmits its early morning rays into the back of the vehicle, filling it with soft light. I feel warm and content for the first time in many months.

"Anything else you want to tell me?" he asks.

"Well, no, that's the main issue," I respond, assuming he's referring to my list of concerns for Marah and her cubs.

"Let me know if there's any other way I can assist," Jason adds, as he starts to stack the coffee flask and mugs in a canvas cooler box.

He's been fantastic. In respect of the long-term scientific process that needs to be implemented in order for Marah and cubs to successfully return to the wilds of their natural habitat, I understand the challenges more clearly than ever. Jason also assisted with the presentations to the Department of Nature Conservation on the importance of the White Lions, and he's initiated all the necessary procedures to get permits for this first-ever White Lion reintroduction back to the wild.

"Time to head back to camp for a snooze if we're gonna be in any condition to monitor through the night again tonight," he concludes, closing the lid on the storage crates and clamping the metal clasps.

We are back on lion time, snoozing the day away and prowling the night.

September 30, 2004. After another night full of stars, dawn's breaking—radiating pristine dewy light over the darkened lace horizon. For the past two days, I've been living like a lioness, catching catnaps in the heat of the day, then tracking the golden lions of Timbavati all through the night, from dusk to dawn. Without real sleep, I should feel absolutely wasted with exhaustion, but I'm exhilarated! I'd gladly spend the rest of my life doing this kind of conservation work. Instead, regrettably, I'm due to return to the city to renew my fundraising drive—against odds that have seemed insurmountable. But for the first time in three months, it feels as if my fundraising objectives are actually achievable.

I have loved being with Jason these couple of days, and I cherish the way he lives, so simply yet so fully. Here, in Nature, everything feels abundant. So many gifts. I realize now that achieving my goal is a matter of aligning my inner nature with Mother Nature, attuning to the real issues, and trusting all will be well in the great scheme of things. *That* is the key to bringing in the resources I need.

After another night of tracking, Jason and I sit in the back of the Land Rover, savoring our last sip of our morning coffee ritual.

He stands up to double-check his telemetry. The lions we've been tracking have settled down for the day.

"All clear," he reports.

I stand up too and shake the dust off my khaki trousers.

"Just wanna get Marah and babes outta there as fast as possible, and into their natural habitat," I conclude determinedly.

"You'll do it," he encourages. "Just remember your track record so far—and keep your eyes on the path ahead."

"Will do—thanks, Jase."

"Yeah. Don't lose focus for a moment—like a lioness on a hunt!"

I smile.

"Come join me," he says, jumping down off the back of his truck and giving me a hand down. "We can chat while I check this out."

On the ground with Jason, I watch him opening the hood of his Land Rover, because a knocking sound has been worrying him overnight.

"Sorry 'bout this. Shouldn't take a moment."

I lean against the vehicle's paneled side, savoring the warmth of the bushveld early morning sunshine.

"No huge rush," I say, smiling.

I am no longer in any hurry. All urgencies can wait. I can't imagine leaving this life behind. A few minutes pass—and Jason emerges from the engine with grease all over his hands, which he attempts to wipe off on a mutton cloth.

"Fortunately, not serious," he says, closing the hood and pressing it down securely. "Sort it out at camp. Important thing is to get you back and on the road ASAP! A shame you've gotta leave today."

Pity. I don't want to think about it.

Jason opens the cabin door for me, gesturing with a warm invitation,

"You can drive, if you like. But 4x4s are very different from city cars—I'll show you low range and when to use the diff lock."

"Great!" I respond, climbing up into the driver's seat.

Jason loves his vehicle, so I know this is a rare privilege. And this battered old 1980s Land Rover does seem something special. He told me earlier that instead of a Land Rover engine, it has a tractor engine—which makes it doubly hardy in this rugged terrain. In the final die-hard days of Apartheid, when the world was boycotting South Africa and South African products, the national defense force produced five hundred army vehicles using Land Rover chassis with Perkins tractor engines, and this is one of the survivors! Because of her bronzed color, Jason calls her Tawny—the color of the golden lions he studies day and night.

"Just give me a moment to fill in the datasheet," he adds, taking a GPS out of one of his trouser pockets and getting a reading, then recording details of last night's tracking session in the clipboard he's removed from behind the driver's seat.

It strikes me that Jason's the sort of easygoing, earthy man who's not frightened of any of the natural functioning parts of life. And if I had a spitting cobra in my bedroom, I know I could rely on him to come to the rescue, without harming the snake or me. The one thing he tackles with deadly seriousness is his scientific work—not only the hands-on field research and data capture, but equally the processing methodology and analysis that follows. I think back to the many challenging run-ins I've had with scientists during my academic career, from my best friend at university to my fastidious neurologist brother and astronomer-in-chief uncle. But Jason's different. His painstaking information collection isn't the ivory tower academia and laboratory test-tube analysis of the kind I encountered as a student at Cambridge University. He doesn't seem to have that scientific detachment that cuts scientists off from their own intuition and instinct. I think of my first morning, when we encountered the dramatic scene of an emaciated old, nomadic lion who succeeded in making an impala kill—a kill that saved him from starvation. Looking greatly relieved himself, Jason informed me that this aged lion (another of his study animals) had attempted many desperate botched hunts over the past few weeks and probably didn't have long to live. I could feel Jason's compassion, almost as if he himself had endured the same agonies as this starving lion.

He climbs down into the cabin with me, and I start the engine with a *vroooom-vroommah!*—and we're heading back to the Timbavati headquarters, where Jason has his base, and where I left my old Mercedes. It's rugged terrain. The Land Rover is plowing through a particularly tricky sandy area, so Jason uses the opportunity to guide me in engaging the differential lock in the gear stick to ensure the weight is equally spread across the vehicle's load.

Once we are safely out the riverbed, I disengage the diff again and drive freely. The landscape opens up ahead of us, with a nearby herd of impala springing one after the other across our path, in choreographed balletic sequence.

"Can't wait for the lions to be back where they belong," I murmur. "But it seems Timbavati's also gonna be full of its own challenges."

"You bet." His tone suggests he knows the challenges only too well.

There's a protracted silence. When he finally comments again, there's tension in his voice, "Wasn't going to mention it, but I'm afraid they're preparing to hunt another lion."

"When?"

"Right now."

"Oh no, not again!" I grimace, feeling that old, familiar chill run through my veins again. "Who is it this time?"

"They're not saying."

"Isn't there anything you can do, Jase!"

Taking my eyes off the uneven terrain for a moment, I glance at Jason again. He indicates frustration with a slow shake of his head.

"As you know," he explains, "I'm virtually persona non grata around here—after I corrected the bogus lion count figures that Timbavati lodged with Nature Conservation, remember?"

"Sure, I remember. They overestimated the figures by more than 70 percent."

"Uh huh. Which would've had serious consequences for the lion-hunting quotas in this region." He pauses, considering. "The facts were wrong, simple. As a scientist and a researcher, well, I had to correct them."

"You never told me what their response was."

"They stripped me of my rights and demanded a public apology."

"And?"

"Of course, I was happy to send out a general email apologizing sincerely if I'd offended anyone. But I also took it as an opportunity to reiterate the facts. Fact is the lion numbers were out by two-thirds."

A tortoise is crossing the path, so I stop Tawny and wait. Jason cautions me that if I lift the little creature—as I was tempted to do—and carry him to the other side, he'd probably pee with fright and lose all his body water, which he can't afford in these dry, late winter months before the spring rains. So instead, I switch off the vehicle, and we wait patiently for him to make his own way across.

"Leopard tortoise male," Jason identifies him by the distinctive spot pattern on his back.

"Adorable!"

Jason takes out his GPS to calculate the time. "You'll have to set out immediately if you wanna reach Johannesburg today. Seven hours' drive from here—wouldn't want you hitting rush-hour traffic on the other side."

After watching the precious little creature finally complete his laborious route across our path, we continue on our way back to camp.

"How're you doing? Ready?" he asks.

"Phew!" I respond, trying to get my mind into city gear. "Don't feel prepared for the concrete jungle right now."

I'd gladly stay here forever in the Timbavati wilderness, tracking tawny lions and watching over leopard tortoises. It's hard to face the city, but being stationed close to South Africa's money mecca is vital if I am to achieve my primary goal of funding Marah's land acquisition.

"Remember: the lions are relying on you!" Jason says.

"Thanks for their vote of confidence, Jase," I reply, smiling and feeling the pull of the powerful engine plow steadily through the rutted gravel surface.

Passing through the dense bushveld scene with dazzling zebra and a small herd of languid giraffe in an open plains area, we are finally approaching Timbavati HQ. A gate guard unlocks the huge grill gates and salutes as he slides them open for our vehicle. We've arrived at the military-style settlement in the bushveld, a cluster of thatched rondavels painted army green, behind predator-proof electrified fencing.

"Better warn you," Jason prepares me as I bring the vehicle to a rather abrupt halt. "There've been a couple of odd types looking for you recently."

"Like whom?" I ask, bracing myself.

"Remember that weirdo we called the stalker a while back, declaring you were his wife from a previous lifetime and he was back to claim you?"

"Yup, I remember," I reply with a flush of embarrassment.

"Well, about a week ago, the warden reported there was another individual looking for you. I made sure it would take the man a while to find you—gave him the aerial map of another region."

I smile. "Thanks."

Jason opens the door and jumps out, and I do the same on my side.

"Thought you should know. He was wafting around in what the warden could only describe as a caftan and a g-string! Didn't go down too well here, as you can imagine."

I cringe and take a good look at Jason's face to gauge the seriousness of this latest intrusion. I suspect he's taken the flack for me again. Ever since my book was published, I've had numerous people try to track me down for their reasons rather than mine. Some were authentic shamans who understood the fundamental importance of the White Lion material I'd handed over and wished to share their own knowledge with me of a related kind, but others were simply looking for cheap thrills. Because I identify the Timbavati area as the White Lions' ancestral homelands in my book, readers captivated by the story sometimes ended up here in search of me: Timbavati HQ! What a conflict of paradigms: New Age faddism and old-school militaristic regime.

With one tanned arm outstretched and holding onto the roll bars, Jason hauls himself onto the back of the vehicle to retrieve my leather rucksack.

"My book's out there, Jase," I observe, meaning it's in the public domain." I need to find a way of controlling people who track me down after reading the White Lion material."

"Understood," he says, jumping down with my luggage over his shoulder. "And people have to take responsibility for their own actions. Just thought you might wanna know."

Under the shade of a tree, next to Jason's tented camp, I spot my old Mercedes. As we stroll over, my mind starts shifting for the first time into another mode, refocusing on my immediate fundraising goals. With a sigh, I consciously start mustering all my inner reserves. Fortunately, I am not short on motivation. Every step I take is determined by one single-minded goal: to get Marah and cubs to freedom and safety. How to purchase her ancestral land still remains a mystery. But my teachings with Maria Khosa have opened me to the possibility of miracles. I'm ready to tackle the challenges again. These last couple of nights tracking the wild lion prides in Timbavati together with lion-man Jason all night until the sun rose, resplendent and new, were a dream come true. Now I'm fully prepared for brutal reality.

CHAPTER 14

Trust and Trustees

It's a chilly spring morning, three weeks since my visit to Timbavati and Jason—and the pressure is on. October 20, 2004. The first, second, and third month of the option passed without success, and I am disconcertingly well into the fourth month. My appeals for funding seemed a solid strategy, but the usual routes simply haven't materialized. All the banks I've approached refused loans, because my nonprofit organization had no guarantee of regular income. As the CEO, I've been working without a salary for the White Lions for over a decade now. No problem with that—it's part of my commitment to the cause, and fortunately I had a nest egg to keep me going—but the difficulty is that my personal record of no income doesn't give these institutions any comfort. They view me, and my cause, as high risk, however worthy my motives.

Over the past two weeks, my persistence generated significant interest from a number of corporate prospects, but not one was workable. In several cases, I got as far as sitting down at the negotiating table with the organization's marketing team to draft terms of association, only to find that, when the chips were down, everything stacked up against the White Lions' interests and in favor of the corporation supposedly offering a helping hand. Mostly, corporations expected to use the White Lions' images for whatever marketing gimmick they chose, however inappropriate: baseball caps, trashy sweatshirts, billboards with slogans and logos. In other cases, the corporation expected to send busloads of staff members on a regular basis into the heart of the White Lions' territory, on the assumption that these rare animals must be at the company's beck and call. My contract with the sacred White Lions won't allow them to be treated as yet another commodity, and acting on their behalf, I simply couldn't agree to these deals. So the bottom line is that in each and every case, the corporations expected more for their sponsorship than they were actually giving. At this late stage in the proceedings, I am becoming really uneasy. This certainly wasn't the unconditional support I envisaged.

Were my expectations too high? Our corporate world seems to have lost all sense of value, so why was I seeking help from those quarters? The truth: deep down I believe everyone in all walks of life—even faceless corporate structures—wants to make a difference, and can.

My main challenge has been my reticence in asking for money. After my trip to Jason and the Timbavati bushveld, the penny has finally dropped. I have to stop asking, because the truth is, I am not asking. Rather, I am offering humanity a chance to help save the most sacred animals on Earth. What a privilege!

After adopting this new approach, the situation has drastically improved. Notification finally came through from our bank that a significant donation has mysteriously been deposited! Out of the blue. Hallelujah! What's so intriguing is that an anonymous benefactor donated the funds—with no strings attached. This amazing validation is just what I've been asking for, daily, in my prayers. The sudden materialization of funds is spine-tingling! True, it is not sufficient to solve the problem, but certainly sizeable enough to give me renewed hope—accounting for approximately a quarter of the missing grand amount.

Naturally, my first feeling is utter and complete delight. Then two days after the funds came in, I had a dream in which Maria Khosa entirely changed my perspective. She showed me two scenarios: The first scenario was a piece of land protected by a fortress wall, with Marah safely in the interior. The second scenario was a piece of land, unprotected, with Marah held in a dungeon far away. I woke up in shock, with a clear instruction: "Erect an electrified boundary fence on the land now, without delay, to ensure Marah's freedom."

That seems simple enough. But the dilemma is that I have only just received this funding. How do I justify spending it on fencing (of all unglamorous things) before the property itself is even purchased?

Since Maria Khosa passed into spirit, I've had lots of communication from her. If I am too preoccupied to take note of my dreams—which is pretty often—she tends to find alternative means of communicating with me from the other side. A number of mediums, or so-called channelers, with whom I've consulted, have inevitably picked up her formidable presence. Often they see a great and imposing queen, sometimes with a sundial or bedecked with a pharaonic lion headdress, seated at a table of elders in the ancestral realm, holding council. I've since come to recognize Queen Maria, and the other members on the council of ascended masters, as a representation of the powerful ancestral entities who continue to work with the affairs of humankind from the spiritual planes. Whenever possible, I actively work in accordance with them too. I regard their guidance as higher council, and information from these rarified sources has guided my actions ever since Maria's departure from this world (and even for some time before, no doubt). In fact, since I committed to serving the White Lion cause, there have been countless occasions when I drew wisdom from these realms. Sometimes, I simply visualized the higher council and their directives came to me so clearly that I had no difficulty in understanding what needed to be done. But the challenge remains how to translate such guidance into everyday reality and convince others in my organization of its merits.

After getting Maria's urgent notification in my dream, I immediately called a strategic trustees meeting in order to reallocate these newly arrived funds—knowing only too well that the trustees would be convinced by results, not daydreams. The meeting was scheduled for 10:00 a.m.

While I am the person driving my cause, there are many respects in which I no longer make decisions on my own. The Global White Lion Protection Trust has a board of trustees and two separate councils of advisors, who have been appointed specifically to give guidance. It is an organizational structure, which I set up based on Ian's sound advice. After a half century of experience in founding and managing nonprofit organizations, he urged me to keep my decision-making caucus lean and mean: a small circle of trusted trustees. That way, decisions can easily be put into action without endless, debilitating debates. But in addition to the trustees, I have two advisory councils: an experts council and an elders council. The first comprises experts in their field—lawyers, conservationists, financiers, and political leaders—while the second comprises indigenous elders from different continents—sages who advise on aspects of good governance and the cultural and spiritual importance of the White Lions. While they don't have voting rights, both councils' guidance is paramount and informs all critical decision-making. However, it is the second council, the wise, indigenous elders, whose wisdom I hope to draw on during this meeting since they would best appreciate that my directives in this matter came from ancestral realms. Sadly none of the elders are available at such short notice, but I've just learned that a couple representatives of our experts' council will be attending today's meeting. Given my audience, I have to be all the more logical and persuasive in my rationale.

I try to calm my breathing as I sit on the high-ceilinged veranda of Harold Posnik's house. From Harold's veranda, I can see his converted garden cottage, which houses the White Lion Trust's office.

Harold generously offered these premises without charge after assessing the pressure I was under in respect to fundraising. Although I was introduced to him just over a year ago, Harold instantly saw the issues for which I'd been campaigning all these years and committed to help. He is like a brother to me, and after all the lonely crusading, that's a great comfort.

I glance at my watch, wondering where he is. I'd hoped to sound him out on this critical issue before the trustees arrive in a half hour's time. He'd be relieved to hear the good news: our first meaningful donation toward acquiring the property has finally come through. But I doubt he'll see the sense in suddenly reallocating those funds toward an entirely different purpose, unless I talk him through the fencing argument very thoroughly. The electric fencing of game areas represents a massive component of overall cost, so naturally, this question needs to be weighed very carefully. Having operated as a lone warrior for so many years, using the trunk of my car as my traveling office, I can't quite get used to the idea that I have a highly effective support system to fall back on.

But how can they support my proposal? If I sink these donated funds into the fencing, where will I find the outstanding amount? I feel that familiar tension gnawing at the pit of my stomach. Waiting for Harold to arrive, I pour myself another cup of tea from the tray and watch the pale wisp of steam spiral up before dissolving into the atmosphere.

Harold's premises have changed my life. His garden, as it happens, is so close to the zoo that I should be able to hear Marah's former brethren, the golden lions, roaring from my office desk. That's if this were the Timbavati wilderness. But it is central suburban Johannesburg, throbbing with traffic on Jan Smuts Drive, one of the busiest roads in the city, so there is no detectable sound at all from the zoo, just over a kilometer away, which, in some ways, is a relief. Nevertheless, the unheard, unseen presence of the living creatures incarcerated there helps motivate my every decision, including the one I have to push through in the upcoming meeting. Marah was once held in those dungeons. I may have secured her release and relocation to a safe haven, but the Queen of Lions is still in captivity, and the longer she remains there, the less likely she is to ever survive in the wild of her natural Timbavati kingdom. All the more reason to press ahead with the meeting.

Harold ambles onto his veranda. We give each other a hug and he settles on the couch opposite me looking serious, his graying, dark hair catching the morning light. He pretends to be tough, but he has a warm heart and a priceless wit. He made his money through aviation—as executive director for aircraft maintenance—then investing in properties and retiring before fifty. While he might live in this gracious and stately Victorian house with an impeccably designed garden, the man himself is something of a rough diamond. Precisely because he's loaded with street smarts, I identified him as my most trusted financial advisor.

I explain, "Realistically, erecting the fence'll take a couple of months, by which time the property deal will be finalized, and we could, in principle, move Marah and her cubs onto the land, without delay."

"Great thought," he concedes. "Problem is the cost of building the electrified fence would clear out our coffers—leaving us unable to buy the land!"

Naturally, he's expressed the obvious.

"Great we've finally received our first significant donation!" he continues. "But the fourth month is over; now the fifth is ticking!"

"We've got to get this fencing up immediately if we're going to get Marah out in time," I urge.

"What's the urgency?" Harold asks. "I don't get it."

"I'm no longer the only one bidding for the property," I explain.

"Don't tell me the canned hunters have wised up to your scheme," he demands.

"Afraid so."

Harold is feisty and straight-talking, and, like Ian, an Aries personality. But while Ian is an old Trojan with a big vision and long-term strategic battle plan for conservation, Harold enjoys below-the-belt tactics in the fray of battle. Both share a concern for my welfare and safety, however, and I know it is secretly one reason Harold offered me his low-profile suburban garden premises. Invisible to the outside world, it is not the sort of place that can be accessed by the public or sabotaged by opponents to my cause. My itinerant existence was successful for the same reason—small likelihood of any antagonist guessing that all my top-secret files were being carted around in my car's trunk! I intend to keep it that way. After hearing of the break-in and trashing of Greg Mitchell's premises last year, his files and hard drives stolen in an attempt to bring him down, I keep an even lower profile. I also ensure that duplicates, in fact triplicates, of all important documents are stored in safe keeping in several different locations.

"So how d'you know the canned hunters are bidding against you?"

"Jason overheard some inebriated comments in The Fort," I explain.

"Local Timbavati pub?"

"Yeah. It's a kind of den of iniquity. Usually all the talk's about rugby, rifles, and hunting, but now the topic seems to be my unwelcome arrival in the region."

"Hmm."

"Main hostility's coming from the godfather of the canned-hunting mob, and others have teamed up with him."

"Damn it, that's not kosher; they're onto you already," Harold says. "I don't wanna unnerve you, but the stakes were probably too high from the outset. You're tackling too big a fish with too small a net."

Harold generally gives me encouragement, but today he can't disguise his concern.

"Well, stakes are raised even higher now, Harry," I concede, "because they've started placing offers way in excess of my own."

"Don't let them get cute with us. Remember: until your option runs out, your claim over the land is secure," he reminds me. "Just sit tight, and get your butt into gear."

"That's what I'm doing."

When Harold's worried, he makes the same point several times over. He is making that familiar point again about the men's pubs in this part of the bushveld being the local equivalent of bars in America's Deep South.

"Watch the testosterone and racial tensions in those places," he's reiterating. "Women—like yourself—and black Africans are at serious risk. And probably Jews too."

As for risk, he didn't have to spell it out. Jason informed me that a young six-foot-four game ranger friend of his had been beaten senseless for arriving at The Fort accompanied by a black colleague. And in a separate incident, another particularly good-looking and seriously heterosexual game ranger was so badly smashed up in a pub brawl that he lost the use of one eye and had his face scarred for life, all because it was arbitrarily decided by the mob that he must be gay.

"This background is important, Harry," I concede. "But today I really need your help and guidance on the strategic financial decision in advance of the meeting—"

Too late—the doorbell rings. My grace period is over, and I have to prepare to motivate this strategic action step that I know is right—at an intuitive level—whether or not it makes sense at an immediate logical level.

Harold's housekeeper opens the door, and Marianne van Wyk steps in first. An impressive lady in her fifties with a pronounced Afrikaans accent, she lives in a two-story mansion full of animals and favors maroon and turquoise for her interior décor. Not long ago, I decided to appoint her as a trustee of the White Lion Trust, after she proved her credentials in levelheaded crisis management and astute business practice. She always arrives at least five minutes early. Today, unfortunately for me, she is fifteen minutes early.

After Marianne has settled in, the doorbell rings again, then again, as one after the other of the lawyers on my experts council arrive. One is a contracts specialist, and the other an envirolawyer and CEO of South Africa's top legal firm.

I make them comfortable, and the doorbell rings again. It's Thembi Mahlangu, the second trustee, arriving late. An eloquent, beautiful woman of Sepedi royal descent, and with a strong, quiet manner, she joins us. After the usual formalities, we begin the proceedings.

I explain the timing is very pressurized for gathering outstanding funds for the land, but that the need to secure the premises and permits for the lions' transfer is more urgent—and in order to do so, we need to erect electric fencing immediately.

Marianne speaks first, with a robust exclamation of disapproval.

"*Yuslike*," she says, using a colloquial Afrikaans expression of shock and dismay. "You've just got the first bit of money for the land; now you wanna throw it all away again."

Her argument, as expected, is that any decision over the fencing should wait until after the purchase of the property. So I provide my most reasonable response, "I wouldn't call it 'throwing money away,' Marianne. It's part of a careful strategy to enable the lions onto the land at the earliest opportunity."

"First things first."

Marianne's position is understandable. With her sound business background, she must view my proposal for use of the funds as premature and rash.

"Why risk money that's desperately required to purchase the land?" Harold speculates.

As the trust's financial advisor, he's shrewd, and he thinks out of the box. But based on obvious financial considerations, the input he offers simply supports Marianne's skepticism. I regret I didn't have a chance to cover the ground with him earlier, so I attempt to do so now.

"We have to erect boundaries, fast. The intention's less to keep the lions in than intruders out. And the immediate objective is to gain an official permit, so we have permission to release the lions on the land—at our first opportunity."

I pause, hoping these imperatives hit home.

"And in practical terms, the fences need to be of a very high standard," I explain, "to satisfy the Nature Conservation authorities."

For the record, I take this opportunity to point out that the permit procedure for reintroducing the White Lions to their ancestral lands was initiated by Jason Turner on our behalf, more than a year ago, and he'd been processing it with dedication ever since—on the strength of which we could expect our official approval shortly. The trustees note that Jason deserves a special letter of acknowledgment.

"Good news is Jason's been painstakingly following due process. But we won't be issued a permit without first gaining approval of the fencing," I continued. "It's a necessary prerequisite."

Marianne, of course, reminds me of our unimpressive fundraising record. "*Yuslike,* my friend!" she says. "So you're telling us we must sink hard-earned funds into land we don't yet own—and we might never own?"

I hear her, but that same pressingly urgent inner voice that Maria Khosa trained me to trust keeps telling me I should delay under no circumstances.

I look to Thembi for backup, but she's sitting in silent thought.

Of course, it's vitally important to consider the lawyers' informed positions. Coming from a conservative background, the contracts lawyer offers an abundance of caution, which doesn't support my argument. The other lawyer, Coenraad Jonker, simply observes and listens intently to the whole scenario. An unpretentious young man with a brilliant, unflashy mind, he had catapulted to the very top of the most distinguished and ruthless legal firm in this country. Renowned for weighing and assessing and mediating all possible options, he tends to take fearless, uncompromising action and never look back.

"Without the fencing in place, we're in no position to move Marah to the land," I summarize. "This remains our primary goal of course—and time's running out!"

In this cosseted, wood-paneled interior in the center of Johannesburg suburbia, I am conscious that my last comment may have sounded melodramatic. But the blistering overhead sun that will scorch the Karoo desert in less than one month's time is just one reminder of the fraught situation in general. In addition, the hotel tycoon who owns the land has begun charging exorbitant fees to accommodate Marah and the pride, evidently hoping that if I'm unable to pay, he'll keep the lions himself. And I am unable to pay. The pressure's building up.

There's silence around the table. From Marianne's posture, everyone can see she's by no means convinced.

"I'm going on gut instinct here," I add. "There's an open window of opportunity now, but I've got a terrible hunch it's about to close."

"If you're wrong, you'd lose the whole deal," Marianne points out.

"Time's of the essence," I continue the same plea. "We have to go on faith that the rest of the funding will come in time and on time."

I'm stumped. I can give no further arguments for taking this action. I know these words sounded feeble to the skeptical mind.

"I've got a problem with this," Marianne announces. "Your view, Harry?"

"It is problematic," he replies, the third time he's repeated this phrase in the meeting.

"Thembi?"

Thembi's no pushover. In the past, she'd shown that she's unswayed by the opinion of others, unless totally convinced by the authenticity and value of what's being proposed. She looks thoughtful.

"I'm considering," she responds in a soft voice.

I observe her closely, no assistance likely from these quarters.

All I can do is call for a brief adjournment before a resolution is passed.

I'm exhausted. Harold and Marianne have been echoing and outdoing each other, like two trainee fighter pilots, competing in the same aeronautical show. And not only me—everyone present must have been suffering from buzzing in their ears.

I watch them shuffle off into Harold's drawing room, where delicious morsels have been arranged on platters. I head out into the gardens to clear my head. All morning, I fought to hold this position, but, alone on my walk around Harold's garden, I am having my own doubts. Why, after all, is this action so important to me? It is a grim paradox that my pursuit of Marah's freedom even necessitates the construction of predator-proof fencing. It doesn't make sense. So why am I advocating it? I feel my whole body weakening. As I stroll under the shaded oaks, I should be strengthening my line of rational argument, but instead my mind is filled with all the emotional and gruesome images I've personally witnessed over the years—of harm done by electric fences. Endangered species, such as leopards, tortoises, and rock pythons, electrocuted on the wires. And other animals, trying to escape, like inmates from a high-security prison, killed against them. Then the scene I'll never forget on my recent trip with Jason: the rarest of rare, a pangolin, curled up in a ball around the lowest electric strand, as a natural reflex, dying an agonizing death from its repeated charged currents. We managed to unclamp this little creature's tortured body from Timbavati's fence line; it was still alive, but there was nothing we could do to save it, and it finally died in my arms.

It appalls me to think of these executions taking place all over the world, wherever electric fences have been erected by insensitive humans. And here am I trying to advocate for the urgent erection of more fencing, which may lead to similar casualties on the lions' sacred lands! What an awful thought.

With these images in mind, I know I'm in danger of losing my resolve. And I know that if I waver, there is no chance of bringing my advisors around to the validity of my position.

My head is aching. I took two aspirin before the trustees meeting and wonder whether I should take another. What on earth was motivating me to pursue this course of action against well-reasoned opposition from my advisors?

That's just it! Suddenly I see it clearly. It is not a rational decision. Cold, hard logic is not going to win this day. The information I received came directly from higher council—it required faith and inner knowing. Therefore, it is higher council I should be calling upon to assist me right now and to intervene where I failed.

Suddenly, I see Maria Khosa's face as clear as day. She is beside me. And beside her, I see my beloved Lion, Ingwavuma, proud and immensely regal—with a kind and kingly smile on his face. They are with me!

"I summon you, Guardian Lion, upon this day," I command under my breath. "Be with my earthly council. Enter into this meeting and reach all those who are gathered around the table that they might hear their own lion-hearts and act to ensure the highest and best outcome."

I feel the life force reenter every cell of my body and a calm descend. I catch the figure of Harold on his balcony, looking slightly agitated. Recess is over.

I stride over to the building and into the elegant conference room. The group has reconvened. There is a general silence, broken only by the rustling and reshuffling of the papers of the day's agenda.

I decide to bring the question to a close by simply explaining, "In respect to the fencing issue, I have no further argument, except to say: what I've proposed is my best council."

In my inner vision, I can clearly see Ingwavuma padding around the table passing each and every person there and activating their true lionhearted natures. He has just passed Coenraad Jonker when I hear the words "You have my vote of confidence."

This from one of the most ruthlessly strategic lawyers in our country.

One of those spine-tingling moments, as if my mane hair at the base of my neck is standing on edge. I catch his gaze in silent acknowledgment.

"If I didn't trust my instinct," he continues, "I'd never have survived hardcore litigation. Been eaten alive, time and again. So I say: if your instinct is telling you to take this course of action, Linda—even if it's risky—just do it."

Ingwavuma passes Harold.

"Dead right," he concurs. "Trust your gut. It's served you before."

Thembi nods her approval.

I glance at Marianne. Still striking her dubious pose, she is shaking her head to indicate high risk. But the words coming out of her mouth are actually—finally—granting approval!

"Okay," she instructs, as she gathers up her papers and prepares to hit the Johannesburg traffic. "Get onto the fencing contractors tomorrow—first thing. Let's get the show on the road."

CHAPTER 15

Law of Miracles

It's two weeks since the watershed trustees meeting. While I don't want to take my focus off the fundraising drive for a single moment, I have something urgent to do. Beside the fortress gates is a military-style guard hut and a sign that shows a skull and crossbones, a dog with bloodstained teeth, a shotgun, and a set of handcuffs. As if these sinister warnings aren't enough, the sign also reads: Trespassers Will Be Shot.

I'm on the borders of Timbavati, about to enter the premises of the most notorious canned-hunting operation in South Africa. It feels like I'm one step closer to the end destination for Marah's freedom, yet a million miles away.

Inside the car with me are Lucia van der Post, a well-known British journalist; Tom Stoddart, an award-winning photojournalist; and Baba Mathaba, a distinguished Swazi medicine man in full ceremonial garb. The *London Times* wanted to do a story on my work with the White Lions, so I forced myself to endure the experience of filming here—in the hope that the article will be helpful in exposing the plight of these critically endangered animals, and hopefully even bring a funder in time for the option deadline.

Bizarrely, this place is open to the public. Since canned hunting is still legal in South Africa, public visits are just another means by which the canned hunter can gain more income for his activities. I'd heard visits to this place are a big attraction for foreign tourists, but mine was the only vehicle waiting for entry.

At a gesture from the guard in his watchtower, I pay the entrance fee through a slot. The electronic gates open slowly, and the guard indicates for me to proceed. I drive down the gravel pathway and pull the vehicle into the concrete parking lot, hesitating a moment before getting out. The Bethlehem canned-hunting camp was a nightmare in the extreme, but I anticipate this will be worse. This is where it all began, where the grand scheme of capturing and breeding Africa's most sacred animals was masterminded and executed. Bethlehem copied this grim prototype, and with the heady smell of blood money, many other canned-hunting operations are likely to follow. But this bleak, militaristic stronghold is where the master plan of breeding the rarest of animals by hand, in cages, in order to kill them, was first configured.

Stepping out onto the concrete parking lot, my body starts to shake like Jell-O. I'm picking up an intense pain and anguish in the atmosphere and I'm chilled to the bone. The last time I experienced this degree of residual denseness was when I visited Dachau, the Nazi concentration camp.

I glance back at the photographer, Tom Stoddart, at the open trunk, preparing his gear. He's a well-known war photographer who has spent his life filming in active war zones, even surviving a mortar attack in Sarajevo. When the *London Times* commissioned him for this assignment, he had just returned from behind the firing line in Baghdad. His first comment when he and I were introduced yesterday at the Johannesburg airport was that he was really looking forward to a break, as he viewed this shoot as a kind of soft "women's" story about a former model playing with White Lions in Africa. I wonder how his view will change after he's finished here.

We'd heard the canned hunter has a violently explosive temper, and a particular hatred for media, especially after the *The Cook Report* exposed some of the malpractices taking place here. So the photographer and I decided our best approach today was to appear to be ordinary visitors and to keep the camera equipment to a minimum.

I feel an involuntary shudder. It's bad enough being filmed in a nightmarish place like this, but what adds to my tension is the presence of Baba Mathaba, seated proud and upright in the back of the car. This powerful traditional healer is one of my mentors, and I visited him last night to set my intention for this important shoot. But when he heard my destination was to visit a dreaded canned-hunting camp, he was determined to join me, so that he might do a ceremonial blessing of protection for the incarcerated lions.

From Maria Khosa's training, I appreciate the importance of such rituals and their far-reaching effects. However, I didn't think it was wise to bring this imposing elder into such a hostile land, where his color would certainly be an issue and where his conspicuous ceremonial dress could cause a riot. The canned hunter is a notorious racist, known to shoot randomly at people he considered trespassers. I tried to dissuade Baba Mataba, but my protestations did nothing to deter him. The distinguished elder was adamant about accompanying me to the site where the White Lions were held hostage. So my best compromise was for him to stay in the car, with the journalist, Lucia van der Post, where he would work in prayer with the lions, while the photographer and I kept our grim visit as short as possible.

Tom and I head off to the farmhouse, which looks more like a military barracks than a family home. We come upon cage after cage of depressed, blank-eyed big cats on display for public viewing. This is where a magnificent, free-roaming White Lion male was imprisoned after being drugged and dragged into a pickup truck, and where he spent the rest of his life in a cage, breeding a royal bloodline, all awaiting execution.

All the tiny cubs are crammed together in a cage no larger than a dog kennel. They have been removed from their mothers and are crawling over each other, with void, unfocused eyes. Instantly, I relive Marah's laser-sharp gaze, which reaches right into my soul. I want to weep. What do other people think when they come to a place like this? Can paying visitors be so thick-skinned as to witness this acute suffering as if it were Disneyland?

Tom asks me to pose with the cages of baby lions, which is what any visitor would do, but I notice a shadowy figure barely visible at the nearby barracks.

"One more session," he instructs. "Over there, with the bigger lions."

There is another cage, with a group of subadults, looking so miserable and undernourished that my heart shrinks in despair. I can't tell whether their condition is the consequence of negligent nutrition or active inbreeding, but I've never encountered more unhappy animals in my life.

After a series of shots, Tom decides that he can conclude his shoot without me and will wrap up quickly. I leave the incarcerated animals behind with their hauntingly brave, sad faces and return to the parking lot. I'm hoping to join Baba Mataba and Lucia there, but as I walk toward them, I notice two trucks pull in, carrying armed troops. The soldiers are dressed in full combat gear. Virtually all are blond, in the tradition of the Hitler Youth. Bizarrely, the sides of both trucks are painted with an inscription in red: South African Army. I stop midstride, frozen, in the center of the parking lot. Something's wrong. Since this is after the fall of Apartheid, these Aryan troops in army gear certainly aren't ANC national forces. This is the canned hunter's private army. I avoid looking in Baba Mathaba's direction so as not to draw attention to his arresting figure in the back of my car. I have to rely on the medicine man to remain obscure there, so my best bet is to actively engage with the vehicles, which are pulled up beside me.

"Where're you taking the troops?" I ask the driver of one truck, also in military uniform.

"Combat training. For a break we're gonna see the trophy lions," he responds, as if this were normal.

He's ready to pull the vehicle out again but ends with his version of polite conversation, "You been to see the cubs? Cute, eh?"

"Yes . . ." I respond, knowing all too well these will be cannon fodder in time.

I wait for the trucks to disappear in the direction of the hunting camps before going over to my parked vehicle. I am about to open the door when Tom approaches, fast. He looks wrecked, a bag of nerves.

"You okay?" I ask him.

"Not at all."

He starts hurriedly loading his equipment back into the trunk of the car, speaking double-time. "Need to get outta here, fast. I know this feeling only too well—in my bones. Same feeling I had in Sarajevo . . . just before the mortar exploded. The last thing I remember—"

I'm with him: we need to leave—now. But instead of erasing this memory, I am going to ensure this grim experience drives every day of my life from this day forward, until Marah roams free in her ancestral lands and her White Lion family are protected by international law.

Black Monday. November 25, 2004. Three weeks after the visit to the canned-hunting camp. The option is days from closing, but we appear no closer to our goal. I'm inside my office in Harold's garden premises, staring at the mountains of meaningless papers on my overcrowded desk. A graveyard of failed prospects and dead ends. As for the fencing contractor, I didn't delay for a moment in bringing him in. With full-on focus on fundraising efforts, I was unable to oversee this complex labor-intensive process myself, but once again, Jason generously volunteered his time and expertise. Based in Timbavati, he took time off his study to assist. First the high-rise, predator-proof, electrified fence around the property's perimeter was constructed. Then, deep in the interior of the property, Jason erected a second fenced camp with quality diamond mesh, designed specifically for the lions and their requirements. He chose an ideal location for Marah and her family—a lovely wooded area, quite extensive, with several thickets of indigenous trees, several of them huge and shade-giving. The internal area is secure and electrified and would be perfect for temporarily housing Marah's pride directly after their arrival.

But as each pole was sunk these past few weeks, and each wire was tensioned, strand by strand, all I could think of was the sand in the hourglass, running out.

I sit at my desk with the checkbook in hand, and my pen hovering before signing off the last installment for the fencing, knowing once this check is cashed, the very last component of the anonymous donation will have been used up.

I pause, momentarily paralyzed, then sign off and place the check in an envelope before sealing it.

With the option nearly expired, our opponents must be celebrating their imminent takeover of Marah's property. Although Jason clearly thought twice before relaying this information, so as not to discourage me, the local hunting mob has been toasting their success for several weeks now—downing pints of lager at The Fort. They took the measure of me a while back. But last week, Jason overheard the hunters drunkenly pronouncing there isn't a hope in hell of "Tucker and her motley crew of New Age bunny huggers" raising the bucks.

I look up from my crowded desk to see one of these bunny huggers arriving, padding over to give me a warm hug of greeting. Xhosa has a characteristic musical jaunt in his step and a particularly huggable, bearlike frame. A young Nguni man in dreadlocks, he painstakingly perused the four hundred pages of my book *Mystery of the White Lions* and, together with his university colleagues, decided these iconic animals would be the route to reviving the youth culture of our nation. One of my most enduring supporters, Xhosa offered his services as my personal assistant for a pittance. It still moves me deeply to think that young intellectuals with straight-A grades and significant opportunities for self-advancement in post-Apartheid South Africa should dedicate their efforts to my cause. Xhosa—whom I fondly call X for short—is also an exceptionally talented rap artist. He and his circle of young intelligentsia had been dedicatedly publishing poetry in literary journals and producing funky programs on national television in honor of my White Lion work. A radio station has now agreed to air his inspired music nationwide.

"It's just the beginning," he tells me, enthusiastically reminding me that his colleagues are pursuing all avenues possible to raise awareness about the White Lions' plight.

"Great news! Well done, X!" I say.

His comment is touching. So much about Xhosa endears him to me. Although art and music are Xhosa's passions, I've known for some time that he actually comes from an accounting background at the university. These past couple of weeks, Xhosa has been particularly eager to do the sums, but sadly, there is little to calculate.

By way of consolation, Xhosa points out now, "At least we've gained the support of quite a number of individuals."

"Yup. They're courageous," I admit. "Clearly they've contributed all they can afford—small amounts given lovingly and unconditionally."

It's not that I undervalue any of it. Every bit counts.

A week ago, we pulled off an exciting and maverick campaign. Members of a well-known British rock band, once called 10CC, came together on short notice to help stage an awareness-raising event in aid of my appeal. It was led by Greg McKewan. In former days, he performed before a crowd of sixty-five thousand people; he'd written a series of songs in celebration of the White Lions. Knowing the urgency, Greg and his band acted very fast and pulled an event together on a shoestring after a couple of weeks of advertising and promotion. They put love and guts into their show, and it has raised huge awareness. But X and I have been assessing the results. I've received masses of emails filled with eager questions, but only a trickle of funds. Every cent is welcome, of course, but all told, these valued contributions are pocket change compared to the amount outstanding.

However, a substantial difference has been made by an American nonprofit organization named Corelight, which raised a significant component of funding and, amazingly, committed it without seeking any form of repayment. Their alliance has been deeply encouraging and supportive from the start, so much so that the founder of the organization, Leslie Temple-Thurston, has unconditionally contributed personal inheritance funds toward securing the land. And following her lead, many other kind people have come in to help, with generous, loving donations. But the bottom line is we are still massively short—owing more than half the funds.

My cell phone beeps. It is a text from Jason.

"DONE & DUSTED. Jxx" That's all he needs to say.

The huge operation of predator-proofing Marah's land, under his supervision, is now complete. I feel all the more bleak. What is the point of this expensive and exhausting fencing operation? And what is the point of imposing on the time and goodwill of this wonderfully obliging and generous friend? I've failed in finding the funds.

I try to pull myself together in a concerted effort to remain positive and to get beyond my personal sense of failure—but the truth is, the option period has dwindled and almost lapsed, and nothing can change that! I feel a crushing sense of defeat.

"X?" I say.

He looks at me from his desk.

"Let's at least be honest. We need a miracle if we're gonna raise the funds before the end of this week."

NOVEMBER 30, 2004. THE LAST DAY of the option's fifth and final month. Five days after writing out the last check for the fencing. Dazed, I open the door to my office, trying to assess the damage. Xhosa is waiting tentatively for me in the interior by his alcove.

"Should we do it, X?" I ask, rhetorically, detecting the nervous tremor in my own voice. Without pausing for his answer, I respond: "Okay. Let's go!"

In desperation, I've resorted to a private moneylender's option. Only the direst of measures could have led me to contemplate this alternative—it was literally the last resort.

We've climbed in my car. Xhosa insists on driving me. He's a responsible driver, so I don't care, but I get the impression he's worried I wouldn't arrive there on my own.

With the vehicle stationary at a traffic light for the moment, Xhosa starts reading my thoughts, as he tends to do, particularly in moments of crisis.

"Not that I'm worried 'bout your driving," he explains, "although your mind's somewhere else right now, admittedly, not on the road. No, I'm worried 'bout this moneylending dude."

"Why exactly?" I ask, exhaling slowly. My whole body aches.

"Just need to be with you to read the small print. That's all."

The light turns green. As we pass by the rows of jacaranda trees on Mandela Drive, I prepare myself for the implications of the moneylender's deal. The advantage of this emergency measure was that the outstanding funds would be available—instantly. In the lead-up to the expiration of my option, this seemed the only solution. The arrangement on offer was a short-term loan—three months—which would give us an all-important extension of our fundraising efforts. But the catch was the sky-high interest rate, calculated on a daily rather than annual basis. And the land itself would be held as collateral by the lender.

I recall Xhosa's concerned and quizzical look when he first handed me the moneylender's faxed contract three weeks ago. The paperwork was not complicated, but as soon as I read it, I felt myself breaking out into a cold sweat. I wouldn't have given it a second glance at the time. But now there's nowhere else to turn.

As the car glides through the crowded Johannesburg streets, my mind keeps flashing back to the seemingly endless preparations that culminated in this grim and fateful day. To no avail. Perhaps these desperate measures will save the day. I am clinging to hope of a positive outcome.

"There's got to be a way out of this!" I say, in a concerted effort to muster my most enthusiastic voice, but bleakness creeps in. The thought of Marah's heartland being reappropriated by the hunting fraternity is too dismal to contemplate.

"I know what you're thinking, boss," Xhosa observes. "But no, you are not going to lose the land, and no, I don't see you giving up. I see you fighting to the bitter end, tooth and nail, rather than handing it over."

Normally, I'd think Xhosa's poetic observation of me a particularly astute character sketch. But what makes it uncomfortable is that those losses are a looming reality. Is this really the bitter end?

WE FINALLY ARRIVE at the monumental Fort Knox–like entrance, with two large eagles, in concrete, balanced on a giant block at either side. An armed guard in uniform comes out and, on telecom instructions, presses the remote to open the wrought-iron grill gates.

Xhosa is shaking his head grimly. "Dunno why we're doing this, boss. D'you know how many friends of mine have been shredded by these scheisters? Out of desperation. They think they're getting a loan—my mother's aunt needed urgent medical care to save my cousin's life—but the interest rate's so high she's chained to repayments for the rest of her life. Slavery. These people are money lords, turning gold into guilt."

"Okay, okay!" I snap, trying not to hear him. "I really need to focus now."

We are standing on the front porch of the overly ornate, neoclassic fortress. The garden around us is barren, apart from rolling emerald lawns as groomed as bowling greens, interspersed with giant coconut palms and monumental concrete sculptures. Another armed guard with earphones lurking behind one of these statues talks into the mouthpiece.

We are exactly on time. Xhosa hammers the brass knocker on the colossal entrance doors. A rottweiler snarls viciously at us, but he's attached to a chain rattling on an eight-meter running wire. The poor animal can only charge back and forth in a fury of aggression. A moment later, the man we've come to see opens the door and steps out onto his porch, barefoot with sunburned, hairy legs and a contract in hand. He is heavily built, with a giant beer belly spilling over his short shorts.

"Sign there, and there," he gestures. "Need to get back to the rugby."

I put down my briefcase on the slablike marbled porch floor in order to take the document and scrutinize it.

The man is underdressed, but I can't help noticing the multiple gold rings on the fat fingers that hold out the contract. Xhosa has been eager to check the fine print, but there doesn't appear to be anything of the kind. The deal is more crass and even more simple-minded than I imagined. The pro forma version faxed to me three weeks ago gave me intimations of trouble, but this is worse. I hand the document over to Xhosa. One clause catches my attention, a stipulation above and beyond the conditions already stipulated (about the land being held): "the lions will also be held as collateral."

Xhosa immediately picks up my briefcase and we make a speedy exit.

The idea of pledging my feline family as commodities sickens me to the core, let alone the gut-wrenching possibility of losing them altogether.

"Shylock!" Xhosa pronounces as we climb back into the car.

"Totally sickening experience," I respond. "My God, X—what a closely averted disaster!"

We exit into the Johannesburg streets again.

"Why do these guys look like they're out of the same box?" Xhosa asks. "For a moment there, boss, I thought it was that canned-hunting operator again—you know, the dude you rescued Marah from."

"Don't I know," I mumble gloomily. He's right. The moneylenders and the canned hunters are one of a kind. If money's your God, no wonder you reckon you're beyond morality.

We are racing past the jacaranda on Mandela Drive again in reverse as we head down the row of high-rise office blocks, toward the zoo.

I would endure every hardship, climb every mountain, face every onslaught of opposition. I would gladly give up everything I possessed for my lions, but I will not risk trading them for anything in the world.

Back at the office and frazzled after our abortive moneylending excursion, I try to resist despair. This morning was, fundamentally, a primary shamanic teaching. Maria once spoke of the lesson, an exercise of faith and trust in the universe. In my prayers to the universe, I had placed only one proviso, that the funds be unconditional. This in turn required that I trust that the unconditional resources needed for the lions would be provided, utterly and completely according to universal law, not man-made law. I realize now that breaking my own pledge and principles—by considering a mercenary moneylender and his unreasonable terms—could have brought about the most dreaded of consequences.

Without other options, I begin sorting the backlog of emails. One of the lawyers on my advisory council wrote to me ten days ago. The email reads, "According to South African law, when an option expires, the seller is required to give the other party fourteen days' notice before laying claim to the deposit money." *Why didn't I see this before?* I have two more weeks. I stare at the computer screen in astonishment.

Doubt creeps in immediately. I've already had five months. What will change in two more weeks? This much I know: the real challenge is going to be containing and transcending my rising self-doubt. Xhosa is loitering, waiting for me to give him instruction. I sit upright in my seat, actively reinstating Maria Khosa's example of the positive vision of a successful outcome.

"The money can arrive now, this minute, X," I announce, snapping my fingers. "If our goals are aligned with universal law."

"I believe you, boss."

With the moneylending episode behind me, here I am, once again, putting on a positive front. But this time, it is different.

ONE DAY BEFORE EXPIRATION of the grace period. December 13, 2004. Thirteen days after the abortive expedition to the moneylender and, for all intents and purposes, nothing has changed. I've stepped up all efforts, focused from morning to evening—and often through the night. Yet I remain dismally short of the target. It is beyond nerve-wracking; it is simply abominable.

Here, in my claustrophobic, closet-like apartment, cramped and bleak, I am in survival mode, stepping out of my business suit. I prepare myself a quick meal, which I eat standing over the counter. I note that I'm "still standing," true, but I am fatigued to the bone.

I take another aspirin and collapse onto my futon on the floor. I look into the eyes of Aslan, King of kings, staring down into my little boxlike space. Holding that image of timeless infinity in mind, I try to settle down under the duvet for the night. Even in the dark, my eyes burn. The tears are building up, and the pressure in my head is nearly intolerable. I rephrase a silent prayer, asking for resolution, fortitude, and lionheartedness. I was granted two weeks' grace, yet am no closer to clinching the property deal. I can feel Aslan's face bearing down at me, but I dare not look up. Not only have I failed to rescue Aslan, but I've failed my beloved Marah too. Maria Khosa should never have handed her mantle of Keeper of the White Lions to me. I feel a total failure.

I shut down everything and wrap myself tightly in the duvet, with the overhead fan turned off, but I'm unable to sleep. All my internal processors are whirring. There is no respite. I can't even toss and turn; I am trying to come to terms with the fact that this past fortnight was, in reality, just an excruciating deferment of the inevitable.

The clock is still ticking in my kitchenette. I drag myself out of bed to remove the batteries.

The hours churn by, a totally sleepless night.

Through the half-opened chinks of the blinds, dawn is trying to break. I might as well have spent the past two weeks in bed. I feel totally unprepared to face the world. I finally get myself up, but it takes ages to get dressed. I stare at my disheveled image in the mirror, drawing my hair back tightly.

I am snarled up in the traffic. I was already late, so the rush-hour jam will set me back another hour or two. When I eventually arrive at the office, I open the door to find Xhosa in work mode as usual. Ever the bright spark, he emerges with a tray of tea. It seems to me he is trying to keep the inevitable at bay, but it's pointless putting on a brave face. I have to prepare myself for the reality that the period of reprieve is well and truly at an end. Marah's kingdom is lost. Despite everything—my life savings, my prayers, my wishful thinking, Maria Khosa's training, Xhosa's dedication, my colleagues' and my own very best efforts—everything is lost.

"D'you perhaps need to sit down, Linda?" he asks, putting the clattering tray on the corner of my congested desk and drawing my chair out gallantly.

I seat myself in silence.

"Good," he says. "I thought you'd be interested in reviewing what our legal advisors have to say this morning."

"I know what they have to say," I conclude. "In closing an option, South African law requires that the seller must send a registered letter of termination, stating that the option will be legally annulled after seven calendar days."

"Correct," he responds. "So, strictly speaking, we still have seven days."

"Sure. Understood. But what good is a stay of execution?"

Without replying, Xhosa stacks new contact details in a pile in my in-tray. Then he departs and busies himself with carrying my files and briefcase in from the car. His idea, as always, is that I should be free to dedicate the whole day—another entire day—to ensuring not a single paper remains unturned.

I stare at my sweet-faced assistant across the battleship of my desk. The obstacles have been too great. I simply cannot begin again! I'd be shuffling papers around an overcrowded deck while the boat sank, with Xhosa piling up notes in my in-tray and jam-packing the desk with tea trays.

Exasperatingly, I hear Xhosa whistling a tune.

This cannot be the end of the story. There has to be another way. But I am at a standstill. A lull before the storm. It's pointless hoisting my sail.

The doorbell rings. My first line of defense, Harold's housekeeper, speaks through the intercom to announce that the sheriff of the court is at Harold's front door. The dreaded letter has arrived. Frozen, I instruct that the official be let in. I wait, my whole head ringing, until eventually an officious knocking starts up on the door of our garden office. I open it. The official asked me for my name and passes the registered letter over. I sign for it. Closing the door, I turn to find Xhosa staring at the document in my hand. For once my loyal assistant is utterly silent, unsmiling, and expressionless. I gave him a faint smile of resignation. I can tell he's trying to summon a state of Zen calm. But there's no easy remedy for lost time.

I throw the document down on the entrance table without a word.

Xhosa stares at me, cracks of concern now creasing his sweet face.

"What, X? What are you thinking? I have no life vest—believe me," I blurt out. "What's the point of clutching onto faith? The boat's already sailed. Nothing short of a miracle can save us now."

"The great one wouldn't have given you more time if you'd already found the answer," Xhosa concludes. "There's a miracle on the horizon—I can smell it."

"Excuse me," I say curtly.

My cell phone's ringing again. I see from the missed calls screen that it rang earlier, coinciding with the moment the doorbell sounded with the special delivery. The incoming caller is Mireille.

"I can't stand the agony any longer," I hear her announce, without introduction. "What's the status?"

"Bleak, I'm afraid dearest Godmum, utterly bleak and pointless."

"Well then, I have a solution."

I stand motionless, phone in hand.

"You have . . . a solution?" In front of me, Xhosa bursts into an impromptu rap song. There's ringing in my ears, so I can't be sure I was hearing her correctly. "Can you say that . . . again, Mum?" I ask cautiously.

"Yes. There's just one last instruction I need to issue in order to make this a reality. I have the solution—and I'm serious."

How is it that at this precise moment—what the proverbs call the darkest hour just before the dawn—that dynamics can suddenly turn head over heels?

Xhosa is hammering out his unrehearsed lyrics, beating his hands on his desk like a drum: "As da hourglass drains da sand, Mireille da Miracle shines da light, breaking da murky darkness God-forgotten world winged sunlight overhead she dives out of blue yonder to save da day . . ."

I feel dizzy. Almost under my breath, I ask Mireille again, "Are we really saved? Sorry, but it's hard to believe!"

For some reason, I never for a moment imagined my fairy godmother would be the one to save the day all over again. She saved Marah and cubs; wasn't that enough?

"I'd be prepared to mortgage my house to secure Marah's land—if that's what it takes," she responds.

I cry, "I can't possibly let you do it, Godmum!"

Her magnanimous gesture has taken me entirely by surprise, like a joker in the pack of cards I'd been playing so strategically. Although I'm overjoyed beyond belief, paradoxically I feel I have to save her from her own rash decision.

"Well, you may be the Keeper of the White Lions, young lady," she replies, sweeping my concerns aside. "But to the Tsonga people in the Timbavati region I'm known as *Kokwane Tangala*—Grandmother of the White Lions. So I too have responsibilities and duties to take care of. Tut, tut—let me get on with them."

I drop the phone, stunned. Xhosa and I do a little jig around Harold's garden: up the garden path, around the koi pond, under the shady oak glade, up the stone steps, onto the veranda! We are in fits of exultant giggles by the time we've finished. This must be the miracle Xhosa envisioned on the horizon. Out of nowhere, Mireille provided the zoo with the ransom money for Marah and her cubs, at a time of dire need. Now she'd do it again. The most important guiding light in my project. She is truly a godsend. I simply adore this formidable matriarch, with her lovable, almost naive, enthusiasm. It is as if we've been mother and daughter, always and forever.

Of course, it had to be Mireille. The miracle. Why didn't I think of it before?

CHAPTER 16

Suspense in Sante Fe

WITH A HEAD BRIMMING FULL OF EXCITEMENT, I set off early to beat the morning traffic, all the while reviewing in my mind the exhilaration of Mireille's unexpected rescue. December 14, 2004. I didn't sleep at all. What a truly wonderful surprise. To use one of Mireille's favorite sayings, "full steam ahead."

Yesterday afternoon, I brought the Corelight organization up to speed with the latest developments. The directors, Brad Laughlin and Leslie Temple-Thurston, were delighted the all-important property acquisition is on track. Having already pledged significant funds to this cause, they've been working around the clock on solutions to cover the shortfall. The organization is faith-based, founded on the premise of the flow of limitless light and resource from the Source. Corelight generates significant funds for worthy causes working in harmony with Nature. I know I have a lot to learn from them. Having kept in close contact with me over the period of my intensive fundraising over the past few months, and after making a considerable no-strings-attached contribution, they came to the rescue again in these final moments, after hearing that Mireille's majority donation required an emergency top-up to clinch the deal. Last night, they confirmed they've raised a further amount to contribute immediately, which, combined with Mireille's majority contribution, will just meet the target. And they were wiring the funds through as we spoke.

Riding the crest of a wave, I'm just ahead of the bumper-to-bumper traffic, buoyed up with irrepressible delight. I'm actually singing an aria to myself, "Ave Maria," at the top of my lungs! Mireille's intervention is truly unconditional. There is no nasty small print; there are no strings attached. She's testimony that this kind of selfless giving actually exists. I'll never forget her hallmark maxim: "I simply give, and don't count the cost." Those were her words on that first landmark occasion when she provided the ransom money for Marah. And she added, "Believe me, I know the reward for this kind of giving is much greater than anything I could ever imagine!" In fact, I did believe her, because I'd witnessed the overwhelming joy and exuberance she experienced in saving Marah—by merely providing the funds for her freedom—and the profound meaning such selfless action had given her life ever since.

From the snippets she revealed to me, I've reconstructed fond images of Mireille as a sunny little two-year-old in a Swiss orphanage, throwing her arms up to be adopted by barren and childless aristocratic parents. But they subsequently denied her their inheritance, because they didn't consider their adopted daughter a blue blood. To me, Mireille's generosity illuminates her true aristocracy of spirit in contrast to their mean-spiritedness, no matter their title.

I stop on my way to the office at the coffee shop close to the zoo. It seems appropriate. My thoughts are with Marah, as always, and her next big step to freedom is finally secured! Precisely 9:00 a.m. That's 8:00 a.m., Geneva time. I start imagining how Mireille's day must be unfolding. With characteristic efficiency, she'd be phoning her banker precisely as the Swiss bank opened its doors, concluding her instruction with a salvo along the lines of: "Get on with it, good fellow—all systems go!"

When I arrive at the garden office, Xhosa is waiting for me, perched expectantly on his seat inside his alcove. A momentary suspense. The phone rings. We both freeze. He's waiting for me to answer. I lift the receiver and before I say a word, Mireille bursts out in sobs on the other end of the line. She is totally distraught. I hear she's in a state of acute distress, her voice choked with emotion even before she completes her sentence.

"I've no choice but to listen to sense! Please forgive me, darling daughter."

In that moment I get a flash of an infinitely reasonable Swiss banker advising his client that no sensible woman would sink her precious francs in a lion project in darkest Africa.

What's there to say? After hearing the cold voice of reason, it's only natural a warmhearted lion matriarch should waver. I'm stunned. My voice is barely audible as I bid goodbye to my beloved godmother. With my last hope snuffed, I clutch my unopened briefcase and leave the office immediately, instructing Xhosa to do the same. Pushing the door closed behind me, I can barely breathe. I've a splitting headache.

The whole journey home is blank. Interminable. Back in the claustrophobic darkness of The Cupboard, I've sealed all the blinds tight shut against the daylight. I stare into nothingness. Too dark to see Aslan's face. I dare not look at the King. After coming so close, I have failed him utterly. The King *and* Marah.

Just when hope was so tantalizingly dangled. I have never felt this kind of excruciating pain before—almost achieving an all-important goal, then failing utterly. Why did I bother to try at all? Maria Khosa must have been out of her mind to believe in me. I've failed her too.

My last glimmer of hope, which flickered for just a moment, has faded to black. I abhor my deluded state, which led me to believe I could actually make a difference to the future of this planet! What a grand and utterly ridiculous scheme. No wonder my godmother got cold feet.

She quite rightly rejected me and all I stand for. And how could

I possibly blame Mireille? She's already done more than could be expected of anyone. It's no one's fault; these things happen. My only mistake was to have held out hope in the first place and to have staked my life on the outcome.

My hateful cell phone keeps peeping and the screen lights up in the dark.

"Congratulations! I knew you could do it!"

It's Ian. Ironically, he's responding to the text I sent him yesterday—the first person I informed of my seemingly miraculous good news of Mireille's eleventh-hour salvage job.

"Ian," I begin typing back. "It's no-go. What can I say . . ." Then I erase the message and drop the phone from my hand. I feel like such a dismal failure.

I can't tell how many hours pass. Too many to care. It seems the day is finally drawing to a bleak and unforgiving end. The final count-down: day two of the extension of the extension. Five hopeless days to D-day.

Now my cell is ringing; I reach out to switch off the noise, but notice that the caller is Marianne van Wyk. Fighter pilot and squash champion, friend and trusted trustee. What difference can she, or anyone, make at this burned-out stage? Best to ignore the call.

Then, as a reflex, against every judgment, I answer it. Marianne has been following very closely the painstaking process of my fund-raising efforts for the land, and, as a trustee, she deserves to be kept informed.

"I'm afraid it's all over, Marianne," I say without introduction, sobbing.

She simply snorts in response, "Huh! It's not over til it's over!'

All I can do is sob.

"I'll take over," she declares, stepping into the cockpit.

She hangs up. I can only assume she is making an international call from South Africa to Leeds.

I am still in the same position, slumped on the futon, holding my aching head in my hands. It's about twenty minutes later, in the blackness, and the cell phone rangs again. Again, Marianne's name lights up. When I answer it, she launches straight into her version of events.

"I told Mireille straight. I said to her, 'Are you going to let some little gray man in a little gray suit in an even littler, grayer office tell you what you should or shouldn't do with your life—and your money—when the future of the White Lions is at stake?' That's what I told her."

I am still tearful, but I can't help letting out a half-spluttering laugh. "And then?" I ask.

"Well. *Wat kan ek se?* I don't think Mireille likes *anybody* telling her what to do."

I want to know more, but I could see from my cell phone there's an international incoming call on hold. I swiftly say goodbye to Marianne and answer the other line.

"Right!" It's Mireille's voice on the other end of the line—assertive and upbeat—and I get an instant picture of my fairy godmother getting back into the driver's seat of her 4.4 HSE Range Rover. "I've just had a call from Marianne to say I should not let anybody overrule my better judgment. Well. Naturally, I was coming to that opinion myself, after a strong cup of coffee and a piece of shortbread. Onward, Christian soldiers! Let's burn rubber!"

So Mireille's steam train is on track again, with all the bells and whistles! The first thing I do after saying goodbye is to splash my face with cold water. And try to get my thoughts into full throttle again.

The challenge is to clear the international transfer through the South African Reserve Bank in time to meet the deadline. Normally, the Reserve Bank allows for a minimum of two weeks for clearance on this scale. We have exactly four working days. In that time, not only do the funds need to be cleared, they also need to reflect in the sellers' attorney's trust account.

Unfortunately, there's nothing more I can do today. Day has become night. Again, the thought of sleep is an impossibility. First thing in the morning, I'll be on to the necessary practicalities.

I've reached a condition somewhere between acute exhaustion and hyperventilation. I wish I could get a breath of fresh air, but it's pitch dark outside, and not safe in my neighborhood to walk on my own. To add to the crisis, I am due to present to an international environmental congress called the Defenders of Wildlife Conference in Sante Fe in three days' time. During the crucial fundraising period, this forthcoming event seemed a secondary priority—so I shelved thinking about it. But I am only too aware that it represents a real opportunity to keep the Global White Lion Protection Trust afloat. If I opt instead to stay in South Africa and the land deal falls through—which, realistically, despite Mireille's best wishes, it's on the brink of doing—I'd lose everything: not only the immediate prospects for Marah and her cubs, but also for the survival of my organization. With everything hanging in the balance, though, how can I even consider going to the congress?

In this cramped carton of an apartment, I feel like a pent-up lioness in the zoo dungeons. The tension is virtually unbearable. There's a new choice to make: whether to go or whether to stay.

December 18, 2004. The day after Mireille's spectacular comeback. Hair unbrushed, I propel myself out of The Cupboard this morning in jeans, a white T-shirt, and a raw silk jacket that could do with extra pressing, but I couldn't care less. At best, sleep has been erratic over the past few months, and unfortunately, last night was another totally sleepless night. If I am to present at the congress, I need to depart later today! My flight to Sante Fe was booked several months ago, so securing a seat isn't the problem. And organizing accommodation for the conference at such short notice is also no challenge, since Corelight's headquarters are located in Sante Fe, and they've long since extended a wonderfully warm invitation. The difficulty is weighing up whether I can risk everything in departing at this pivotal moment.

I've made arrangements for Xhosa to meet me at Marianne's house. After driving down the panhandle of her entrance drive with its purple plastered walls, I climb out of my car. It's a blazing summer's day, and I prepare myself to be slobbered to death by Marianne's fierce guard dogs: one a miniature version of the other. I see them propelling themselves toward me now: a huge shaggy dog with long black hair, a drooly mustache, and bright button eyes behind dreadlocked fringe; and a tiny shaggy dog with the same hair, drooly whiskers, and button eyes: a black-haired Bouvier and Scottie. Sure enough, they launch a twin assault, nearly toppling me over—but I am rescued by Marianne, who calls them off.

"*Ag shame,* just see it as part of the design," Marianne announces, referring to the additional muddy paw motifs all over my white T-shirt, some big, some small.

No point in trying to dust myself off.

"Hellooooo!" I hear a cry as I enter the front door. It's Marianne's cockatoo, Pumpkin, shrieking a greeting at me from his colorful jungle gym.

I sit on Marianne's couch and the two panting, dribbling dogs leap up to join me.

"There's nothing more you can do. Leave the country," Marianne instructs. "Sign any relevant document. And sign a couple of extra blank sheets, while you're about it. *Gaan maar.* Go! Pack your bags. Get the hell outta here! Go do what you have to do at the congress—and leave this little matter to me."

I wonder whether I am really in a position to do so. "You do realize, Marianne, that whatever überqualities rocketed you into national squash championships in your late teens will be needed, and more, to pull off the impossible timing?"

My response to Marianne's firm answer was not exactly encouraging, true. Nevertheless, the champion fighter pilot is not deterred.

"Let me get my hands on those bankers," she demands. "And Corelight? How're they doing?"

"Well, if anyone can swing it at this late stage, it's Brad and Leslie's organization," I explain. "They've an SOS distress call out to their entire circle. But now the timing's excruciating!"

Suddenly, the front gate bell is ringing, and the hounds leap off the couch in unison, tearing into the front yard. Xhosa has arrived and is bowled over by the guard dogs, who are giving him an exuberant greeting, with barking, jumping, and dozens of kisses sealed with slobber. I would assist, but my phone rings; it's Mireille. Breathless, I explain the impossibilities of our timing to her.

"Mission impossible?" she responds in her Swiss-British accent. "Absolute nonsense!"

She's adopting a haughty tone, and it's a relief to see that her characteristic bubbly enthusiasm has returned, en force. I recognize that it must have taken every last ounce of matriarchal lioness courage to go ahead with the decision she just committed to.

"Regrettably, dearest Mum," I explain, "We have to face the reality that the timing could just be too tight now."

"Bulldust!" she announces, the matriarch's way of encouragement. "Darling daughter: ever since a child, I've gone by the dictum: If it's possible, it's already done. And if it is impossible, it shall be done!"

Allowing myself a momentary smile, I explain to Mireille my thinking in respect to the congress, where help and resources may be available for the fragile survival of the organization. She agrees there wasn't much more I could do to process the funds. She is satisfied to leave the final details to Marianne and Marianne's connections in the Reserve Bank.

It's decided. After Mireille's encouraging phone call, I begin sorting files, packing, giving Xhosa instructions, and signing documents for Marianne.

"Okay," Marianne instructs. "Put your signature on those blank sheets as well—just in case."

I give her the binder full of relevant background material. Xhosa carries my bags to the car.

"Hellooooo!" shrieks the cockatoo as we depart.

"And goodbye, Pumpkin!" I reply. "Sorry, can't stop to talk today."

As the rows of suburban houses flash by, Xhosa announces, "Can't let banking formalities and procedures halt the perfect solution in these final critical moments. That's inadmissible."

"True. Inadmissible," I reiterate. "Simply can't happen."

Despite the tensions, I can't suppress a moment's amusement at Xhosa's highfalutin language. He's such a delightful concoction of Rasta-cool and scholarly intellect.

The prospect of thirty-two hours in transit is exhausting but, in reality, this might present my first and only opportunity for significant sleep in several days. However, there's still the congress to consider. Normally, presentation at such a high level of exposure would require a lot of preparation and careful thought. With my entire focus on the all-important property purchase for Marah's freedom, I'd given it no consideration whatsoever. In this respect, I'm totally unprepared.

Lights off, shutters down, Xhosa ready in the car, but I feel I've forgotten something. I pause in the doorway, trying to identify it. I desperately need rest. I am grateful and relieved that Xhosa is driving me to the airport, because I doubt I could have made the taxi drive without stopping to gag. My stomach keeps churning, and my throat is so hoarse that I can't even make conversation. I am utterly overtired and disoriented. My wits are hanging by a thread.

IN A STATE OF FATIGUE BEYOND JET LAG, after two days' traveling, I have arrived in Sante Fe. December 19, 2004. I'd gained a day in traveling across time zones, which means that in South Africa, the final day of the option has already dawned.

I have absolutely no idea what measure of success Marianne has achieved with the banking processes. But I know she has a way with words, which can make or break any deal. On the flight, I was imagining her instructing her colleague at the Reserve Bank, "If you close the doors of the bank today without clearing these funds, *ek se vir jou,* I'll have your balls for breakfast."

While Marianne tended to be upfront with friends, she was even more direct with rivals. I was imagining Marianne's instruction to the sellers' attorney: "If you close your office before registering these funds today, I, Marianne van Wyk, will personally make the rest of your life unlivable."

I picture it clearly, but I can't visualize the outcome. Have we or haven't we succeeded? I am too mentally and physically depleted. I've even stopped praying with my every last gasping breath for divine intervention. My primary objective now is to somehow hold myself together and get to the congress. I determine not to phone Marianne, in case the bad news knocks the last stuffing out of me. Mercifully, I am staying in a loving and warm environment: the guesthouse of the Corelight organization, known as The Casa; an elegant abode filled with inspired paintings and large, comfortable furniture.

When I arrived at The Casa twenty minutes ago, Corelight's right-hand woman, Victoria, a warm and highly wired enthusiast, made sure she brought me up to date on the status. I sit on a high barstool in Corelight's ample kitchen, mug of cocoa in hand, and she informs me that Brad and Leslie have held up their end of the deal, with "the speed of light." I marveled to hear of their swift and effective action—they wired through additional funds, which were safely received in the sellers' account in the nick of time. With these in place, it only leaves Mireille's master loan pending to clinch the deal. I'm trying not to assume the worst.

I'm eager to see Brad and Leslie again, to thank them personally for their support. But, as fate would have it, I'm due to present to the congress this evening, so I politely excuse myself from Victoria and retreat to my room to try to rest. My presentation was hurriedly put together on the flight, leaving little time to doze. Now, in my spacious suite in The Casa, I pause for a moment in the bathroom, inadvertently catching my reflection in the mirror. Wide, staring eyes and matted hair in a tangle, the face of Medusa! I am in a state of utter collapse. I slump into the queen-size bed and sink into a state of suspended inertia.

I hear my alarm sounding. I drag myself out of bed, drape my cashmere suit on a hanger behind the bathroom door, hoping that the steam from my shower will soften the travel creases. After showering and drying myself, I step into the suit, comb and forcibly gel my hair back into a ponytail, preparing to set out with my laptop under my arm.

I calculate the time difference between Sante Fe and Johannesburg and realize the last working hour of the final day has closed. With a grinding sense of relief, I finally shut my mind down to any further options or saving grace. After the close of business in South Africa, on this seventh day, the option is well and truly at an end. Whatever the outcome, it is now a fait accompli.

I try to put the property deal entirely out of my head. It is pointless agonizing. I need every last wish and will to keep my dwindling composure together and deliver a coherent presentation shortly. I force myself to focus on getting through the presentation, as if this were a distant light at the end of the darkest tunnel. I am halfway to the congress building before realizing that I've left the power cable behind. Retracing my route, I'm in a rising panic. Back at The Casa, I stumble into the interior only to find Brad Laughlin and his partner

Leslie-Temple Thurston, cofounders of the Corelight organization, looking astonished to see me. They appear unusually tense today.

"Linda, thank god you're here!" Brad exclaims. "We couldn't reach you en route to the congress. You miscalculated the time by an hour. South Africa close of business is twenty-five minutes off. A call has just come from South Africa—sounds desperately urgent!"

He's holding out the receiver in his hand.

"They're still on the line!"

I step forward anxiously.

The South African caller is Marianne's sister and acting personal assistant, Marlene. Her voice is tense.

"Thank heavens it's you, Linda! Here's the status: in one moment, the South African Bank's going to ring you at this number in Sante Fe. Marianne's had a lot of trouble convincing them to push this thing through in time. They won't—because they want to confirm it's really you who's the signatory of these documents, okay?"

"Okay! Anything you say!" I respond, my whole body convulsed with anxiety.

Marlene too sounds as if she's barely suppressing a panic attack. "Please listen carefully. Bank's on the phone to Marianne right now as we speak. They'll ring you in a couple of seconds! Everything depends on you saying yes!" She draws breath for the first time. "Got it? Yes?"

"Yes, yes. Understood," I respond. "I'm completely—"

But she interrupts me, "Oops, gotta go—Marianne's just put down the phone to the bank."

It is literally the last hour of the last day of the last extension of the extension. How is this possible?

I stare at Brad and Leslie, and they stare back at me.

"The bank's waiting for authentication." I explain breathlessly.

Both nod in silence. They know what's at stake. Time's ticking by. An elegant, old walnut grandfather clock in the hallway taps out the time with the exaggerated *tick-tock, tick-tock* of bygone eras.

Meanwhile, destiny has sped up and is racing ahead, the cogs of great and small Mayan calendars, churning, turning, and grinding at an incomprehensibly inexorable pace.

The phone rings again. It's the bank. Trembling, I give the go-ahead.

The receiver is back in its cradle now. I stare at Brad and Leslie again.

"Bank said they'd put it through right away," I report back.

Suspended silence. Time standing still. We all turn simultaneously to stare at the grandfather clock. If the hands are accurate, it's just over twenty minutes to the hour. Close of business, South African time. Tick-tock, tick-tock, tick-tock, tick-tock. Fifteen minutes, ten minutes, five minutes to the hour.

Suddenly, the phone rings again. It's the bank again—to confirm that my authorized instruction has been authenticated. Heaven knows how many arms were twisted and regulations broken, but the remaining funds were transferred into the sellers' attorney's account, effective immediately.

The professional voice at the other side of the receiver confirms that the transaction was on record in the sellers' attorney's account.

"Thank you! Thank you! Thank you! Thank you! Thank you!" I say long after I put down the receiver. Then I look up at Brad and Leslie who are standing holding onto each other, wide eyed and expectant.

"We've done it!" I splutter, stunned.

This, moments before the sounding of the final gong!

A little door on the grandfather clock springs open, and a partridge pops out its colorful, decorated head, crying: "Cuckoo! Cuckoo! Cuckoo!"

"Just in time for Christmas!" Brad announces, hugging me enthusiastically in congratulations, shaking with laughter and relief.

"What an incredible birthday present for Marah!" Leslie exclaims warmly. "Christmas baby!"

"What an incredible gift for humanity!" Brad pronounces.

"We've done it!" I repeat, on the point of tears.

Marah's sacred lands have been secured. The Bethlehem baby is safe. I can shut down completely. I can simply stop. I imagine I can hear Xhosa singing a Marley jingle: "Everything's gonna be all right; everything's gonna be all right now. Everything's gonna be all right; everything's gonna be all right now."

"No woman, no cry," I say to myself.

All the energy has drained from my body. I'm ashen and trembling, moribund with fatigue. Next thing I know, I'm crumpling into bed. I intend to sleep for a week. I imagine that Marianne and Mireille must be doing the same in their respective countries, but I have no strength to even lift the phone. Brad and Leslie will contact the organizers of the congress and offer my apologies. I'm unable to present. I cannot stand, let alone think, a moment longer.

In an exhausted delirium curled up in bed, I delve deep into the collective unconscious for meaning behind this grossly unnatural crunch on timing. Faith tested to the ultimate extremes of endurance seems so unnecessary, with all the other challenges the White Lions have to face.

From the ancestral realms, I hear Maria Khosa's voice and familiar, uproarious laughter, "Why, you ask? Ha! Because you wished it would happen with all your heart, yes—good—but your head still doubted you could do it. Now you have done it anyway. Ha! You see, daughter? Reclaiming the sacred lands is, after all, your destiny."

I'm vaguely beginning to understand. Somehow the whole exercise seemed yet another of Maria's Herculean initiations, but I am still unsure of the lesson.

"So why'd I have to be bailed out by Mireille a second time?" I demand in my mind. "It seems so unfair that she should be the one to make the sacrifice all over again."

I see Queen Maria now at the head of an ancient engraved stone table, in full ceremonial regalia with lion headdress and ankh in hand, seated beside a council of esteemed elders, who remained somewhat hazy in my vision.

"It was always ordained," she pronounces. "For your godmother of light, it's not a sacrifice, daughter. She gives unconditionally. This is who she is."

I am confused and aching to understand. Does this mean I didn't have to go to all that inhuman effort to try to get an alternative form of funding? Too exhausted for decorum, I demand of Queen Maria, "So could I simply have spared myself, knowing all along that the savior of the day was always going to be Mireille?"

"Not so, daughter. You needed to prove your commitment. She needed to see your dedication. You needed to be yourself in order for her to be herself."

The vision fades, and everything fades. I simply allow myself to dissolve into nothingness.

CHAPTER 17

Highway Hennie

BACK IN SOUTH AFRICA, I FEEL REFRESHED, confident, calm, and very focused. January 4, 2005. Two weeks after the property deal went through in the closing, penultimate, twelfth-hour moment. I've spent almost a fortnight resting and celebrating, and even the thirty-two hours of return travel seemed like a cruise. After receiving the fabulous news from the bank, I slept for days, waking momentarily, then dropping off again in the tranquility of Corelight's refined and peaceful premises. For the first twenty-four hours, I slept around the clock in the cocooned, nurturing environment. When I finally emerged, it gave me an opportunity for quiet discussions with Brad and Leslie, which put a lot into perspective. Highly enlightened individuals, who have raised significant funds for humanitarian causes including conservation and AIDS relief, Brad and Leslie encouraged me not to underestimate what has been achieved. In their view, raising money is relatively easy—if one doesn't calculate the cost. By contrast, giving or receiving unconditionally, like unconditional love, was one of the most rarified attributes humanity could ever learn.

We also had a chance to talk through the implications of the White Lion work, and what it means to have reclaimed the hallowed heart of Marah's kingdom. In the course of my work with Nature and the White Lions, everything I thought I understood about the teachings and dogmas of Judeo-Christian doctrine has required reinterpretation and reevaluation. I suspect Brad and Leslie have gone through a similar process, in their own way. They spoke about the concept of Christ consciousness not being limited to the masculine principle, but equally represented by the feminine Christos force in Mother Nature herself. In the context of Marah's arrival on Christmas Day in Bethlehem, and the belief among the African elders that she's the sacred lioness for whom they've been waiting, Brad and Leslie's enlightened philosophy made a great deal of sense. Right from that awesome moment when Maria Khosa prophesized I was destined to become the guardian of the Lioness of God, I've lived with the fear of being misunderstood. And this fear grew stronger with the fulfillment of Maria's prophecy. Following on Marah's birth on December 25, 2000, in Bethlehem, and the subsequent all-consuming rescue mission, the sanctity of Mother Nature became radiantly apparent to me, as did the inherent symbolism behind this divine birth as a manifestation of the Goddess. But at the same time I found it understandable why others might dismiss me as totally delusional. Suddenly, I no longer care if I am misunderstood. I have the validation I need, validation of the most heartwarming kind. Mireille has given me her generous backing, not once but twice over—despite being the daughter of pious and staunchly conservative Christian missionary parents. And others of high standing have come forward, the most notable being Corelight, prepared to pledge its funding in support of my cause.

Leaving The Casa after five days of tranquility and meditative discussion, I headed back via Britain, just in time to celebrate Christmas with Mireille. And boy, did we celebrate! Without doubt, it was the most wonderful and meaningful festive season of my entire life. Gone are those gaping Christmas nonevents of my early childhood, vacantly suspended between Christian and Jewish beliefs, where neither tradition was honored or upheld. Gone are the tinsel commercialism and frenzied shopping sprees characteristic of my student years, in a desperate bid to share the meaningless rituals of our consumer society. This Christmas, I knew something huge had fallen into place. And it felt so right! I didn't have to prove anything. Christmas was a joyous, momentous celebration like never before.

Then New Year came around—what an unbelievable new beginning! Mireille and I drove through the rolling landscape surrounding Leeds for hours and hours on New Year's Day, sweeping through the snow-covered dales in her royal blue Range Rover, reminiscing, planning, dreaming, talking, strategizing, and, finally, when we realized we were totally famished, stopping at a hearty roadside pub for lunch beside a roaring fire.

Back in South Africa again, I finally feel ready and more able than ever to take the next unhesitating steps toward securing Marah's freedom and her homeward journey back to her natural Holy Lands.

When I return to my desk, my very first task is to sweep all the piles of papers with lists in scrawled handwriting—some ticked, others crossed out—directly into the garbage, leaving the surface clear for the first time in six months. What a relief! A tray of fresh tea arrives for me on the pristine cleared surface, and a breezy light streams in through the open window. I literally roll up my sleeves and settle comfortably behind my desk, with a clear plan of action formulating in my head. I can't help sending an affectionate glance in Xhosa's direction. There he is, a cuddly bear tucked into his alcove, wearing a bright red woolen beanie cap. I notice he's put on his academic glasses before turning to me, so I know he has something serious to say. He ambles over, with the file of official-looking documents that have built up while I was away. He hovers a moment, as if trying to find the right words.

"Over the past two weeks," he tells me, "while you and I and the rest of our team recuperated, our opponents celebrated their victory. Apparently, they thought they'd seized the property and couldn't register the prize has slipped their grasp, milliseconds before the winning post!"

"I can understand their total disbelief, X. The timing was absolutely absurd."

He gives a slow, deliberate nod. "Agreed. However, the sellers' attorney must've then conveyed the bad news to our bad guys."

"Oh," I respond, bracing myself. I can imagine the trophy hunters' initial shock and outrage. Then, once the truth hit home, I can imagine how nasty they've turned.

"The officials obviously couldn't get anything issued over Christmas and New Year—so *that* gave us a breather," Xhosa explains. "But as soon as the regional authorities were back in their offices yesterday, January 3, the pressure was on. Check out this attorney's letter."

Xhosa cringes as he opens the file and slides the fax to me. "It's for you, boss, and I'm afraid it's spitting mad."

"But this is probably more urgent," Xhosa adds, pulling out the next letter from his stack of officious-looking documents. "You'll see it was sent to the Department of Nature Conservation."

I scan cautiously through the contents. In sudden shock, I notice that this letter demands that our White Lion project "should be prohibited from any permissions or permits—under any circumstances." The opponents are citing as grounds for objection the fact that they, as neighbors, have "the right to be consulted, and the right to protest."

I don't feel good about this, and I am trying to assess just how bad I should be feeling.

"Done some homework," Xhosa continues, pulling out a printed copy of a Government Gazette. "Here's a copy of new South African conservation policy—being redrafted currently. You'll see it does allow for the written opinions of interested and affected parties."

"Understood," I comment.

In fact, a while back in my efforts to secure this property, when the threats from the hunters in the region first started erupting, I discussed this particular clause with one of our legal advisors, and his advice was that public objections could prove highly influential in the department's decision-making process—particularly if the objectors were to employ intimidation tactics, bribes, or both.

"Not cool," Xhosa continues. "But it gets worse."

The next letter indicated that the irate neighbors are, in fact, threatening the Department of Nature Conservation with legal action if it issues us with a necessary permit.

"Hmm. Looks grim," I mutter under my breath, feeling my morale about to take a dive. Or should I take my cue from Xhosa, who is still looking quite upbeat for a messenger of bad news?

"Remember, boss, there's one factor the bad guys haven't banked on," he points out, placing his pen behind his ear at an almost smug angle. "We've already been granted permits!"

"I'm aware of that," I say cautiously.

"But d'you remember the reason, boss?" Xhosa asks, revealing a dose of pride and just a little glee.

"I don't get you yet."

"It's an anomaly—that's what I'd call it. Remember that intrepid decision you took when you risked all our funds by erecting fencing on land you didn't own, right? Well, that did it! No fencing; no permits. But with the fencing, you've beaten them to the goalpost! Bottom line is we've already got the permits!"

In a bizarre twist of events, it seems the gamble I took in the trustees meeting, based on that inner knowing alone, could prove the saving grace of the project and the key to the lions' freedom. I ponder a moment; that must have been why my instinct told me it was such an overriding imperative to erect the fences in advance. On the strength of fourteen kilometers of immaculate predator-proof workmanship, the Nature Conservation officials had already approved our facilities and granted their permission for the reintroduction project. Whether or not I held title over the land at the time was not an issue.

Xhosa produces two more official-looking papers, which he's kept until last. These two I am, in fact, familiar with. They are our permits. But calming my breathing, I take a closer look at each of the stamped and approved documents, scrutinizing their stipulated conditions in fine print. The first is the export permit. This granted permission to transport Marah and her cubs out of the Western Cape province. The second is the import permit, granting permission to transport Marah and her cubs into the Limpopo province, where Timbavati is situated.

"And the holding permit, X?" I ask. This third and final permit granted the importing party permission to keep the lions on the Timbavati land.

"Ahem. Not yet."

"What!? I was informed that this would come through while I was away," I say, tapping my pen on the desk in frustration.

"True. Under normal circumstances," Xhosa explains, "this final permit is a formality—a procedural consequence of the other two permits. That's the exact wording the permit officer told me. Naturally, it follows that if an organization has been granted permission to import lions into a particular province, that same organization has permission to hold them there. That's what he told me. So, at the end of the day, boss, I wouldn't worry. We've got the other two permits, that's the important thing."

"Precisely," I say crisply. "The latter permit is premised upon the former permits. So where is it?"

"I'm saying that's what the official told me."

"But it hasn't been issued?"

"Well, no. Not yet."

Adjusting his glasses, Xhosa concludes, "I didn't want to bother you on the day of your return, boss. I'm sure it's all okay, but. . . . Well, now that the hunters are knuckle-dusting the departmental officials, Nat Con has—understandably—gone a bit cold toward us for the moment. Don't expect any breakdancing from officialdom right now. But you already did the fencing and got the permits, so who cares?"

I waste no time in phoning the permit officer in question. In my experience, any effort to get through to bureaucratic departments tends to hit brick wall after brick wall, so connecting with him on my very first attempt now feels decidedly lucky. After the initial formalities, I inquire why there's a delay on the outstanding permit, fully expecting good news.

But instead the official informs me that, "following hostile action taken by nonconsenting parties to the proposed project, the issuance of the final permit has now been suspended.'"

"Suspended?" I ask, still not following.

He continues, "All departmental action as pertains to this application is halted and on hold."

"Halted and on hold? For how long, officer?"

"Indefinitely."

I would ask for further explanation, but I'm speechless. There is no point protesting until I understand the full implications, so I thank the official and put down the phone, muttering to Xhosa after I do so. "The authorities haven't gone cold, X. They're cadaverous, frozen stiff."

"Sorry to hear that," Xhosa says. "You look like you're chilled to the bone yourself."

"I just can't believe what I'm hearing! After four years—and five months and twenty-two days—of patient endurance, are we saying that Marah's long-awaited freedom is going to be revoked again!"

"Not if you can help it, boss!"

I wish I had the same confidence. When I arrived home last night, I was fired up and willing to face any challenge, to take any intrepid step required of me to secure Marah's destiny. Now, face to face with this blockade, I am ready to weep with even more dire frustration! I feel so cold I have to find Harold to borrow a pullover.

This threatening stalemate is creating an entirely new dilemma. I suspect that the lethal merger of hunters' aggression with bureaucratic inaction could bar the way to Marah's freedom—indefinitely.

I feel bewildered and frustrated, but I am not prepared to stand by and watch as all the bureaucratic doors—which I had taken such care to open over so much time—slam shut again in an instant. I have to take action—but what?

MIREILLE SITS BESIDE ME on the couch in the bedroom of her Pretoria hotel, squeezing my hand tightly. She's barely let go of my hand over the past eight hours. She joined me from England yesterday to lend moral support. It is still relatively early on a hot summer's evening, and we are talking through the seriousness of our situation. March 5, 2005, 9:30 p.m. It has been three months since my return from Leeds, and the intervening period has lapsed without any thawing on behalf of the authorities. Despite ongoing intensive communications and representations on my part, no further permit has been issued. The situation has become desperate, as the export and transport permits have a three-month validity and are therefore due to expire in two days' time. Since our organization has long since provided the department with all the documentation they officially require, I have been hanging onto the conviction that the last outstanding permit would belatedly come through. We've made numerous appeals to various authorities. Alas, nothing. My faith held until close of business yesterday, Friday, when the finality of the situation loomed. By Monday the permit will be invalid. There's no denying we are in deep trouble.

Though Mireille has chosen a particularly warm and friendly hotel, with bright décor and wallpaper in florid sunflower motifs, the gaiety of our surrounds does little to lift our mood. We've been forced into a perilous corner. With our prospects shattered and the permit withheld, there are only two dread alternatives: go ahead as planned before our two existing permits expire, or rethink everything. Through Harold's aviation circles, a private plane has been procured for the scheduled epic flight tomorrow, a classic old DC3, generously sponsored, this time by the pilot himself. Our trusted veterinarian Tindall has agreed to fly his own plane and join us in the Karoo mountain lands, and from there accompany us and the pride on the last leg of their homeward journey in the DC3. A specialist in lion tranquilization, Tindall is prepared to donate not only his expertise, but also his fuel and the use of his plane to the cause. It is astounding. I feel overwhelmed by the support I've received from these like-minded people. It is partly their faith in me that prevents me from giving up on myself at an impossible juncture.

Meanwhile, no less than nine international television productions and fifty-two channels have asked to cover the story. So as not to create a media circus and risk negatively impacting the lions themselves, I agreed that only one production company—Animal Planet—may film the transfer, for Discovery Channel.

The preparations have been painstaking, and we've covered all bases. Jason has been processing all the scientific aspects. Since early yesterday, his scientific team has been on the ground in Timbavati, on standby to receive Marah and her cubs once we land and transport them safely home. Jason has made sure that the GPS collars, which will ensure the lions' safety once they are released, are ready to be fitted. Even the electrified acclimation camp erected in the interior of the land has been double-checked and switched on in anticipation.

The summer months of searing heat came and went in the Karoo semidesert, and all I had for comfort was JJ's weekly reports that Marah and cubs were doing absolutely fine—lions being much hardier animals, he said, than I gave them credit for. With the new pressures on, I dare not take even a brief break to visit my lion family. Instead, I've been doing everything possible from a practical perspective to ensure a positive outcome for their future, making absolutely sure that every last detail has not been overlooked for their historic return home.

Every day I've prayed that sense would prevail, and the permit would be issued as originally promised by the authorities. But the nagging turmoil in my mind has been building up to a fever pitch—in fearful anticipation that, despite every effort to gain final authorization, I might end up being faced with precisely the nerve-wracking decision that now faces me. Everything is in place—apart from the official stamp of approval!

Sitting on the sunflower-yellow couch in Mireille's hotel room, holding her hand, I rehearse all the vital and necessary components undertaken in order to make this trip a reality.

In talking through the options with me, Mireille has been holding strong, radiating faith and hope. But even her tried and tested solution of getting practical can't solve this crisis. In Swiss precision mode, she's been ticking off our checklist of last tasks in her notebook. But having successfully been through the list, she holds her silver pen up in her hand, suspended, and glances at me again, mouth pursed in consternation. She and I have reached the same stumbling block as always: we are ready and able to relocate Marah to her rightful homeland, but we have no authority to hold her there.

Without the holding permit, it could be argued we are breaking the law. To add to our tensions, I received, just before close of business yesterday, a legal letter stating that law enforcement would be waiting for us on arrival if we attempted to import the lions into the province. The letter was sent by an aggrieved pro-hunting neighbor. Unnervingly, he'd also somehow extracted everything he needed to know about our permit situation, as well as our scheduled arrival at the local airport, which indicated he must have an inside track with the authorities.

With our list of procedures safely ticked off in the notebook in her lap, Mireille has let go of my hand momentarily to pour us both a glass of water. I am still sitting on the couch of the sunflower room in agonizing indecision. Do I go ahead with the risk of bringing Marah and her family home—a risk that will invoke accusations of illegal activity and even conceivably result in the confiscation of the lions? I think through the consequences once again. If Marah and her cubs were to be seized by the authorities, they'd be held in cages until their fate is decided. A series of court cases over a number of years would follow. Most devastating, if I were to fail in defending my case, the authorities could elect to euthanize the confiscated lions. How could I possibly proceed with such excruciatingly high stakes? But the alternative to euthanasia could be a fate worse than death: incarceration for life. After all these years of struggle to secure Marah's freedom, could I really cancel all our meticulously laid plans for returning her and her children to their natural kingdom, and watch the prison doors bolt shut again? Probably forever?

As customary when I feel stressed, I try to calm my breathing. The pressure is utterly overwhelming. I glance at my watch. It's after 10:00 p.m. I've been on the phone since early afternoon, to our advisors, one after the other. My decision has been fraught with mixed advice. Personally, on gut instinct as usual, I feel ready to implement our prearranged plan. And Marianne, in full throttle, also advocates taking action tomorrow. But Harold and Ian call for extreme caution. Given Ian's lifetime in conservation, I have to take his cautionary advice with due seriousness. Personally, I believe he understands, but professionally, he can't agree with taking action in this case. He has put his reputation behind my cause, which other experts tried to dismiss as entirely "lacking conservation value." And since Ian has spent over a half century fighting for conservation issues, it has been encouraging to see how his firm public support of my efforts has subdued those scientific loudmouths proclaiming that White Lions are "freaks of nature," unworthy of consideration. Inevitably, the caution he expressed earlier is giving me serious cause to reflect.

"So, what's to be done?" Mireille asks, in her most efficient, officer-reporting-for-duty tone. She hands me my glass of water.

I drink it gratefully. It's a warm evening, and I hadn't realize how parched my throat was. Having just arrived from the frozen Northern Hemisphere, Mireille is reacclimatizing, because, while I'm in shirtsleeves, I notice she's wearing a red bomber jacket. Or perhaps she is simply preparing for battle.

Personally, I have a clear and comprehensive understanding of the options, but it strikes me I haven't brought Mireille fully up to date, and that is the most important priority before we decide our course of action.

"Okay, this is the state of play, Godmum," I explain. "Legally, the only safe way forward is to keep the lions in captivity. If we release them to freedom, we risk their seizure and confiscation."

"What's the position of our legal advisors?" she asks, standing with her back to the window, where the flickering city lights shine in.

"The only legal advisor I could reach at this hour was adamant we should withdraw from this risky course of action—immediately."

"You agree with him?"

"No," I say, uncompromisingly. "If security means a lifelong jail sentence for the lions, I'd prefer to take the risk of seeing them freed."

"Absolutely. But they could be jailed on arrival. Why don't we simply wait til we finally get the permits reissued?" she asks sensibly.

"Realistically? Absolutely minimal chance of that. And once the two permits expire, we have no leverage."

Jason has alerted me to the fact that lapsed permits are seldom reissued. Without any valid permit, it would be impossible to move the lions, this lack of compliance being exactly the kind of weakness the hunters are aiming for.

"There's another worry," I add, putting my glass down on the table. I open my briefcase and retrieve the notification from Jason, alerting me to this new danger. "Take a look, Godmum. Because of the chaos over the canned-hunting issue with worldwide conservation organizations objecting to these malpractices, notification has come from the government that issuance of all permits is now on hold—for all lion activity, nationally. That means the end for Marah's reintroduction to her natural homelands for the forseeable future."

"No permits at all in the whole country?" Mireille asks.

"Apart from existing ones."

"What rot!" she concludes, deeply offended. "This means Marah and her little ones will have to stay locked up in that camp in the desert, forevermore?"

"That's the status quo."

"They'll never be free?"

"According to the new regulations," I confirm grimly. "But forget how unjust this is; we need to remain focused on strategy."

I appreciate my dearly beloved godmother trying to come to terms with our limited options; I've been weighing them constantly over the past three months and know all too well what's at stake.

"But things could change," she suggests. "If you manage to change legislation in this country, like you've been campaigning for?"

Hearing her hopeful question, my heart is torn with the grindingly familiar quandary. "I've fought to change legislation for years now—the law isn't going to change overnight. Even if we succeed in changing regulations in future, which I sincerely hope we do, by that stage it'll be too late for Marah. Her chances of hunting and surviving in the wild would've been ruined."

"That's tragic," Mireille declares, outraged.

"Let's get a breath of air, Mum," I say, opening up the sliding doors to her balcony and taking her by the arm.

"Surely Nature Conservation's job is to conserve nature," Mireille demands emphatically. "After all, conservation's what they're there for."

"That's what I used to think. But the situation's very messy in

South Africa, and the canned-hunting mob seems to have infiltrated the conservation authorities at every level. Remember the story I told you? About the attempt to free Marah's siblings, which went horribly wrong?"

"Good god, yes!" she replies, with a rising sense of outrage, as we stand looking out over Pretoria's lights.

I don't want to raise this deeply depressing topic again, but Greg Mitchell's failed attempt to rescue eight golden lions from the Bethlehem killing camps underscores my own desperation.

"That poor man was simply trying to save those dear lions from being killed," she recollects. "After you yourself managed to rescue Marah from that same despicable extermination camp."

"Precisely. He'd bought them, legally, and transported them out of the province, legally. He and his American girlfriend spent millions of rand acquiring a massive property for them. They applied for permits, legally. But after nine months or so, they still weren't granted issuance. Madness. Canned-hunting operations are being issued easy permits all over the place, so why deny a legitimate sanctuary?"

"Shocking!" Mireille admits. "They weren't doing the lions any harm, or any humans for that matter. They just wanted to save the lions by moving them onto their wildlife reserve. Somehow, the canned hunters were in league with certain officials, or so it seemed. What happened to those dear cats?"

"Confiscated." A shiver runs down my spine. "All efforts on the part of Greg and his girlfriend to get them back to safety failed. They spent several million rands on court action. Worst is that their lions are back in the canned-hunting system."

"Good god! Simply can't credit it."

"Regrettably, yes."

As a champion for the disenfranchised, Mireille can't suppress her outrage. "Meanwhile, all those canned-hunting hoodlums are doing just as they please with these precious animals!"

She flashes me a look. "Don't tell me they'll end up as trophies on a wall?"

"Who knows their future. They've disappeared into the system. Greg's lost them forever."

"Appalling state of affairs!" Mireille concludes. Then, suddenly looking terribly alarmed, she asks, "You're not saying the same thing could happen to Marah! Are you?"

"Godmum," I respond carefully. "We have to believe good will win in the end. It has to. Nature may not be treated in this way."

"Absolutely! No denying that . . ."

Exhausted, we return inside from the balcony and settle on the yellow couch. But we are sitting in silence now, pondering.

"So, you'd rather take the risk?" she ventures, taking my hand again.

"Yes, if the alternative means life imprisonment for Marah and her cubs. Absolutely yes."

"Would you?" Mireille quizzes. "Really? Even if freedom risks their lives to euthanasia?"

I wince. Would I really risk the lions' lives in the hope of achieving their freedom? I wasn't prepared to offer Marah and her precious cubs as surety in securing their heritage land, so why am I preparing to put their lives on the line now?

Time is running out, and I need to face up to this dread decision—without further delay. Drawing on all my courage, I identify two last advisors, whose trusted input I urgently need to consider. The first is Advocate Phathekile Holomisa, the president of South Africa's council of traditional leaders. A king among the Khosa people, Holomisa is a formidable figure in South African politics, and has been a member of parliament since Nelson Mandela came to power. As a member of the advisory council of the Global White Lion Protection Trust, his advice means a great deal to me.

"Excuse me, Godmum," I say, giving her hand a last encouraging squeeze. "Two last calls to make."

Standing outside on the balcony of Mireille's hotel room now with my cell phone to my ear, I take care to explain the gravity of the predicament to Advocate Holomisa; then I hold my breath for his response.

"You know my vote, Ms Tucker," he replies, in a regal Xhosa accent. "If you've followed all due procedures with officialdom as far as they can go, then keep doing what you're doing. I believe you shall win in the end, lioness."

I allow myself a faint smile at his bold encouragement. African kingship has always been associated with lions and lionhearted values and, as the head of South Africa's traditional leaders, my friend, chief of chiefs, often portrays lionlike qualities himself.

Taking heart, I thank him, bid him goodnight, then pause a moment to digest his words.

The other call is to Jason. At this time, he is en route to Pretoria, driving seven hours from Timbavati in preparation for the lions' historic flight home. Over the past few months, he's dedicated much of his personal time to assisting us with the permit process. Truly lionhearted, Jason also has predominant Taurus qualities: strong and immovable, with a thorough systematic mind that follows through to the very end. Gentle, but no pushover, his approach to any problem, whether scientific or bureaucratic, is to apply increasing measures of perseverance, determination, and expertise. If anyone could get a permit through the corridors of red tape and rubber stamps—legally—it would be our lion ecologist. But Jason sounded particularly crestfallen earlier today, having to break the news to me that the authorities will not budge on the final permit issuance. In response to my phone call now, he confirms that he's still on the road from Timbavati and will join us in a half hour to talk through the options. I thank him and return to the bright interior of the hotel room.

"We've got the go-ahead from the chief of chiefs," I update Mireille, but stop short. Her expression remains stalwart, but the sparkle has gone from her eyes and the color completely drained from her cheeks.

"You all right, Godmum?"

"Darling, I know full well the consequences for Marah and her family could be a lifetime of captivity," she replies, ashen. "But the risk of losing them is too great. One wrong move, and—no, I just can't condone it! Regrettably, I've come to the conclusion we should cancel all tomorrow's plans—"

"—for the lions' rescue?" I respond. What a shock! I can't believe I am hearing this from her.

In my heart of hearts, I simply cannot agree, but I am not prepared to overrule my godmother's cautions, and besides, I feel them too, excruciatingly.

I am alone in my unbearable dilemma, burdened by the weight and consequence of this impossible decision—which is ultimately mine to make. Or is it? If I go ahead with this risky step to free the Lions of God, as Maria called them, can I rely on the creator to protect his precious creatures from human brutality? Can I hand over responsibility to higher causes, in faith that the sun god's holy children will be protected, as they deserve to be? What would Mother Mary say? A mother who must have wrestled more than anyone with questions of what it means to call for protection of her beloved son from humanity's brutality?

I close my eyes, praying with all my heart, and I receive a clear vision of Mother Maria, standing before me in all her traditional regalia: Black Madonna, loving but fierce.

"How seriously must I take these threats?" I implore Maria Khosa. "Are the stakes too high? Must I call off Marah's rescue?"

Unhesitatingly, the guidance from Maria is clear and firm, but so disparagingly dismissive that I couldn't translate it for Mireille without blushing.

"The canned hunters are just farting in the wind," Maria reports. "Get on with the task at hand!"

Ah! At least that is unambiguous.

As time passes, the thumping of my heart subsides and I feel my courage returning. My eyes are still closed, but if Mireille were to glance at me now, she'd detect a humorous smile on my face.

There is a polite knock at the door.

Jason is standing in the doorway, with pizzas!

"Good evening, dear man," Mireille announces, unloading the three flat boxes cradled in his arms. Neither Mireille nor I have eaten since breakfast, so our blood sugar levels must be very low.

"Fuel up, ladies," Jason says, stepping inside. "We've got a long journey tomorrow."

The turning point!

After a few hearty bites, Mireille is back on the frontline. She stands, with a huge slice of pizza in hand, informing Jason that I was absolutely right to choose action over inaction.

"After all," she announces firmly. "Marah, exiled lioness of Timbavati, has a divine right to return home. And I, Mireille Vince, Grandmother of the White Lions, am certainly not going to stand in her way."

"Right you are!" Jason concurs, as if he never had any doubt.

"What God brings together, let no man draw asunder—or something to that effect," she adds, smiling heartily.

Jason has a broad grin on his face, despite the tensions of the occasion.

"Let's get to it then," he instructs.

I fling my arms around my godmother, feeling my resolve strengthen like never before. I feel strong and clear and determined. My commitment to Marah's freedom has seen me through many challenges. But singleminded and lonely as my journey has been up until now, I was never alone. From the start, I had the support of my loving sister, Mae, an astute professional psychologist who understood and encouraged my work, even during those years when my colleagues from high-powered advertising and marketing arenas thought I'd gotten heatstroke in Africa and gone insane. And over time, as the project progressed, people offered assistance in many different capacities. Now, after ten years of lonely campaigning, I have enormous momentum behind me, and so many special people have come in to assist. I have so much to be thankful for. How can one measure the support offered me by Dr. Ian Player, and the credibility he's lent to my project? Of course, most immediately, I have dearly beloved Mireille to thank, whose unconditional funding has freed the lions and the land. And then there's Corelight and all the others who have been prepared to commit significant funding, as proof that the cause to which I've dedicated my life is worthwhile to them too. Reinforcements have truly arrived at last. But the watershed was Jason's appearance in my life.

Padding into my world and my project like a quietly confident territorial male lion, he's brought with him eight years of specialist scientific study—six of which were spent specializing in the Timbavati lion pride dynamics. I'd imagine that's why Jason has unconsciously developed leonine qualities himself.

I think back on the past couple of years, how he's assisted my ongoing efforts at the most crucial and challenging times with the construction of the fencing, the applications to Nature Conservation officials, and the harnessing of scientific support and expertise. And after completing his master's degree in wildlife management three week ago, Jason joined the Global White Lion Protection Trust as a full-time scientific advisor. He's taken each step with careful consideration, never looking back. After many months of careful long-term scientific planning, he heads up the scientific team assisting me in relocating Marah to her promised land.

Jason Turner has no intention of backing down now.

Mireille, Jason, and I stand on the runway of Lanseria private airport, under the tilted metal hull of a DC3 troop carrier. Mireille is hanging tightly onto my hand. The tarmac shimmers; despite the heat, she is still wearing her favorite red bomber jacket. Our plan is that the plane will first transport us ten hours into the Karoo mountain land, and from there, collect the sleeping lions and transport them another nine hours to Timbavati, and freedom!

The pilot of the solid old World War II aircraft, Henry Delport, stands beside us: short, dark, and hardy-handsome, with what seems a slightly maniacal streak of heroism in his eyes. Magnanimously, he's offered his historic plane and his services free-of-charge, for which I'm deeply grateful, as a flight of this nature would have cost a small fortune. With funds particularly thin on the ground, his generous lift-off swept Mireille and me off our feet. However, I recently learned from Harold that this feisty personality was known as Highway Hennie in aviation circles after famously landing his aircraft on the N4 triple highway, due to engine failure. The reputation that precedes him may be unnerving, but I have more serious things to worry about.

Everything is on track, for better or for worse.

A film crew, who flew in from a great distance last night, are due to join us on the tarmac at any moment. I fortify myself, knowing I am going to have to break the news to them on arrival, and reveal that the entire expedition is in jeopardy.

It is 10:00 a.m., our scheduled departure time. Highway Hennie buckles up his leather jacket and pilot's helmet and clambers into the cockpit, unusually through a door in the hull itself. He'd spotted the film crew's panel van speeding down the entrance road, then swinging onto the tarmac and honking on arrival.

What lies ahead is a life-and-death action-step for Marah's future, more utterly agonizing than any I've taken before. But I no longer feel afraid. I have my team beside me. And I feel the full weight of the responsibility that Maria Khosa handed me in passing on the ancient title: Keeper of the White Lions.

CHAPTER 18

Presence of the Leopard

MARCH 6, 2005. THE FLIGHT IS HARROWING. I am trying to avoid the smell of engine fumes that keeps churning my stomach. We've already spent eighteen hours in the droning old troop carrier—first to the Karoo to collect Marah and cubs, then onward to Timbavati. I felt ill with anxiety on the outward-bound journey, and I've been physically sick, repeatedly, on the second leg. That feeling of dread lurches in my stomach again, and I reach out for another sick-bag.

Not knowing what awaits us on the landing strip is awful. I've been trying to get the menacing legal letters out of my mind, and the recurring image of incensed pro-hunting neighbors and officials persuaded by intimidation tactics—and very possibly fat wallets—to seize the lions on the runway. I dab my mouth with a paper towel, trying to shed the unpalatable acid taste of fear from my system. Through my fits of vomiting, I catch repeated flashes of Mireille's red bomber jacket as she tries to offer me water. And there are other flashes, of Jason advising Tindall, who has set up a drip for each of the tranquilized lions. I focus on the positive. Having once transported soldiers and arms, this old craft now carries the most precious of cargos—four snow-white lions, angelic and soundly asleep under blankets—to their promised land.

In the sweltering heat, I peer out of the small window at the wilderness below, wondering what fate lies ahead. All the while, I have had to navigate the demands of the film crew, who've shown minimal care for the lions' welfare and no clue of what's truly at stake. At first, they seemed a fairly pleasant, if rowdy, bunch. But when they tried to refuse Mireille and Jason access to the plane, pronouncing that "these extras and personalities aren't needed in the documentary," I felt a lioness's fury overtake me.

"Not negotiable," I instructed them and turned away to climb the stepladder.

I was fuming. My life's not up for negotiation, nor are Mireille's and Jason's; they aren't "extras" but utter lifelines of support and encouragement. Having an insensitive film crew with me on this profoundly personal occasion isn't what I would have chosen, but we'd all agreed in advance that Marah's return to her natural kingdom is a historic moment that shouldn't go unrecorded. So I compromised. However, the only way I manage to calm myself is to focus my attention, as always, on my lion family, and their all-important rescue. These exquisite cats are sublimely peaceful, sleeping like angels. Watching Marah's serene, majestic face, I notice her eyes flickering; she's starting to stir. I turn to Jason, but he and Tindall are already out of their seats and by her side, gently topping her up with Zolitel, the long-acting tranquilizing drug.

I watch Marah's vision fade again, and she passes into tranquilized sleep once more.

The film crew has had cameras trained on me since before the takeoff. But fortunately for the past couple of hours, when the nausea really hit, they've all been asleep, en masse—director, assistant director, cameraman, presenter, and presenter's makeup artist. Thank goodness for a little privacy.

Jason returns to his seat, together with Tindall, their watchful eyes still set on the lions. I seize this opportunity. I've been holding myself back for hours and hours, but I can't fight the urge to leave my seat and join Marah on the cabin floor, under her blanket! I crouch down next to her. Feeling her closeness, I lie on the floor and cuddle up, with my arm around her taut muscular body and warm, snowy fur. Pressing against this magnificent creature, I breathe in that same exquisite scent I remembered from Marah's cubhood—that fragrant blend resembling talcum powder and freshly cut hay. The airsickness fades away and I feel deep inner strength and courage revive in me again. I am as close as I'll ever be to the lioness I love with all my heart! Intertwined with her, and breathing in her fragrance, I am transported back to that amazing day when I managed to free Marah from the dreaded canned-hunting camp for just one day with the covert assistance of Greg Mitchell. She was a little subadult then, nine months old, and it was her one and only day of freedom! Releasing Marah from her cage, in secret—under the very noses of the canned hunters—into the surrounding fields! I'd remember that eternal day: running with her through the fields, bounding and tumbling and rolling together in the long grass—forever! What an indescribable feeling. I feel it again. How could I ever forget the most exhilarating day of my life?

What will be the outcome of today's great trek? What if incarceration rather than freedom lies at the end of this journey? I have to remember Maria's training. Release fear and doubt. Instead of visualizing the worst, I have to focus on aspirations and dreams for the future. If all goes well, Marah's freedom will be secured—not only for one day, but forever.

Freeing Marah has offered its own challenge, one that Jason had tried to prepare me for, over and over. With freedom as my endpoint, the only way I could be physically close to Marah was when she was unconscious. Wrenchingly sad as it is for me, I know with absolute clarity that Marah and I must remain physically separated. In her best interests, she has to break all dependency on humans and take up her position of sovereignty in the wild. Despite the bondage she once had to the human world, she can no longer cross back into that world. Magnificent lioness, now in her prime, she would be at risk of being destroyed by those same humans.

From where I lie on the cabin floor, I can see Highway Hennie seated in his open cockpit. At least, I can just see his feet—he's wearing shiny black Italian-style shoes and bright red socks with racy Snoopy images on them. Definite type-A personality. I have discovered over the years that the lions tend to bring out heroism in certain people, and our highwayman pilot has hatched a feisty scheme to avoid the risk of officials waiting on the runway to seize the lions. He is planning to make a last-minute diversion to an undisclosed destination, without informing the local airport. With this brainwave in mind, Jason conveys the new coordinates to his ground team, using mobile telephones, which don't affect World War II aviation technologies. So, things are looking up—and help will be waiting for us on arrival!

"How're my puppies doing?" I hear our daredevil pilot announce through his crackly World War II microphone.

He is referring to the magnificent great cats slumbering on his aircraft floor beside me.

I watch Jason and Tindall give him the thumbs-up.

The cameraman has woken up again, and all of this is on film. Suddenly, the craft starts tipping over the edge of the precipitous Drakensberg Mountains.

"Seat belts on, everyone," our pilot announces. "Prepare for landing. ETA: fifteen minutes. Destination: unknown."

Relunctantly, I leave Marah and return to my seat.

Mireille is wide eyed, gripping onto the armrests of her seat. "Unknown landing strip—off the charts? How exciting!"

The craft has dipped from the so-called highveld plateau down to the vast expanse of flatlands laid out below. Our gallant pilot sweeps the plane over this expansive lowveld area, finally hovering it above a magnificent serpentine feature, the only perennial watercourse carving through the massive expanse of wilderness. He broadcasts through his microphone that this is the Klaserie River; I remember it from the area map I scrutinized so many times: the one single arterial river that carves through the White Lions' sacred homelands, delivering much-needed water to this entire thirsty bushveld region. Maria called this river Tsau, the river of the starlions.

We circle over this snaking artery one more time before finally dropping down to land in our secret destination. It's Sunday. God willing, the private airstrip will be clear and deserted.

The cameraman is still rolling his camera, and the director and producer are up too. When they learn our plans have changed, they're not happy, no real reason, it seems, except it puts their schedule out. I peer out of the small portlike windows at the land below. We are about to touch down on Timbavati soil, and the gravel runway rises up to meet us.

WE'VE LANDED! In a flash, my mind suddenly fills with images of Ingwavuma, my ancestral guardian, who was brutally hunted on these lands at the time of the setting sun on the last day of Leo. Suddenly, I recognize this as the same remote runway where I first spotted Ingwavuma—where the great King stood with the windsock blowing behind his majestic head, as if to signal that he had landed! I still feel the acute tragedy of this starlion departing these sacred lands, under such cruel circumstances. His slaying coincided with a date sacred to the pharaohs—when the sun crosses Regulus, the heartstar of Leo—that moment the Ancient Egyptians believed the soul of the Great King returns to the stars. Here we are bringing the starlions back to Timbavati once more.

Both cameras are rolling now. Mercifully, we seem to have landed safely and in secret, without incident. There are no unwelcome parties lurking on the runway in this remote spot, except a family of warthog, which was digging up the tufts of grass on the landing strip, and even they beat a hasty retreat after the troop carrier dropped from the skies, in a spray of dust and gravel.

Our pilot brings the plane to a standstill. Out of the small windows of the craft, I spot Jason's trusted ground team standing by, as arranged: three scientists, professionally dressed in khaki uniforms and bush caps.

Their specialty is GPS tracking, which turns out to be of great advantage, given that they must have needed the devices to locate this unexpected new destination. They've drawn up the vehicles alongside the grass landing strip: a rented passenger transporter for the humans, and two closed-back, long-axle panel vans for Marah and family. The cubs have grown so much since that first transfer from the zoo to the Karoo mountain land that the whole pride no longer fits into one panel van.

Jason and Hennie open the door under the hull of the DC3 to a burst of blazing bushveld atmosphere. Looking out, I see the three scientists coming forward to help. The cameras are rolling again, and it is all hands on deck, lifting the lions onto stretchers in the hull, then carefully handing them down to ground level.

The heat outside is so intense it radiates off the gravel landing strip, stinging my face as I step down. Holding one pole of Marah's stretcher, I help carry her into the waiting transport vehicles. As before, it takes six of us to transport Marah this way, five men and myself. Then Jason and Tindall return to lift the first of the cubs. None of the scientists has ever seen a White Lion before. They are professional, efficient-looking specialists, but I can't help notice their faces glowing with excitement and reverence, having become unlikely ceremonial bearers of these magnificent sleeping cats.

Everyone's drenched in sweat. It's approaching late afternoon, but the sun is still high in the sky, and the heat shimmers off the scorching bushveld around us. It may be the rainy season, but there isn't a rain cloud in the sky. Mireille sensibly packed several large cooler bags with provisions as part of her list of priorities, anticipating rightly that we'd have no opportunity for food after arrival—and possibly for some time to come. These bags of provisions are being loaded into the third vehicle.

No obvious danger in sight, for the moment. I'm with Jason in one panel van, together with the director, cameraman, presenter, and Marah, while the cubs are with Tindall in the other panel van. Mireille is with Hennie and the rest of the crew in the passenger transport vehicle, along with the provisions.

Jason leads the way, with the other two rented vehicles following us. He doesn't need a GPS to navigate the Timbavati region; after more than four years of traversing it, he knows it like the back of his hand. Unlike the previous cavalcade with a police escort through peak Johannesburg traffic, there are no other humans in sight—and no need to keep the sliding doors of the vans closed. So the doors of our vehicle and the one directly following us are standing wide open to aerate the interior for the sleeping lions. The cameras are still rolling. In the cloying afternoon heat, our convoy meanders through the dense bushveld, past a grazing herd of zebra and wildebeest, who raise their heads and stare before getting spooked and suddenly galloping off. Gusts of heated atmosphere funnel through our moving vehicle, clammy and fragrant. We pass a herd of giraffe, who stare down at our vehicle over the leafy treetops. From that angle they can see into the back of the vans and are tilting their heads curiously—having spotted snow-white lions!

Behind the wheel, Jason shifts his leather bush hat, to peer up at them. "In the '70s, Chris McBride reported he'd sometimes use giraffe to locate the White Lions in the bushveld," he informs me. "They'd be curiously staring down at something, and he'd follow their eye-direction—then find the Machatan pride nearby, with their white cub."

Maria illustrating for Linda the ancient ancestral knowledge through the bones of divination

Carrying the Lion Queen's mantle

Photo by Richard Wicksteed

Linda beside African high priest Credo Mutwa, who holds his eagle staff in contemplation

Below:
Linda with newborn Marah, pledging to secure her freedom and return her to the land of her birthright

Photos by Richard Wicksteed

Photo by Jason A. Turner

Linda with Tsonga tracker Jack Mathebula, who holds the tail of the last White Lioness seen roaming the Timbavati Private Nature Reserve, in the 1980s

Photo by Richard Wicksteed

Linda with serious-faced Aslan, promising she will not forget him

Long walk to freedom: Linda in the dungeons of a South African zoo, offering the Timbavati soil to be placed under Marah's paw

Winged lion landed: Linda with Mireille and Jason, transporting Marah in a stretcher just after the DC3 has landed

© Global White Lion Protection Trust

Joyous return: Linda with tranquilized Marah, finally being transported to her ancestral lands

© Global White Lion Protection Trust

Jason and Linda carrying a tranquilized cub to safety

Photo by John Liebenberg

Marah's daughter Zihra, now almost fully grown, tranquilized in order to secure a radio collar for her safety

© Global White Lion Protection Trust

Sleeping beauty: Marah slowly awakening to her kingdom

Photo by Philippa Hankinson

Linda with Jason in their reeded bushveld camp

Outdoor classroom: schoolchildren gathering for a cultural celebration of Marah's return

Sepedi dancers in the heat and dust

Tsonga children holding up their White Lion puppet in a gesture that indicates "Order is restored"

I find this amazing. "You mean the giraffe distinguished between White Lions and the golden lions in the region?"

"Appears so. Those were the days when White Lions still roamed freely in these lands . . . before their technical extinction in the wild."

I had read that Chris McBride was responsible for removing three lions from Timbavati in an event surrounded by much secrecy and later described in his book as "Operation White Lion." I imagined he did so with the best intentions, as White Lions were at risk from hunters and poachers—and he mentioned this fact in his book in the 1980s. But the tragedy is that these White Lions were relocated from the wild to a zoo, where they later died. And shortly afterward, the private reserve itself voted to introduce lion trophy-hunting as a means of bringing in income, so the numbers of White Lions remained precariously low, then disappeared altogether after that last birth on November 10, 1991.

"Well, you're about to change that now!" Simon, the scientist beside Jason, comments encouragingly.

"Okay, repeat that!" says the film director, and the cameraman swings his camera back onto Simon—a short, academic-looking scientist in his seat beside Jason.

"The White Lions were technically extinct in this region. Linda, Jason, and we—their team—are about to change that," Simon says on camera.

I cringe slightly at the exposure—but there it is, on film, forever.

"It's a big day for me," I explain, trying to put my inexpressible feelings into words for the camera. "I just wish it hadn't been such a struggle. These lions have a right to be here."

Heading for the epicenter of White Lion territory, our convoy is well on its way to successfully deliver Africa's most sacred lioness and her cubs home! We are through the gates of our newly acquired property. The director stops us, and we have to do that scene of entering the gates again, then a third time. The heat is indescribably oppressive. I dab my forehead again on my T-shirt. We are winding slowly down the dust road, imprinted with a multitude of different animal tracks. What a blessed relief—we are almost there! Our destination is that secure shady *boma* in the very pulsating heart of the lions' indigenous heartland.

The cameraman clambers out first, heaving the high-definition camera onto his shoulder in order to film us carrying the lions: first Marah—I carry one side of her stretcher together with Jason, Tindall, and his three-strong scientific team. The cameraman focuses in on me as I lay her royal head down gently in the long, green grass. Tranquil and asleep, she's never looked so at home. I wipe the perspiration from my brow again. It's burning my eyes. Then we return for the cubs, one by one. The cameraman walks with us, filming, as we settle the first cub down in the long soft grass beneath a leafy thicket, beside her mother. Zihra—she looks gentle and content, so angelic one could forget for a moment how fierce this little lioness can be. After she's settled, the cameraman returns with us to film the other two siblings being carried. We made sure we placed all of them close together to avoid disorientation when they awake.

"How're you feeling?" the presenter asks me, on camera.

"I'm just relieved they're home," I reply. "That's the important thing."

"Just do that scene again," the director instructs the presenter. "Bring the mother in again on the stretcher. We didn't get the right angle. And Linda—give us your answer again. Ready. Roll. How're you feeling? Got it?"

"Got it," the presenter replies.

I take another deep breath, the sweat dripping down my brow.

Jason and Tindall were busy checking the cubs' temperatures and pulses. With the assistance of Hennie, Simon, and the other two scientists, we carry Marah into camera again, lowering her down, and I gently laying her head once more on the Timbavati grass.

I glance over to Tindall and Jason. The vet is putting eyedrops in the cubs' eyes, while Jason is gently shutting their lids with his fingers to ensure no dehydration, placing hand towels over their faces. The camera is still rolling. Jason finishes taking blood samples from all four lions, which we'll send for testing in a lab to make absolutely sure of their optimal health. He carefully sizes Marah's neck for a radio collar, to ensure her safety out in the wild. We also agreed he should take this opportunity to insert a tiny hidden microchip beneath the skin of each lion, as secret identification, should there be any need to prove their identities in the unknown times ahead. He and Tindall have completed that simple operation. Run over the lions' bodies, the scanner beeps, detecting the hidden device, complete with a secret code for each family member.

They are home! This is the critical turning point in my project's history.

Still, I dare not let my guard down yet. The sun has sunk low in the sky, assuaging the blazing heat. The end of the first day on White Lion territory is gradually drawing to a close. Caught up in my own inner world, I feel dazed but deeply, profoundly relieved.

I refocus as I hear the film director demanding we reverse the tranquilizing drug, so that they can film the scene of the lions waking up at sunset. I can't get a grip on what I'm actually hearing! After all the careful implementation of our emergency plan, this has to be the lowest point in the whole journey. Tindall and Jason are denying his request, pointing out that they won't consider putting the lions' lives at unnecessary risk—for any reason. Jason explains it's vital to ensure safe recovery from the tranquilizer, which must wear off slowly overnight. The risks of casualties are high after such a long trip under sedation and searing heat, and the lions have endured enough trauma already.

I would have thought that explanation was enough, but I watch the film director's petulant response. He loudly gripes about his lost opportunity to film. Then he begins complaining to his colleagues that he can't see why, given that the lions have already been tranquilized, that they can't simply be woken, then tranquilized again—"to sleep it off," as per the vet's requirements. I have no trouble understanding the director's filmic needs, but his demands are so out of tune with the real purpose of this day, and any concept of respect for Nature—or life itself—that it saddens me. Fortunately, both Jason and Tindall silence his complaints. They proceed with the step-by-step program, asking that everyone move out of the *boma* now and keep voices down. I watch the director and his team exit, still grumbling.

Fortunately, Mireille is preoccupied with sorting out refreshments for the group outside of the *boma* and entirely missed this episode; otherwise she'd have marched over like a sergeant major, wagging her finger and ordering the director off the property.

I look up to the sky. Vultures are circling high above us in a haze of copper and golden light. Realistically, there is little likelihood of any movement from the sedated cats for several hours, and the sun is dropping fast. Given that there is no further lion action to record, the film crew opts to conclude their first day's filming with a sequence of me instead—at the ancient baobab site nearby, of which they'd heard me speak. Nelias, the elderly farm worker who'd been on this land for fifty-three years, showed me this huge, wise, upside-down-looking tree on my first visit to the land. Estimated to be around fifteen hundred years old, this tree holds a wonderful presence, an ideal setting for an interview. Spectacularly, it straddles the entire rock frontage of the dry ravine and can only be approached by walking down a long, dry riverbed.

With great difficulty, I leave my lion family, knowing they are safe in Jason and Tindall's trusted hands, and I head off to this baobab site, together with the film crew. It is about a twenty-minute walk. I'm still shaken and slightly quaky at the knees from the flight, and their insensitive demands aren't helping. At the end of this long, momentous day, watching the film crew trudging up the hot riverbed toward the incredible baobab tree, I find myself increasingly desperate to secure a moment to myself, to connect with the Earth, the lions, and the ancestors.

Marah's home! Do I dare savor this unbelievable moment?

We are nearing the ancient tree site. I watch the director and crew walking ahead of me, in a better humor now, yelling to each other, cracking jokes, and guffawing so loudly that the sounds create echoes in the ravine. I let them get ahead. They reach a point where the ravine takes a sinuous curve, and they are just about to disappear from view. I take this moment to briefly sit down, alone, in the soft, warm river sand. I so badly need a still space—just a brief moment—to center myself. I am calling upon the spirit of Maria Khosa to show me that all is well, despite the immediate threats and uncertainties that surround our arrival. And I ask my beloved teacher—with all my heart—to give me a sign that she, after all, presides over these lands.

As often occurs on such occasions of communication with the ancestors, a gentle, warm breeze suddenly starts to blow. And I can feel her presence. But I can also hear the film crew calling my name in the distance, so, reluctantly, I stand up again.

A moment later, I hear screams and shouts. Alarmed, I break into a sprint to join them.

When I round the corner I find the film crew standing, looking shocked, all shouting at me simultaneously. Apparently, just ahead of them in the riverbed, a leopard darted straight past and made a kill in the impenetrable riverine bush, meters away. From the squealing in the bushes, the cameraman indicates it must have been a warthog. I can't believe what I'm hearing! Apart from being extremely reticent and actively keeping away from humans, leopards are nocturnal predators, by nature hunting at night. The likelihood of such an event occurring in daylight, and with all the disturbances of loud human noises, is probably a million to one. I can't help laughing out loud, although I don't attempt to explain my exuberance to the others. Maria always had a particular penchant for spectacular drama, with a humorous twist. Without a shadow of doubt, I know she is here with me!

I called for her presence and received the affirmation I was looking for. It happened as if by pure, natural magic, and it signals that all is well, despite the challenges. That's enough for me.

I am not alone in my mystical belief that Maria, the most powerful priestess, who was imbued with great catlike qualities, can take on lion or leopard form at will. Not long after Maria's death, a friendly leopard came visiting the staff quarters in Timbavati, padding right up to the inhabitants' rooms and even lying on the threshold of their barracks. The Tsonga staff members who knew Maria Khosa in her lifetime maintained that this great medicine woman had returned to visit her beloved people in the form of a friendly leopard. And they actually left a dish of milk, or their favorite staple meal—*mieliepap*—outside their doors in acknowledgment of Maria's presence. I am still looking forward to one day sharing with Jason that the leopard who sat with him and me under the stars on the night we first met was, I believe, Maria Khosa herself. She was presiding over my welfare and, in so doing, was giving Jason, my special friend, and me, her spiritual daughter, her blessing. I knew this without any doubt at the time, but I imagined my intimacy with Jason still required a certain level of understanding before I'd risk sharing it with him.

One day I'll tell Jason. As for now, newly arrived on sacred lands, in the riverbed, with the distant film crew screaming from shock at the sudden appearance of a leopard apparently out of nowhere, I silently thank my shaman teacher, again and again, for providing the confirmation I yearned for on this day, the most day important of my life.

CHAPTER 19

Return of the Lion Queen

PEACE, AT LAST! NOTHING BUT THE STARS. It is the night of Marah's arrival on her sacred lands. Filled with relief and gratitude for the sign from ancestral sources, I glance at Jason in the darkened Land Rover's seat beside me. He's viewing the lions through a set of infrared binoculars so as not to disturb them by shining a spotlight. Hennie and the scientists headed back to camp, together with the film crew. Jason and I kept insisting that each of us would prefer to do the night's monitoring shift; then we finally agreed to do the shift together. Having put aside a cooler of food for us at the back of our monitoring vehicle, Mireille headed off with Tindall to get some sleep. Tindall has a radio at the ready, should we need backup.

At last, I'm starting to feel myself again. Jason's presence in the driver's seat beside me is warm and supportive. Only a man of courage and integrity could endure the journey we've just been through. So much is in jeopardy, and I fully recognize that among the risks is Jason's scientific reputation. But he didn't hesitate to weigh up the criticism his peers might have for this unusual project, which doesn't conveniently fit into any scientific category and hasn't been rubber-stamped by the authorities. Instead, he willingly took the necessary action steps together with me, whatever the consequences.

Jason and I intend to take turns monitoring Marah and her family all through the night. I offered to take the first shift. . . . But I open my eyes again . . . and I realize I must have fallen asleep from sheer exhaustion. Still in the passenger seat, I wonder whether, when I keeled over, I had my head on Jason's shoulder all the while or if I'd been drooling into his lap, but he gallantly gives no indication of it. Straightening myself out, I sit upright. It's after midnight.

"Any movement from the lions?" I ask him, back in efficiency mode. "I'm awake now. I'll take over."

"All calm," he responds. "I've set my alarm so I can take over the shift in a couple of hours. Wanna sandwich?"

I gratefully take one of Mireille's chunky cheddar cheese sandwiches from Jason's hand, and am about to ask him a question about how to work the telemetry equipment, only to find that he himself has completely passed out now—upright, in the seat beside me, out for the count.

The hours tick by, tranquil, warm, and sublimely peaceful. It's pitch dark. It begins to rain. A gentle hazy rain, falling, falling, falling, all around me. Suddenly, I shake Jason awake.

"What? Tell me!" he says, sitting up and focusing immediately.

It is still dark. Predawn. But the cats are beginning to stir for the first time! The cubs seem to be waking first. I watch them through the infrared. They are pretty bewildered, looking around with wide eyes and heads lolling slightly from the tranquilizer. A low growl—that's Marah's waking.

I think back twenty-eight hours, how she fiercely resisted the tranquilizing drug. God, how my heart wept for her then. She fought and fought the drug's debilitating effects, requiring three doses from Tindall's dart gun, before finally succumbing. Now, with the same determination, she is actively fighting off the drowsiness as she emerges from the drug.

I hand the night-vision equipment over to Jason, who takes it, and says, "Look how focused she is!"

"But she's still staggering," I point out, concerned. "Her legs seem to buckle under her weight!"

"That's quite normal for the dosages we've used. Remember the Karoo? This time, the journey was much longer, so we unfortunately had to top them up more than once. Don't worry—" he says, putting down the night sights momentarily and turning to me with a comforting smile. "Don't underestimate her!"

Her cubs attempt to make their way over to their mother. She's not far away, but with every step they take they keel over. As usual, I want to rush in and help prop them up—and cuddle them. Fortunately, after staggering a couple of paces, then lolling and toppling over again, they finally reach her. All four huddle together for comfort. They look drowsy and dazed in their new playground but, thank God, they are all very much alive and well!

Being with them on this groundbreaking occasion makes me feel relieved and so very proud. No mother watching her child take his or her first teetering step could possibly feel more proud.

Jason is beaming proudly at them too as he views them through his infrared binocs.

For the first time, I become aware of a long-forgotten joy rising through my body—and suddenly I burst out loud, uncontrollably, "Marah's home! Marah's home! Marah's home!"

Jason turns to look at me, grinning.

I'm bouncing up and down on the seat next to him. I don't care what he might think of me and my excitement. It's taken every bit of self-restraint not to leap out and run toward my darling lions with my arms outstretched! I'm forcing myself to hold back.

"Yes, I know, Jase—they have to remain un-human-imprinted!"

Not only does an electrified fence separate Marah from me now, but, more importantly, we have a self-imposed separation, which I have to honor, even if it goes against every imaginable yearning. Once committed to Marah's rewilding, I have to maintain my purpose—minimize every and all human intervention, so that she and her cubs might return to the wild without dependency on humans. So instead of running toward them—as I continually yearn to do—all I am able do is simply watch!

I stare out at them in the soft dawn light. They are wide awake, bright-eyed and staring straight back at us, their coats translucent in the first light. Morning has broken. The mist has lifted and the skyline is pink and golden. It feels like the first morning on Earth!

Crisscrossing the tall grass and treetops in the lions' *boma* are a thousand finely spun nets from the golden orb spider. Sunlit from heaven, the dew droplets catch the first beams of light, suspended on fine golden threads, like twinkling gems, fracturing into a spectrum of different hues. Ah! Sunlight! Dawning of the first day! The mother of the sun herself, Ma Ra, has awoken! And the first rays of sunlight on Earth—Regeus, Letaba, and Zihra—are shining bright as on the day of creation. I am speechless. So is Jason.

Finally, reluctantly, Jason clears his throat and radios to the camp to inform the film crew that the lions are waking up. To settle the lions and encourage them to feel at home as soon as possible, Jason planned to use the same technique as in the Karoo: discretely leave a wild game carcass for Marah and her family to "discover" in the far corner of their *boma*—their first meal on native soil. He organized with Simon and colleagues to place it here while I was away with the crew filming at the baobab tree. It was a whole kudu cow and the belly has been cut open to assist Marah in picking up the scent. Again, like my first attempt in the Karoo, there is no wind. But this time, Jason expects it to be different.

And sure enough, a little steadier on her paws, Marah determinedly makes her way over toward the hidden carcass, through long, green grass and dense foliage, her head held high to pick up the faintest scent on the air. She looks around her anxiously to check for danger. It's all so unfamiliar. But then, suddenly, she looks back at me and Jason, and her face softens, as if comforted.

The hungry cubs are not waiting behind this time. Instead, they pad after their mother on unsteady legs.

For observation purposes, Jason had his team slash the grass in preparation for the lions' arrival. But even so, in some places, the cubs are only discernable by the movement in the long grass through which they are moving—and tails flicking up above the grassy fronds.

Marah's located the carcass.

"Phenomenal progress!" Jason observes proudly.

Although clearly still weakened by the tranquilizer, she's started dragging her prize back toward her expectant cubs.

"Isn't she simply amazing!" I bask in her glory.

It is a clear indication that the Queen of Timbavati is settling back into her rightful role—from the moment her paw touched down on her ancestral homelands. Fortunately, she doesn't seem to need to check the electrified fence this time around.

The sun is starting to rise, and the film crew pulls in. Following our long night of quiet observation, their raucous arrival inevitably feels like an intrusion into our magical world. But this land is so powerful, and the spirits of the place are so very present, that absolutely no one could destroy the magic.

Understandably, the crew didn't see any message in yesterday's leopard drama. They looked shell-shocked that a lethal predator should have made a kill so close to them. And they were also equally disappointed at not being able to capture any aspects of the dramatic leopard incident on film. The fact they have nothing by way of record of the incident makes me smile. In shamanic circles, Maria's elusive appearance and disappearance would be recognized as the work of a "spirit leopard."

Not surprising that the film crew has nothing of Maria's visitation on record; but this particular morning, they are being blessed with particularly great lion footage. The cubs are total stars: they're up and about and playful—truly amazing under the circumstances—running circles around their mother, who expertly provided them with their first banquet on home territory! A delightful scene.

Having filmed for almost an hour, the crew must have captured some really heartwarming interactions. In fact, they seem more than satisfied and have called it a wrap.

We assist them in packing up their camera gear and they head off back to camp, waving their goodbyes and all revved up to join Hennie the hero on his return flight.

Back at the farmhouse, we should be celebrating. We should be cracking the champagne, lighting the fireworks, leaping for joy! Instead, by sheer necessity, we are gathered around the camping table in the dingy kitchen, like an emergency war council, strategizing and planning next steps. Mireille, Xhosa, Harold, and I—together with Jason and his team of scientists. Jason and I returned from the lions' *boma* a half hour earlier, having left the pride contentedly asleep in the deep shade, with Simon watching over them. We've been joined by Xhosa and Harold, who drove down from Johannesburg to be of assistance. All of us hear the droning overhead now, as the DC3 circles one last time, and I picture Hennie peering down from the cockpit trying to detect his white "puppies" in their *boma* from the air. Satisfied that the danger period for the tranquilized lions is over, Tindall joined Hennie and the others on the return flight back to Johannesburg.

Feeling the full weight of responsibility for the pride's safety, I've gone quiet and pensive, my head heavy. I can hear the intensity of human voices all around me, but I am making no effort to follow the debate. I watch the armies of ants in a frenzy gathering grass seeds and breadcrumbs from the concrete cracks of the kitchen floor, as if preparing their underground bunkers for a long, hard winter of sustained attrition. They may have been planning ahead, but all I can think of is the heat and stress of the day. Despite the soft, refreshing rain overnight, it is already swelteringly hot. The kitchen door stands open. This isn't the gracious, colonial, *Out of Africa*–style farmhouse, with generous yellow wood floors, spacious verandas, and high ceilings. It's more of a barracks. The floors are concrete, bare, and cracked, allowing through the legions of ants. The previous owners were hard-working Boers who clearly struggled to survive in an environment they must have found particularly hostile. The whole place is barred up, a patchwork of corrugated iron and bricks and mortar, and there's no real living space. It has clearly been built piecemeal over the years, by a determined hunter-farmer who had no resources, nor any apparent need for recreational space, while toiling and battling the total onslaught of aggressive forces he imagined were invading from Nature outside.

I step outside to phone Marianne.

"Tell her all quiet on the Western front!" Mireille calls after me.

In the blazing heat outside, I have to climb a giant termite mound to get a signal. It is a beautifully erected pyramidal structure, about five square meters at its base, and provides a great vantage point over the expansive Timbavati wilderness to the Drakensberg Mountains. The thought of Johannesburg and my existence in The Cupboard, just one of so many live-in boxes, seems a lifetime away.

"The eagle has landed!" I inform her.

"Phew! That's *lekker* news," she exclaims in delight.

"And Mireille asked me to tell you not to worry: all's quiet."

Then I start updating Marianne on the vulnerability of the present status. We don't know what the next move of the authorities and canned hunters will be.

"*Eish!* Just keep your head down," she instructs. "And keep your eyes on the project."

From my new vantage point, I take an all-encompassing glance over the rambling bushveld wilderness on all horizons, shimmering with midmorning light. I imagine Ian must be anxious to know how our mission fared, having voiced his caution over taking these risky steps. I leave a message on his cell phone, informing him of our success thus far and indicating that I would be grateful to talk through some of the challenges facing us now that we've succeeded in avoiding detection from hostile opponents and officials. My next call is to my friends and supporters from the Corelight organization in the States, to inform Brad and Leslie that Queen Marah is safe, and to ask that they continue to pray for her welfare and protection.

I feel bolstered by the support of a dedicated network of supporters and specialists from different fields and from all corners of the globe. But locally, here on the land, on all borders of the ancestral White Lion kingdom, we are under siege.

I'm about to turn back to camp but change my mind. It's too hot to be out in the midday sun, but Mother Nature lies stretched out to the distant horizons, emitting an overwhelmingly majestic resonance. I take Mireille's sage advice and settle down in the dense shade under a huge gnarled jackalberry tree to make a list, once again, of everything I have to be grateful for.

First on that list I write: Marah's safe return! Hallelujah! Unbelievably, I am here—and she is here too. But the real celebration will be the first day the Lion Queen roars her presence over the land, signaling her command over her rightful territory. May that day come soon!

Next, I give grateful thanks for the land itself. It's hard to believe I'm the custodian of many kilometers of indigenous bushveld terrain, the heart of the original White Lions' kingdom. The habitat is savanna land, but much denser than the open plains of the Masai Mara—particularly in the late summer months, with the foliage lush and verdant like a jungle in the river areas. Although I can't see the Tsau River, I can feel its awesome power: the Nile of the south, some two hundred meters spanning bank to bank, carving its way though this great uncharted land. At my very first opportunity, I'll walk through the dense bushveld terrain to these riverbanks, to place my feet in the water and pay my respects.

I wipe my damp palms on my khaki shorts and continue writing. Next on the list, I scribe one word of my own coining: "lion-love." There's no better word to express my thankfulness to the great Maria Khosa for passing on to me some of her wisdom and all of her love for lions. Without her lionhearted lessons, nothing in my world would have made any sense. And I thank her for guarding over this project, forever and always, from the ancestral realms.

Under the jackalberry tree with my pen in hand, I hear the alarm call of the purple-crested loerie in the branches above me and wonder whether its cry signals that a predator is moving this way through the undergrowth. Rather than fear, I realize I feel a warm, loving glow at the thought. Sadly, no lions roam this property as yet, unless they've escaped from the neighboring reserves, and most of the other predators resident here—leopard, civet, caracal, genet, serval, and hyena—are nocturnal hunters. So I conclude that, being daylight, the stalker is very likely to be a little black-backed jackal. I stand up slowly to see if I might spot the lovely slinking creature. Nearby, there's a scurrying, and I catch a glimpse of the black and white coat heading through the lush undergrowth. It's not a jackal, but a honey badger—unusually out during the day! Certainly a great omen—Maria told me that badgers signify the meeting of day and night, the playing out of light and shadow in God's plan. Their favorite food is honey, but they're omnivorous and will eat all sorts of insects, eggs, plants, and even some small mammals. I wonder what he is after. But as I move forward in the hope of seeing him more clearly, the purple-crested loerie suddenly starts into the sky in a flash of wine-colored wings heading for the river canopy, giving a distinct alarm call in reaction to me. It is disconcerting to be reminded that the most ruthless predator, both on the savanna and in the concrete jungle, is, after all, human.

I have no intention of ever returning to the city, with its crime rate, street muggings, car jackings, and smoggy skyscrapers flickering with TV and computer screens. Here I am, home at last! Ever since Maria Khosa's teachings, I've lost all fear of Nature. Instead, a sense of wonderment infuses every given moment. As I settle down in the shade of the jackalberry again to complete my list of thanksgiving, I notice two scarab beetles rolling their earthly possessions around with them in neat dung balls near the base of my tree. Like the Ancient Egyptians, the Bushmen people consider the scarab beetle sacred, because it converts waste into wealth and keeps the world turning. From Jason's description of their characteristic behavior, I determine that the female beetle is standing by, assessing which macho male she is going to partner with. I wish Jason were here. His innate instinct for Nature—and for lion behavior in particular—fascinates me. I've always appreciated a natural man. But what I find so rare is the intensity of his feelings for the lions. Over the past few months, it has been something of a revelation to discover that Jason's overwhelming love for these great cats probably equals my own. First he identified the urgency; now he's put all his scientific credibility into helping save this genetic rarity from extinction, recognizing that Marah holds the key. I imagine, somehow, that it is Jason's passionate nature that protects him in life. Without his love for lions, Jason would never be able to withstand the immense personal and professional challenges that he'll be required to face for involving himself in my project.

Realizing how much time has lapsed, I stroll back through the long, green grass, feeling utterly revived. The air is hot and fragrant in my lungs and the earth, solid and supportive underfoot. And with Jason's support of the project, I feel bolstered and protected like never before.

The group is still congregated around the farmhouse table. I am beaming again—I feel so lucky to have this team of dedicated supporters, all exceptional people in their own right, all united with me on this intrepid journey. As I join them at the table, everyone's attention is suddenly focused by my presence. There's a sense of expectation, and I can tell the group is preparing to settle back into the intensity of tactical discussion. Feeling refreshed from my walk, I muster the stamina to discuss the urgent next steps lurking in everyone's mind.

"Queen Marah has returned to her ancestral heartland—as prophesized by Maria Khosa," I begin. "But her long walk to freedom is far from over."

My intention is to set the scene for everyone by applying the symbolic level of my work first, the legendary aspect in which Maria trained me. I can feel how this raises the vibration of the consciousness around the table, with everyone's attention totally directed. Then I get down to the nitty-gritty.

"Here's our problem: If our actions are deemed illegal by the authorities, a law enforcement officer could arrive at our gate, without notice, at any time, with a summons to confiscate the lions."

Understandably, a shudder runs through the group. But it is best for us to be prepared. My guess is that we'd be granted no more than a few days' breathing space before the legal battle would begin in earnest. I've determined from my legal advisors that the only way we could prevent confiscation under these circumstances is through an urgent interdict, which a judge unsympathetic to our cause might not be prepared to issue in a hurry. I know this appalling thought will keep me awake tonight. There's no getting around that, but I've got to be careful not to alarm anyone else and instead equip them to deal with eventualities.

"Be aware, everyone. If any official arrives at our gate, he's not allowed access to the land—unless he has a legitimate warrant."

I make a mental note to inform Xhosa, who left to get us more provisions, of this procedure too. "If, in fact, the official is carrying a warrant, with authorized stamps, it's imperative you notify me immediately—because we'll need to act urgently in applying for an interdict. We probably have no more than twenty-four hours to stop the confiscation."

"Everyone got that?" Mireille reiterates.

My darling godmother has been appointed chair of the Global White Lion Protection Trust, having chaired many church groups and charity committees in her day. It is a tough position for which she is ideally suited. I hope she'll always hold this position, chairing our organization. Our overriding objective, as always, remains the lions' safety and welfare; step by step, we intend to put all the necessary procedures in place to protect not only Marah and her family, but also their next of kin all around the globe, held in captivity against their will. It feels like we are the Resistance, surrounded by electric fences, waiting for invasion.

There's a momentary silence, and the scientists look particularly grave. True to form, Jason uses the lull to add something encouraging: "We're gonna get through this. Just take it step by step."

"We can expect a play of light and dark," I caution, making a reference to the badger I'd just seen, who showed himself as a meaningful sign from Nature. "We should recognize this as a chess game, and be very careful and strategic about every move we make."

"Got you!" Harold responds, clearly enjoying the challenge.

"Our main difficulty is," I continue, "it's impossible to anticipate next steps. Will we be granted the outstanding permit necessary to proceed with the White Lion reintroduction, on the strength of our first two permits?"

There's a suspended pause, as I take a deep breath to complete my sentence. "Or will the objections lodged by our neighbors sway the decision of the authorities, who could then proceed with action against us, and the lions?"

A grave silence.

Again, I feel the shudder of fear run through the assembled group. Knowing that White Lion conservation relies on lionhearted action, and not fearful inertia, I look to Mireille to provide cheery guidance.

"Chin up, everyone," our chairperson announces on cue. "It'll all work itself out. Remember, we've got Mother Nature on our side!"

"Okay," I continue. "So we've covered protocols for dealing with Nat Con officials hammering at our gates. What's important now is we need to get beyond the immediate challenges and look at the bigger picture, and what Marah's return really means for this region. Although we're not in attack mode, we are ultimately poised for a territorial takeover."

I unroll my topographical aerial survey map of the entire region and pin it to the wall, the same map I pored over so many nights in succession, when I was holed up in The Cupboard. Only now, it makes real, solid, tangible sense. Standing so everyone can see, I identify our exact position. Sweeping my hand over the whole region—a massive million-acre area of largely unspoiled wilderness known as the Kruger to Canyons Biosphere Reserve—I pinpoint the land I've secured for Marah, at the epicenter.

"That's the ultimate purpose of Marah's return to this region, to create peace and unification. We won't exactly aggressively claim and reclaim the White Lions' heritage lands, but we'll invite in any party who shares our vision of protecting these sacred animals for the future of our planet."

Harold looks quizzical, balanced precariously on his three-legged kitchen stool. "If the biosphere region were a dartboard, this property'd be bull's eye, right?" he points out. "That's how it looks to me."

"Quite so, Harry. Highly relevant," I concur.

I point out our location in relation to neighboring wildlife reserves, illustrating how we share a border with neighboring Timbavati, while Timbavati itself borders the Kruger National Park.

With everyone's attention focused on the map, I sweep my hand over the strategic area in question, illustrating how Timbavati's lands are vast, some 120,000 acres, stretching out to the east.

"But there's one huge problem," I point out. "D'you see?"

"The whole of modern-day Timbavati is cut off from its water source." That's Jason's voice.

Even coming from a scientist, this sounds so unlikely that the group experiences a momentary hesitation. I turn to the map again, and point to the Tsau River, drawing my index finger from the top of the map all the way to the bottom, following the river's path. It flows from the south to the north in direct alignment to the great River Nile, the sacred river of the Ancient Egyptians. There will be another occasion to explore with the group why this correlation is of absolutely vital importance. For now, it's critical I follow the strategic thread of argument.

"The issue is simple," I explain. "But potentially catastrophic. This private reserve exists entirely without any access to surface water."

Harold is frowning, beads of perspiration creasing in his brow. "Can't tell me that's true? It's suicide."

I nod gravely. "The Tsau River is the only river in the region that flows all year round. Present-day Timbavati Private Nature Reserve is cut off from it by its many kilometers of predator-proof electric fencing!"

The seriousness of this observation strikes everyone at the same moment. Harry in particular shakes his head slowly, as if weighing up the gravity. There is a protracted silence, which Jason breaks in order to discuss the practical implications.

"Timbavati's dry riverbeds flow only once or twice a year, after rain," he points out. "The inhabitants survive by tapping into a fragile network of subterranean streams through the use of boreholes, which often run dry."

From his position, seated with the others at the kitchen table,

Jason ponders a moment before continuing to address the group. "I'm not sure the current landowners really appreciate the extent of their vulnerability."

Then he stands and joins me at the map, in order to further focus the issue.

"This fortified veterinary fence is known as the Red Line," he explains, drawing his finger down the thick, nearly straight line, marked in red. "There on the map—see it clearly? That demarcates a massive electric barrier, running north-south, carving through many kilometers of wilderness."

"Fitting name, isn't it?" I can't help commenting, wryly. "The Red Line is yet another man-made barrier to complicate our efforts to secure the White Lions' protection—just like all the others . . . whether cages, electric fences, bureaucratic brick walls, or red tape."

Perched on his barstool, Harold is about to pipe up again. Being an aviation specialist, he's fascinated by topographical details. "You've said this important area was declared the third largest biosphere region in the world. Am I hearing right? The Red Line literally carves this natural biosphere in two!"

"Correct, Harry."

"Okay," he says, swinging his stool squarely onto the concrete floor again, with an emphatic clunk. "Walk me through solutions."

"Important thing is our founding property shares a border with the Timbavati Private Nature Reserve, alongside this Red Line," I explain. "We'd consider dropping our joint fences—but this could never take place until the reserve prohibits lion hunting."

"Agreed," Jason concurs, respectfully. "But that basically means changing the mindset of this whole region. Don't see that happening in a hurry."

"Hmm," Harold summarizes. "What we're saying is: Timbavati's a protected wilderness region without any protected water? Suicide."

"Worse," Jason says, illustrating his point on the map again, "since all the water originates from the Drakensberg Mountains here in the west and flows across this whole unprotected region here," he sweeps his hand over the land west of the Nile meridian. "What it means is all the water for the entire region—including the Kruger National Park—is basically unprotected!"

"What a balls up!" Harold retorts.

"How seriously should we regard the ecological impact of this fence line?" Simon comments.

"Possibly the most serious ecological concern for this entire wilderness region," Jason responds. "There're ongoing casualties against this artificial fence line. It cuts off the natural migration routes of herd game, like wildebeest and sable antelope. As a result, species like sable, which were once abundant in this region, are all but extinct."

Simon looks shocked.

"We're saying these horrific casualties might continue forever, until the massive wilderness area on both sides of the Red Line is united."

"Precisely. That's why this Tsau River, running north-south, is so absolutely vital," I conclude. "And that's why our longer-term vision has to be the uniting of east and west across this artificial man-made barrier."

"Phew!" Simon responds, wiping his brow at the enormity of the problem.

"Right," I continue. "Let's look at our immediate challenge."

I reach down to collect another map, this time an enlarged schematic of the game property itself. I unroll it and pin it up against the wall alongside the other. Everyone scrutinizes it. I've seen it before, but that was only in theory; now we are on the very land charted by this map. It's deeply exciting. Standing where everyone can view the map and the lay of the land, I point out our location in relation to that of the lions several kilometers away on another sector of the land.

"In addition to the threats from our neighbors," I continue, "you'll see our own protected land itself poses an immediate challenge because it's divided in two by a municipal dust road."

Personally, I knew this to be highly significant: Maria Khosa prophesized, like the sacred lands of the Ancient Egyptians once known as the Divided Land, the separated lands on either side of the Tsau River would be unified through the return of the true monarch. This heartland, torn in two at the present time, she told me, would one day be united like two chambers of the same heart, healed and made whole by the lion-hearts themselves. But until such time as Maria's prophecy comes about, the heart of the White Lion kingdom remains in a state of separation.

In the greater scheme of things, Maria's prophesized unification of these divided lands is pivotal to the future of our project, and to the hope for unity in these lands and the greater ecosystem. But it is important for our immediate goals to focus on practicalities, not prophecies.

"Let's look at the planning for the lion reintroduction," I continue. "Over to you, Jase."

"Okay. We're dealing with two pieces of land separated by a fenced-off dust road. Personally, I don't believe the division of the land poses a problem for our project. It means, at this beginning stage, that the lions can be free-roaming on the one side, and the humans on the other—without us worrying that the two might unexpectedly meet."

Nervous chuckling all around the table.

Unperturbed, Jason continues, "We're looking at implementing a carefully phased scientific reintroduction program—"

"What d'you mean: phased?" Simon pipes up.

"Many factors to consider. We'll talk you through them in due course," Jason responds. "For the moment, I think it's enough to say the layout of the property, currently, should be viewed as an advantage, not a disadvantage. The parameters will eventually change when more land comes in."

"More land," I smile hearing Jason's wording. "Comes in," as if property has a mind of its own! As Jason wraps up, I think about how little doubt I have that all the surrounding land wants to be included in the White Lion project. What an incredible thought. So, in my mind, momentarily, I warmly invite all neighboring lands to join us.

Xhosa's vehicle pulls in. We all get up from the farmhouse table to help offload the provisions, all of us feeling a little more upbeat. But Xhosa climbs out of the truck, looking ashen. He's empty-handed, apart from the rolled-up copy of the local regional newspaper, which he clutches, staring at me. He unrolls the paper and holds it out to me, speechless. On the front page, the banner headline reads:

White Lions Return to the Region,
Neighbors Threaten Legal Action

CHAPTER 20

Vernal Equinox

MARCH 21, 2005. VERNAL EQUINOX. Two weeks after our arrival. I am walking down the sandy riverbed toward the ancient baobab tree, in preparation for a sunset ceremony together with indigenous elders from different cultures. This is the other side of my work for the White Lions: the symbolic side, the reverential and meaningful side, which supports each ruthlessly practical action step I have to take.

In the madness of my trials and anguish on behalf of the White Lions, it is these quiet times of ceremony that bring order and significance to my world. Padding barefoot through the soft river sand, I think back over the shock tactics of the past two weeks—beginning with the poison-pen journalist and the newspaper headlines threatening to bring down my life's effort. Instead of launching a public counterattack, or even attempting to defend my position under such damaging misinformation, I chose to gather my strength and fight another day.

I have to draw on Maria's teachings like never before. Rather than declaring open warfare, Maria's example has trained me to recognize fear (my own and others) and to manage the inherent danger of giving in to it. The way to overcome fear is through love. And love is the force that has sustained me through the traumatic days after arrival here.

I think back to the moment of seeing the damaging newspaper headlines. My first response was to cut further strategic discussions and get back to monitor the lions. Jason and I took turns. I took the first shift, Jason the second. Then we swapped at midnight, and I slept, tucked up in a sleeping bag in the back of the truck until first light. Given the onslaught from my neighbors, I was dreading the dawn, but then—the moment I opened my eyes I was greeted by the most heartwarming sight imaginable: magnificent Marah and her brood, well fed, content, and alert, shining like the rising sun—all staring brightly at me!

It was the second day after arrival, and the effects of the tranquilizer had entirely worn off, leaving them radiant as sunlight. After noticing I was awake, all three cubs turned to investigate their new environment. None ventured near the electrified wires, as if they all knew the fence and nasty wires were out of bounds. But everything else piqued their interest: the new habitat, the cry of an owl overhead as dawn broke, the distant snort of a grazing wildebeest herd. In contrast with my very first view of Marah's cubs as frightened little bundles hiding in the straw of their concrete cell, these adventurous youngsters were soon bounding excitedly like scrub hares through the thick undergrowth. Frolicking, tumbling, mock-hunting, even climbing trees and dropping down on each other in staged "attack" mode, then returning excitedly to their mother for kisses and cuddles and affectionate cheek-rubs. I knew that whatever the future may hold, being with them is worth a lifetime! And that sense of loving celebration helped me gather my strength after the media attack, and refocus.

There have been other challenges since then, but always the lions have seen me through. With the same sense of clarity, today's ceremony of thanksgiving for the White Lions and Mother Nature will be built on the work of Maria Khosa and that mysterious instruction she gave me in the early days of my White Lion initiations—before I could possibly understand what it truly meant: she said the way to protect the White Lions is to celebrate them!

I am just beginning to understand. Celebration is the oldest form of unity with the Divine, an acknowledgment of the wonderment of creation, thereby reinstating law and order at the highest level. What could be greater protection than to call upon the highest authority, the overarching presence of the creator, in protecting his perfect creations?

Earlier today, in preparing for this evening's ceremony, I buried a sacred stone in the dry riverbed beneath the baobab tree, just as Maria instructed me shortly before her death. It felt deeply meaningful, although, as ever, I tried not to rationalize the full symbolism behind such a timeless act. I sat alone for a long while, yearning for Maria's lost companionship and guidance. Finally, I called upon my great shamanic teacher to give me a sign of her presence once again, just as I did with such dramatic effect the day of Marah's first arrival on these sacred lands—to the utter astonishment of the film crew.

Now as I return down this soft, sandy riverbed to complete the ceremony, I wonder what sign Maria will give me, and I pray that I won't overlook it, as is so easy to do with signs and messages from the other realms. I am accompanied by an indigenous woman from the Dakota tribe who traveled all the way from the States to be here after receiving a message in a dream about the White Lions. It is not the first time people have tracked me down after receiving highly evocative White Lion dreams. Walking just behind her are two exquisitely fine-featured men, each holding an ostrich egg in both hands. They have brightly colored beads in their hair and torn clothes over beautiful copper skin. They are representatives of the last surviving Bushmen or San people, a lineage as endangered as the White Lions. They themselves have made a pilgrimage all the way from the

Kalahari Desert, over several days, in order to pay homage to Queen Marah, the sacred lioness who has returned to her natural kingdom, bringing back hope and courage to the indigenous peoples of Africa. I marvel at the great lengths and distances undertaken by these people, and it's still a mystery how some of them heard of this place. Following the Bushmen people of the !Xam clan walks an Inuit elder from Greenland in full traditional dress and, trailing him, a medicine man from the Ndebele people of South Africa's northern territories. All united with one single intention.

I too am in ceremonial dress—draped in the lion-printed fabric that Maria Khosa once gave me in a loving act of handover I'd never forget: that moment when she intimated I would be taking over her mantle after I met Ingwavuma for the first time. In my case, there's no single culture that I represent. Maria Khosa informed me that in serving the universal spirit of the great White Lions, I would one day come to represent all peoples.

Our shared intention is to honor the return of the White Lions at a time of profound cosmic sacredness, the vernal equinox, an occasion which has been celebrated by indigenous cultures the world over since time immemorial. By celebrating the equinox, the ceremony we are about to undertake is intended to help restore balance on Earth. It is also intended to reinstate the Golden Line that exists between the White Lions of Timbavati and Ancient Egypt, linking the modern-day mystery of the starlions in this unique region with the everlasting riddle of the Sphinx.

It deeply saddens me to consider how modern humans have erected an electrified barricade, the infamous Red Line, along this very north-south golden meridian—the selfsame longitudinal line recognized and honored by the ancients as the most sacred ley line on Earth! Poignant as this may be, it is indicative of the many imbalances contemporary humans have imposed on our Earth and, conversely, the rebalancing role the White Lions are destined to play.

Maria Khosa's prophecy that one day the two sides of this massive ecosystem will be united as one great body of ancestral land—a kingdom governed by the King and Queen of all animals—is in line with Ancient Egyptian beliefs. This precise ley line, which links Timbavati with Giza, is understood by the Ancient Egyptians to be the prime meridian. Known as *Zep Tepi*, it was believed to correspond with a subterranean seam of pure gold, holding the Earth's axis in place. At a level of prophecy, returning the White Lions to their original sacred lands means these magnificent creatures can once more perform their role as divinely appointed protectors of this subterranean seam of pure gold, the age-old guardians of the Earth's axis.

I estimate it is still a little way off before we reach the ancient baobab tree. Watching my footsteps imprint in the dry river sand, I can't help thinking how sad it is that present-day Timbavati has no flowing rivers. Symbolically, as a medicine woman and natural healer, Maria Khosa always drew analogies between circumstances in the outside world and conditions in the human body. She viewed the Tsau River as the spinal column holding together both sides of the body of these lands, just as the Nile runs through the sacred lands of Ancient Egypt. Without access to this source, Timbavati reserve had severed its connection with not only its own spinal fluid, but also its very lifeblood, which no longer ran in the land's veins. Equally, the fortified fence blocking the life force that flowed between East and West was analogous to the left-brain not communicating with the right, or the right side of the body not coordinating with the left. Maria viewed these conditions in the way she would view a critical illness; the difference was that this illness had a remedy. I know that this body of the natural kingdom will remain unbalanced and divided until the great overarching spirit of the White Lions unites it and restores health to our Earth.

After our slow walk down the dry riverbed, my companions and I clamber up the tufty riverbank, coming to stand on high ground beside the baobab tree, preparing for the ceremony. Feeling a gentle breeze across my face, I glance down to the site where I buried Maria's crystal earlier in the day. I feel her presence. And suddenly—astoundingly—I see a leopard stretched out in the riverbed below us! She is languidly lying right over the crystal I'd buried earlier in the day. I am dumbfounded. The very sign I've been waiting for. Queen Maria. Awaiting us!

This time, it is impossible for me to miss the sign. Everyone else is equally overawed, and the two Bushmen drop down in a state of prayer and gratitude. All shamans see spirit in Nature and know the mysterious ways in which the ancestral world manifests in our own. They think in symbolic language, so at this moment I appreciate that the higher meaning of such a blessing must be resonating with each of them in their own unique way. It is truly amazing! In the brutal everyday world of this region, where leopards are mercilessly hunted, these exquisite cats are habitually furtive and shy. And besides, they're nocturnal, so again, late afternoon is way too early to spot such an elusive creature at the best of times. All the more amazing that this magnificent cat is so serenely sitting, waiting and watching, her paws outstretched in a guarding position directly over the stone site where I myself sat only a few hours ago. She seems totally unperturbed by our presence. She gives a most glorious yawn and a full, languid stretch, glistening like liquid gold in the late sunlight. Standing up, she graciously pads down the riverbed, with her tail casually swaying behind her. I watch her tracks imprint in the dry river sands below as she disappears out of sight—and then I see it—her paw prints pad right over my own footprints from earlier in the day! I feel utter jubilation seeing how the Queen of Timbavati, Maria Khosa in leopard form, is walking in my own footsteps—just as I have followed her path.

Tears of joy stream down my face, as I take a deep breath of Timbavati's pure, fragrant air, knowing with every fiber of my being that Maria Khosa will be with me in spirit throughout this sacred ceremony.

I'M IN THE CENTER OF A CIRCLE OF CRYSTALS, reminding me of the occasion years back that coincided with the birth of the Blue Star. These powerful stones have been placed in geometric formation on the surface of the Earth by elders from different indigenous cultures, while Maria's buried crystal remains down in the riverbed beneath the white sands, unseen. Candles are being lit at the four corners of the cardinal axis—north, south, east, and west. And the !Xam bushmen have placed the ostrich eggs, balancing like sentinels on their pointed bases, symbolizing the moment of creation, when all was in perfect equilibrium.

Night equals day; the sun sets while the moon is rising. My world is held in balance by cosmic timelessness. The indigenous woman from the Dakota tribe, in ceremonial dress, is presiding. She steps toward me, with a flame in her hand, that I might light the burning center of our sacred circle.

"Are you ready, sister?" she asks.

"Give me a moment," I respond, taking the burning flame in my hands. I need to center myself.

I remember those nights with my shaman teacher, how Maria and I would sit beside the Tsau River, with Orion and the Leo constellation so brilliant above us, and the Milky Way overarching like a river of stars. This ceremony is lit by another such star-shimmering night—only Maria has since gone, and the angelic lioness, gift from above, has returned to her kingdom.

But Maria's words live on, and I draw strength in the knowledge that tonight we celebrate Queen Marah's return as ordained in the heavens. Here, on the sacred land of White Lions, the land where the starlions came down, I feel the wonderment of this celebratory event.

In the secret knowledge, these luminous creatures are understood to be guardians of the Earth's axis; that's why they were depicted in this way in all the great squares of the Earth, whether Trafalgar Square in London, St. Mark's Square in Venice, Singapore's Merlion Park, or Giza's Sphinx. They are true avatars of enlightenment who will bring all people together in harmony, and in this way unite the four root nations of the Earth. Poignantly, here tonight, on the sacred lands, I picture my four lions, two female and two male. By force of circumstance, they are still held captive in their fortified *boma,* but this fenced area in the heart of their ancestral kingdom is located precisely upon the prime meridian—the golden ley line understood by the Ancient Egyptians to be the central axis of the globe. And it seems to me that, despite humanity's confused and fearful efforts to stop the workings of a higher plan, these four lions are literally guarding the four corners of the Earth here, now, forever.

Under the infinite stars, my anxieties about the hostile neighbors, and their intimidation tactics emblazoned across the local papers, are dispelled. The blazing headlines seem so miniscule. I am fully equipped with the spiritual weaponry Maria handed over to me, and I will never forget her words: "Love is the greatest force!"

"Are you ready, sister?" the Dakota medicine woman asks again.

I am.

Drawing on an inner knowing, a connectedness with everything around me, I prepare myself to lead this ceremony of celebration, giving thanks to the creator for all that is. Holding the flame in my hand, I light the fire at the center. With eyes closed, I visualize the east and west coming together and uniting along this great divide. And then north and south. I put out a prayer to the universe for healing and unity among all people, and a prayer of protection for the White Lions, newly returned to their sacred ancestral lands.

In the shadowy presence of the baobab tree, the luminous aura of the leopard presides, and I take Maria's lead in this thanksgiving ceremony, calling upon the spirits of our ancestors to join us in celebration, inviting representation from all the animals, plants, and minerals, and the angelic kingdoms. With the thrill of the big cat's presence running through everyone's veins, I do not need to speak. Instead, I allow Nature's voice to speak for itself.

We settle down, cross-legged, for an all-night vigil. The Bushmen, normally irrepressible with excited chatter, have long since gone into a state of reverential calm. Above us, the Milky Way spans the north-south horizon, a massive river of shimmering stars. All of us hold the silence.

I visualize the future. One thousand years of peace. I call upon the vision of a golden age: a verdant paradise, where love and respect bind all beings and humanity is in harmony with Nature. Listening to the night sounds around me, I let go of worldly images and gradually attune to the entire biosphere of land, undamaged by human impact, and protected, loved, and nurtured. A deep contentment and calm overcomes me as my mind expands into unfathomable realms.

When the dawn breaks, we, the initiates who've been gathered all night around this stone medicine wheel in wordless meditation, break our silence. One after the other in different languages, a prayer of peace and unity sounds in praise of Mother Earth. We don't share a common language, but our prayers sound with one mind and one heart. And it seems the great shadowy baobab tree, its ancient branches reaching out into the heavens like a giant tuning fork, amplifies our prayers many times over.

As the first rays of sunlight take form, the Intuit elder begins humming, and all parties join in. My eyes are still closed, and the vibration of this continual humming resonates throughout my body, filling my being with celestial sound. It feels as if I am one with the life force all around me, with the creative essence of all creation.

When the humming draws to a close, I open my eyes again to find that the Bushmen elders have disappeared. Their tracks head off into the bushveld, in the direction of the rising sun. In fact, it's the same direction as the distant *boma,* a kilometer or so away through dense bushveld terrain, where Marah and her cubs are housed. I know they are going to pay homage. But since Marah didn't sound her roar yet, I wonder what telepathic means will navigate them to the Queen of Lions.

The sun bursts over the horizon, a gilded disc rising on the cardinal axis, due east. With it, the great river of stars has fast faded from view. But Maria's prophecy remains crystal clear in my mind.

May 10, 2005. With the radio clenched in my hand, I stand at the base station, summoning security. Mireille is beside me, dressed in her trademark red bomber jacket, despite the warm morning temperature. She has postponed her return flight several times over these past couple of months—in order to satisfy herself that the lions are settled, and that we ourselves are set up as best we can be in the dilapidated, old farmhouse on the property. Despite her staunch aristocratic background, she flourishes in these humble circumstances, rallying the troops with encouraging philosophies and preparing sandwiches and flasks of coffee for Jason and my late-night lion-monitoring shifts. She's donated a radio communications system to the project. This way, we can communicate with any member of our team, wherever they are located on the land, particularly in times of emergency.

She stands by my side for moral support, holding my left hand. There's a crackle over the radio. Then nothing.

"Nelson, Nelson! Come in, Nelson!" I repeat my call over the radio, gripping the unit with my right hand. The subtropical climate has eased a little, but I feel myself instantly breaking out into a sweat.

The last few months have probably been the hardest in my life, focused on complex and perplexing legal strategy for which I feel totally unprepared. The warning emblazoned in the headlines of the local paper was no empty threat. Fortunately, the top legal firm in the country under the leadership of Coenraad Jonker has offered the services of its environmental law department pro bono. Without this assistance, we'd be sunk financially, since every last cent has already been spent securing the property, with virtually no fallback for funding daily subsistence.

Standing at the radio base station, urgently waiting for Nelson to respond, I feel that nervous tingling start up in my feet again. It's bad enough facing a legal battle, but today Jason was tipped off in town that neighboring hunting farms have intentions of actively sabotaging our project. He's just phoned from Hoedspruit, advising that we check our southern boundary immediately. He'll be back shortly to take over for us, a comfort and support in particularly trying times.

There is another crackle over the radio in answer to my call—and a gravelly Tsonga accent responds: "Nelson, standing by."

"Nelson, please check the southern fence line with Thornybush. Now please. We think there could be poaching activity there."

Most of the time, I struggle to comprehend the reason behind such ferocious opposition. It's difficult to pinpoint exactly who these opponents are, and exactly why the reintroduction of White Lions to these lands should be so threatening to them. At least a legal battle is open and declared—we can manage that. But the shadowy, nefarious activity at our borders is more unsettling. I continually worry what form this might take. One lighted match thrown into the parched winter grass could lead to an uncontrollable veld-fire raging through our land, trapping Marah and her cubs in the interior. This prospect is utterly appalling. Then again, if my beloved lion family found their way to the fenced borders, they could be at risk from a hunter with a rifle taking a shot at them. Marah and her children mean everything to me, but their value in monetary terms is what worries me most. In a context where money drives all kinds of illicit activity, it is a reality that a poacher might dart the White Lions with a tranquilizing drug, cut the fences, and remove the cats from the property for trophy purposes. Each lion has been carefully fitted with a numbered transponder just under the skin, which, when scanned, would identify them. However, if they were kidnapped, and we were unable to trace their whereabouts, for instance, we'd have no way of applying the microchip device in proving their identities.

Security, and guarding our borders, have become paramount. We've decided not to bring in an independent security firm, because there's no guarantee of its allegiances. Post-Apartheid South Africa is full of armed-response units comprising supporters of the old regime, trained in deadly weapons. These men are often big hunters themselves, with racist inclinations. There have been frequent reports of security guards caught red-handed, poaching the very game they were meant to protect. So instead of employing a specialized armed-response unit, we decided our best security was to make use of our own trusted staff. Fortunately, we have Nelson Mathebula, a well-built Tsonga man in his midfifties. Nelson has a broad smile and an infectious laugh; he'd been with my family for many years, working in an all-around capacity as gardener, caretaker, and security officer. He's weapons-trained and a specialist in antipoaching techniques after years of field-ranging in this part of the bushveld in his younger days. If I'd looked far and wide, I couldn't have found a more comforting right-hand man. Yet amazingly, I have two such stalwarts, backing each other up as a security partnership. The other is the delicate-framed Nelias Ntete, the dignified seventy-three-year-old Sotho man and expert tracker who has lived on this land for the past half century. He's an ideal back-up to Nelson.

Nelias' expertise is not book-learned—in fact, he's never been to school—but he knows every tree, every termite mound, every bird and animal print of this intricate ecosystem. He is the man who showed me the site where the ancient baobab tree resides when I first set foot on these lands, even though the previous owners never made mention of it. Working for the hunter-farmers, Nelias was required to track down game for trophy hunters; now he is on alert for human footprints.

"Okay, we'll *famba lapa* southern fence, Mama Linda," comes

Nelson's voice. His manner of titling me is a Tsonga token of respect. The staff tend to call me Mama—even though I am younger than most of them.

Mireille has just picked up the radio receiver and given an additional instruction with her pukka Swiss-British accent. "*Famba, Famba!* Chin-up, Nelson and Nelias! D'you copy me? To the borders, everyone!"

As she waits for Nelson's response to crackle back over the airwaves, she informs me, "Just giving a bit of encouragement over the walkie-talkie."

Mireille's technique over the radio is cause for much mirth with the rest of my team. She addresses Nelson and Nelias using a scramble of Tsonga words she remembers from childhood and other obscure expressions seemingly dating back to World War II.

"Nelson, standing by for *Kokwane*," he responds to Mireille's instruction. *Kokwane* means "Grandmama"—an even greater sign of respect than "Mama" in Tsonga culture.

"Security men," Mireille instructs, "if anyone gives us any trouble, just tell them to Foxtrot Oscar!" She catches my eye and giggles delightedly, believing she has wickedly transgressed some social code of her generation.

She concludes the radio communication with "Roger, over and out!"

Nelson and Nelias find this expression very funny because there is no Roger on our staff.

On a daily basis, Mireille's matriarchal quirks give us many moments of light relief. But no one doubts the seriousness of the situation. Some of Nelson and Nelias's security report-backs over the past few weeks have been particularly troubling. On one occasion, they picked up from the tracks on the ground in front of our main gate that a large 4x4 had pulled up and a man with army-style boots had gotten out and tested our padlocks before pulling off again in his vehicle. On another occasion, Nelias picked up a device attached to the fence that cut the electric current, indicating sabotage. Such evidence makes me wonder about motives. Suddenly, it seems we have adversaries on all frontiers—some declared, others unknown and secretly subversive.

In a strange twist of fate, however, our greatest threat has suddenly been removed from the playing field. Within weeks of our arrival, our direct neighbor to the southeast, the notorious "king" of canned hunting, who gave so many threatening warnings in the fort and bid directly against me for these lands, suddenly relocated and disappeared to another dark corner of the country. No stranger to scandal, this significant adversary lifted his entire canned-hunting operation and hurriedly departed. It turns out that a staff member, who was savagely beaten, was then thrown to the hungry lions. When the police found the unfortunate victim, only his skull remained. Under the glare of the international press, the canned hunter vacated and moved, lock, stock, and smoking barrels, in trucks crammed with caged lions.

At one level, the head honcho's removal from the region, directly after Marah's return to her sacred lands, seemed fortuitously coincidental. But at another level, there's no coincidence about it whatsoever. To me, it seemed a key piece has been strategically shifted on a chessboard, with the "dark warrior" being removed at the critical moment of the White Lions' return. It reminds me of Maria Khosa's imperative that this heartland is part of the body of a kingdom, which needs to be reclaimed and reconstituted to ensure the sovereignty of the true monarchs—the White Lions—and the plan of light ushered in by these enlightened and consecrated Kings and Queens of Timbavati.

It's the morning after Jason was tipped off on the threat of sabotage. Nelson and Nelias have combed the southern border through the night. They reported back in the early hours that they picked up three different sets of boot prints entering our property by breaching the electric fence, and indications that the intruders were armed (a rifle case left at the point of entry). The tracks traversed the southern fence line, then finally exited again a few kilometers farther on, where they doubled back, possibly intending to return for their equipment another time. Perhaps the intruders aborted their mission because they were skilled enough to realize they themselves were being tracked, or perhaps their purpose was simply to "stake out the joint." Either way, it doesn't help my comfort levels. Jason has evaluated the situation carefully and is considering bringing in a colleague of his who operates an armed-reaction unit to ensure our safety and that of the lions.

CHAPTER 21

Showdown with the Safari Suits

May 14, 2005. A warm, tranquil night. I am totally serene, lying in Jason's arms. We're under the African sky, beneath the great ancestral presence of the baobab tree, under a fleece blanket on a roll-out mattress on the earth. There's a crackling fire beside us, sending sparks up to join the fireflies and the twinkling stars above. We've just spent the most heavenly night together.

So deliciously serene, my thoughts drift back to that unforgettable night we first met. It was platonic then, but it went on and on forever. Now it seems, that same dreamy night has never ended. Whatever dangers exist beyond my borders, they dissolve by comparison with the safety I feel in Jason's arms. I am so content, there's nothing to say. I wonder whether that ancestral presence of Maria is guarding over us again, in leopard form, nearby. I feel sure she is.

In the spot where the sacred fire burned in ceremony and celebration during the equinox, our fire keeps us warm. The world is at peace, the resonant silence only enhanced by the exquisite gurgling of a nocturnal bird, whose nightingale sweetness has been serenading us for the past few hours.

"Fiery-necked nightjar," Jason acknowledges its celestial presence.

It is one of the sweetest calls I'd ever heard.

"So what's a glamorous Paris model doing with a bushman like me?" Jason asks, with humor in his voice.

"Isn't it obvious?" I respond and give him another warm, lingering kiss.

"What took you so long to wake up?" he replies with that same gentle humor.

I just nestle closer, savoring his warmth and the full, resonant silence. Then, suddenly, as if to answer for me, I hear a distant roar. It's an utterance I know so well from the many nights in Timbavati with Maria Khosa in the days of Ingwavuma. I know it deep down in my soul, a voice resonating across the Earth that speaks to all creatures great and small—the command of true royalty. But this roar is different from all the others; I've never heard it's formidable vibration before. It is the voice of Queen Marah, roaring her sovereignty over her kingdom—for the very first time!

WE DRIVE THROUGH THE AUTUMNAL SAVANNA, along the sinuous dusty road. Nelson and Nelias have been doing regular sweeps in the bushveld for signs of poachers and continue to discover hidden traps and cages, and evidence of hunters' camouflaged hides in the riverine areas. But many of these date back to the days of the previous owner, a hunter-farmer. Some cages still have a dangling chain in their interiors, with a piece of desiccated bait attached. Each time I see one of these hideous contraptions, I'm reminded of that initial sense of trauma I felt when first setting foot on White Lion territory, which should be a place of peace and protection. I hope that every time we remove another of these killing cages and dismantle it, we shift some of the negative energy still lurking in various parts of this land.

We approach the run-down old farmhouse, where we now live along with a number of volunteers. We call it Base Camp. Entering through the farmhouse gate, still hanging loose and rusty on its hinges, I make a mental note that we need to remove and replace the shabby gate sometime, but there are much more urgent priorities. As we enter our makeshift headquarters, I see several cages piled up alongside other junk that our team has extracted from the wilderness—rolls of barbed wire, old tires, off-cuts of corrugated iron, snares. Jason plans to dismantle all these cages and utilize the metal grills to seal up river outlets, those exit points that are most tempting to big cats infinitely capable of digging their way out of reserves. I shudder as Tawny passes these macabre mechanisms. It brings back vivid memories of my first and only meeting with the previous owner. He took the opportunity to boast that he'd single-handedly killed sixteen lions during his occupancy of this land—a half century—and he added that he'd be pleased to hunt down my White Lions, if I gave him the chance. If he were still capable of executing his threat, I might have been worried, but he'd become quite decrepit with age, and his wife confessed to me—just between us ladies—that her husband was "leaking out of several orifices." I remember standing there, wordless. With my colorful imagination, I couldn't help picturing the hunter himself riddled with symbolic bullets, as a kind of poetic justice for all the lions he'd shot. The old boy told me he intended to use a bunch of the money from the sale of the property to live out his life's dream of going to Zambia to hunt the "Big Five." But fate didn't allow him the luxury, as it turned out, and he died shortly after the funds for the lions' land were transferred into his account.

Jason has parked Tawny, and as we walk toward the farmhouse, two dogs come careering out to greet us—Sam and Cibi, their hot breath visible in the chill morning air. Sam, my loyal and dearly beloved dog of many years, is an Alsatian with a stumpy tail, originally from the SPCA, and Cibi, which means "dog" in Sotho, is a little female we found attached to a two-meter chain when we arrived on the land. As a conservation project in the wild bushveld, we had no intention of keeping domestic animals, but I couldn't leave Sam behind, and there was no way that Jason and I were going to turn our backs on this excitable little creature—a Doberman cross, tugging at her chained wire collar. So unshackling Cibi was what Jason jokingly describes as our first scientific release program. After warm greetings all round, Sam and Cibi, tails wagging, follow us down the dry gravel path to the farmhouse.

I get the impression that the old hunter built his house with his own two hands and minimal resources, except for an exceptionally hard-working staff, piecing together a patchwork of corrugated iron and bricks and mortar over the years. We discover that it leaks like a sieve during the rainy season and roasts in the summer heat. And we've just starting to suspect that it freezes in winter. Yet this hodgepodge of different structural components is all we have for the moment.

It's our operational nerve center: our living quarters, guest quarters, offices, scientific research center, and headquarters all in one. The phone lines are regularly down after stormy or windy weather, which makes communications with the outside world very challenging. And electricity is intermittent, so we often shower with cold water.

Today, we're going to need a cold shower. We're preparing for an occasion where hot-headed tempers could boil over.

JUNE 10, 2005. MIDDAY HEAT. Three months after arrival. Jos Macs is a bush pub with a deck overlooking the Tsau River, and also our local meeting point. We've chosen this setting in an attempt to ensure that a highly volatile occasion remains as cordial and informal as possible.

We've decided to call a "public participation meeting," open to everyone. In this way, we'll be able to answer any questions and hopefully dispel any misinformation neighbors may be harboring about our project. Over the past couple of weeks, we've posted an open invitation in both local newspapers to "all interested and affected parties." We've also made sure that specific invitations were sent to our most direct neighbors. Mireille took it upon herself to make courtesy calls to many properties in the vicinity, so as to inform them of the White Lion reintroduction taking place nearby. Typically, she'd leave Tsau property, armed with an apple tart and a factual brochure or two on White Lion conservation, which we compiled and printed a couple of weeks ago. Her missionary background proved ideal training for mustering recruits.

Word has gotten out, and quite a lot of people have shown up at Jos Macs, but I wonder how many have come as friends. The crowd has gathered in the billiards room, where heavy benches have been dragged into rows. I feel the tension building. It's another blazing hot day—a bushveld winter day. I was prepared for this occasion, but nevertheless feel a cold sweat breaking out on my forehead.

We are just about to start proceedings when we hear the spray of gravel and dust outside in the parking lot. Pulling up in their 4x4s, a cavalcade of hunters has arrived—ten minutes after the appointed time. All four of them barge in, dressed in safari suits and crunching boots. I see at a glance that these men are PH's (professional hunters): the "safari suit" has been the unwritten uniform in the region since Paul Kruger's day, over a century ago, only now the style is to mix and match safari colors oddly on the same items of clothing. Khaki shorts tend to ride high in the crotch, stretched tight over hairy rugby player's legs, and tempers tend to rise even higher.

We are about to start our introduction again, when a couple more late arrivals join forces with the others, kitted out head to toe in full hunting camo-gear. Who knows which, if any, of these army boots breached our borders and staked out our southern fence line? The late arrivals are so rigged up with camouflage equipment, it is not difficult to imagine their crossbows and rifles lurking, still warm, in the back of their pickups.

I try to breathe evenly. We've made sure we've provided ample fruit punch, without alcohol, for everyone attending. However, a lot of booze was clearly consumed prior to the meeting, and I brace myself at the thought that beer and cider will be freely swigged throughout our introductory presentations. The late arrivals seem to have come straight from The Fort, fortified with lager and *witblits*—white-lightning liquor, 80 percent alcohol.

Putting on a brave front, Xhosa reopens the meeting with his modern version of a "Song of Praise" in the old African tradition. His delivery is flawless, and he finishes with a characteristic flourish and a curt bow. But his prayer to the lions is followed by an intimidating silence.

Mireille is chairperson, striking a diplomatic if slightly schoolmarmish figure behind her table. After Xhosa's praise song, Mireille introduces the panel. It comprises Thembi, our trustee representing the cultural view of the White Lions as sacred animals; Jason, presenting on the scientific aspects; and me, whose task is to introduce the project and its objectives.

Unfortunately, Marianne was unable to attend. Her spitfire personality would have relished the opportunity to represent our position to the gathered macho men, who are mostly, after all, Afrikaners like her. I feel a vast gap without her presence.

In preparatory discussions, it was decided that we absolutely need a fourth member of the panel. As such, we were expecting a female scientist and habitat specialist from the Timbavati region to join us. Over the past few of months, she was commissioned to assist in our project as a paid consultant and had provided in-depth expertise on methodology for restoring damage to the land—knowledge vital to the long-term sustainability of the White Lions' survival in the wild. However, yesterday, the day before the public participation meeting, she suddenly lost her voice. She indicated that the cause was a sudden onset of flu, but we are all the more sympathetic knowing it was actually an attack of fear and tension. Either way, it means she is unable to speak on behalf of the White Lion project.

That leaves just the three of us.

But these members of our panel are not the only lion representatives in this space. Beside the panel's three chairs stands an empty chieftain's chair. Maria told me that in the old African tradition, when a group of traditional elders convene to discuss an issue of consequence to Mother Nature, they ensure that Mother Nature has representation. They place an empty chair in their midst to indicate that Mother Nature and her creatures are present and represented. Since Mother Nature's creatures use language that is not that of humans, they're in effect "silent stakeholders." Every important decision taken on their behalf, therefore, has to consider the position of these silent, unseen representatives. Maria made this clear to me with one powerful phrase, which she often repeated: "Who shall speak for the Lions? Huh, daughter? Who shall speak for the Lions?"

So, before beginning this public debate, I invited Maria and the lion ancestors into this space. It is not difficult for me to feel their tangible presence, even in this packed room of rowdy humans, and that of Ingwavuma, in particular, who is seated on the chieftain's chair beside me.

THE CROWD IS FIRING QUESTIONS without listening to any of the answers. I had anticipated there'd be a clash of cultures and ideology, but I hadn't realized quite how antagonistic things could become. The aggression in the room is palpable. When Thembi or I stand to speak, we are shouted down. Thembi managed a couple of eloquent sentences about the importance of the White Lions as a universal symbol of love and unity, but no one wants to hear it. It's become clear that the safari suits are only prepared to talk to Jason, man to man.

Or, more accurately, fifty men to man. By nature, Jason has a steady, methodical way of talking, considering his words carefully to ensure their accuracy. I watch him now, patiently providing answers, only to find the same drunken question fired back at him from another safari suit in another corner. He responds again, slowly and factually. The tension is building, and the firing squad is so bitter and angry, I feel like ducking on Jason's behalf.

I dart a glance at him, with his clipboard resting in his lap. He's long since stopped making notes because the same questions just keep being fired back: "What you gonna do with the lions?" "Why you messing with nature?" "Why you bringing these freaks into our territory?" "What you gonna do with them?" From his exhausted expression, I can see his reserves are in tatters. He's still in the firing line, but nothing he says made any difference. The lack of logic in the room is starting to scare me. It is dangerously incoherent.

Mireille taps pointlessly on her glass for silence and order.

Feeling Maria Khosa's presence, I ask myself whether I am willing and able to put a cat among the safari suits.

Suddenly everything becomes quiet as I tune into higher logic, above all this noise and aggro energy.

"Famba!" comes Maria's emphatic answer. *"Go!"*

While alive, Maria Khosa once showed me how to break such waves of aggression by following a time-honored procedure of great power. But I'm not sure I'm brave enough to use this technique in this atmosphere of violent men seemingly held together by fragile egos and deep self-loathing.

Prompted by Maria's voice in my head, I glance at the carved wooden chieftain's chair, standing empty beside us. The chieftain's chair has been in this position, unoccupied, throughout the meeting. I would have explained its significance to the gathering at the outset, but the atmosphere clearly wasn't right. Now I can hear Maria Khosa's voice urging me on. On the spur of the moment, I follow Maria's lead and interrupt proceedings. I stand up suddenly.

My heart is pounding so loudly, I can't hear my own voice. After a hush falls around me, I explain to the group what the chieftain's chair signifies. No one is physically sitting on it, but the presence of authority resonates from this seat. Everyone glares at it. It's not difficult to visualize the King of kings, Lion of Judah, sitting there, overseeing this gathering of mortals.

I ask for a moment of silence so that we might give consideration to what The Lions may have to say on this matter—which, after all, concerns these creatures directly.

My appeal is followed by a fiercely indignant silence. It's as if all the gathered men in their multitoned safari suits are taking a shared gasp of oxygen. It's a stunned, rather than comfortable, silence. I feel like cowering, because this unnatural hiatus is building up like a tsunami drawing itself back before the renewed wave of aggression suddenly hits me with full force.

"We haven't come here to be force-fed African voodoo—Jesus Christ! Don't waste our fucking time, bitch!" bellows one voice, reinforced by others. "Who the fuck do you think you are, huh? And what the fuck are you doing with our fucking lions?"

Fortunately, Mireille is experienced enough to call a halt to the proceedings before they became physically violent.

Battered and exhausted, I retreat together with my team to the sanctuary of the White Lions' heartland.

A COUPLE OF HOURS HAVE PASSED since the public participation meeting, and Jason and I sit with the lions as the heavy sun dangles behind the filigree of bushveld savanna. We are outside the pride's enclosure in Jason's Land Rover, a little distance away so as not to disturb them. My primary objective is to try to regain my emotional equilibrium, which has been entirely destabilized by today's public assault. I suspect Jason is as seriously shell-shocked as I am; he's quiet and downcast. To add insult to injury, directly after this afternoon's hostile pounding, a microlight has been flying low over our land, circling and doubling back again and again, staking it out. It was so low that Jason could see the color of the two pilots' helmets, but as yet we've been unable to make out the license number on its wings to identify the culprits and take action against them. Sitting with the lions as the spying machine flew over, we watched, fuming, as Marah and her cubs cowered, then fled for cover under the acacia trees, huddled together out of sight. This intrusion over our airspace added to the general sense of foreboding, which has darkened these past few months. Many mornings I wake up with a start, dreading feedback from Nelson and Nelias and wondering whether the electric fence has been breached again, or whether they have picked up alien footprints branding their imprint on our land, intending to do damage to property, or worse, lions.

These highly endangered innocents urgently call for humanity's protection. Yet the entrenched pro-hunting mindset on our borders holds a different opinion. I often think of Ian's warning, prior to my purchasing land in this region. Despite his caution, I went on to secure the heart of the White Lions' ancestral homelands as a protected area, an isolated bastion, under attack on all sides. Still, I don't regret it. It's a foothold in the White Lion kingdom, infinitely better than having Marah exiled in a dungeon or cooped up in a cage with other animals awaiting the hunter's bullet.

And I know protecting the heart of this kingdom is simply part of my shamanic work as the Keeper of the White Lions, the next step in the process toward creating a better world for Nature and humanity. So, while Jason has been in discussion with his colleagues about setting up an armed response unit stationed on our property, I've been working with alternative methods to secure our boundaries. The shamanic techniques I was shown by Maria Khosa, Credo Mutwa, and a number of other high-level African medicine people have enabled me to establish an invisible forcefield around our perimeter, which barricades against access by dark forces. In fact, the energy shield

I have activated on our borders works with the frequency of love, thereby converting "all guilt into gold," such that no one holding negative intention toward us or the White Lions can gain entry. Only by converting this base intention into love and light would access be made available to them. Above the land itself, a pyramid of pure light has been created, rendering the White Lions invisible from the air, so in my estimation, the invading microlight over our airspace is more of a nuisance than a real threat to these radiant sun creatures.

In the golden glow of sunset, these playful animals lift our morale. Just for fun, the youngsters have made a daisy chain of three parts, holding onto each other's tails. It's simply adorable! Marah's loving bond with her cubs is so strong, they seldom leave her side. They dote on their mother, tugging at her to join their play, attempting to grab onto her tail as it sweeps by. If her children stray too far for too long, Marah summons them back with a soft, guttural grunt, lovingly licking their faces and nudging them on their way again. Then, spectacularly, she springs up the trunk of a tall marula tree, climbing to a height of about seven meters, where she settles comfortably in the branches.

Jason and I watch totally spellbound. No doubt she hoped to grant herself a bit of peace from her overexcitable brood. Regally she stands, high in the tree's branches, staring out over the Timbavati wilderness and the distant Kruger National Park. I can hear her thinking, "One day, all this will be reclaimed and brought together under the White Lions' supreme governance."

Despite the pride's fun and games, it's sobering to remember that Marah and the cubs are still housed in a mere five-acre enclosure. Albeit dense with trees, this area is not much larger than the camp in which they were housed in the Karoo for nearly a year. It was designed simply as an acclimatization area, originally intended to provide temporary housing for a couple of weeks before releasing the lions onto the surrounding bushveld wilderness of Tsau's protected area. But in the current climate, with the legal battle pending and hostile neighbors making claims that we are introducing lions illegally into the region, we can't risk freeing the pride from this confined area.

"Sometimes I can't get over the absurd paradox that Marah's freedom means that I, of all people, have to build fences," I observe, trying to suppress my rising frustration, but I can't stifle the pain that wracks my heart.

"It's the only way to ensure their safety for now," Jason reminds me.

"Yes . . . true . . . but . . ."

What more is there to say?

There's an overwhelming sadness burning in my chest, as I watch these loving creatures make the most of the forced captivity unenlightened humans have imposed on them. The cubs have gathered at the base of the tree, looking up at their mother before darting off to play. Marah is in the tree's highest branches with her eyes closed, fast asleep. What a scene.

Squeezing my hand encouragingly, Jason mutters, "This makes everything, absolutely everything, worthwhile!"

CHAPTER 22

Not Forgotten

July 5, 2005. The public participation meeting is long since behind us, as Jason and I pass through the fortified gates of a property abandoned by the godfather of the canned-hunting industry. Dislodging himself suddenly from the region, he'd left devastation behind him: empty cages and desolate land. It remains incomprehensible to me that a concentration camp like this could exist in this region for decades without neighbors objecting or Nature Conservation authorities shutting it down. Observing their aggression toward our project, I wondered why they were so afraid of the light.

The canned hunter's property is up for auction. Corelight has courageously offered to put in a generous bid, so we are here to represent them. While it would be good to rescue this besieged land and lovingly restore and nurture it, we've heard the canned hunter has placed an astronomical figure as his reserve, so it's unlikely we'll be successful. Nonetheless, I need to return to these lands to remind myself what I'm fighting for. This time, the parking lot is vacant; there are no troop vehicles, and the electrified gates to the crowded cages and coops that held the lions captive over a period of several decades stand half open.

Jason strides ahead of me on the gravel path, so as to fill in the auction's registration forms at a trestle table set up on the concrete patio. While he fills in the details, I force myself to walk over to the house itself. Approaching this grim residence, I recall visiting two years earlier. I can still vividly see the image of that shadowy figure, leering out of his house, itself a fortified cage in the middle of the surrounding lion coops. Looking at the structure more closely, it occurs to me that even the warden of a high-security prison would not live in such barricaded incarceration.

I step across the threshold into the interior of his private world. A grim stuffed elephant head greets my arrival in his home. Glancing from left to right, I'm saddened to see lion trophies on either side of the entrance hall. It grips me as a gruesome parody of Egyptian sacred architecture. In Giza, everywhere one looks is a marvel of magnificent marbled guardian lions in Sphinx poses, serenely protecting every temple gateway. Here, by contrast, living lions are stuffed and positioned in simulated postures of killing each other, mouths grotesquely opened to show their impressive incisors.

It's hard to imagine what his friends and guests must have thought, arriving to this macabre welcome. I vaguely wonder what the other prospective buyers must be thinking. Looking through the grills fixed to the window frames, I catch a glimpse of several safari suits clutched into a gathering outside, each gripping a can of beer. Which one, I wonder, will be the proud new owner of this blood-stained fortress? If Corelight were to be the highest bidder and claim this property, the idea is to turn this stronghold into a monument, so people were reminded of the atrocity that canned hunting represents.

Stepping into the dark interior, I notice that pinned in the middle of the wall ahead is a painting with two elephants fighting to the death. All around me, the windows of the hunter's house are barricaded against the sunlight. Not only are the outside entrances of the house grilled up; every room in the dark interior has its own security grates and bars, barricade after barricade. The entire house is a mausoleum, stuffed with trophies of animals in dreadful grimaces of anger and trauma. The entrance hall, lounge, dining room, each and every bedroom I force my way through is crammed with taxidermies. Even the so-called "living room" is stuffed with dead creatures. Entire cheetah and leopard families of taxidermies are clustered together. Then, with a wave of nausea, I see the stuffed subadult white lioness and the stuffed baby white lion cub—will it ever end?—wherever I look, I feel like choking!—stuffed vervet monkeys and stuffed baboons with snares around their necks and rugby caps, as if a macabre joke. Soon I am gasping for breath, trapped in a morgue.

I hurriedly depart the house. Outside, amidst the safari-suited bargain hunters, I feel hemmed in by the intensely oppressive sense of incarceration all around me, and the feeling of entrapment hits me in the belly like a wallop of nausea. I experience the pathology behind it all, the condition of fear and inner hatred that wreaks havoc on the outside world. Caged human, caging all of life.

Only by healing ourselves can we humans stop wounding the beautiful creatures that surround us. But the dreaded question remains, Will humanity actually reach this point of understanding with our natural environment and fellow man?

Jason is outside too, finishing the forms, and I hasten to join him. I tug at this arm, recommending a walk into the surrounding grounds. I notice the concerned expression on his face and try to straighten myself out. I am desperate to escape and suggest we drive out to view the property.

It's a relief being back in the Land Rover and moving, but I notice that the lands too have been raped and carved up into multiple fenced sections, denuded and overplowed. I tell myself all is not entirely lost, remembering how Mother Nature recovers in response to love. The indigenous trees will grow again over time if allowed to, and the soil has not been entirely stripped of its fecund richness. As usual, Jason is offering some encouraging comment about the land having every potential of being nurtured back to life. It's a soothing thought. We drive around a clump of alien gum trees and there, suddenly, unexpectedly, we are faced by another fenced camp. Somehow, I've let my guard down, so I am caught totally unprepared. This electrified camp is one of the last lion camps remaining on the grounds, separated from the other coupes we'd already seen—and there, ahead of us, are the lions, waiting. Oh god, the lions! I didn't realize that the canned hunter had left five lions behind on his land, two white and three golden, allowing a last opportunity for the new owners to enjoy a bloody trophy hunt. The lions standing in front of us are the last members of the surviving bloodline, from that original proud White Lion male stolen from the wild!

On spotting us, the two White Lions separate from the others and move quickly right up to the fence, facing us squarely. They are making direct eye contact, and it is extremely painful. It is like looking into the eyes of a wrongly convicted death-row prisoner, a desperate prisoner who is moreover one's close relative. Still watching, the subadult female starts retching and retching, her stomach contorted in pain, right in front of me. I can feel my own stomach turn. I know intimately how she's feeling. My whole being feels sickened.

Then the male starts digging at the fence line, as if making an urgent bid to escape. The tears are burning down my face, but I simply shake my head at him. Escape is pointless—he'd just be tracked down and shot, or returned and flung back into death row. The helplessness I feel is excruciating—there is nothing, absolutely nothing, I can do to relieve his desperation. With Marah's own life and future at risk, how can I plan any further action or rescue attempts? As if hearing my thoughts, the young male suddenly stops digging. He looks at me with a pitiful expression, but with supreme dignity. I see that he and the young female are badly damaged, not only psychologically, but also, I fear, physically or even genetically. But his soul and true spirit are unbroken. He knows exactly what is at stake. Looking straight into my eyes, he communicates courage and perseverance, as if he knows that behind the madness there is a plan. It is not the White Lions who need to escape their shackles; rather, these great beings are waiting for humans to free themselves. I tell this beautiful creature, and the young female in pain beside him, and the three golden lions who have remained huddled together in the background, watching: "You are not forgotten; you are not forgotten!"

I am weeping copiously, sobbing my heart out. I beg Jason to take me home, as fast as possible. Jason has submitted Corelight's bid, so I can't see any point in lingering for the auction itself. My helplessness makes me burn with anger and frustration. I simply can't see a solution. I need to get back to Marah and our lion family, as fast as possible, to try to settle my distress.

I'M BACK ON THE WHITE LION HEARTLAND, sitting in the Land Rover with Jason. He is trying to comfort me with words I can't even hear. Marah and her cubs lie close to the dense thicket at the center of their *boma*. I am heartbroken, totally shaken, as if nothing in the world will alleviate the pain. But seeing the family shining with contentment and serenity encourages me to wipe away my tears. I am snivelling without a tissue and Jason has taken off his T-shirt, chivalrously presenting it to me to dry my face. I feel the first inklings of humor and love returning. Queen Marah has her back turned to me. Her daughter, little princess Zihra, is lying snuggled up with her brothers. Zihra's paw is flung over one of her brothers affectionately, while all three contentedly doze. Their luminous white coats glow in the afternoon sunlight. I try to suppress my miserable snuffling as their beauty begins to instill a calm back into my soul.

But suddenly, as if she's heard something, Zihra springs up on all fours. She looks anxious rather than alarmed and comes padding over toward me, as if to gain clarity on something that's bothering her, something that I've said, or shown her. She looks up, right into our vehicle, and intently makes eye contact with both Jason and me.

Her gaze is totally direct, as if reading our minds. Then suddenly she begins retching and retching right in front us. Her stomach contracts again and again, as if in agony. We are both dismayed. Neither Jason nor I have seen this behavior before, in the many months of observing them. Jason's immediate reaction is concern for her health. He's ready to speed back to base camp, to call in our veterinarian. But, watching closely, he changes his mind. He's thinking what I'm thinking. This is no coincidence. This behavior completely replicates that of the young female in the dreaded canned-hunting camp a couple of hours earlier. I'm stunned, wondering what it could mean. After a few bouts of repeated vomiting, Zihra quickly recovers. She gives us a lingering look with intense sapphire-blue eyes, then relaxes and turns tail to join her brothers. She shows no signs whatsoever of prolonged discomfort. I scrutinize the other lions. They are all sitting up, watching her. Most especially, I take my cue from Marah's regal expression. She transmits a serene knowing, the corners of her mouth curled up into a hint of a smile. Zihra flops back down next to her brothers and characteristically flings her paw over one of them, again. As if to say, "Okay, job done. Back to cuddle land."

I can see the loving care etched in Jason's face and I feel his relief that Zihra recovered so quickly. He's holding both my hands to his lips, kissing them gently, sighing with relief.

I breathe deeply too. From my training with Maria Khosa, I can only conclude that Zihra's unusual behavior is a form of "distant healing," specifically aimed at assisting the ailing lions in the canned hunter's stronghold. The most powerful shamanic healers, like Maria Khosa herself, are able to alleviate pain as well as heal wounds, long distance.

Time and space are no constraint for them. I realize this painful episode was yet another lesson in White Lion magic. For me, it confirms Maria Khosa's view that White Lions—like all great avatars, including Christ—are supreme healers, working miracles, performing

CHAPTER 23

Waiting Game

July 10, 2005. The sun is rising, silhouetting and gilt-edging the dry bushveld. A fish eagle calls high above us, circling. And the pride lies contentedly in a heap. Since our venture into enemy territories two weeks back, we've managed to raise the funds for a second-hand Land Rover. For the purposes of our project, it has been custom-altered: closed in at the back, which is ideal for all-night observation, with bunk seats that easily convert into a double bed. Awake after one of many wonderful nights out with the lions, Jason and I need to get on with the practicalities of the day. We reluctantly head back to base.

The kitchen door stands open, and Cibi and Sam come careering out as usual to greet us. A little disheveled from our night out with the lions, Jason and I enter the farmhouse kitchen. Everything begins really early in the bushveld, and our team rises with the sun. The only missing team member is Mireille, who had to depart just before the auction two weeks prior in order to attend to her affairs back home. She left a huge space, and everyone's hoping she'll return soon to add vibrancy and good cheer to our gatherings.

Sitting around the table are Jason's colleagues, hunched over steaming mugs of coffee, rubbing their hands together from the cold.

"Join you in ten minutes for the meeting," I say as I head out of the kitchen to the shower room.

In the icy shower water, I have little encouragement to linger. So, pulling on woolies and a fleece over my khaki clothes, I return to the breakfast table, where Jason is preparing the practical steps for the day. He's poured me a hot mug of coffee too. I clasp both hands around it for warmth.

The dogs settle on their mattresses on the kitchen floor. Since leopards still roam the area nocturnally, Jason and I decide it is safest to keep both dogs inside at night. Glancing affectionately at Cibi, I remember how poignant it was to learn that during the period when she was chained, she broke free several times after sensing a prowling leopard in the vicinity—and managed to escape the predator, even dragging a chain around her neck! Her tenacity is an inspiration to us all.

"What a survivor!" Jason praises her with a big hug.

He's the only person I know who treats dogs as if he's one of their pack. He buckles down to their level, kissing and cuddling Cibi and Sam in turn, and rubbing noses.

He finally stands up again and, walking over to the table and taking his files out of his rucksack, prepares to plan the day with his colleagues.

"Okay," he says, decisively. "First priority's to sort out the radio communications network. For some reason, it isn't operating today."

Despite his easygoing temperament, I can see the strain starting to show on Jason's face. It is also a reflection of my own inner tensions, which I've been trying so hard to keep in check. Month after month has dragged by since moving onto the lands. My days have been fraught with worry and strategy, and many nights are sleepless. I miss Mireille's warm presence, even though she makes sure to call for an update nearly every night. There's always plenty of feedback for her—the burning of firebreaks, clearing of alien plants, patching of erosion sites. What I'm struggling to keep secret from her are the thatched rondavels Nelson and Nelias are lovingly constructing for her return—beautiful rounded huts built through traditional Tsonga techniques, with traditional African screeded floors. They spend a couple hours each day building, between their early morning and afternoon security sessions. Meanwhile, the rest of us focus on getting everything possible in place for the lions' release from the *boma,* so we are ready and prepared as soon as the moment arises.

A lot has been achieved, but in some respects, there's been no progress at all. We are all playing a waiting game. Sometimes, the only way I can deal with the seriousness of the situation is to see it as a game—a chessboard of opposing pieces, played out one dangerous move after another. Strategically, we have to close ranks and hold a defensive position, ensuring all our key pieces are in place to protect our Queen. Over these past months, our lawyers have persistently continued sending letters to the authorities, respectfully requesting issuance of our outstanding permit. At the same time, the most litigious of our opponents has stepped up their demands on the authorities—threatening to take the department to court if these authorities don't shut down our project. All the while, the final permit remained unissued.

Meanwhile, over time, Jason has gathered a scientific team around him in support of White Lion conservation, specialists in their field who give their time freely and voluntarily. Their support is deeply gratifying and helps us focus on priorities. Thomas, an ecology student from Canada, has joined Jason's team as his scientific assistant. He's a tall, lean, good-looking youth with heavy eyebrows and a scarf flung around his neck against the morning chill. He's also an excellent scientist, but from my perspective, Thomas's cynical, rational mind sometimes gets in the way of his higher logic. I notice that Xhosa is not with our team this morning. He's probably already at his computer, checking through emails. I myself am hesitating about going to my office, bracing myself in case there's some menacing fax lurking in the machine.

"So what new missile d'you reckon's gonna be hurled at us today?" Thomas inquires, with an arched eyebrow but no emotion.

"More of the same," Jason responds, with a gentle smile. "We'll just continue to get on with the job."

"Well, at least we can't complain it's boring," Thomas retorts. "Being under constant enemy fire."

Over the last months, legal missives have been rapidly exchanged, like cross fire from the trenches. I feel out of my depth in this tortuous legal arena. Despite legal letter upon letter, the painstaking process of permit issuance, which was so debilitatingly slow over the lead-up to Marah's relocation, is at a total standstill countrywide. So, despite the tenuousness of our situation, which risks officialdom arriving at our gate at any moment with a court order to remove our lions from our land, I have absolutely no shadow of doubt in my mind that I made the right decision to stick to my guns and bring our pride home. Failure of heart would have denied Marah her freedom, forever. While I know this for sure, it hasn't been easy.

We are holding firm, but we have no way of knowing from where and how the next attack will be launched. Or what new ploy might emerge to stall or even shut down our program. We've regularly made efforts to follow up with the government department, but our White Lion file keeps getting mysteriously "lost" in the works. In fact, we've had to submit and resubmit our case several times over—a box file, hundreds of pages thick. It's been particularly unsettling to discover that information from our several files lodged with the department "somehow" found its way into the hands of opponents. The hunting fraternity has since used this material as leverage against us in subsequent letters of demand. They've also handed it over to their local poison-pen journalist.

Unfortunately, the front-page headlines six months ago had been one of many such nasty stories over the intervening period. Not surprisingly, it turns out the journalist in question is, in fact, the mouthpiece for some particularly vicious and frustrated pro-hunting entities who have made further published inroads in attempting discredit us on home territory.

While every day has seen a new drama in our neighborhood, there's still no resolution from the authorities. Without a permit, all they need do to render us "noncompliant" or "illegal" is to do nothing. The only grounds the authorities offer our lawyers for delaying our permit is that some of our neighbors have lodged complaints that our land isn't large enough for free-roaming lions.

"Interesting argument," I muse out loud to Thomas. "Particularly since not one of these neighbors have ever lodged a complaint about the canned-hunting operations keeping lions in small cages-for-killing on their borders."

"We're applying for sanctuary status, right?" Thomas asks.

"Yes. Fifteen hundred acres doesn't represent the full extent of White Lions' original kingdom. True," I continue, "but it's a safe haven. And it's the heart!"

Routine daily events provide some comfort from the unmitigated stress, and it's heartening to watch Jason take his work file out now for his colleagues and proceed to list the actions for the day in order of priority.

"What's the status on the thorn-tree barricade?" Jason asks.

"Complete—as of yesterday," responds Thomas ultra-efficiently.

"That's a relief. Worth all the effort and torn uniforms?"

Jason's referring to a massive undertaking, which involved setting up a bush squad of field workers—mostly volunteers, together with some paid contractors from the local Tsonga community—who spent the past couple of months dragging hewn thorn trees and stacking them against each other to form a long barrier.

The barricade was lined up inside the fence itself—about ten meters in—and was part of a carefully laid strategy for protecting the lions. This monumental job is finally complete.

I open my briefcase and double-check the names on the paychecks one more time—Nelias Ntete, Nelson Mathebula, and eight other names from the Tsonga and Sotho people: the bush squad, who will be returning from the field at the end of the day. It's been challenging working on a shoestring, but this month there's just enough income to pay our contractors well. And it was the same the last month, and the month before. There's nothing left over to pay Jason, and he doesn't expect payment, but that can't go on forever.

I look up at him appreciatively. Together with his team, he's scrutinizing the map of the property, rolled out on the kitchen table.

"Once the lions are roaming freely," Jason explains, "the primary risk areas are here on the west and here on the northern frontier, where our electrified fence borders a dust road. These perimeter fences pose a serious danger zone, because they can be easily accessed by humans. But the thorn-tree barricade should act as a protective screen."

"Hope it keeps Marah and cubs away from dangers at their external boundary," I add. "And out of sight from any humans accessing the boundary road."

"Can't pussyfoot around when it comes to saving lions," comes a smart comment from Thomas.

"Too true, Tommy," Jason concurs. "So, in terms of prepping the environment for Marah's release, we're more than ready. Our only headache is waiting for the permit. Big headache. For our reintroduction program to be successful, timing's absolutely essential."

The threat of possibly losing Marah and cubs, combined with the endless incapacitating delays in securing the final permit for her release, has worn me down. In all these agonizing months of waiting, there's been no tangible shift, only legal pressures intensifying, and the department's tone toward us hardening, as coercion from our pro-hunting neighbors amps up. We've managed not to lose ground in the face of threats from adversaries and intimidating letters, but without the go-ahead from the authorities, it's difficult to gauge how we might drive the process forward.

Having the backing of a legal firm with such a formidable reputation provides some relief: their name alone on a litigious letterhead has kept the onslaught at bay. But I've come to the conclusion there's much the lawyers don't understand about the nature of the White Lion project. Bottom line is: we don't have the luxury of time.

All the while, Queen Marah waits.

There's a twang of electric wires and a sudden scuffle.

"At least the dogs can practice their hunting techniques!" I observe.

Outside the kitchen window, Sam and Cibi have charged after a family of warthogs, the local version of the European wild boar, which have wandered out of the winter landscape into the farmyard in search of greener pastures. The hogs scatter, dogs after them. I've trained both Sam and Cibi not to chase animals in the surrounding bushveld wilderness, but in their home territory—Base Camp and its surrounds—they have free rein. Chasing warthogs, however, can be risky, as these fierce little pigs have been known to unseam or disembowel dogs with their vicious tusks. Fortunately, the hounds come trotting back, grinning with victory.

The constant daily list of vital improvements and preparations for the lions' free roaming on these lands is never-ending: the security measures, fence maintenance, erosion control, and many other aspects of habitat management. But in the absence of resolution from the authorities, there's nothing more we could do for the lions' urgent release except wait. We've looked at the challenge from all angles. Without a way forward, the uncertainty is becoming intolerable. Personally, I'd be prepared to put up with the department's indecision, if it weren't that these delays could have a hugely negative impact on Marah's future survival in the wild.

The team is wrapping up their plans for the day when Xhosa steps out of our office and gestures to me. Something's not right—he looks like a bear with a sore head today.

"Be with you as soon as I can, X," I respond.

He doesn't look happy, but there are other urgencies that must take priority—most immediately, paying the staff.

At the end of another month, it's pay day again. Nelson and Nelias have been waiting outside for some time, dressed to the nines in preparation to head home. If I don't pay them now, they'll miss their bus home, which travels on this remote route only once a day.

I call them in to join Jason and me for a quick cup of coffee. Nelias is in his neatly pressed Sunday best, standing hat in hand. Nelson is all smiles and brawn, muscles rippling through his T-shirt and crisp denims. These two dedicated men are the backbone of this project; it would be impossible to implement the next steps without them.

From the beginning, directly after taking them on, Jason and I decided to double their former pay. I wished I was in a position to pay more—both men are worth their weight in gold. Nelson proved his loyalty, courage, and total dedication in the years he worked for my family; and Nelias, to my mind, is an invaluable asset. How do you put a value on this elder's support? He's one with this ancestral land, its wildlife, and its very lifeblood. Over the past few months, I'd come to regard this simple laborer as one of the most dignified and intelligent men I'd ever met. Without his tracking skills, our project would be at much greater risk. Even Jason, who's worked with many skilled indigenous trackers from different tribes, including the Bushmen in the Kalahari Desert and the Zulu from Natal, confirmed that Nelias's tracking abilities were exceptional. His understanding of Nature and her ways are unsurpassed, and I've seen him read her signs like a book. Yet Nelias is illiterate and can't spell his own name.

We discovered this at the end of our first month here, when we were issuing him his first paycheck. He couldn't sign his name, but he confirmed that an inscribed name on the envelope, in the handwriting of the previous owner, was his name.

The previous owner, the hunter-farmer's wife, had told me his name was Alice, and she and her husband had called him by that name for a half century. After I queried this as an odd name, she insisted, and wrote his name down on the envelope for me. She didn't know his surname, but not knowing the staff's surname isn't so unusual in the old South Africa, with its Apartheid mindset.

Turned out he had been called by the wrong name for most of his life, but, poignantly, Nelias's dignity was such that he was prepared for Jason, me, and our team to continue to call him by this ridiculous misnomer until we saw from his ID papers that his real full name was actually Nelias Ntete!

I observe Nelias for a moment, standing upright and proud, beanpole thin, enjoying the light banter and the strong coffee into which he is dunking his buttermilk rusk. In African culture, calling someone by a woman's name would add insult to injury. Yet I marvel how Nelias embodies natural strength and quiet dignity and how even this unimaginable insult has not affected his true identity.

I hand over the two paychecks, which Jason has reviewed for me. Nelson will keep his safe under his mattress to share with his girlfriend who is coming to visit that weekend, and Nelias will hide his in his shoe so that no *tsotsi* (thief) could steal it from him in the minibus taxi on his way back to the community township where his family lives. For the next month, we've committed to take Nelias into town to assist him in opening a bank account for the first time in his life.

Jason cracked a joke in Zulu—something about tracking Nelias all the way home to Swaziland if he leaves the country with all that money in his shoe—and the three men simultaneously break out into peals of laughter.

Nelson finishes his coffee and washes his mug, leaving with a wave and a broad smile. Nelias does the same, stepping out into the broad daylight with Jason, who's offered to give him a lift to Hoedspruit, an hour away, where he'll catch his taxi back to his family.

Xhosa emerges from our office room again. I have the same nagging feeling something is seriously wrong, and now I determine to act on it. Entering, I sum up Xhosa's mood in one glance: dead serious. At first I imagine he must have checked the fax machine before me, but there's no fax in his hand. Then I see the registered letter. Grim-faced, he hands it over, explaining that last thing yesterday afternoon, while Jason and I were out monitoring the lions, a registered parcel suddenly arrived, hand-delivered by a conservation official at our gate.

"Did the official come onto the property?" I demand, my heart plummeting like never before.

"No—handed it to me through the gate, and I signed for it."

"Oh, Heavens, X! They didn't physically deliver the summons onto the property, as we've been warned?"

"That'd have been over my dead body!"

"Hopefully that won't be necessary," I retort sarcastically, desperate and angry at the thought that thirteen precious hours have passed. "Why didn't you alert me before?"

"Tried, but couldn't reach you on the radio network—lines were down! I haven't told anyone—my rationale was that you should be the first to know. I didn't want people panicking, but I've spent a sleepless night, worrying—"

"Okay, okay!" I interrupt. "Give me that."

Snatching the sealed document from him, I see at a glance that the envelope, with its official crests, and stamps, and signatures, is marked "Final Warning." I have to hang onto the nearest chair for support. Like a death sentence, the thought that this official letter might be the dreaded summons announcing the confiscation of the lions splits my head in two.

I open it. As it turns out, this “Final Warning” demands that our lions be removed back to the province they come from, failing which, action will be taken against us. It’s one step away from the summons I’ve been dreading—the drastic measure from the department that tore Greg Michell’s lions from his safe haven and dumped them back into the killing industry. I know only too well that he never got them back to safety, despite taking the matter to the highest courts in the land. Xhosa stands beside me in silent consternation, chewing his nails through his cut-off woolen gloves. Seated, without gloves, I’m doing the same, my mind in turmoil. Finally, once I’ve reconstituted my thoughts, I come to a firm resolution.

“Sure, X. It’s sinister. The hunters are pressuring the department for results.”

“Upping their aggro,” Xhosa concedes, his shoulders slumped, defeated.

“On the positive front,” I observe, “at least now we’ve something concrete to work on.”

CHAPTER 24

Unsettling Questions

THERE'S A CRACKING SOUND AND A HUGE FLASH in the dark. Then the smell of charred human flesh. A voice is wailing and I recognize it as my own. Everyone on our team has had to accept the occasional unpleasant jolt while tending to the electric fences, so this is nothing unusual. But tonight, when I opened the electrified gates, my silver bracelet caught on the electric wire, which amplified and protracted the effect. The smell of burned flesh comes from the last two fingers on my left hand. I couldn't jerk free on reflex. Examining my fingers in the light of the Land Rover's cabin, I discover that the burns are not so bad after all. With some ointment, they'll probably recover in a couple of days. Jason, behind the wheel, gives me a comforting hug of sympathy.

July 30, 2005. It's a crisp winter's night in the bushveld. Almost three weeks after that last threatening letter from the department. Jason and I are out on a late-night check again, between 11:00 p.m. and midnight. Jason has established a roster, whereby a member of our team tests the fences every night at around this time, as well as dawn and dusk, to ensure there is no breach of our borders. It's a grueling schedule. Tonight, and every night since my arrival in Timbavati, my most pressing objective is to get relief from the human tensions and to connect with the lions.

The past few weeks, in fact the past few years, have been a continual emotional rollercoaster. Just when I feel optimism returning, something else goes wrong and my morale takes another dive. The obstacles stacked up against Marah's freedom, one after the other, have been so relentless.

On the positive front, our legal team has been effective in countering the department's final warning and, thereby, staved off the executioner. The last ten days have passed without further reprisal from the authorities. However, we remain entirely in the dark as to whether the department will authenticate our project by issuing the outstanding permit, or shut us down. We are still bound in a tug-of-war. On our side, we don't tug; we simply hold fast, our heels dug in deep so as not to shift our position. But sometimes there seems such a tearing frenzy of aggression on the other side of the rope that it's taken all our reserves just to keep holding on. All told, we haven't given an inch, but nor have we gained ground.

My only respite is to get out into the unspoiled wilderness and try to forget the darker side of human nature. Entering the realm of these luminous lions helps me maintain an inner calm and equilibrium. Everything stands still and human commotion dissipates. At night, Jason and I are in lion-time.

Having passed through one set of electric gates on the western property, we cross the Guernsey dust road and unlock the second set of electric gates on the eastern property. Each time we cross this road from west to east and east to west, I know we create an energetic link between the divided lands—like an artery between the two chambers of the heart—knowing that one day this heartland will be united as one. And each time we do so, it reminds me of my studies of Ancient Egypt and the attempts by the pharaohs to unite the divided lands.

Jason jumps out of the driver's seat to open the gate on the other side, wearing a miner's headlamp so he can see in the dark. For safety reasons, the gates Jason has erected run along a metal rail, rather than swinging open into the land. In fact, the safety design Jason engineered for our project means we enter into a cagelike space before opening the second security gate into the bushveld wilderness. He's momentarily in the cage, having opened the external gate, and is sliding the internal gate open, grinding along its metal rail. On the other side, Jason drags the internal gate closed along its rail and locks the padlock. With Jason back in the driver's seat, we are in the primary reintroduction area and steadily traversing the property in the direction of the lions' *boma.*

Reaching the *boma,* I'm still licking my fingers in pain, but once I'm in the lions' presence, I know I'll soon forget my woes. Jason settles the monitoring Land Rover close to the southern fence of their *boma,* and we soak in the lions' presence like starlight. It's magnificent under the frozen night sky, with Scorpio stretched out above us in a shimmering sequence of dots.

Suddenly, he indicates for me to keep perfectly still. A gray duiker, a tiny antelope with dainty pointed horns, has ventured too close to the pride's enclosure. The unwitting little creature is drawing intense curiosity from the cats. The duiker, looking up with a shock, suddenly stares four predators in the face and darts off in alarm.

"Hmmm, would've liked to see more instinctive predatory behavior from Marah," observes Jason.

"And the cubs are still so innocent, all wide eyed and curious."

"True," Jason allows a note of concern to creep into his voice. Then adds, facing into the impenetrable moonlit darkness of the bushveld, "Really hope they're gonna make it on their own. It's challenging out there."

"You're concerned they might not survive in the wild?" It's my greatest fear too.

"They should crack it," he ponders, "if humans don't prevent them from ever getting started."

Concerns about Marah's survival in the wild have been a long-standing topic of intensive discussion between us, but tonight the subject takes on a new urgency.

"Without any training period for her to practice her hunting skills," Jason spells out the problem, "she's missed her prime learning opportunity."

We've been through the issues ad infinitum—the urgency, the risks, the intolerable delays. I am worried about Marah, but knowing her true identity and her prophesized destiny in reclaiming her natural kingdom, I keep praying that our gracious Queen will succeed against all the odds. Yet it's hard to remain optimistic when there's no end in sight.

I catch a glimpse of their glowing bodies, luminous in the moonlight. I can pick out the boys by their scruffy manes, backlit in a lunar halo. They all look restless and hungry now, but tomorrow they'll be happily feeding. Until Marah is released and can hunt for herself, Jason continues to provide for her and her cubs. After discussing it carefully, we decided it would be an unacceptable cruelty to artificially place a live animal, like that little duiker who scampered away a moment ago, in the relatively small confined area of the *boma,* together with four hungry lions. Instead, Jason gives the family carcasses of a variety of different prey they might expect to encounter naturally in their land. The carcasses are given whole, together with their innards and stomach contents, to ensure the lions are getting their proper nutrition.

To minimize association between humans and feeding, Jason's standard scientific protocol dictates that the carcass be dropped into the lions' enclosure from behind a screen, without humans being visible. And to prepare them for the contrasting times of plenty and scarcity in the wild, he varies these feeds, sometimes waiting as long as ten days before providing their next meal. Tomorrow, he'll treat them with the carcass of an adult wildebeest that we've purchased and transported from a game area some distance away, the species that Jason determined in his master's study to be most favored by lions in this bushveld region.

We've observed that Marah is strangely altruistic when it comes to feeding, unlike most lionesses Jason studied in the wild. She tends to stand over her cubs, watching attentively to make sure they've eaten their fill before she herself tucks in. This is very unusual. Although it's touching to watch her selflessness, this unusual behavior adds to Jason's concern that she might never develop that killer instinct essential for a predator's survival in the wild.

Because the cubs were raised by their mother, and not by interfering humans, their instincts appear naturally sharper than Marah's own, particularly her feisty little daughter, Zihra. We've watched many chasing escapades in an effort to claim the same piece of meat—which is natural. But last time they ate, a little squabble developed between the two brothers over the last remaining piece. At this age, the boys are quite a lot larger than their sister, and they made sure they let off a low insistent growling to warn her off their food, rising to an impressive crescendo. But, undaunted, Zihra suddenly swooped in and seized the last piece right out from under her brothers' noses! I reassure myself that these survival traits will stand them in good stead once they are released. If they are released.

Suppressing my frustrations, I adopt lighthearted conversation.

"Jase, let's presume we open those gates right now?" I prompt him. "Just hypothesis, right? Who'd you think would be first out?"

"Hmm. Could be Letaba," he responds, thoughtfully. "He's dominant. Could make the first move."

"Good bet," I concur.

Letaba always showed himself fearless of mud or blood on his face. I remember him as a little fluff-ball in the concrete dungeons of the zoo. Even then, he "fiercely" threw himself against the bars to protect his mother. So I wonder whether Letaba, lion-heart, will venture first out of those gates. Or will it be his mother, Queen Marah, who's waited so graciously through seemingly endless trials to recover her heritage and reinstate her monarchy?

"Or Zihra?" Jason muses.

Both Jason and I glance through the Land Rover's window toward Zihra, Marah's beautiful daughter, who takes after her mother in looks but not in caution. She is an emerging leader in every sense, graced with an incorrigible curiosity, continually outwitting her floppy-pawed brothers with feminine stealth and strategy.

"I'd put my money on Zihra," comments Jason. "But no bets on Regeus taking the lead, I'm afraid."

Regeus is the handsome "mama's boy," King in waiting. He's incredibly good-looking, and we all love him dearly. But, true to form, he always adopts the regal attitude of presuming the rest of the pride owes him a living, while he need not bother to lift his velvet paw. So we doubt he'd risk putting that paw out first.

Enlivened by this discussion, if only in theory, I gaze into our lions' camp and suddenly notice that Marah has been watching us intently from a distance. She is so closely engaging with us, it feels she's somehow overheard our conversation. She's serene and glorious in the moonlight, physically glowing like a beacon, so it's no wonder the White Lions are known as "Spirit Lions" *(Ngonyama Moya)* by indigenous peoples.

"D'you notice the white highlights under her eyes?" Jason points out. "To reflect the moonlight. Great aid to nocturnal hunting . . . one day soon."

"Hmmmm, one day soon," I respond.

Many critics of my project—particularly those holding White Lions in captivity, and now even some well-known scientists—proclaim these "freaks" would never survive in the wild because they lack camouflage. This argument continues to rile me deeply because the fact is that they did survive and flourish in this region until humans removed them for purposes of gross material gain. What's more, in the silvery winter landscape, their white coats are fitting and not at all out of place, and if they choose to lie down out of sight behind the dry grasses, and upwind, no unsuspecting prey animal would guess their whereabouts.

Jason's instinctive and innate knowledge of lions means I can easily share with him some of the shamanic techniques Maria Khosa once entrusted to me. Despite his scientific training, I've observed that these more intuitive interspecies techniques come naturally to him, since his instincts are already primed over the years by his closeness to the lions themselves. Then again, I respect his scientific precision, which helps me sharpen my own observation. There are behavioral aspects of our lion pride that I might never have noticed without his careful observations. A twitch of an ear indicating mood change; the "follow me" signs of dark fur on the back of the ears that act as flags during a strategic hunt; the whisker spots, like fingerprints, an identification entirely unique to each individual cat. Noticing every detail brings me closer and closer to my feline family—a warm, loving feeling that crosses all barriers.

Tomorrow morning, it will be back to the bureaucratic stresses of securing Marah's legal rights to return to her land of origin, and the mounting practicalities of managing this project. But out here under the stars, we've reentered the magical world of the lions, in dreamtime. In the lions' presence under the night sky, we find our spirits reviving and soaring! When we are together with Marah and family, we're invincible. Human issues seem so pitifully small. Our love for the lions, and each other, deepens by the day. This soul bond is eternal, beyond time and space. It knows no limits, nor can the petty minds of men impact it. Love is the greatest force, and the force is with us!

Cosseted in the Land Rover with Jason asleep and my adorable lion family wide awake and playing under the stars, I try to imagine what life would be like without love. What would it feel like to detest oneself and the world so much as to feel unworthy of love? We all have moments of self-doubt and self-loathing, sure. But what would it feel like to hate oneself so acutely that the only way to enjoy beauty is to shoot it and put its head on a wall? We all have dark or "shadow" aspects. We've all made mistakes. But, again, I'm trying to imagine what it would feel like to be so dark that the only way to experience light is to destroy it, plunging oneself into fathomless darkness once again.

I shudder at the thought. In my mind, at this very moment, I return to that caged cell of the canned hunter's house again. What damaged consciousness could construct vile cages to trap sensitive, living, flamelike creatures? And I begin to imagine what it must be like to be that tormented inhuman being, ensnaring himself in his own cages. It must be extremely painful. Surprising as it is to me, for the first time I start to feel compassion rather than anger, fear, and even hatred. This is a totally new feeling. These depraved people, brutally murdering sacred animals and blocking every step I attempt to take in forging the way to their freedom, desperately need nurturing and understanding. My dreaded opponents, brutalized and brutal, are crying out for love. And if they can't earn love, they'll steal it or kill it. Ironically, it is my overwhelming love for the lions that is helping guide me toward compassion for those who are perpetrating such terrible crimes against them. It doesn't excuse anything, but it helps me understand.

Following this unlikely thought process through, I'm also coming to see why there is so much resistance to our project in the neighborhood. After the godfather of the canned-hunting mafia hurriedly relocated himself from the region, I'd mistakenly imagined our opposition was removed. Not so. Instead, the darkness that concentrated around this man seemed to have shattered into a myriad confusing fragments, coming back at us from all angles. Since most of the surrounding game farms remain under the ownership of staunch hunters, it was logical to expect a clash of ideologies from the outset. Yet it has always perplexed me that the return of these rare animals to their rightful lands should have the pro-hunting fraternity up in arms. This was, after all, the lions' original endemic homeland! These majestic creatures were artificially removed from their natural habitat, and therefore have every right to return. So why so much aggression and obstruction to reinstating what is rightfully theirs?

Tonight suddenly, for the first time, I think I understand.

Coming back to the present time and place, I watch the lions radiating outside in the starlight—my pride and joy! Inevitably, the radiant White Lions' shining light exposes shadows that some prefer to keep hidden.

With the lions' return, uncomfortable questions are being raised: Why were the White Lions removed? Who was responsible for removing them? Who secretly benefited from their removal? Why were these rare animals allowed to go extinct? What vested interests were really at stake? Why were they not protected in the past? Most immediately, why are they still not protected?

These are the questions that demand answers at a ground level. At a higher level, I am identifying another overreaching question, one that simply won't go away until it is truly addressed by humanity. If the children of the sun god are indeed enlightenment bearers bringing messages of light and truth to humanity, they pose an ultimate challenge to those resisting change. The question is: Are we humans ready to receive grace and higher learning? Or will we fight to the end in an attempt to hold our egotistical position of control and domination over our Earth and her precious resources, thereby destroying everything, along with ourselves?

CHAPTER 25

Shock Tactics

August 27, 2005. Nine days after I shocked myself on the fence line, and my fingers, which are pressing the viewing slot open to see the lions in their enclosure, have healed. Jason's standard protocol is to drop a carcass over the screen for them to feed on, and I have stood behind the monitoring screen numerous times during these occasions. This method has been working perfectly well. But this time, the impala carcass has mistakenly fallen on the electrified wire, and Marah is approaching to retrieve it for her cubs. She reaches out her paw to place it on the meat. Oh no! The shockwaves pass through the electrified carcass into her body and she recoils in agony, like she did that first time in the Karoo camp, but this time she won't let go! I watch in horror. This food is her prize for her cubs, so she's refusing to take her paw off. I watch her body jolt with pain. Jason and his team leap back into the pickup truck, speeding to the shockbox in order to turn off the current. All I can do is stand helplessly behind the feeding screen, horrified, trying to communicate to Marah to back off.

The pain from the electrical charge must have been too much for her. Thank heavens she finally releases her paw. She's shaking angrily and looking in the direction of the pickup truck speeding around her *boma* fence to the shockbox on the far side. She steps back and clears a patch of grass. I don't know why, but this seems significant.

She's starting to coat the pads of her paws, and perhaps the cool earth acts as a kind of balm. It's thick and almost dry, claylike. It seems she's using it as a fast-drying coating, like gloves—because, having covered her paws, she's returning to the carcass. Where are Jason and the team? I'm trying to assess their progress, praying for them to please, please switch off the shockbox. She puts her paw back on the electrified carcass. Seems the caked mud cuts the current, because she suddenly manages to drag the carcass clear of the electric fence.

Moment later I hear Jason's voice crackling through the radio to confirm that the electrical charge has been disabled. But by this time, Marah has already dragged the carcass, under her four quarters, to her three hungry cubs.

Jason returns shortly, together with the team, and we review the situation. She seems content now. She has stopped that angry flicking of her tail and is feeding together with the cubs in the interior of the *boma* under their favorite clump of trees. Phew! Everyone sighs with relief.

It's day's end, and we decide to head off to the local restaurant in search of our own supper. We all feel thoroughly shocked ourselves—not an experience any of us would like to repeat. We drive off together, all five of us—Xhosa behind the wheel, me beside him, with Jason chatting to his team, all squeezed into the back of the Land Rover.

It is only a twenty-minute drive along a dust road that follows the Tsau River, but the road is so corrugated that every bolt in the Land Rover's chassis and every joint in our bones seems to have rattled loose by the time we arrive.

The nearest and only restaurant is Jos Macs—nowhere else in a hundred-kilometer radius for locals to meet. Located in the middle of the African savanna, it's the only local watering hole, for humans and animals alike. Since the grueling public participation meeting some months back, we've paid many visits to old Jos. It's not a place for the fainthearted, but mostly, the ghosts of that challenging day have been laid to rest.

It occurred to me recently that, in defending the lions' case, we ourselves have been forced to become fugitives. We've been on the land for nearly ten months, yet this very morning, as Jason and I searched through our clothing for clean T-shirts, we realized we haven't even unpacked our suitcases. The lions' premises are immaculate, of course, and despite our financial constraints, we haven't spared any expense in ensuring the maintenance of their camps and fencing, but we ourselves are still camping in one room in the ramshackle old farmhouse.

Our colleagues, who've generously come to assist over the months, sleep on foam mattresses on the floor. I can't help smiling to myself, visualizing the indignities that some of our esteemed advisors have been prepared to put up with in order to willingly offer their services. Despite the meager circumstances, we continue to have many lively gatherings around the kitchen table, which help lighten the tensions.

We walk through the reeded, cavelike interior of Jos Macs—dense with smoke and alcohol fumes and blaring music—onto the wooden deck, perched on long, stilted, wooden poles, which stretches out over the Tsau River. It's beautiful there on the deck, under the vast canopy of ancient jackalberry trees; any variety of wild animal may find its way through the tall reeds of the riverbank below and suddenly reveal itself. The shrill of the cicadas and other nighttime melodies reach us, although their melodious notes are no competition for the raucous blare coming from the humans' quarter inside the pub, where the television is tuned into the sports channel. Gathered at the bar, locals in safari suits hang over the counter, beers in hand, and tipping back shooters (shots of mixed liquors). Under cover outside, the billiards table and dartboard that were cleared for our public meeting are back in action. It's a place for carnivores, with "freshly shot" specialties and no vegetarian dishes available.

The colloquial nickname for the lowveld is slowveld, and that certainly applies to Jos Mac's kitchen. Our group settles around a long, wooden table and, having learned from experience, we place our order immediately. Then we start sharing theories on what occurred earlier with Marah. Based on the afternoon's evidence, the scientists are analyzing whether or not Marah could possibly have an innate understanding of electricity. Jason estimated that the team must have taken five to seven minutes to reach the transformer. By which time, amazingly, Marah had assessed the situation and acted.

"Okay, so tell us again exactly what you saw," says Thomas, running his fingers across his brow quizzically.

"I saw Marah pull the carcass off the electric wire after coating her paws with clay," I recount.

"So, we're saying she deliberately made use of a tool—clay coating—to aid her predatory behavior?" Thomas postulates.

"Perhaps. I'm saying she deliberately cut the electric current, which suggests she may understand how electricity works."

"Some of the charge must have been transmitted through the water particles in the caked mud," Thomas points out, skeptically.

"Sure, but the insulation must've been enough to relieve the pain, and cut the full electrical charge," observes Xhosa, perhaps feeling the need to leap to my defense. "Because Marah went back to the carcass after coating her paws and pulled it away from the wire without hesitation."

"They're sun creatures; of course they understand the nature of energy," I explain. "What happened was amazing, whether you give it scientific credence or not."

Personally, I don't doubt what I saw. It reminds me of how diligently Marah conveyed the warning about the electrical charge to her cubs, by use of telepathy, that first day after waking up in her new *boma* in the Karoo. I describe that event for the team now: how Marah tested the electrical charge first; then communicated telepathically with her cubs to prevent them from getting hurt.

"Certainly was amazing," Jason agrees. "She definitely communicated the danger to her cubs, so they didn't get the shock treatment."

"Do we accept that she somehow got the message across? Telepathy? Maybe," Thomas pontificates. "But that doesn't prove she understands electricity."

I can see Xhosa is about to take up the cause again, and I decide to leave him to it. He is discussing how we humans used to believe we were the only creatures on Earth capable of utilizing language, ritual, and tools; then we discovered that animals did all these things, and more.

I've long since stopped trying to put animals into human constructs and concepts of intelligence. Shamanic techniques had given me a glimpse of the higher abilities of the other creatures on our planet, and it was mind-altering.

Based on Maria Khosa's training, my understanding is that electric shocks are even more offensive to White Lions than they are to humans, precisely because these creatures function at such a high frequency and intelligence. Being a creature of pure light energy must be continually testing in such a dense and base environment. Yet Marah continues to shine her light, unfailingly. Much as I value the stringency of scientific methodology, sometimes I simply let doubting Thomases exhaust themselves in their circular scientific debates, as I drift into my own space. I've spent too much time in the debating societies of Oxford and Cambridge to be diverted by intellectual conundrums any longer. The real world is calling, and I'm tuning into the night sounds, allowing myself to enter the arena known to shamans as dreamtime, where I can meet with the lions on their terms and speak the language of souls.

There have been many unusual incidents over the past few months that led me to appreciate that "survival" in Marah's world functions on a higher level than humans give her credit for. Admittedly, on the everyday level, there is Marah, the lioness, held captive in a *boma* after many years of imprisonment, disadvantaged in all her natural predatory instincts. But on another level, there's an extraordinary creature, a great sun-being of pure light and love, who is able to employ technologies and frequencies way beyond normal human comprehension.

I glance momentarily at our assembled group. Xhosa has his intellectual's thinking cap on and is vigorously engaging in an increasingly heated debate, but I don't believe it is my task to convince anyone. To me, it's clear my work for the White Lions entails two levels of comprehension, which function in parallel. The mundane practical level involving bureaucratic obstacles, legal procedures, and numerous man-made challenges and threats on an ongoing basis. Contrarily, there is the level of magic introduced to me by Maria Khosa and the lions themselves. And in the magical world of the lions, everything is possible!

I feel the force of Nature all around me. Magic's natural and Nature's magical—that's the primary law of the shaman! Maria illustrated this for me in real time. And living with the White Lions themselves, magic is my daily reality. The distant healing I witnessed between the traumatized lions held captive in the canned hunter's stronghold and our own lion family was one example of Nature's miraculous workings. But there have been many others. Over this period of waiting and watching, it is gratifying to realize I can truly communicate with Marah. Telepathy is the transmission of a mental image or word without making a sound. I've always known this. But what I didn't know—until Maria showed me—is that telepathy functions on the love vibration. This is not something I feel necessary to convince anyone else about. It simply is. I originally discovered this ability in my communications with Ingwavuma. But I do believe most of us have experienced this in one way or another. Even the densest doubters. For example, one might think fondly of a loved one who's been away for some time, or who's living on the other side of the globe; then a moment later the phone rings—and that loved one's on the line! Telepathically, they've picked up our positive thoughts, which created an instant connection, and they responded to the mental message. Telepathy's able to cross time and space in an instant, and the frequency on which this silent message travels is that of heart-consciousness. In fact, working with Maria Khosa taught me there's an entire technology of love, which links all of creation in an intricate web of intercommunication. Most importantly, I believe forces of darkness cannot tap into this interconnecting web of love. Only by transforming themselves into love can such forces gain access. And in so doing, they have, after all, transformed themselves!

At first I didn't see the immediate application of this kind of higher wisdom in my daily trials and tribulations. Then I discovered how important such knowledge was to me, especially at times of greatest need. Recently, there's been a concern that our phone lines are, in fact, being tapped. At first our team thought this far-fetched, but then we all agreed there was cause to assume it was true. We started to take it seriously after an associate, who once worked for the Special Forces, instructed us in due diligence. This man pointed out that radical right-wing operators, once equipped in surveillance techniques by the former regime's armed forces, haven't lost their skill in post-Apartheid South Africa.

Not that there was much one could do about it. That's where the other level of operating becomes important. Maria's training showed me that sinister forces are ill-equipped to tap into my telepathic lines of communication with the lions or with people I love, since these negative entities can only break into the codes of love by themselves becoming love. Applying these methods may be a different way of approaching life—but, as always, the golden rules apply.

"So, how does one know one's receiving a telepathic image, rather than simply a thought process?" I hear Thomas address a skeptical question to me, and I drag myself out of my reverie.

"It hits you here—right between the eyes," I respond. "And here, in the heart."

More accurately, in my experience, telepathy reaches us through that invisible entry point known as the third eye and through the heart chakra. To best receive a telepathic transmission, we have to develop and open both these chakras.

"So what verification's there to confirm we've received the message correctly?" Thomas asks.

"Well, firstly, it's important to stop doubting oneself by using words like verification, quantification, proof, and measurement," I explain. "To telepathize, you simply listen internally."

I'm watching Thomas's quizzical eyebrow.

"Seriously, Thomas. Stop your rational mind doubting for a moment—and that in itself'll allow your intuitive mind to receive messages more clearly, without interference."

"How?" he challenges, sounding more dubious than ever.

"Well, best way of testing is to practice it, of course. See how it works. But beware: as long as you limit your mind with restrictive rational thoughts—like you're doing right now—you'll prevent telepathic transmissions coming through."

Based on Maria's teachings, I know the White Lions are the greatest masters and mistresses of telepathy, precisely because they're beings of pure love. And I'd witnessed Marah employ telepathic techniques on many different occasions, not only with her cubs but also directly with Jason or me. Her transmitted mental images were so powerful that she was able to enter my dreams and convey transformative symbolic messages of love and hope at those times when I most desperately needed them. More incredibly, she was able to enter other, unfamiliar people's dreams. Reports of dreams of this kind are shared with me so regularly that I've been gathering a whole dossier of records sent to me by readers and supporters. And I realize part of her purpose is to deliver profound archetypal wisdom to humanity at large.

Jason stands up from the table to buy everyone another round, while we wait for our dinner to arrive. I'm not ready to go into this debate at great depth, since in some ways the activity of endlessly deliberating on the merits of ancient shamanic knowledge demeans the profound lessons learned from Maria Khosa, which have long since proven themselves to me. But I provide our team with some examples to help clarify.

"You know I've been gathering records of White Lion dreams sent to me by various people? Well, it's interesting to record just how powerful these dreams are—so powerful they can change the dreamer's life," I explain. "For me, White Lions entering people's dreams is part of their telepathic powers of communication."

"How so?" interjects Thomas.

"Well, the White Lions can reach humans in dreamtime and deliver a message that these same people might take no notice of during waking hours."

"Maybe these people have simply read your book," concludes Thomas, adding, "So now they're hooked on your idea of the spiritual importance of the White Lions."

"Maybe, Thomas. But, in fact, what's so fascinating is many of these people were previously completely unaware White Lions existed. Then, after their life-changing dream, they made contact with me through the Internet or some other means. Generally, I respond by sending them a photograph of Marah. And that's where it gets interesting. They often write back, saying they recognize this specific lioness as the same unknown majestic presence who visited them! She's usually described as a light-being of sorts, filled with love and compassion."

Thomas looks more skeptical than usual.

"Yes, Thomas. Strange, agreed, but true. Offers us intimations of how vast and significant Marah's mission is, certainly much greater than I can fully comprehend."

Personally, I believe that all animals come to Earth with a greater purpose than we humans give them credit for. Maria Khosa once explained to me that not only the King and Queen of animals can telepathize, but every wild animal species, to a greater or lesser extent. Knowing this helped me understand how even household pets attempt to communicate with us telepathically. To me, it's deeply saddening that we humans tend to be too "busy" or distracted in our man-made worlds to hear their insistent messages.

"Okay, so there've been some scientists, like Pavlov and Sheldrake, working on animal responses," continues Thomas, "but how'd you go about proving their intelligence in the way you're describing now?"

"Personally, I don't need validation," I respond. "If I ever doubted animal intelligence, I just remind myself: they're the ones who learn our human language, while we're unable or unwilling to learn their dog, or cat, or bird language!"

"Yup, that speaks volumes!" quips Xhosa, waxing poetic as usual.

Supper still hasn't arrived. I need air, so, with my juice in hand, I excuse myself and take a stroll from the wooden deck into the surrounding land. Outside, the magnificence of the bushveld wilderness presses in, with every imaginable creature living its existence in an intricate tapestry of magic and wonder. These lands are truly magical. I can feel their primordial power; there's a consciousness in every single object around me, animate and inanimate.

It's not that I feel superior or arrogant about participating in these intense rational debates. Rather, it's that I've observed how the arguments tend to go around in circles while missing the mark entirely. My training has taught me that the key to understanding is to open your heart; it's that loving heart-connection that bridges divides in this world. And intellectualizing simply won't get there.

Fond as I am of Thomas and his interesting and complex character, in some ways he's typical of the scientific mindset that tends to fear matters of the heart and soul. He's afraid of trusting his instincts, following his heart, and believing in his dreams, because, scientifically, he believes he is stepping beyond the boundaries of acceptability. I observe that he tends to be physically quite fragile and sickly, probably a result of this inner conflict. Having spent so much of my life in academic pursuit, I sympathize with the need to rationalize everything, but I also recognize that rational thought is only half the story. I'd share this observation with him—how psychologically unbalanced it is to attempt to justify our entire existence by man-made, scientific constructs alone—but I worry that pointing this out may be so close to the bone, it could leave him deeply wounded.

Since we humans lost our telepathic love bond with Nature—that creative force that gave birth to us and sustains us throughout our living, breathing, functioning lives—we ourselves have been left feeling unloved and meaningless. That's the danger. When a discipline separates itself from its natural source—which science tends to do in order to analyze, dissect, categorize, or label—it inevitably limits its own validity. Of course, there's value in test-tube experimentation, analysis, classification, and categorization, but it's the connection between things, rather than the separateness, that interests me.

I can hear a hippo grunting in the river nearby and the pearl-spotted owl calling in its unique crescendo; then the sports channel is turned up to a deafening pitch, with some raucous cheering blasting from the bar area. The racket takes me back to the gang of pro-hunting neighbors in this same venue eight months ago, kitted up in their khaki safari suits, firing questions at our panel on the frontline. Over the months, we too have somehow developed our own unspoken uniform. It amuses me that I haven't once had cause for a designer outfit since my arrival. Those are long forgotten in boxes in the storage room outside the kitchen door. Every day, without fail,

I've worn shades of khaki—tops, shorts, longjohns, jackets, T-shirts, pullovers, caps—and suede hiking boots. I can barely imagine wearing anything else.

I walk to the bar to order a last round for our group. Propped up next to me on the barstool is a large, glum figure of a man in standard safari-suit gear, and in an advanced stage of inebriation. We haven't met before, so I introduce myself while we wait.

"Sssso you're that arrogant bitch, Linda Tucker?" he retorts, spluttering in disgust.

Of course I'm taken aback, but my first feeling is defiance rather than fear.

"Don't you think you should meet me first, before you decide?" I inquire, with a slight curious smile.

"Ya wanna come pisss in our patch, huh, Lady? Make fucking sure you can aim."

Before I know what's happening, the man suddenly grabs me by the back of my crown and pulls me closer. I don't know whether he's about to kiss me or smash my head into the bar counter. But he's seriously intoxicated. His rapid action throws him off his balance and he teeters over backward, off his barstool, nearly taking me with him. Just before he crashes to the ground, his grip loosens, and I pull myself away in time to see three of his buddies step forward. Next thing, they're carrying him out of the pub.

I'm pretty shaken but more saddened than threatened. There was so much suppressed rage in such an individual that I can only feel concern for his health. What exactly have I triggered? Returning to our group outside, I make a conscious decision not to mention the incident that's just occurred. At all costs, I want to avoid a pub brawl that ends violently. Not that any member of my group—despite appearances in their khaki fatigues—has a tendency to act with testosterone-driven violence.

Outside now, I find that the food's finally arrived. Meanwhile, the discussion has turned to the question of hunting, and I sit down, bracing myself for this old, wounded topic. Having spent so much time watching lions devour their favorite meal, and even witnessed lions make their kills in the wild while on tracking sessions with Jason, I don't have an aversion to occasionally eating meat myself. To me, the key is "conscious eating"—being totally and completely aware of what one is ingesting and accepting this sacrifice from Nature and the life that's been taken, with utmost reverence and gratitude. My objective remains a commitment to serve Mother Nature, just as she served us.

So I take a moment to contemplate my dinner—grilled calamari steak and salad comprising lettuce, baby tomatoes, olives, and feta—and offer a silent prayer of thanks to Nature for all she provides.

But I'm shaken up and I have pretty much lost my appetite. I can still feel the man's viselike grip around my skull and neck, before he toppled back. I actively try to get this image out of my mind, and enjoy the rest of the evening.

The group has its teeth into the big, bad hunting issue, always a raw and emotive topic. But for the moment, the hunting our team is discussing is the predation strategy expected of Marah in order to feed her cubs, once she's released into the wild. I feel everyone's burning frustration. For Marah to hunt successfully and survive in her natural habitat, she has to get out there as soon as possible. After nearly nine months of waiting, the pressure is mounting among our team members. I keep thinking the stress on Marah herself must be enormous. Because she's so highly telepathic, she must be picking up everyone's tensions, worry, and creeping doubt about her ability to command her natural environment. Our entire team's hopes are pinned on her, yet in reality, after her five years of forced captivity from birth onward, everyone is secretly wondering: what hope is there?

In our morning meetings, the group regularly expresses concerns for Marah's survival in the wild. Their worries are valid, of course, but

I believe our group is seriously underestimating her abilities. Thomas and the team are on this same subject again now. Their sense of doubt has grown, so I focus my entire mind on conveying an encouraging warm image of success to Marah, which I trust she will receive on the ether, rather than their negativity.

"You can do it, Queen—I know you can!" I tell her telepathically.

"Why's it we've no problem with the idea of predators hunting, yet humans with rifles and crossbows are so repugnant?" Thomas postulates.

I find myself tuning in to the group again, and realize that Thomas is directing this query at me, on behalf of the others.

"C'd'you repeat that, Thomas?" I ask, getting my thoughts into rational gear again.

"Well, I'm just noticing you're not vegetarian?"

"I do eat meat occasionally."

"No problem with that?"

"I think the key's to recognize where food comes from," I explain, slicing another strip off the calamari steak. "Not the supermarket, but from Nature."

I pause, before continuing. "This may sound obvious, but I think if we were to acknowledge, and show real appreciation and gratitude for, these gifts from Nature—without which we'd all be dead—most of us would stop damaging Nature. It's the key to our sustainability."

"Okay," replies Thomas, carving through his last chunk of sirloin. "So why do we have a problem with hunting? Predators do it all the time in Nature."

"Well," I ponder again, finishing my mouthful. "In Nature, predators hunt, but the laws and rules are totally different from humans—not so? Today's trophy hunter claims the life of an animal for money, or for pleasure. Whereas in the wild, predators hunt for survival. That's the fundamental difference."

I always try to harden my heart as this old, painful issue opens up again. For emotional reasons, I'm utterly opposed to trophy hunting. I simply can't see any reason for blood sport—killing for fun—in our civilized world. On a different tack, Jason opposes trophy hunting for scientific reasons—because it works against Nature's laws. And that's the reasoning behind his argument at dinner.

"Natural predation's the process," Jason explains, scooping a dollup of butter onto his baked potato, "by which natural balances of interdependent species are maintained. It has intrinsic conservation value."

Xhosa responds, "I know what you mean, Jase, but I'm not quite following yet."

In his years of study, Jason witnessed many kills made by lions in the wild. Although he applies scientific knowledge rather than mysticism to his first-hand experience of Nature, both he and I tend to reach the same conclusion.

"I don't see anything ghoulish in a predator taking down its prey," he elaborates. "It's totally natural. You'll find it's the young and weak, or elderly, sick, or decrepit, that are predated on by the cats."

"Darwin's principle of survival of the fittest," observes Thomas.

"Precisely," Jason continues, swallowing his last mouthful of grilled chicken. He pauses a moment to consider, before continuing. "But the trophy hunter's objective is to get the biggest prize as a trophy—the lion with the biggest mane, the eland with the biggest horns, and so on."

"So trophy hunting acts against natural selection," Thomas points out.

"That's my major problem with it," Jason concludes, pushing his plate aside. "It destroys the genetically superior animals—and weakens the entire species."

Having finished supper, we stand up to leave. There's another subtle aspect I've chosen not to venture into: the soul connection in the predator–prey relationship. In the wild, where commerce has no place, hunting's the most natural process in the circle of life, something to be honored and celebrated. It has both sacred and scientific value. Maria Khosa explained, through her time-honored understanding of Nature's higher laws, that a lioness hunting her prey is a celebratory act: a sacred exchange of energy between souls. In the true order of things, the prey actually offers itself up to the predator, by agreement and according to a soul contract. How could we modern-day humans, whose animal products arrive in portioned packages from supermarkets, begin to understand this? We, who have broken our contract with Nature, time and time again: taking without giving back, receiving without thanking, and consuming with such avarice and greed that we've all but destroyed the fabric of love and life that connects all things on our planet.

Once we remember the love bond that exists between all things in creation, we'll be on the path to reclaiming our own souls. I know that is what Marah and the White Lions are here to teach us.

CHAPTER 26

Tsau: Starlion River

August 30, 2005. Out walking with the dogs in the bushveld, I encounter human footprints ahead of me in the sand. It's less than a week after our outing to Jos Macs and the incident with the drunken neighbor. As I study these tracks closely—the imprint from army-style boots—stabs of tension seize my body. Summoning my shamanic shielding technique, I reinstate the forcefield of love I've created around the heartland's perimeter, surprised that an antagonistic intruder could have invaded my territory.

True, I've been suffering from a creeping low-grade depression for weeks, and I may have let my guard down. Normally, I'd feel no fear whatsoever—neither from man nor beast. This is my home now, in a deep ancestral kind of way. And the power of these lands makes it easy to believe Maria Khosa's unusual instruction that there are vast ancient civilizations buried deep beneath the Timbavati soil. The earth holds such resonance. Down in the riverine areas beside the magnificent Tsau River are two-thousand-year-old trees, reaching up into the skies, gnarled and knotted, like ancient pillars of wisdom holding up a green and golden canopy over the sacred lands.

Picking up my tension, Sam looks up into my face, questioningly, waiting for instruction. The track doesn't resemble any of our staff's familiar shoe prints. The damp earth clearly records army-issue imprints—which passed here very recently, since frost fell this morning. I immediately draw my radio from my belt to put out an urgent call to our security duo, Nelias and Nelson, now armed.

"Nelias-Nelias-Nelias Ntete or Nelson-Nelson-Nelson Mathebula, come in," I radio urgently, waiting for their response to crackle back.

Nelias responds immediately to my radio call: "Standing by."

Describing my location and the nature of the prints ahead of me, I am greatly relieved to discover that these tracks, in fact, belong to the new patrol boots issued by Jason as part of our security uniform a few days ago. I wasn't aware that Nelias and Nelson had already changed over. By unlikely coincidence, it turns out that Nelias himself is out on a foot patrol about five hundred meters ahead of me, heading for our northern border. These are his tracks.

I radio back and ask him to stand by. Then Sam, Cibi, and I beat a path through the riverine undergrowth, following Nelias's tracks until we catch up with him. There he stands, a familiar comforting figure, reed-thin but strong and upright. Never having had the luxury of a warm shower in his life, he looks great in his security uniform and new army boots. It's an honor and privilege joining this distinguished man on his patrol—suddenly every animal track comes alive, and every broken twig or scratchmark on the base of a tambotie tree tells a story. Leading the way, he walks bolt upright ahead of me now, reading both the skies and the Earth for signs.

It's the tail end of winter. The bitter cold has eased, but the drought hasn't abated. Timbavati has a summer rainfall, so one would expect a dry winter season, but this excessive drought is unnatural and perturbing. At the river's verdant edge, the soil remains moist and fecund, but beyond the evergreen borders of the Tsau River is a wasteland in drought, stretching out on all horizons.

To add to my worries, the continuing drought has created a famine, and the prey animals are beginning to die. In the bushveld, the parched grasses are now being eaten down to their roots, and the earth is tinder dry. Waterholes have become dustpans. Nelias and I have just passed the second skeletal carcass of a bushbuck succumbed to starvation.

As I trudge behind the elderly tracker, I look beyond the fringe of green leaves to the parched wasteland all the way to the horizon, lying dormant and fallow, awaiting the Queen's paw print to revitalize it. This sustained drought might have seemed like a natural disaster, but Jason has explained to me the dire consequences are the result of human mismanagement. Under natural winter conditions in a vast wildlife region such as this, starving animals would normally migrate to greener pastures, sometimes crossing great distances—provided fences don't block their way. Instead, relatively small units of land have been carved up and fenced in by people who believe they can "own" a piece of nature. An unintegrated patchwork of properties formed, without any coherent overarching plan in support of Mother Nature.

Each piece is individually managed for short-term commercial purposes, like farming and trophy hunting, where overstocking with prey animals has led to overgrazing and denuding of the food base. And with the true fabric of Nature torn apart, the complex interrelated ecosystem started unraveling.

Because I am living so close to the land and its wild creatures, I can't ignore the issues I readily glossed over when I worked as a model in Paris and an advertising exec in London. It's easy to hang onto illusions when you're living in a virtual world. But here, Earth issues are all too real—and they demand urgent attention.

Over the past few weeks, every time our team sits down to a meal around the kitchen table, I can't help thinking of those animals outside in Nature, dying. Not only here on the lionland, of course, but everywhere. Witnessing the drought, first-hand, forces a new perspective. In the past, I simply selected food and paid for it over the counter—never pausing to think about this food's real production cost and negative impact on our Earth. I'd get my nourishment from the supermarket—a mass-produced and bulk-packaged product, grown and farmed somewhere else on the globe, then transported over many carbon miles to my particular location. I now know that the combined contents of an average shopping cart has been around the world many times. But back in my modeling and advertising days, I never once paused to consider the real cost of that product in terms of waste, chemical fertilizers, artificial preservatives, plastic packaging, pollution, not to mention jet fuel and carbon emissions pumped into the atmosphere simply to get my little packaged item to me wherever I might choose to live on Earth. And I didn't pause to think for a moment of compensating Mother Earth for this real cost. My transaction for the consumables I bought took place only between humans. The fact that I should be repaying Nature for providing everything didn't occur to me. Now I wonder what on earth I was thinking, or wasn't thinking! While our natural resources are dying out, our consumer society continues to demand more and more and yet more choices, stockpiling delusions of plenty while we incrementally destroy the Earth's real wealth.

What a frighteningly dangerous, delusional world we've created for ourselves. As a fashion model in Paris and London and New York, I used to feel the global crisis was hypothetical, but here in the lions' land it's all too real. In the very heart of the animal kingdom on Earth, I can't afford to buy into those delusions any longer. I have to give back to Mother Nature and help restore some of the damage—that's my life task.

Suddenly, Sam and Cibi charge off after some unidentified wild creature. Squinting through the riverine shade, I see two jackal youngsters bound through the bushveld to get away from the dogs, with Sam and Cibi high-tailing it after them. I catch a glimpse of the jackals' adorable pointy faces and luscious bushy tails—despite the dogs' best efforts, they've managed to establish an increasing distance, before finally disappearing out of sight.

Meanwhile, I summon Sam and Cibi back with a firm maternal voice and sit them down for a talking to. Both expectant faces look up at me, knowing they've transgressed our code of conduct. I take care to explain the following:

"Those jackals are your wild relatives, understood?"

I get a "yes" and a guilty expression.

"You may not chase them, right? You have your food dished out in bowls for you every morning and every night because you're part of the human world now. But your family in the wild has to find their own food. It's difficult work—and you've just chased after them—and used up all the energy they need to go hunting scrub hares and squirrels."

Very guilty expressions.

"Understood?"

"Understood. Understood."

We proceed on our way now, Sam walking one step behind me, and Cibi obediently taking up the rear.

Ahead, Nelias stops for a moment to pick up a coil of rusted wire, which he winds into a knot and inserts into the impala-skin bag he has slung over his shoulder before moving on. Jason's instructions are that any and all man-made debris must be collected on any patrol, to minimize damage to the land. Following the figure of Nelias, I think of the biblical description of a prophetic time on Earth when drought and pestilence will ensue. Often it seems we are approaching that time, the epoch described as the time of Revelations. Species going extinct at an unprecedented rate, large numbers of livestock eradicated en masse due to mystery diseases, including avian flu, bovine TB, and mad cow disease.

In this region, a tuberculosis pandemic has broken out. All the wildebeest and buffalo to the east of the Red Line—those herds in

Timbavati and the other protected areas in the greater Kruger National Park system—are at risk now. What is deeply concerning is that little to no measures are being taken to rectify the situation, and information on the seriousness of this outbreak in the national park system has been suppressed for years.

Through discussions with veterinarians called in to assess TB-infected animals, Jason and I have determined the crisis is far more serious than authorities are admitting. And the incidence of this disease has increased incrementally over the years.

For me, the immediate horror is that lions preying on TB-infected animals contract tuberculosis themselves—and usually die as a consequence. If Marah and her cubs happen to feed on an affected carcass, they'll face the same risk. For this reason, Jason travels long distances to purchase disease-free game from outside of the Red Line. Today, he's on the road again for this purpose, traveling several hours in a westerly direction to ensure that the wildebeest carcass for Marah and her pride is TB-free, having first gained a stamped permit from the Nature Conservation offices for this transfer.

Again, the sad truth is that the TB pandemic was another man-made crisis. The wild game originally contracted the disease by being forced into close proximity with humans and their livestock. Now these wild prey animals, and the predators preying on them, can be shot on sight if showing signs of the disease.

It seems to me animals always bear the brunt of human folly. Following the course of Marah's long walk to freedom, I'm reminded of Dr. Cloete and his joint specialties of taxidermy and DDs (dangerous diseases—passed on by animals to humans). As far as I know, no one has done a comprehensive study of the dangerous diseases we humans pass to animals. Recently, the lions in the National Kruger Park region started contracting a debilitating ailment known as FIV (feline AIDS), which attacks their immune systems. Little, if nothing, is being done to remedy this disease.

Nelias is walking ahead of me, but he suddenly stops, intently regarding the skies. Outside the leafy canopy of the river, vultures circle. He shakes his head. Sam, Cibi, and I head out with him into the dry bushveld to see what's attracting these spiraling scavengers.

Before long, we find an adult wildebeest female. She's lying in the fragile shade of a sickle bush, having died giving birth. Her exhaustion, frailty, and lack of ready nutrition were a deadly combination. I instruct Sam and Cibi to sit, and they take up an obedient sitting position, although highly excited and interested in this discovery. I feel exactly the opposite. Already wrestling with depression over these past few weeks, I'm left totally bereft by this sight. The calf's tiny head is half out, and it wrenches my heart to see this delicate little creature die unborn.

I'm gripped with a sudden fear and panic and sense of indescribable loss—is my project also going to be stillborn? I turn away so that Nelias does not see my tears. He's seen so much hardship in his life: drought, pestilence, famine, poverty, loss; yet, through my tear-filled eyes, I notice how proud and upright he still stands, staring down at the earth and the most recent casualty.

Nelias begins to drag the carcass of the pregnant wildebeest mother out into the open, so that the vultures, at least, could feast. I know the pack of jackals will probably be here tonight, and by morning, little trace will be left of this poignant scene. Nelias uses the knife attached to his belt to open the wildebeest's ribcage to check her lungs for polyps, indicative of TB.

Fortunately, there are no telltale signs of tuberculosis. Nevertheless, I am fighting a rising sense of despair. The story of a wasteland resulting from the dethroning of the true monarch is a timeworn fable, recounted in Ancient Greek times, Ancient Egyptian times, and well before. Even *The Lion King* was a reinterpretation of this same story. After the true king, Mafasa, is dethroned and the false monarch, Scar, seizes power, the lions' territories are laid to waste.

Only when Simba, the rightful heir, returns to reinstate order and balance in the natural hunting grounds does paradise return. Standing there in that moment with the land lying barren all around me, I feel the profound truth of this mythical tale. In this real-life story of the White Lions, the removal of the true rulers of the wilderness from their ancestral homelands has also resulted in devastation. Under oppressive dominion, a wasteland has ensued. What deeply distresses me at this moment is the solemn realization that it is we humans who have played the role of the false monarch; we are the "Scar" on our pristine Mother Earth, having pillaged, raped, ruined, and left behind deserts where once there were wilderness paradises. I know, with that unfailing clarity, that Marah's return will reinstate order and balance to the natural ecosystem. But with vested interests at stake, will this restoration of natural order ever be allowed to take place?

Nelias is standing, ready to move on, but I can't face him yet. Turning away from the sight of the dead mother and calf and focusing instead on the distant horizon, I wipe the tears from my eyes. I am trying to reinstate my long-term vision of reclaiming lands on all borders. Through these means, I will dismantle the electrified barricades that separate these lands from the rest of the White Lions' kingdom. Stilling my aching heart, I concentrate on reaffirming my pledge to Marah, not only to ensure her divine right to freedom, but equally, to assist in restoring balance to her sacred heartland, which was so brutally ravaged in her absence. And I call on great Mother Nature, Gaia, to assist me.

Feeling my strength returning, I tell Nelias I am ready to go. I follow his trail back to the river, gaining some comfort in reminding myself that the land has already begun to flourish under our guardianship. The brief period we've been here has witnessed life return in many subtle ways. Every time Nelson and Nelias remove an animal trap or snare on their antipoaching patrols, or a barbed wire wound tight around a tree, Mother Nature can breathe more freely. And I know that one day, under Marah's silent padded paw print, life will sprout and blossom and flourish in abundance once again.

Drawing on my courage, I focus on watching Nelias place his boots one step at a time on the earth, while he scans its surface for traces of those creatures that have used this path before him. And I begin to take heart from his dignified example. With our lion family protected in the epicenter of their ancient ancestral lands, there's no going back. Only forward, one step at a time.

CHAPTER 27

Canned Hunting, or Caged Slaughter?

SEPTEMBER 10, 2005. THE MINISTER OF THE ENVIRONMENT has finally announced his intention to prohibit canned hunting, and he is instituting a public participation process to consolidate the issue. Our team has urgently convened to try to evaluate what, if any, headway this announcement will make in actually shutting down the monstrous industry.

The assembled group is the usual that gathers in the kitchen every morning—with two differences. We are gathered around a table at Jos Macs, rather than Base Camp, and Mireille has rejoined us! My godmother returned from England to the lionland two weeks ago, hale-hearted and disseminating good cheer like relief parcels to soldiers on the frontline. Having her with me again has revived my flagging spirits. She arrived with gusto, only to find—much to her delight—that the rondavel Nelias and Nelson have been secretly working on is almost complete. She's now expressing a long-standing wish to move out to the lionland permanently. Matriarch that she is, there are moments when Mireille suddenly resembles that golden-haired little urchin who spent day after day alone with her loving Tsonga nanny in the remote rondavel, singing Tsonga songs and telling animal stories, or sitting outside in the dust with the bugs and other creatures, while her austere adoptive parents went on their missionary rounds. She may be a formidable *Kokwane* now, but she's never lost her childlike enthusiasm, which proves a huge support in our challenging project. She wakes up early, hearty and enthused, no matter what bombshell was dropped the previous day. But recently, even Mireille's warm enthusiasm has been put to the test. In the face of the government's suspension of our permit approval, the relentless to-ing and fro-ing of tense legal letters between our lawyers and the authorities, and the never-ending threat that our project could be shut down and Marah and the cubs seized, I've noticed she has to rest more frequently and sometimes is unable to rise before 10:00 a.m.

But all of us are up early to catch the first morning news. Mireille stands at the head of our table, putting in an order for breakfast. In fifteen minutes, a program on national television will be aired, addressing the issue. We don't possess a TV at our camp and haven't invested in a booster aerial for reception. So our nearest option is Jos Macs, where for once the incongruous television screens in this sonorous natural environment are an advantage. Fortunately, there was no competing rugby event at this early hour, and the pub's entirely empty, apart from our group.

Jos Macs's kitchen staff is looking worse for wear after another late night. One waitress has taken up a broom to sweep around our feet. Another carries out a tray of coffee mugs. Having laid it down on our wooden table, she gives the surface a cursory wipe with her damp dishcloth. Jason is lugging in a comfortable chair for Mireille, who is standing, orchestrating from the head of the table as usual. The rest of us are seated on the hard, wooden benches around the table, edgily watching the screen. Television's not high on our team's agenda, but this is a matter of life and death to our cause, so we've all shelved our immediate practical plans for the day.

This will be the first television program I've watched in the nine and a half months I've been on White Lion territories. It was such a relief having broken my dependency on TV. I often think of humanity all around our fragile globe, glued to their boxes, staring into a virtual world while our real world gasps and cries out for help. In the months when I was stuck in The Cupboard in the city, trying to fundraise, I'd often fall asleep to the inane flickering of the television screen, in an attempt to distract my anxious mind. But then I'd wake up an hour or so later, feeling even greater exhaustion and clutter. These days, when I'm not out monitoring with Jason, I fall asleep to the gurgle of the nightjar, the hyenas whooping and laughing, or the gentle rustling of the wind in the leaves. The comforting sounds of Nature instill calm and peacefulness, as they've done since time immemorial. And most recently, with Marah making her presence known, sounding her rulership over her kingdom, I fall asleep to the impressive roars of the Lion Queen. Her three cubs have just started joining their mother in a formidable chorus of roaring. I pause momentarily to see if I can hear their distant rumbles from Jos Macs's wooden balcony, but the sound of the TV intervenes once again.

Our group is in deep discussion, waiting for the program to commence. Frankly, no one is holding their breath, as the government has made promises of this kind in the past, without delivering.

Ever since the shocking exposé almost a decade ago, when this massively well-funded industry first emerged, we've been gathering petitions and letters of protest from around the world in order to fight the lions' cause. In an act of showmanship, the government immediately placed a "voluntary" moratorium on canned hunting, but it studiously avoided taking action. Finally, under intensive pressure from our organization and others, the government agreed to reassess the issue. More time elapsed, while the subindustry burgeoned into an uncontrollable monster. All the while, regulations were not put in place to curb the escalating atrocities.

In one of many cruel twists, *The Cook Report*, which first laid bare these atrocities to the world intending to alleviate the crisis, was in fact ruthlessly exploited as free advertising by the canned-hunting industry. At the time when canned hunting was first exposed, only a handful of operators existed in South Africa. Less than ten years later, more than one hundred canned-hunting operations have since established themselves. And they are still aggressively expanding under the guarantee of fast money.

So in terms of our greater strategy, this breaking news is one of the most important developments so far. Under the escalating barrage of outrage from the public, the government has announced its intention to outlaw canned-hunting practices, but before anything concrete is actually put into effect, it has invited a public participation process, which could go on for several more years. Meanwhile, the torture and killings continue.

Seizing the tension of the moment, with all of us focused on the same issue, Thomas poses a question, "At a time of ecological crisis, like now, d'you think any individual person can really make a difference?" He tightens his woolen scarf around his neck, pausing for effect, before continuing, "Sure, if that person holds the position of premier or minister of the environment, he can change policy—but I'm talking about the rest of us—the ordinary layperson. Can any of us actually change things—or are we simply moving deck chairs around on the *Titanic*?"

"Certainly, everyone can make a difference, my lad," announces Mireille cheerily. "In any walk of life, in your own unique way."

Having pondered this question long and hard, I know she's right. I myself have witnessed how incredibly responsive Mother Nature is to love. If we show her loving kindness to the best of our abilities—whether by watering the emaciated tree in our backyard, recycling our waste, or rescuing the stray dog we spot desperately navigating the highway—Nature rewards us lovingly in return. And Nature invariably gives much greater gifts than we ourselves have given.

"First rule is to remember our Earth is sentient," I respond to

Thomas's question. "She's conscious, like a mother. So when we become conscious, we work in harmony with her."

"Don't get you. We're all conscious."

"Well, yes. Barely. I mean 'conscious' as in wide awake—and responsible."

I pause momentarily, savoring the vibrant natural environment all around us. There is a momentary inhaling of breath in the surrounding wildlife.

"The 'Mother Earth' expression is totally right," I continue. "She protects us, heals us, feeds us, nurtures, and loves us—just as any true mother would."

Thomas nods slowly, trying to pick a hole in my argument.

"That's the fundamental law behind saving our planet," Xhosa chips in, holding his coffee mug with both hands, in his trademark woolen cut-off gloves. "In saving her, we save ourselves."

For Thomas, I should have perhaps tried to formulate something in more scientific terms, but the TV program is beginning now, so like everyone else, I turn my attention to the screen.

First there's an interview with the minister of the environment. He is a white South African from Afrikaner stock who has somehow found his way into the ANC government, and he is announcing that this trophy-hunting industry is now under assessment, and the pros and cons are being evaluated. Our team groans with a single voice—this process has already taken ten years of assessment and so-called evaluation, and we've heard it all before. But then, when the minister goes on to announce that he is drafting policy to keep canned hunting under control, there are some sighs of relief. Perhaps something positive will come from this public participation process he has initiated. Following the minister's speech, there is an interview with a canned hunter. The man has been filmed standing in front of a caged camp full of aggressive and utterly miserable-looking lions. I brace myself to watch. I know somehow I have to come to grips with the mindset behind these appalling activities. How can I oppose this mindset without understanding it? I remind myself of Nelson Mandela's studied and strategic approach during his twenty-seven years as an imprisoned activist. He was insightful, despite his appalling circumstances, in persuading his comrades that it was crucial to appreciate the mind of the oppressor, so that they could face their formidable foe and overcome it.

Trying to suspend judgment now, I observe the canned hunter gesturing toward the caged lions behind him in justifying his actions:

"This's how I make my living," he objects indignantly. "Why can't I do what I like with those things, there? I paid for them."

I am absolutely spellbound by his argument. Where do you draw the line between commodity and sentient being? If money is the only justification, does absolutely everything have a price? If so, where do you stop? With your dog? With your mother? Your child?

It fascinates me that this man is prepared to go public with his views, openly, and in his way, honestly. By contrast, most canned-hunting outfits operate clandestinely, through secret networks that the public, and possibly even the authorities, are completely unaware of. We simply can't fathom a fraction of the wheeling and dealing. Many are so brazen as to publicly advertise themselves as kiddies' theme parks or "petting" zoos, while trading behind the scenes as barbarous trophy-hunting operators. I've witnessed the Bethlehem canned operator lie about his activities, straight-faced and on record, publicly claiming he'd never shoot a White Lion, while at the very same time advertising for this lion's head as a trophy on the Internet. Lies and deception are rife. However different these views are from my own, I find this particular man's approach refreshing, in a bizarre way.

"They've a wonderful life!" he continues. "When they get born, my wife bottle-feeds them, like babies. Then they get to play with my kiddies in the house—they even sit at the table or sleep in the kids' beds. When the things are a bit bigger and they start messing the house, we put them in a cage with other lions the same size so that they can grow," he gestures. "So what's the problem? The things can sleep as much as they like, and eat and f—ck. Then, when their manes are big enough, we shoot them." He pauses, with an expression of astounded indignation on his face. "That's how we make the trophy that hangs on someone's wall for a long, long time." Again he pauses, as if that were justification enough, then continues. "I tell you, people are prepared to pay big bucks. So I don't see why's anyone jumping up and down! Huh? Must be just they're jealous of the money I'm making."

The man has a thick South African accent, with a high-pitched voice.

Thomas picks up on this and asks, "Why's it so many of the butchest hunting goofs suffer from squeaky voices?"

I pause, then quip, "We girls have our theories."

Which results in a tittering laugh from the men in the group, and the inevitable comeback from Thomas, "Now that's below the belt, Linda."

"Let's just put it this way," Mireille announces in her most uppity tone. "There's something disproportionate about the size of their guns."

Another titter. Fortunately, I've noticed that the team members—including Harold himself, when he was present—tend to temper their language when Mireille is around, but I've also observed that our matriarch is not incapable of her own colorful expressions.

The hunter is still talking. "The mark-up on speed-bred trophy lions is much better than battery chickens. I tell you: give me one good reason why should I do anything else?"

"It's like saying he makes a good profit through child prostitution, so why should he refrain?" snorts Mireille, outraged. "We don't have a right to make a living out of any activity!"

Unprepared to watch any more claptrap, she marches off in a huff and busies herself in discussions with the Tsonga kitchen staff.

The interview is coming to an end in any event, and the man has his own trademark way of concluding: "Thank you and f—ck you," he declares to the press reporter.

Then the program switches to include a very brief interview with an advocate fighting for animal rights before turning to other matters. I notice there is no word from my lionhearted colleague, Gareth Patterson, the man who relocated George Adamson's lions after this iconic figure (of *Born Free* fame) was assassinated in the '80s. Patterson went on to publish seven books on lions, leading up to a grueling exposé entitled *Dying to Be Free,* which uncovered some of the atrocities behind the canned-hunting industry, almost a decade ago. Since the publication of his book, Patterson has gone underground, weary and worn out both by the death threats he received and the total ineffectuality of the authorities in doing anything meaningful to stop the killing of innocent lions.

"So?" Mireille has returned. "Is this positive news?"

"Hard to say," I comment.

I provide background by explaining that in the '90s, when the first deplorable reports of canned hunting hit the press, the government declared a "voluntary moratorium."

"How can any moratorium be voluntary?" Xhosa asks. "Contradiction in terms."

"Exactly," I respond. "All it meant was ethical operators who respected the law were obliged to cease all lion-related activities, while for canned-hunting operators, it was the ideal black hole of opportunity. In over a decade, nothing whatsoever's been done to curb this industry."

I can see the expression of outrage in Mireille's face, and the group looks increasingly hotheaded. If the government's intention is to place on hold any activity involving the transfer or relocation of lions, the exact reverse is taking place: the breeding, international trading, and killing of captive lions has exploded into a massive industry, virtually overnight. Alas, it has only gotten increasingly worse as the months and years pass.

"One wants to be optimistic about the minister's announcement of a provisional hold on lion activities, of course," I pause, feeling my own anger rising. "But probably all this means is that reputable operators are again denied permits—while for canned-hunting operators, business is at an all-time high."

Even Jason looks hot under the collar.

"Worst is: canned hunting remains legalized," he points out. "Until the government has officially abolished these malpractices, any individual or organization's free to make a successful career out of breeding endangered animals—for slaughter."

Mireille stands, hands on hips, listening with an intense matronly expression of disapproval. The grim facts speak for themselves. The proliferation of these killing camps has made a mockery of the government's supposed moratorium. In just over a decade, an entire pitiless industry has boomed by exploiting animal misery. The vast majority of the imprisoned lions are golden-colored, while the number of White Lions incarcerated in this way has remained a closely guarded secret, despite the fact that the Global White Lion Protection Trust succeeded in focusing media attention on this appalling state of affairs.

"Disgraceful," Mireille finally concludes. "It seems to me this industry's shot up overnight, and the authorities are conspicuously doing nothing about it!"

She's looking more determined than ever. "Most important thing now's for all welfare groups to join forces."

Having myself been one of the lonely voices of protest for years, I've watched the wave of animal welfare and environmental groups suddenly rising to campaign against canned lion hunting. However, the result of this overwhelming political tension is bureaucratic chaos, with authorities undecided which way legislation should turn.

Without clear directives from government, permit officers are approving or withholding lion permits at will. Underhand dealing is commonplace, and in some cases, entire permit books have disappeared, unaccounted for. It's a world gone mad.

"We're in the middle of a bizarre and frightening nightmare," I'm forced to admit, "which doesn't only affect Marah and her family. It's a national crisis."

The enormity of the problem weighs heavily on the whole group. Unfortunately, the issues around my captive-born lioness and her right to freedom are not isolated; they reverberate through an entire malign industry.

"An additional problem is the impaired genetics of many of these captive lions through aggressive speed-breeding," Jason voices the grim truth. "So there's no conservation reason to return them to the wild."

There's a bleak silence.

"But what's to become of all these dear creatures, snatched from nature," Mireille demands, "and held captive in a pitiless system?"

Another silence.

Xhosa stands up, and for a dread moment I think he's about to break into a rap on the subject. But instead he offers one of his gems, "One day we'll look back on these atrocities, like America looks back on slavery and South Africa looks back on Apartheid—and we'll cringe at our legalized misdemeanors," he forecasts somberly.

"True, X," I concede. "But for the meantime, we're trapped in the middle of this insanity—with the majority of people totally oblivious to the problem."

"And blithely unable to comprehend why it's so completely and totally unacceptable!" Mireille adds indignantly.

I stand up, pointing out, "Question's not why some morally bankrupt individuals get pleasure out of killing beautiful animals. Unfortunately, there're always gonna be unsavory people, like murderers and rapists. The real question's why the rest of humanity lets them get away with it. I agree with you, Godmum. Every single person can make a difference. So why don't we?"

"Because so many of us have lost touch with Nature," Xhosa concludes.

Solemn silence. I notice the waitress, who was slumped behind the bar counter, staring at the sports channel, now that it's been switched back on.

"And our own natures," I add. "Most people don't realize how powerful they are when they awaken the spirit of the lion within them."

"Precisely!" Jason says decisively, standing up and reaching for his bush hat on the table. "Right everyone. We've got a program to get on with. Let's move."

There's a general reorientation as the team refocuses on the day's schedule: bush clearing and fence maintenance. We pay the waitress, then march down the gravel path, one after the other, and pack into the back of the Land Rover, Jason driving with Mireille in the front passenger seat.

Once on the land, Jason drops Mireille, Xhosa, and me at Base Camp, while he heads off with the team into the bushveld for the day. My godmother and my assistant immediately start busying themselves opening our post to check there's nothing sinister, while I make my way to my office.

I go to my desk to check my voicemail, picking up a message from a journalist, wishing to interview me on these recent developments with the minister. As always, my first reaction to exposure in the press and media is resistance. Then I start to think of the canned-hunting camps I've visited and countless untold tales of atrocities unnoticed. The current situation is almost too much to bear, these orphaned and imprisoned animals in the brute hands of our own inhumane species. Every time I witness an atrocity, or even have it reported to me, the injustice tears at my heart. And compounding it, because the country's laws are not on the side of the lions, I feel helpless and handcuffed, as if I'm right inside that cage with the incarcerated cats, facing the mindless cruelty of my jailors. What a world we humans have created! Where's the solution? In this context of ignorance and apathy, the solution lies in collaboration with a network of enlightened people. With this in mind, I recognize that the media has been a great assistance in closely monitoring Marah's amazing story, because publicity has helped protect her.

We have poisonous journalists targeting us at the behest of the hunting industry, but equally, in fighting Marah's cause, the press and media have also been our greatest ally. So I embrace the opportunity.

I actively calm my mind once again, in preparation for a barrage of questions, then I call back. A woman answers, with an efficient voice, and starts off rather upbeat, explaining her thinking. First she indicates the story will be published in a popular women's magazine, not a newspaper; then she goes straight into the pitch.

"So—I told my editor, yours is another *Born Free* story."

"Not exactly," I comment. "Unlike Elsa, Marah wasn't born 'free,' but a prisoner."

"Oh, true," observes the journalist.

"Unfortunately, the tragedy's that Marah's not alone," I point out. "She may be unique—that's for sure—but she was hand-reared in captivity along with many other rare animals, bred specifically to be killed."

I go on to explain that in fact, the challenge we face is entirely different from challenges at the time *Born Free* was written, when Elsa, the lioness, was hand-reared by Joy and George Adamson in Kenya in the 1970s. Canned hunting didn't exist in those days. It's a product of Apartheid-type separatism, and it emerged once the Apartheid regime fell. I also explain that canned hunting is the inevitable endpoint of consumerist thinking, which presumes everything—however rare, endangered, intelligent, and sentient—can be sold and packaged like a commodity on the stock exchange. I wonder how she is going to respond to this blunt information. I've had dealings with responsible journalists who recognized their crucial role in positively influencing public opinion at a time of dire need, but others who simply saw mine as another story before moving on to the next flavor of the day.

"Okay," she responds cautiously. "I wasn't intending to get into all that political stuff. But, yeah, I suppose it's important to put your lion story in context."

I pause. "It is. Really."

Choosing my words carefully, I go on to discuss the challenges of my project in brief: the canned-hunting opponents; the common exploitative view that natural resources, including White Lions, are there for the taking; the similar view among some scientists today that White Lions, by virtue of their unusual coloring, have no conservation value; and, most glaringly, the gaping lack of spiritual connection with Mother Nature that allows people to treat animals like merchandise.

Her response is somewhat vague, as she explains she was interested in my own personal story and not the wider issues. So I redirect my focus to first-hand details. In some ways, these are the most difficult to talk about. Taking care not to become emotional, I describe the taxing step-by-step process from the day Marah was born to her present incarceration, and the multiple ways people contrived to keep this rare creature under brutal lock and key. The facts speak for themselves. But what I have difficulty explaining is my own inner conflict, each and every day, at having removed myself from the lioness I love in order to ensure her freedom. Elsa, the lioness born free in the wild, orphaned and then raised by the Adamsons, lived with humans. She slept in the Adamson's tent, traveled in their vehicle, ate with their staff, and finally was left to fend for herself alone in the wild, where she eventually died. Much as I would have loved to have the same privileged relationship with Marah, by force of circumstance I've had to choose a very different route. Ever since Marah was in my care, Jason and I have actively resisted any kind of taming, or habituation. We're ensuring human contact is minimized, to give her and her family the greatest chance of survival in the wild. But with every passing day, the bond grows stronger, and the physical separation between us becomes more difficult.

The journalist is now fascinated by the differences between my own story and that of the Adamson's in *Born Free*. I explain Elsa was a lioness caught between two worlds—the human and the animal—showing humanity how Nature's love can cross the species barrier. But in our day, humans have breached and disrespected that barrier by bottle-feeding and hand-rearing cuddly cubs as if they're family—with the specific purpose of slaughtering them in their cages as adults. For me, direct contact with these loving animals is the most powerful experience of unconditional love imaginable. So it is indescribably painful to witness the callous betrayal, taking place all over our country. In shamanic terms, when humans break the sacred contract with lions, King of beasts, they commit the ultimate sacrilege. There is probably no greater taboo. For the shaman, it is not a life for a life, but a human soul for every lion's life taken in this profane bargain.

That is the greater picture. I keep my response to the interview simple, and when I pause for breath after describing my goals and dreams for Marah's rewilding, the journalist is satisfied she has the material she needs.

"Okay, that's about it," she sums up. "Don't forget to send me some cutesy pictures of you hugging Marah and cubs."

I wince at the thought. I'm not sure how much she's really understood, and I'm particularly concerned the public shouldn't get the wrong idea.

"There are pictures of Marah and me as a baby," I venture, feeling an involuntary shudder at the thought of that little lamb-like creature singled out for her snowy coat to become a prized commodity. "And there're also some photos with Marah at nine months when I released her, for about one hour, from the canned-hunting camp."

As I offered this option, my mind flashes back to that unforgettable day. The pictures themselves give no clue of the secrecy and high risk surrounding that brief encounter between me and the most beautiful cat on Earth, a subadult lioness full of innocence and wonderment.

"But I'm concerned not to give the readers the idea that it's okay to pet lion cubs," I explain. "Problem is, so many cubs are handled these days—in zoos, petting parks, even supermarkets—and no one seems to understand the gruesome truth: that these same animals, hugged as babies, are put in cages to be killed for fun when they grow up."

"Sick," the journalist concedes. "You sure this is really happening?"

"On a large scale, unfortunately. It's a massive, well-funded industry. If we allow it to continue, it'll be the end of wildlife as we know it."

"Okay, I'll see what I can do," she responds in closing.

I thank her and say goodbye, feeling an indefinable gulf in communication.

I'm wondering how my life's story will be chewed over, digested, and regurgitated to the world. After replacing the receiver, I sit in my office chair, head in hands, suddenly overwhelmed by the enormous burden of it all. Ten months waiting for the go-ahead to release Marah on her own sacred lands, and am I any closer to my goal? What is the point of engaging media when canned-hunting exposés are used to promote canned hunting? What is the point of engaging authorities when they have no authority? I feel I am teetering on the edge of despair. As always, I yearn for direct contact with my beloved lion family. But those who have the closest contact with lions these days are the same people who torture and crucify them! So the greatest love I can show Marah and her cubs is to avoid direct handling, or human imprinting—and give them back their freedom! That is the paradox I live, day after painful day—like an overprotective mother whose life purpose is to release her children, so they might be free to express their true natures, unattached to her apron strings. If you love them, truly, set them free.

CHAPTER 28

Silent Stakeholder

OCTOBER 29, 2005. NEARLY TWO MONTHS AFTER the minister's announcement, nearly a year of waiting for resolution on Marah's release. The drought in the lions' land hasn't abated, and the intensity around the canned-hunting issue has reached a point of national crisis. Everywhere there are people politics, while for the lions, the prospects have only worsened.

After months of tense engagement without any tangible end in sight, over and above years of relentless campaigning, Jason and I are fatigued and battle-weary. Today, we are away from home—fighting the White Lions' case at the national level. We are attending a national forum, convened by the government with the purpose of presenting the minister's new draft proposals and hammering out the issues with potential stakeholders.

On the legislative front, national rules and regulations are in deadlock. Permission continues to be withheld for Marah's release, and all over South Africa, authorization has been withdrawn for lion sanctuaries or any lion-reintroduction programs in the wild. By contrast, captive-breeding operations (breeding lions for trophy hunting) have sprung up without regulation everywhere—a nefarious subindustry that knows no mercy and no restraint—aided and abetted by officials without mandate.

Since the minister's announcement, a policy for regulating "the management of large predators" was drafted and comment was invited from "interested and affected parties." As a lion ecologist, Jason was identified as one of several experts in the field and asked to submit scientific papers for the minister to review.

Jason's report was painstakingly well researched and comprehensive. He addressed key issues: acceptable practices in large-predator management; natural lion behavioral traits; size of enclosures that might be considered humane for holding captive predators; minimum period for their scientific rehabilitation; and other aspects vital to the management of large predators in captivity.

That's the good news. Hopefully, once a prohibition of canned hunting is implemented, it will not only regulate widespread malpractices, but it will also be applicable in our unique case and finally free up Marah—the sacred lioness trapped at the dead center of this raging debate. However, the bad news is we don't have good reason to believe we can rely on government action. I've watched over the last few years how legislation outlawing canned hunting has been proposed, revised, postponed, and then proposed once again. Meanwhile, there's little to no policing of this subindustry, which brazenly acts outside of any ethical constraints. Accustomed to getting their own way by killing, the canned-hunting mafia continues to explode into a thriving multinational business, and the international trophy price for captive lions has skyrocketed once again.

Over the past few months, more public participation meetings have been held; polls have been taken; and a panel of experts appointed. However, the findings of this panel of experts were not made public. Disturbingly, these and other irregularities over nearly a decade of procrastination point to vested interests at top levels.

ON ALL FRONTS, A BLOODIED CAMPAIGN is raging, internationally, nationally, and right on our very doorstep. As if the dangers from the international canned-hunting cartels are not enough, the White Lions are also at risk here in the wildlands of their origin, where they should be celebrated and cherished as this country's most precious and protected animal.

Finally, last month, a breakthrough occurred. Several landowners in the region broke rank and approached us in a private bid to club together in an anti-hunting campaign. Their initiative followed a spate of incidents of unethical lion hunts in these parts, which were boldly reported in national papers. Using those botched trophy hunts as leverage, the breakaway faction has managed to achieve a temporary moratorium on lion hunting in the Timbavati and neighboring reserves, while the minister of environment assesses the validity of their claims. Their argument is a commercial one, and for this reason they've reached the ear of the minister, at least temporarily. They argue that since Timbavati and other neighboring reserves share an open border with the adjacent Kruger National Park ecosystem, whereby the private reserves allow national game to roam freely onto their land, the very same animals protected by law in the national park can be trophy-hunted once they cross into private territory. In other words, these reserves are hunting national assets for private gain.

While it is based on a commercial rationale, we view the moratorium as a huge step forward, even though the White Lions' protection isn't specifically part of the equation yet. Not surprisingly, it has further intensified the negative atmosphere on our borders, enraging many private landowners in the region because suddenly, trophy-hunting activities they've enjoyed and benefitted from for several decades have been provisionally outlawed.

Over the past few months, we've been to numerous government-led forums, where we've sat for hours at a time in government-issue chairs arranged in rows in dreary bureaucratic halls, alongside officials, scientists, some leading conservation entities, and a number of animal-welfare groups, following a seemingly interminable agenda, and engaging in endless debates on this highly inflammatory subject. It's understandable that formulating and promulgating legislation is a slow process, so, until today, we were still hopeful. However, a government meeting we have just attended took a serious downward turn.

Jason and I arrived well before this morning's meeting opened and were joined by the usual seasoned campaigners. But one look at our allies this morning and I noted they'd given up before we got started. We also noted that, among the so-called "interested and affected parties," there was representation from some well-known trophy-hunting outfitters, the most famous being Safari Club International operating out of Las Vegas, so we knew the debate would heat up. From the outset, the forum had the makings of an orderly dispute, but as the morning agenda rolled out on the merits of the legalized misdemeanors, it soon was met with an excruciatingly combative atmosphere. By comparison, the Jos Macs gathering seemed like a tea party.

After a Nature Conservation official in a safari suit pronounces the meeting officially open, secondary officials proceed to hand out the revised policy document. That is the first disappointment. On carefully reviewing the official document, we notice that none of the recommendations made by Jason and the Global White Lion Protection Trust's scientific team, as part of a panel of experts and direct stakeholders, have been included in the new policy. In fact, from a conservationist and animal-welfare point of view, the policy is an unmitigated disaster. While the document begins with clear declaration of intent—"to prohibit the activity known as canned hunting"—the rest of the policy is so riddled with loopholes and inconsistencies that, in reality, it allows for this malpractice to continue unabated.

So the meeting opens at a low point, and then it gets worse. The moratorium on trophy hunting in Timbavati and neighboring reserves isn't officially on the day's agenda, but Jason and I intend to raise the issue, while lodging an appeal for the White Lions' urgent protection. However, as the morning's program unfolds, we don't get close to broaching the topic.

When the first tea break is called, Jason and I group together with some other anti-canned-hunting campaigners. By contrast with most of these activists, we started the day optimistic, believing this government forum was an opportunity to influence positive change in government policy. Most of the other activists argued, by contrast, that it was another elaborate cover-up—behind the process was a hidden agenda with a cynically predetermined outcome. Unfortunately, after assessing how little the policy document reflects the submissions from the panel of experts, we are fast reaching the conclusion the animal activists are right.

A bell has just sounded to indicate the session is reconvening. We've walked back into the stuffy auditorium, and I have to actively summon my strength. The official in the safari suit now proceeds by giving a point-by-point explanation of the new draft policy. I'm in a terrible dilemma.

Having finally concluded his explanations, the official invites any contributor to the debate to provide their name and that of their organization, before going on to offer their input. Where should I begin critiquing this policy document?

Having done comprehensive background research into the issues prior to the meeting, both Jason and I have prepared detailed input to contribute to each and every clause in the draft policy document. So I have little trouble formulating a simple, clear argument in support of White Lion conservation. That is not my difficulty. The problem is that the drafting of this policy document is so biased toward commercial rather than conservation practices that the very foundations need reevaluation.

The rationale is founded on short-term material gain for an avaricious few, without any regard for sustainable long-term economics or preservation of natural resources for the future of our planet.

In such a banal, materialistic context, and faced with an argument based on crude money only, I'm wrestling with how to formulate a counterargument. If people have lost their hearts and souls, how can one appeal to their value system?

Our justice system is based on the premise of fairness: give and take. So how could any document, based on principles of unfairness, be worthy of the term "legislation"? A one-sided policy that legislates how humans may lawfully take from Nature without giving anything back—would any right-minded human sign such a document?

I feel utterly appalled by the injustice of it all. While we humans debate whether lions as a species may live or die, the great cats themselves have no say at all. The lions are the primary stakeholders in this process. Stakeholders without a vote. In a country where 90 percent of the population was denied a vote until Apartheid was overthrown and Mandela came into power in 1994, surely the lessons learned from lack of representation count for something?

I glance at my watch. It is 3:00 p.m. A gang of canned hunters has suddenly marched in, in a characteristic posse. They never come alone. Or at a respectful hour. After their dramatic entrance, the semblance of bureaucratic and orderly atmosphere has held tenuously for the past fifteen minutes or so, but they are lurking at the back of the auditorium, directly behind me. I can feel their repressed aggression like a powder keg, waiting to ignite.

I'm angry too. I'm sitting at the edge of my seat, fuming, struggling to find the right way to voice my outrage at the inherent injustice of these policies drafted to "manage" lions, without considering their rights. Or offering them a hearing. Since lion language remains foreign and unlearned, we humans behave as if they—the Kings of all animals—have no voice.

I know Maria would cut to the chase, and demand: What would the *lions* have to say today?

I need to get that same message across, in my own way. Somehow,

I have to make a bridge between our crass human world of self-serving policies and legislation, and the lions' God-given world of mystery and magic. But there is such discrepancy between modern-day conservation protocols and age-old shamanic belief systems that I'm not convinced even Maria could make that bridge, and nor can I in this grim, bureaucratic government building. Here, where humankind hammers out lion legislation. Maria Khosa handed over her mantle to me, but am I really mandated to speak on behalf of the great cats? Can I represent their case? I'm burning, fuming, feeling so conflicted. Am I up to the task? I prepare myself to stand up and speak out. But as I do so, I feel my voice choking in my throat. If I can't speak for the lions—here, now, in this context—then who can?

I clear my throat. What would the silent stakeholders have said of this document? Their almighty *roar* of outrage and despair at the human condition would be deafening!

There's a painful pause. Behind me, like a smoldering fuse, I feel the canned hunters' rage and indignation mounting. This policy condemns their newfound livelihood, at least on paper. A livelihood that made them many millions in virtually no time. From their viewpoint, what right does anyone have to deny them such benefits?

Standing, I hear myself speaking now. Deep-down sadness chokes my voice: "White Lions are a cultural heritage. A national treasure. They may not be destroyed for commercial reasons."

The official, taking minutes, asks me for my name and the organization I represent.

"CEO of the Global White Lion Protection Trust—I'm here to represent the lions." I say. Now, summoning courage, I add: "Today, we're deciding the fate of South Africa's—no, the world's—lions. Question is: what would they say—the lions—if they were given a voice?"

There is a shocked silence—like at Jos Macs, only bigger, and still rising. A collective response of outrage building. I resist sitting down. I hold my ground, feeling emptied out. A massive shockwave washes over me, tsunami-like, but has anyone heard? I feel flooded then totally drained with exhaustion and oppression. Finally, I sink back into my seat, still breathing. Alive. But all around me, there's that collective loss of breath.

The official makes a note, at least on paper, then looks up. My contribution hasn't helped the brimming tensions. Behind me, the representatives of the canned-hunting industry suddenly erupt. First it was the tumultuous water of emotion; now, as they inhale again, it's fire. Ignited, they're all suddenly standing, inflamed and fuming, and one marches forward and delivers an attorney's notice to the official. Although in uniform, the official looks intimidated, and he reads it aloud. They demand to meet the minister himself, face to face. Do they mean a meeting in the Supreme Court or in some dark alley someplace? I note the outrage in their attorney's tone, as if his clients have been betrayed by government and sold out by the Afrikaner minister himself, and will employ bully-boy tactics to ensure the traitor complies. After a confused, hot-tempered scuffle in the aisle, the lynch gang storms out.

It's late afternoon, and Jason and I are on the national road, driving back from the government forum in Polokwane. We are relieved to be released from the confined bureaucratic time bomb that exploded in those last moments. Beaten and bruised, I feel unsure whether this high-stress public event represents a step forward, or two steps back. It's a six-hour drive back home. At least the long drive is an opportunity to unwind; it'll give us a chance to talk through the escalating pressures and analyze where things are heading.

"So the officials asked you to submit yet another report," I note, as Jason and I follow the twisting road through the mountains back to the lions' land. "What's the point, Jase? None of your recommendations were incorporated in that policy. It's just greenwashing—who do they think they're fooling?"

"We've got to believe it'll make some kind of difference," Jason responds, his eye on the road. "Perseverance and factual accuracy."

"Sincerely hope so."

Jason's driving is steady and focused. I watch the winding road ahead, and wonder where this journey is really taking us. Jason and I have always made sure we equip ourselves with the factual information around highly charged lion conservation issues, so that we are well informed before taking action. But there is such a dark cloud of smoke and mirrors surrounding these issues, it is unlikely many of the concealed facts will ever see the light of day.

"You know, there are times when I almost feel sorry for those canned-hunting guys," I observe.

"They're dangerous," Jason replies.

"And damaged—I think *that's* why they cause all the harm they do."

I think of the man who expressed his view so emphatically in the TV interview, and the formidable mafia boss in his caged fortress on our borders. And, with a shudder, I think of the canned-hunting operator in Bethlehem who once held Marah—and still holds Aslan, together with many other exotic and rare animals, some in coffinlike cages—carving out a flourishing livelihood by taking their lives.

"In my next submission to the government, I'll need to look more closely at the IFAW report," Jason is thinking out loud as he drives, planning ahead.

"Good luck, Jase!" I respond, admiring his perseverance. "That's another document that makes for grim reading."

In preparation for today's meeting, Jason and I ensured we were armed with various documents for reference, so I heave my briefcase onto my lap now in the car, snap the clasps open, and remove the report from its folder. Behind us, the low sun is dropping toward the mountains in the west, but there's sufficient daylight left to read for a while longer.

"Can you check out the section on predator camp sizes and numbers held in those captive camps?" Jason asks.

"Will do."

The IFAW Report is a comprehensive study by a courageous journalist friend of mine from university days, a trained economist commissioned by the International Fund for Animal Welfare. It was published a month earlier and has made no attempt to detail the atrocities; it simply documents facts and figures for the government's review. But in some respects, these telling factual details make for the grimmest reading of all. For instance, the report established that there are an estimated four to five thousand lions cooped up in cages waiting to be butchered as trophy heads. These sickening records of legalized crime against wild animals make a farce of the department's authority to govern this issue in any meaningful way to date. And now there are links emerging between canned hunting and other elicit activities: gun-running; mercenaries into African countries; trade in animal parts; and, perhaps worst of all, child-prostitution rings.

To solve the crisis and shut down the canned-hunting operations, the minister is advocating mass euthanasia of all the lions held in the captive camps. When this solution was raised at today's forum, it was firmly supported by a number of the scientists present. To me, it was additionally gruesome that so-called purists in conservation and scientific circles, who'd done nothing to stop this escalating runaway industry, were now arguing that these speed-bred animals should all be exterminated because of the probability that their genetics are impaired. Underneath these heartless scientific pronouncements, I sensed a rising hysteria, and deep-seated fear of Nature and the consequences of meddling with her and her precious creatures.

"Is this appalling 'final solution' the best we can do, Jase?" I pose the question, forcing myself not to get overly emotional.

"Under the circumstances, it might be the only solution," he responds, dropping a gear and overtaking the truck in front of us with grim determination.

The sun drops out of sight in the rearview mirror and dusk falls heavily.

"Better than keeping the killing camps operating, granted," I concede. "But what a nightmare's been created—"

"All because the authorities haven't been willing, or able, to take responsible action," he observes.

What is the solution? It seems to me it is not the activities themselves, but the consciousness behind them that most urgently needs to change. Why is it that the same practitioners who were once involved in human crimes in Apartheid times are now granted free rein over animal cruelty in the new South Africa? The post-Apartheid government has been so preoccupied with human rights issues that the shocking abuse of animal rights is given carte blanche under their very noses. Worse still, many newly appointed ANC politicians and dignitaries have greedily lined their pockets, without care for human—let alone animal—rights, as if in an attempt to outdo the atrocities of the Apartheid government before them.

"What, if any, progress was made today?" I ponder aloud. "What's the point of all this discussion of canned hunting? It's like debating a draft policy document on slave management, when there shouldn't be slavery in the first place!"

"Not everyone sees it that way," he responds.

"Hmmm. Amazing what arguments people will concoct to support their commercial interests."

"Sure. Money skews people's judgment. Even some of the environmentalists—how was that argument today? Couldn't believe it. Some conservation group arguing that canned hunting's a good thing—because breeding lions for commercial hunting in cages will protect other lions from being hunted in the wild!"

"Grotesque!" I concur. "So twisted. Like saying we should legalize pedophilia in order to protect street kids from being molested!"

Driving in the dark along the treacherous mountain pass, now the gravity of the situation is hitting home. With or without permits, the factory farms have continued to prosper. And the canned-hunting industry's threat of suing the government is no empty one; through their nefarious activities, they've amassed a substantial war chest to execute it. Clearly, a court case is a cynical strategy to keep the government tied up in litigation for another ten years, while the malpractices are given free rein.

"D'you think government's actually in on this strategy?" I question Jason now.

"Elements of the government," he responds. "Certainly looks that way."

"Even if the outcome of the court case is ultimately successful," he adds, "another decade of these malpractices would destroy the genetic integrity of the world's entire lion population."

I can't see his face, but I feel Jason's gloom.

The road ahead is dark, and our headlights don't help us see any farther down the way.

CHAPTER 29

Stonewalled

OCTOBER 30, 2005. AS DAWN BREAKS, the first thing I see when I open my eyes and look out the Land Rover's window is the crisp winter sun rising and gilding the bushveld scene—and all four lions lined up, nestled together under a clump of trees, watching the sunrise. What a vision!

"Don't wanna leave the cats," Jason murmurs, giving me a warm hug upon waking. "Could stay here forever."

In the aftermath of the government forum we attended yesterday, Jason and I feel frazzled. The storm out by the canned-hunting troopers and their demands on the besieged minister will be all over the papers by now. Jason and I may be untrained and ill-equipped, but we've developed seemingly inexhaustible stamina when it comes to protecting our lion family. So I gather myself for yet another day of red tape and legal battles.

The shamanic forcefield I set up around our perimeter has held. There've been no more invasive breaches of our fence line, and everyone who has set foot on the land has come in support of our cause. But beyond our borders, it seems a kind of lawlessness and insanity reigns, with humans riding roughshod over Nature's rights to survival.

With all my heart, my only wish is to be alone with Jason and our lions, in paradise. But Marah's story is being played out against a vast political backdrop, as the raging national debates around the issue of canned hunting reach a new ferocity. I don't have the luxury of time, or retreat. With the urgent new developments on the boil after the government forum, we need to get back to camp to manage the issues. So we roll up the duvet and straighten ourselves out. As Tawny moves off, all four cats pop their heads up above the bleached grasses to watch us leave, and I look back at them with a yearning heart. The sun is backlighting their furry heads now, like halos.

What's their future?

Through our love for the lions, Jason and I have somehow managed to remain optimistic, but our resistance has reached its lowest ebb. The endless applications to the authorities, combined with the unrelenting threats of law enforcement shutting down our operation, have worn our nerves and our morale thin. Of all frustrations, our inability to take action in respect to Marah's release is our worst constraint, magnifying the drought of the parched lands all around us into an internal landscape of desperation and despair.

When will the merciless drought break? We head back to Base Camp now, through the barren landscape of dry skeletal trees, toward the eastern boundary. The magic guarri tree, so-named because of its medicinal powers known to traditional healers like Maria Khosa, is one of the only bushes that keeps its green leaves in winter. But I see these leaves too have shriveled and dropped off under the interminable heat. There are so many animal carcasses along the way that I find myself despairing of the rains ever falling again. Desiccated remains in the dust exposed to the pitiless winter sun. It's desperate.

Still, we keep going. Every morning, we identify more tasks to be undertaken in preparation for Marah's big day. The team of field workers whom Jason put together to assist—mostly voluntary, some employed by the White Lion Trust—have been working intensively. For security reasons, we've made sure field staff members are relatives of Nelson and Nelias, selected from the nearby Tsonga community, so they are trusted additions to our existing team. Mercifully, each month, sufficient income somehow comes in to pay them fair salaries.

Heading along the perimeter, Jason takes the opportunity to check the thorn-tree barricade, running parallel and about ten meters in from the fence line itself. The hewn thorn trees are all stacked against each other to form a long barrier, as planned. He's pleased with the massive bush-clearing exercise.

"Hmmm. Worried 'bout territorial male lions coming to court Marah," he comments, as he brings Tawny to a halt and climbs out of the vehicle to test the perimeter fence with his voltage tester. "Would be really challenging for her sons."

"Natural threats I can live with," I respond. "It's people I worry about."

"Sure, but I'd like to minimize all the risks. Remember, lions growing up in the wild suffer from an 80 percent mortality rate—and that's before humans even start interfering!"

Because we share our eastern and southern borders with neighboring reserves, there is a danger of possible territorial encounters with neighboring lions, which would pose a threat to Marah's subadult sons, Regeus and Letaba. Jason has established the internal thorn-tree barricade as a protective screen, to keep Marah and cubs away from hazards at their external boundaries, and out of sight from any humans accessing the boundary road on the northern and western borders.

"Looking good," he comments as we drive on, running his eye over an area of habitat selectively cleared by the bush squad.

While the primary intention behind the barricade was protection, Jason also used this procedure to effectively clear out invasive plant species, redressing the historical problem of habitat imbalance, which was a consequence of the previous owner overstocking his land with game for hunting.

"These huge game losses we've suffered in the drought are largely the result of previous land mismanagement," Jason reminds me. "We'll get the balance right eventually."

I try not to sound too bleak. "Hopefully, things will start to improve once the habitat recovers."

"You watch—this bush-clearing program'll have huge impact on the recovery of the habitat," Jason responds, optimistically looking at the skies. "Once the rains come, this cleared area could become the ideal hunting grounds for the lions."

"Yup! We know they can do it!" I respond. In that moment, I visualize our pride in a carefully strategized hunting party, crouching down behind bush cover, stalking, chasing, and successfully taking down their prey. Just like a wild pride! Of course, they can do it.

Jason and I encounter the bush squad themselves. It's early, just past 7:00 a.m., but they've already started their day's work: patching up sections of pipeline. They look up and wave at us, and we stop briefly to give them encouragement. Jason engages freely with the field workers in fluent Zulu, talking through the challenges. Zulu is the communal language everyone shares, although some of the team are Tsonga and others Sepedi. Several of the bush squad are women who work even more effectively and determinedly at this hard labor than the men. These amazing people have become the mainstay of our organization, and the women, particularly, have earned my deepest admiration. Without fail, each morning before they begin their daily work, everyone prays for rain, no matter his or her religion.

Due to the relentless drought, the priority this month was laying water pipes, and maintaining dams and water points. Before Marah and her cubs arrived here, we ran a five kilometer-long pipe to deliver water from the Tsau River to the troughs in the lions' *boma.* Further preparations for their release meant extending this by several more kilometers. The intention was to supply a crucial centralized area, which had completely dried up during the drought. But even as this pipeline was laid, starving prey animals were digging it up in numerous places in a bid for moisture, which means we've been unable to get the water supply to its destination. In some areas we've managed to keep waterholes replenished, but even here animals die right beside the water, because there's so little to forage on in the parched winter lands.

"Must check in with fire protection services as soon as we reach camp," Jason mutters as we leave the bush squad and drive on, adding another item to his seemingly endless list.

With the bushveld so pitilessly dry, fire is a real and terrible threat. Later today, we'll be burning firebreaks around all borders, as a precautionary measure against a veldfire. It is a high-risk procedure in itself, which, if not managed impeccably, can go horribly wrong, with staff getting burned or runaway fires causing havoc. Today's weather forecast indicates no wind factor, so Jason's call to fire protection services is simply a formality and additional safety measure.

As we approach the camp, we pause to let a giraffe mother and calf cross the dust road.

"Next step will be their translocation," Jason notes, referring to these elegant creatures, looking down at us with their gentle, doey eyes under long lashes.

We've been putting off the daunting exercise of moving the herd of seventeen giraffe as long as possible. It will be a harrowing exercise involving helicopters, massive transport vehicles, significant costs, and stress on animals and humans alike.

"Gonna be seriously traumatic for the giraffe," I murmur.

"Agreed. Sadly, I don't see an alternative."

Reluctant as we both are, now that winter is finally on its way out, we can't delay any longer, because the likelihood of casualties when moving giraffe in summer months is much higher than in the cool season.

One kick of a giraffe could prove a fatal threat to the lions as they attempt to hunt. Jason has given this careful consideration, having witnessed a wild tawny lioness with a broken jaw die of starvation in the course of his studies. But the greater threat is that a fleeing animal the size of a panicked giraffe may breach our predator-proof fences—pursued by the pride. And, once free of our protected area, the lions could be shot on sight by our unfriendly neighbors. As always, the natural risks we are prepared to tolerate, not the man-made ones. All the other creatures on the land will stay: the many herd animals and prey animals, the browers, grazers, antbears, and badgers, and even the other large predators, like the hyena, leopard, jackal, serval, and caracal cats. The creatures in this natural habitat are exactly what Marah would expect to find in her endemic homelands, except the huge herbivores, like the elephant, rhino, and water buffalo, not presently resident on this piece of land. Until we expand our borders, it is too small for them to live natural lives here.

"The lions' survival has to be our primary goal," Jason adds.

"Understood, Jase. I just feel for the giraffe! They've a right to be here too."

"And one day they will be, and the whole fragile ecosystem'll be reestablished. But for now, one step at a time, right?"

"Right. And one day, Marah and cubs'll meet up with wild lions," I say. "But for the moment, that'll only happen through electric fences on our borders."

"Yeah. Remember, lions are territorial. We'd risk wiping out our lions, particularly the males, if they have direct contact."

"Back to human issues," I note as we arrive at the farmhouse.

Through the kitchen window, I recognize Mireille's figure even from a distance. Great to see she's up and about, rallying the troops as usual. For several days, she's been out of action, probably needing some emergency treatment herself, but any of my attempts to bring her a tray in bed were dismissed with firm instructions to "kindly stop all this fussing."

Harold is also at the table. He's been visiting over the past few days.

And I can tell from the general flurry inside the kitchen there is quite a lot of anxious excitement from the group, waiting for feedback from us on yesterday's government forum meeting. Sam and Cibi come hurtling out of the kitchen door to greet us. The last remaining remnants of the lawn have long since been uprooted by the warthogs—even the dogs' repeated "Charge of the Light Brigade" failed to keep them at bay. I just hope the desperate hogs have found fodder elsewhere and that their numbers aren't among our growing fatalities.

We walk into the kitchen now, and Xhosa holds up last night's *Mail and Guardian* newspaper, which he brought back from town after doing the weekly supply run this morning. Our government forum is featured on the front page—with a picture of the minister of the environment, confirming his intention to prohibit canned hunting.

"Window dressing?" comments an ever-cynical Thomas, as we seat ourselves.

Mireille pours coffee all around. "What d'you think, goddaughter? Is Mr. Minister telling us porkies again?" she quips, using one of her favored Yorkshire expressions.

"Sincerely hope not," I reply.

Our voices are upbeat, but underneath I am fighting deep-seated depression. A formidable group of allies has gathered around my project now, with Mireille at the helm, but there are times when all our united and dedicated efforts seem entirely unsuccessful.

"Is our minister lying to us?" I ponder out loud, taking up the national paper and running my eyes over the article. As a former hunter himself, the Afrikaner minister was quoted conceding publicly that "practices are taking place in this country that are not only unacceptable but utterly despicable."

Before I've finished reading, Harold has a rejoinder. "Well, you yourself said the minister's protestations have been completely ineffectual. No doubt a deliberate cover-up."

"True, Harry, he hasn't delivered in the past, but the minister's one of the only people in a position to change the status quo, and—well—it's good to finally see some genuine emotion coming from a man in his position."

Mireille stands behind my chair, drying her hands on a dishcloth. "His desk must be flooding over with hideous horror pictures. But will he prohibit the malpractices?" she demands.

Deep down, I also dread nothing further would be done.

"Where d'we stand?" she prompts.

"Well, firstly," Jason takes up the challenge, "we need to assess if the new draft policy document will effectively make any real difference. Then we could look at how to plug the loopholes."

"Even then, can we afford the luxury of time, waiting for these processes to roll out?" I retort.

"Hold that thought!" Mireille responds before I have a chance to further discuss the state of play. "I'll be back in a jiffy, once I've assisted with our hot breakfast." She disappears into the scullery. Miraculously, it seems, she's managing to rustle up a large saucepan of scrambled eggs and sausage over the single flame on a gas cylinder.

"So what exactly happened?" Harold asks Jason, while Mireille is out of the room. "Did the canned hunters stand up, clutching their nuts, and demand a showdown?"

"Pretty much," Jason responds, with a slight grin.

He goes on to describe in some detail the previous day's government forum and how it ended in disarray. The canned hunters' thinly disguised threats were a greater echo of the same intimidation tactics that had forced our project into deadlock.

Harold clears his throat conspiratorially. "Just between us girls—I think they're running scared."

"Wouldn't presume so, Harry," I retort.

"No, seriously, those guys're running out of testicles!" he concludes.

An amused grunt from the other men around the table—Jason,

Thomas, Xhosa, and a Dutch student who was volunteering his help.

Noting he's onto a good thing, Harold continues, "Now's the time to hit 'em where it hurts. They're on the run. I say go straight for the ghoolies!"

"Ow, that sounds painful!" responds Xhosa.

"No, seriously. This new legislation's got their testicles in a brace. Now's the moment to tighten the clamps."

There's a general titter, but I shake my head at him. "Harry, this is serious."

But he's on a roll, and I'm not sure he's even heard me. "You've been rattling cages for too long now, Linda. Stop the petitions and gentlemen's tactics, and go for the jugular, or better: the testes. Do a badger! Or even a Bobbitt!"

Peals of laughter.

"Okay. Let's get real here," Jason responds, bringing the group's attention back to the issue at hand. "Our problem is that the canned-hunting industry is dominated by the Afrikaner right wing—"

"Agreed," Harold notes, sobering up. "The *boytjies* with pro-hunting neo-Nazi affiliations."

"And international mafia links," Jason continues.

There's a pause.

"No, you're right," Harold responds, sounding very sober all of a sudden. "They have their sights set on the minister."

"Exactly," Jason replies.

Another pause.

"How seriously should one view all this?" asked Thomas, for whom the political maneuvering and intrigue remains somewhat baffling and academic.

"I'm saying," Harold continues, pointedly now, "if the minister's genuinely taking this on, he'd better watch his back. They'll be gunning for him, and his family."

A chilling silence is finally broken when Mireille returns with a breakfast tray of plates with steaming eggs and sausage on toast, sprinkled with chives and parsley from Nelson's surviving herb garden outside the kitchen door.

"Yum, *that* looks yummy!" Xhosa observes, standing up to help.

Relieved and grateful, I pass the plates to the others around the table. Everyone's focus for the next fifteen minutes is on their food, with occasional grunts of appreciation and disparate chit-chat.

As the plates are being removed, I take a closer look at the front-page story, with the minister's statement and an account of the dramatic events of the government forum. After the cover story, I turn to page five, where a responsible journalist reports on some of the legalized atrocities perpetrated against wildlife in our country. I force myself to read the article, bracing, as always, even though I know this review doesn't come close to exposing the extent of the horror.

"So where d'we stand, darling daughter?" chirps Mireille again as I lay the paper down again on the table, shaking my head grimly.

"Well, we mustn't let our guard down for a moment. This is far from over," I respond.

Already, Xhosa has discovered advertisements being posted on the Internet, inviting the international hunting circuit to participate in "what could be your last opportunity to trophy hunt the endangered White Lion." He has printed some gruesome evidence out and slaps the stack down on the kitchen table.

"Like a dead fish," Harold comments, taking up the papers to peruse the distasteful ads. "Only less appetizing."

"So what's the status?" Mireille prompts me persistently, her dish-cloth flung over her shoulder. She's on a mission; I don't know what it is yet, but I know she won't stop until she has the answer.

"Unfortunately, to the canned-hunting mind, this's just another opportunity to exploit," I summarize grimly. "The international trophy price for lions has increased—as from today."

"And here in Timbavati, what's the status?" she insists. "Is this ban on lion hunting going to be enforced?"

"As you've gathered, Godmum, we didn't even get close to addressing the question of trophy hunting in Timbavati in the government forum before all hell broke loose in the canned-hunting sector."

"Question is, if there's a moratorium imposed on hunting on our neighboring farms," Harold asks, "will we consider getting into bed with these neighbors?"

"Not exactly, Harry," I reply, with a raised eyebrow. "If they commit to a non-lion-hunting policy in some irrevocable way, then yes, of course we'd consider affiliation."

"But only on the basis that Marah, her cubs, their offspring, and any future White Lions born in the region would be protected by law, in perpetuity," Mireille comments, backing me up.

"What's the likelihood of that?" Harold asks. "Even with the nut-crunching pressure of the moratorium?"

"To tell you the truth, I don't see it happening," I conclude. "Money rather than ethics is the driving factor."

The *Mail and Guardian* article has printed a statement issued by the spokesperson for our neighboring private nature reserves, demanding the government revoke its moratorium because of the financial impact on their private reserve. Picking out a relevant sentence, I read: "We [the Timbavati Association] have sold permits for hunting to overseas visitors, and we have clients hunting in the veld as we speak."

I turn to Mireille. "So, to answer your question, Godmum, that's the current status." I pass the newspaper back to her with a shudder. "Hunters are in the field as we speak."

"So, to answer your question, Godmum: that's the current status," I pass the document over to her. "Hunters are in the field as we speak."

Outside, the incessant monotonous call of the tinker barbet, also known as the suicide bird, is starting to worry me because of its distinctive communication, like a tap drip-drip-dripping in one's head. For sanity's sake, I've been trying not to think of Aslan, King of kings, and the price that must have been escalating on his royal head.

Against this grim political backdrop, Marah's unique story is playing itself out. Watching the odds mount against her survival in the wild, my frustration has built up to breaking point. In my dreams, I've already opened the gate to her freedom, over and over again. But the reality is more challenging. This step may have seemed utterly simple, but the consequences could be catastrophic. By opening the gates and releasing the lions into our extended property, in defiance of the permit process, I could seal Marah's fate by bringing about law enforcement action against us.

"Trouble is, as our lawyers keep saying, 'Lions are dangerous animals, so they should be contained until we get full permission,'" Thomas points out.

"Yup—that's our lawyers' opinion," I reply.

I rethink their argument one more time. Keeping four dangerous animals captive on our land without the final permit is one matter; allowing these dangerous animals to roam free on this same land—which, though well fenced, is also surrounded by antagonistic neighbors—is another matter entirely.

"Their view is that this rash action could provide precisely the ammunition our opponents are waiting for," I explain further.

"So that's our legal advice, then?" Mireille asks.

"Yes," I explain. "But while their caution's valid, I'm starting to see the issue differently."

"How so? Please tell," Mireille encourages.

"Well, if I look back, I don't regret a single step I've taken," I explain. "But I know I'd live a lifetime of regret if I avoided taking action and failed to move the lions to our property when we had the chance."

Based on hard experience, as well as intuitive knowledge, I know there was no option but to forge ahead.

"True," Harold concedes. "Doors have slammed behind us. Thank our brass monkeys we took the gap. That momentary lifeline we seized of transferring lions into a sanctuary's now dead and buried. Problem is, we still don't have a permit."

Mireille backs me up. "Okay, so we still don't have a permit, but the royal family's safe. That's all that's important."

Jason sits opposite me at the table and he clears his throat, thinking carefully before he speaks. "Agreed, the lions are safe in our care. But I'm afraid we have to accept that keeping the pride in a five-acre safe haven's not the solution."

Everyone looks up at him keenly, anticipating what he's about to say.

"So, where to from here?" my godmother prompts.

"What's our alternative?" Harold inquires.

We all know the answer. It's been nearly a year, without the authorities making any decision on the future of Marah and her cubs. If there's any hope for Marah's future in the wild, we have to take the next bold step to freedom. Jason and I have been carefully weighing up this outcome, agonizingly watching the pendulum swing again and again.

Gathering my strength, I look at my colleagues hunched around the table like a war council worn out from attrition. It's much the same group that was gathered in council the day after our dramatic arrival in the DC3 troop carrier eleven months ago. But something in the bunker has shifted.

"Is there anything whatsoever still to be done vis-à-vis the permit process?" Mireille prompts Jason. "Any stone unturned?"

"Sadly, no, Godmum," I confirm, thinking back through the arduous and seemingly endless process. "We've done absolutely everything imaginable—and everything possible—to get that permit stamped."

"Stonewalled," observes Xhosa. "Simple. Been through the same process one hundred times now. There's nothing more that can be done, realistically."

"Interaction with authorities is an inevitable part of this process," Jason points out, invoking a communal sigh of frustration among our team. "We recognize that."

"But they mustn't get cute with us," Harold snaps. "How long's the permit process been now, two 'n a half years?"

"The bureaucratic red tape, or should we say red herrings, never ends," adds Xhosa. "Something's wrong."

"Chin up everyone. It'll all work out," Mireille affirms, with her most stalwart expression. "As for Marah, with our loving confidence and pride in our lioness's unusual abilities, she'll surely manage in the wild, and impress us all, when the time comes."

"No doubt about her unusual abilities," Jason concurs, with an unusually somber tone in his voice. "But all things considered, it's unrealistic to expect Marah's natural survival instincts to remain intact, especially after the sustained human imprinting she's had to endure."

"It's time to act," I conclude.

With her hands on her hips, Mireille looks deadly serious. Then she regards Jason, and every member of our team, in turn, before focusing on me again. "Are you saying we're prepared to open the gates to Marah's freedom, with or without a final permit?"

"Precisely," I affirm. "I'm the Keeper of the White Lions. I know on whose authority I act."

There's a solemn and intensely protracted silence.

CHAPTER 30

These Restrictions

NOVEMBER 1, 2005. AFTER A YEAR OF NAIL-BITING SUSPENSE, we are finally going ahead with the final stages of the release program. Tindall is carefully removing a dart of tranquilizing drug from Marah's flank. The final step of preparation for the lions—fitting their radio collars—is about to take place, in the cool early hours to ensure they are not put at any risk during the heat of the day.

Fortunately, the darting procedure has gone smoothly. To minimize the trauma, Jason and Tindall tranquilize all four members of the pride simultaneously. I'm not objecting—but nevertheless I can't help hovering over my sleeping cats now, like an overanxious mother. All four cats are asleep beside me. It's predawn, and I am right in the middle of the *boma*, together with my lions!

Jason looks up at me, and I note his face is emotional too. In all these months of waiting, he's often caught me unwittingly fixing my gaze on those metal gates and the ridiculous padlock that has held them shut.

"One little turn of the key—and our family'll be free." I whisper to him.

"Yup. Know what you're saying. Or we could simply leave the gate open 'by mistake' and let them walk to freedom right now. Believe me, their time's finally arriving. The collars are the last step."

I look down at Jason's agile hands, lovingly securing the device around Marah's neck. Jason's scientific colleagues have generously donated two leading-edge solar-powered GPS collars, which operate on sophisticated telemetry readings—and he's fitting one now. I stand anxiously, moving from foot to foot—calling on the presence of Maria to protect our sedated and vulnerable Lion Queen. Jason glances up at me with a broad grin. The collar fits. I smile back, nodding. This is an unspoken reference to our initial unsuccessful attempt to collar Marah on the day of her arrival. At the time, Jason argued it was the best opportunity to fit her collar, since she was already tranquilized. For health and safety reasons, he wanted to avoid darting her to do so later. He'd arranged with his colleagues to have the collars carefully made up and sized according to average lioness measurements.

However, when it came to actually fitting the collar that first day after landing in the DC3, Jason discovered Marah's neck was more than ten centimeters larger than average. Of course, I never doubted Marah was an exceptional lioness, but this came as an unexpected confirmation of her unusual size. Ever since then, Jason has been pondering whether White Lions might, in general, be larger than their tawny counterparts. Determining the accuracy of this hypothesis will require careful ongoing scientific study, which he and his team intend to pursue in due course.

For today, fitting the collars while the pride is still in their *boma,* asleep, allows us a chance to ensure the device is operating correctly before Marah and her pride disappear into the wilderness. And in order to limit Marah's period of sedation to an absolute minimum, Jason ensured the GPS function was already activated prior to entering the *boma.*

I look down to watch Jason tightening the screws with a custom-made device. It is vital Marah's collar isn't too tight, because it could strangle her if she gains weight, but it can't be too loose either, as it might get caught on branches, or her paw could get stuck in it while scratching her neck.

Jason moves on from Marah to tighten the screws on Letaba's collar now. We decided Letaba should wear the second tracking device, since he's the most daring of the two brothers and therefore most likely to stray in the eventuality of territorial patrols and showdowns with other lions. With Marah and her one son collared, Jason's thinking is that we'll pretty much know where to find the other two family members at any given time. Both collars are on, and Jason and Tindall move on to the other two cubs for routine checks.

Alone with Marah as she sleeps, I linger for a moment in the early morning light, crouching down to press my hands against her taut, muscular body. I feel her heart beating. I glance toward Jason and Tindall, who are putting drops in Regeus's eyes. On impulse, I lie down beside Marah again, just as I did during that epic flight over the highveld. Laying one arm around her warm, soft flank, it occurs to me this is exactly what Zihra did when dozing with her mother. Again, I breathe in that exquisite talcum-and-fresh-cut-hay scent. I don't care what anyone else may be thinking. This exquisite creature has determined every step I've taken since we found each other, five years ago. And now, for just one brief moment in cosmic time, I am able to be with her again! Words are totally inadequate—only purrs and roars could begin to express how I feel. The tears start welling and I simply can't stop them. That indescribable yearning to be cuddled up with her, as a member of the royal pride, is actually realizable—just for the briefest star-crossed instant. Every day the mother–daughter bond between us intensifies, and if I were granted just one wish, it would be to shapeshift and join Marah's pride in lioness form, forever one with my sublime lion family. I can understand why people want to tame, cage, hold, trap, box, and keep captive beautiful wild creatures, in the hope of capturing their essence. But, surely, the greatest gift you can offer your loved ones is freedom, so they can be themselves in all their magnificence.

Jason and Tindall have reversed the tranquilizer on all four lions. Over the past eleven months since the translocation to Timbavati, a new tranquilizing drug—Metadromedine—has been tested, which does not require that lions sleep it off overnight, and can be reversed by use of another drug, Ketamine. Having tested this out a number of times, Tindall is confident this combination is preferable to Dormacan. After he delivers the reversal drug intravenously to Marah and her cubs, he and Jason are promptly retreating, advising everyone else in our team to do the same. With Marah starting to emerge from her drugged state, I feel the full life force returning to her lithe body, and the umbilical bond between us growing ever stronger. When she was a cub, I thought of her as my daughter, but now it seems she is my mother—either way, no love in my life has ever felt so strong. Yet, in defiance of this overwhelming feeling of bondedness, I know I have to withdraw to allow Marah to wake up naturally with her own cubs. Tindall and the scientific team have already pulled out of the *boma,* and Jason is patiently waiting for me at the open gates, gesturing, with a hint of concern. But I can't resist lingering just a moment longer. Their moment in the sun will come! Lying here in the long, dry grass, as one of them, I glance toward those gates standing open. My emotions are totally overwhelming me again. Being here among my family, I can so clearly picture these four glorious sun creatures, padding their path into the rising sun, through the open gates, wild and free—as if I am walking alongside them.

Feeling Marah suddenly stir beside me and lift her head, I realize that, in my modest human form, I have to move out—now.

I force myself to extricate and walk swiftly through the grasslands toward the gates.

"Move!" Jason instructs. "Marah's already on her feet!"

"Soon," I say as I pass through, remembering those words I once heard Marah speak, while held captive in the dungeons of the zoo. "Soon they'll be free."

He snaps the padlock shut behind me.

From the safe distance of the viewing hide, out of sight, Jason and I watch and wait for the rest of the pride to wake. Our team returns to Base Camp, with Tindall on standby should we need him again.

Though the chink in the viewing hide, we observe beautiful Queen Marah move over to her cubs, anxiously, on slightly unsteady paws. Letaba wakes, lifts his head, then flops down again. Zihra shakes herself awake, then staggers over to the carcass Jason left them. Finally, they are all wide awake and we watch closely to see how they respond. The two boys have joined their sister in feeding. They look absolutely fine, including Regeus, who tucks in with gusto. But Marah has positioned herself nearby, standing stern and intimidating, without eating at all. I'm hoping she'll accept the newly fastened contraption around her neck without too much resistance. Instead I find myself flinching as I observe her displeasure. She shakes her head, without attempting to dislodge it with her paw. She wears her encumbrance with dignity, but from another toss of her majestic head, it's clear that she's not impressed. And when the Queen's not impressed, there are consequences.

Jason and I continue observing to make absolutely sure the lions have emerged fully from their tranquilized state. With the cubs contentedly feeding on the carcass, Marah finally settles down to join them, momentarily distracting herself from the uncomfortable band around her neck. Carefully assessing the situation, and concluding all's well, Jason and I decide to head back to camp ourselves for a quick lunch.

I'm keen to return to see how my Godmum is doing. It's entirely unlike her to have missed today's big event. She insists we go ahead with our careful plans for the collaring, even though she doesn't feel strong enough for the early rise this morning.

Nearly twelve hours have passed since we fitted the collars first thing this morning. The sun's setting, and we've returned to our lions. Jason, Godmum, and I. She spent the day in bed, but says she's "fighting fit" again. Thomas was monitoring in the interim. We take over, and Jason tests his telemetry equipment to ensure the devices are operating. Jason points the aerial out of the Land Rover window toward the pride, now full-bellied and sleeping contentedly. He suddenly turns to me, looking perplexed. Both radio collars are malfunctioning. He tries the equipment again, shaking his head.

"I don't get it," he comments, totally flummoxed. "Thomas and I activated the collars, and just to make sure, we tested them three times this morning before going into the *boma*. They were working perfectly. Then I tested them one final time when we fitted them in the *boma!*"

Jason unhitches the radio from his belt and crosschecks: "Thomas, Thomas, come in Thomas."

"Thomas standing by," crackles back.

"Did you check the radio collars this afternoon, Tommy?"

"Affirmative. Working fine."

"Hmm, neither is working now," Jason ponders, turning to us. "They're guaranteed to function minimum eighteen months."

Mireille and I consider a moment. Meanwhile, Jason tests the equipment one more time before laying it down in frustration. Both collars are malfunctioning.

"So where's that leave us?" Mireille asks.

"Catastrophe," Jason replies factually. "We'll need to replace the collars with new ones, which means tranquilizing the lions all over again!"

"Oh, dearie me!"

"Wouldn't do it before one week's time," Jason notes, shaking his head. "Really important not to dart the lions too soon after today's tranquilization."

I'm concerned but can't help smiling to myself. That little "inner voice" tells me Marah herself may have "scrambled" the technology.

"Give me a moment, please Jase," I ask. "And Godmum, if you don't mind: no talking please—we need to concentrate our minds on the lions."

To test my hypothesis, I have to sit in absolute stillness, tuning in to Marah and her cubs. Accordingly, our usually chirpy chairperson forces herself to keep dead still. Jason has also fallen silent, with a mixed expression of bewilderment and frustration on his face.

I calm my mind and open my heart to my lion family. They are stretching languidly now, with full stomachs, reluctantly waking up again after their day's siesta. Letaba gives a massive yawn, displaying his pink tongue and impressive not-so-juvenile teeth. His fluffy mane is now partially pressed down by the radio collar fastened around his neck. He yawns again even wider than before, and I imagine he's going to get up in a moment, but instead, he flops, with all his weight, onto his brother, and promptly falls asleep again. Again, I concentrate on clearing my head of rational concerns and worries, and try to reach that meditative pranic state of peace and calm. And, as always, a surge of overwhelming love fills my heart. The cubs are still asleep, and I focus on Marah's majestic face. She's sitting poised, with her paws straight in front of her in the classic sphinx position. Suddenly she looks up at me, and those Nefertiti eyes beam straight into my soul. At that moment, her transmitted words resound in my head, just as they did on that occasion when Mireille and I visited her just before her rescue from the zoo. I have her answer about the radio collars. It's crystal clear. And it's not surprising:

We don't appreciate these restrictions, the Queen informs me. *Why d'you use telemetry when you could employ telepathy?*

As always, I feel utterly humbled. In my mind, I try to explain to Queen Marah that the telepathic skills of our monitoring team (myself included) would be hopelessly inadequate in tracking the pride in dense Timbavati bushveld.

"Please understand, Marah," I murmur under my breath. "For your family's safety—as well as our peace of mind—we need you and your cubs to wear these tracking collars."

From her demeanor, I see she's heard me. She remains poised in her statuesque, regal pose, intently transmitting that searing gaze like a laser beam straight into my soul. But suddenly she relaxes, and I watch how she gives a deep sigh, as if to say, with utmost tolerance: *Hmmm. Your limitations are understood, beloved daughter. So be it.*

After gaining Marah's sanction, I turn to Jason, encouraging him to go ahead with replacing the radio collars.

"I'm sure we'll have better luck next time," I say, studying the queen closely. "I don't imagine we'll have any more resistance or interference from Marah."

"Hmmm," Jason ponders.

It is so idyllic with our lions that all three of us are reluctant to head back to camp. Instead, we stay on, watching. Before we know it, a half hour has passed. While Marah endures this band around her neck with grace and dignity, I'm beginning to suspect, from his audacious behavior, that Prince Letaba, by contrast, is secretly proud to have been singled out as the dominant male over his brother. Marah is suddenly directing her gaze at me again, and once again I hear her transmitted message. It seems clear enough.

"Jase," I request on impulse. "Test the collars once more, if you don't mind."

"You serious?"

"Yes. Seriously. Try them again."

Patiently, Jason removes the aerial and once again points it out the window in the pride's direction. Then he joins the aerial to the handheld telemetry set and examines the screen carefully, just as he did many times in assessing the malfunction.

"You're not gonna believe this," he comments, turning to me. "Both collars are suddenly working!"

Mireille and I laugh out loud, while Jason simply shakes his head. He's come to accept more than the odd weird and wonderful occurrence around Marah and her family.

NOVEMBER 2, 2005. I sit on a spectacular promontory of precipitous rock frontage, looking out over a vast expanse of lowveld, stretching out to the faraway Drakensburg Mountains in the east, without a single human dwelling in sight. It's been a long, hot day in the dry, winter sun. Day's end. With the radio collars fixed and functioning as from yesterday, no practical detail remains to delay the release of the lions. We are ready! On my own now, I'm preparing for the biggest moment of my life: the freedom of Marah, the lioness to whom I've pledged my life! Alone, apart from Sam and Cibi, and all of Nature stretched out before me.

I called this vantage point Lion Lookout. It was two hours' walk from Base Camp, and one of my favorite places to meditate and dream. From this high point, I can see the sun sinking down toward the horizon. Beyond the lush evergreen Tsau River snaking its way below me, the bushveld lies dry and parched, like the skeletal scene from *The Lion King* before the return of the true monarch. These past barren months have reminded me of Scar's derelict wasteland, many times over. All the while, internally, my heart mirrors this desolation and frustration at being denied Marah's reinstatement to her rightful lands. Now, all this is set to change!

In just two days' time, Marah, Queen of Lions, will walk free!

This outing with Sam and Cibi will be my last before the grand opening of the gates, and I have no doubt that this high promontory where I sit now will soon become Marah's favorite haunt! From here, the lions' *boma* is about eleven kilometers away—and I imagine the queen restlessly pacing her eastern fence line in anticipation of her imminent release.

Putting my binoculars to my eyes, I survey the open stretch of savanna laid out below me, which Marah will soon roam. We've named it in her honor: The Marah—a lighthearted play on Kenya's Masai Mara. From here, I can see a newly settled herd of some sixty wildebeest, brought in two weeks ago from a nearby reserve by articulated truck, as a final preparation before the pride's release. Like the other three herds already resident, they look totally at home now, although struggling to find grazing. I spot a herd of waterbuck in the distance, distinguished by the white rings around their rumps. It's a relief to see these lovely creatures have weathered the drought. And there's a small dazzle of zebra and some last surviving impala rams in a bachelor herd, on the distant plain. No kudu herds to be seen, nor bushbuck, warthog, or nyala. These species have been particularly hit hard by the drought, but I pray there are some survivors. Despite the long months of attrition, the atmosphere feels very different now, on the brink of our biggest step yet.

Up here, overlooking the natural hunting grounds, I can't help thinking of that grand opening scene from *The Lion King* when all the animals of the bushveld gathered to pay homage to the newborn royal cub, as the King and Queen of beasts stood high above them, looking out over their kingdom from the edge of Pride Rock. Sitting on my log, with Nelia's walking stick in my right hand, like a matriarch looking proudly out over these lands, I feel the tingling parallels in my fingertips—knowing that the real-life Lion Queen will lead her cubs up to this promontory, and here she will stand tall, surveying her pridelands to the distant horizon, as all other natural kingdoms gather in homage.

The radio crackles; Jason asking for my ETA. I inform him of my location, and the route I'll be heading back. He indicates he'll collect the dogs and me by Land Rover at Mamba crossing, before night closes in completely.

Heading back down through the darkening undergrowth, I think of Mireille, and how elated she must be feeling. No doubt, the Grandmother of the White Lions will be preparing a hearty supper. It will take a lot of doing to persuade her to retire early tonight.

With the epic event scheduled for the morning after tomorrow, the intervening day has been declared a Day of Rest in anticipation. But no one in their right mind could sit around resting while waiting for this big moment! Not least our fired-up team, and least of all Mireille Vince herself. She has plans. A while back, my Godmum was invited to be the honored guest at a prize-giving event at our local community school, and she is not going to let them down. Besides, in her mind, nothing could be more appropriate on the eve of Marah's Big Day than to celebrate with the local Tsonga community. I wholeheartedly agree. We've had forty White Lion fluffy teddies sewn up, along with one hundred T-shirts and three thousand White Lion badges manufactured for the occasion, so I'll be joining her tomorrow to help hand these out.

Not one to wait around while bureaucracies shuffle paper over the past eleven months, Godmum has been drawn into educational and poverty-relief programs with the local community. In between all the White Lion duties, she and I have been developing an ecoeducational curriculum, using the iconic White Lions as a motivational symbol. Recently, the neighboring community area around the White Lions' ancestral territories was declared one of the "poverty nodes" of South Africa. In some of the schools with which we'd worked, the classrooms are no more than empty shells, crammed with children attempting to get through the syllabus without the aid of a teacher or even textbooks. Some of the classes take place outside on the dry, dusty earth, under a tree. Tragically, many of the children come from child-headed households, where both mother and father have died from AIDS, and these little ones are left as the sole breadwinner for their entire family of younger siblings. The program we've been developing is designed to bring assistance and hope into the schools, as well as the greater community, in these poverty-stricken areas, where morale is low.

During the last few months, Mireille and I have made countless enthusiastic visits to several Tsonga schools in the region to pursue this challenging but deeply fulfilling work, which I view as directly related to the White Lions' spirit of hope and enlightenment. Funjwa Lower Primary is our most exciting project. The little school's situated in the small village of Acornhoek, approximately an hour's drive south from the lions' land. The principal, Daphne Mhaule, is a miracle worker who constantly seeks to improve the lives of both her pupils and their families. Watching Mireille and Daphne meet for the first time was, for me, like witnessing a reunion of old souls. They soon discovered the Tsonga community in this region attends a Swiss Mission Church, which, amazingly, was one of the church buildings built and established by Mireille's missionary parents over sixty years ago when she herself was a little adopted urchin.

Daphne sings in the choir at the Swiss Mission Church every Sunday, and Mireille and Daphne began regularly attending services together in the simple brick-and-mortar building, which pulsates with African choirs and is well attended by people, goats, and chickens.

Somehow, everything has come full circle, and Mireille has found her life's purpose. So, there's no point arguing with the *Kokwane* of White Lions when this matriarch has her mind set. Instead of a Day of Rest in the lead-up to D-day, Mireille will be celebrating in the heat and dust, with the people she's loved since childhood. And the lions and I will be celebrating with her.

CHAPTER 31

Mireille Star

NOVEMBER 3, 2005. THE DAY BEFORE THE LIONS' RELEASE. Outside in the dust, under a large tree, Mireille, Xhosa, and I wait expectantly for the celebrations to begin. Around us, more than one thousand faces are spellbound, in anticipation.

What with all the excitement building up to Marah's big day, it's not surprising my Godmum has been temporarily out of action. She's recovered her robust strength, and true to form, she is at the center of everything, orchestrating events.

Daphne Mhaule stands in front of all her students, directing and smiling warmly as she looks out at the milling ocean of eager faces. Then she swivels on her heels and beckons to Mireille.

"*Kokwane,* come here!"

"Yahoooo?" Mireille calls back.

"Come and sit here with me, *Kokwane tangala tobasa,*" Daphne instructs, using the phrase Grandmother of the White Lions in Tsonga.

Mireille marches across the makeshift performing stage of grass mats laid out in the dust so as to join the sturdy, warm-hearted schoolmistress on one of the two plastic chairs. I smile, watching them seated side by side, two matriarchs, yin and yang, waiting for the proceedings to begin.

The teachers wander around, settling the children into their respective places. Many kids are crammed under the ample shade of the huilboerboon's vast natural canopy, but others have to make do with the heat and dust. On wooden tree stumps around the periphery are parents, aunts, uncles, grandparents, and other local community members, all seated under colorful umbrellas, having gathered from far and wide to hear the children's tales and watch their performances.

Everyone participates in our ecoeducational programs, teachers and students alike. Our approach is to encourage them to create expressions of joy and celebration for the return of the White Lions to their natural habitat. With permission from their teachers, our first step is to invite each child to express themselves in whichever medium or subject is their strength: painting, dancing, writing, beadwork, pottery, or wood carving.

As Maria taught me, the legends of the White Lions go back into the hazy mists of time, but much of the great knowledge has been lost, since the storytellers themselves have died out, leaving no legacy. But a new story is being scribed.

Daphne stands up and calls for silence. The excited chatter of nearly a thousand five- to ten-year-olds immediately dies down . . . and if the proverbial pin were to drop on the dusty ground, I believe I'd hear it.

Xhosa steps forward and gives an exaggerated bow, invoking roars of giggles and laughter. Then he swings into his rap performance in dedication to the White Lions, as mounting excitement swells in the sea of children. Everyone is standing to get a better view, and soon the spellbound little bodies are swaying to the left and right, in waves, clapping their hands in time to the rhythm Xhosa is creating. After he brings his performance to a close, there's a momentary hush.

"So," Xhosa announces in his most theatrical tone, feeding into the eager silence as he looks out into the crowd. "Where d'you think . . . the White Lions come from?"

"From God," announces one bold little voice.

"Aha!" responds Xhosa.

"From Timbavati," says another.

Suddenly, the crowd shouts in unison. "Timba-Vaaaaati!"

"So tell me, young ladies and gentlemen: what does Timbavati mean?" Xhosa asks.

"Stars! Place of Stars! Starlions!" Different versions come back.

"And what sound does a lion make?"

Momentary silence.

"Huh?" pronounces Xhosa. "Are there really no lions out there, ladies and gentlemen? Only sheep?"

He peers into the crowd again, as if searching.

"I'll ask again," he says. "What sound does a lion make?"

Suddenly the hush transforms into a monumental *Roooooooo-aaaaaaaaaaarrrrrrrrrrrrrr!*

The young voices reverberate in unison—a cacophony of small cubs suddenly empowered by the great lion spirit. I think back to the frightened little urchins I met on my first day at this school. A few months back, these same brave, little souls were so withdrawn and timid that many were too afraid to put their hands up, let alone speak out. But when we showed them pictures of Marah, the Queen who has returned to her royal lands, together with her cubs, I watched a flame ignite in each child! The White Lions did the rest, transmitting their sublime and radiant force of love, hope, pride, and leadership. Now most of these little lion-hearts are roaring their courage and excitement into the world.

Suddenly there is a little White Lion character, with a body costume made of a recycled maize-meal sack. Then, after some jostling, one child steps forward, like a news reporter making an announcement:

"Marah was born in Bethlehem on Christmas Day. She was taken away from us and sent to the United States, England, China, Russia, etc. She was imprisoned and the sun didn't shine! But in 2004, an angel came to her rescue."

And all the kids break into song!

> Alala! Marah, Alala!
> Marah, Marah, you are the Queen of Lions.
> Like Nelson Mandela, you spent your whole life in prison,
> because people are scared of your greatness!
> Now you're gonna be free, Marah!
> Alala! Marah, Alala!

We are witnessing a cultural renaissance out of the humblest circumstances! When the story of the lions was introduced to children, it rekindled in these little ones a connection with Nature and heritage and knowledge, bringing out leadership qualities and self-worth. They visibly lit up—little lion-hearts performing with all their hearts and souls . . . simply adorable!

I smile as I spot Mireille, perched on her seat beside Daphne, glowing with excitement. I can't help thinking of that once-orphaned child, returned as an elder to give something back to the orphans of Africa.

Mireille is radiating delight—clapping her hands in time to the rhythm, shifting her weight from side to side in her plastic seat. This work is deeply inspirational and so wonderfully heartening. For Mireille and me, it is such an invigorating contrast to the embattled conservation arena. I simply can't imagine my life and this project without my beloved godmother—her wisdom and constant encouragement keep me focused on the positive aspects of this challenging work and keep me driven to continue the legacy created by Maria Khosa.

Another child steps forward, shiny faced and bright eyed. He's hanging on to a miniature Land Rover he's constructed out of recycled wire. It is complete with turning wheels and opening doors—a superb piece of craftsmanship—to which he's attached a long shaft and steering wheel, enabling him to drive it around in the dust. In our program, we've actively encouraged the use of recycled materials in the kids' presentations, to promote a sense of inventiveness as well as environmental awareness. The results are innovative and delightful.

After more jostling, additional performers appear, dressed in different animal guises: the crocodile's scaly costume, made of recycled metal bottle tops; the tiny elephant's flapping ears, made of cardboard; zebra costumes, made from recycled wire frames and strips of discarded rubber tire. A group of kids hop around in hessian sacks, representing a pride of tawny lions. A performance begins with a whole tapestry of different arts—dance, drumming, poetry, singing, acting—all woven together to tell a delightful tale, with different characters playing different roles. I haven't seen this story before, but shortly after it begins, I notice there is a medicine woman figure, dressed up just as Maria Khosa once dressed, in colorful fabrics with lion motifs. Suddenly I realize that, in fact, this little actress *is* depicting Maria Khosa, who has become a legendary figure in these parts.

The child with the wire Land Rover comes to center stage, driving his miniature wire vehicle through the dust with great dexterity. But now his vehicle is surrounded by the gang of kids in lion costumes, all growling and snarling. A simulation of my own story! I'm dumbstruck. It's a retelling of that night in 1991, when a group of terrified companions and I were trapped in the middle of a pride of agitated lions, with no way out—until Maria Khosa, Lion Queen of Timbavati, came to our rescue. This story has become famous in this community; the children from Funjwa School are reinventing it in their own unique way!

So heartwarming! The little Maria Khosa figure walks through the gang of lions, parting the predators like the Red Sea and shaking their hands as she walks, muttering in Tsonga: "You are my mother, my father, my family. My lion brothers and sisters, you will never harm me. . . ."

The little actress has a doll strapped, like a baby, to her back—just as Maria had on that bizarre night more than a decade ago. Suddenly, there's a little Linda figure! She walks like me, she talks like me, she's bossy like me, she's odd like me. Only she is seven years old, dark skinned, and all of three-foot-three tall. I catch Mireille's eye—she's laughing delightedly, and I can't stop a fit of stomachaching giggles! It's so delightful to see myself translated into history in this quirky way.

After the play ends, the teachers and performers and audience all look exuberant with the results of their shared efforts. It's prize-giving time, and my doughty godmother is on her feet again, handing out the white lion teddies. "Still on my pins, and going strong!" she declares. "Lovin' every bit of it! This is my moment, wouldn't change it for anything!"

Concerned about her stamina after a day in the heat and dust, I offer to take over from her, but she's in full swing.

Giggling heartily, she announces, "If my stern old parents could only see me now!"

As the prize-giving draws to a close and Mireille bends down to pin a White Lion badge to a tiny child, a document slips from her shoulder bag. I reach into the dust to retrieve it, but before I can hand it over to her, everyone is on their feet simultaneously, stamping up clouds of dust and dancing delightedly to the pounding of drums. The celebratory singing reaches a crescendo of excitement, and Daphne puts a whistle to her mouth—*Phewwwww! Phewwwww! Pheww—Phewwwww!* Not to silence the throngs, but to up the noise levels, in time to the African rhythms. A livewire of a headmistress. What a treasured moment! I am totally overwhelmed by the vibrant, joyous sharing of this communal moment! For me, this moment will last an eternity.

In among the throngs, Mireille turns to me, flushed with excitement, rhythmically shifting her weight from side to side with an exaggerated waggle.

"Nowhere but Africa can this joyous rhythm be found!" she shouts. "Goddaughter, thanks to you and the White Lions, I'm back!"

Again, I reach out to her to give her the document I retrieved, but she's whisked off again by the ocean of excitable children in the heat and dust and dancing—and, suddenly, there are a multitude of little bobbling heads between my godmother and me.

Looking down at the document, I register some of the contents. It is a diagnosis from Mireille's British doctor . . . and, to my absolute incomprehension and rising horror, I read the words ". . . with sincere regret that we inform you that the clinical tests have confirmed advanced Grade 3 malignancy of the duodenum . . ."

Immobilized, I am in complete shock. All around me, the cultural event is in full swing, but I am frozen stiff, unable to move in the midst of the jostling fray.

I look at these all excited little faces—this heightened moment could be the turning point of their lives!

The drums pulse. Everyone's singing. I am anchored in place as the ocean of school kids circle all around me, stamping and clapping and beating up the dust to the rhythm of the pounding drums. Mireille can't be kept down. In the distance, I see her swaying back and forth in the midst of the gyrating children, side by side with her dear friend Daphne, two matriarchs dancing with primal rhythm, joined by teachers and community members, engulfed by dancing kids.

Dancing like there's no tomorrow.

JANUARY 2006. Bereft, I'm with Daphne, Axon, Nelias, Nelson, Jason, and our team, preparing to walk the slow route to the baobab tree, the sacred site so beloved by Mireille, and where she always said she wanted her ashes to be spread one day. With us is Mireille's beautiful daughter-in-law, Liz, and her beloved son, Ray, whom I've met only once before in my life. He carries his mother's ashes.

Ray and I are almost exactly the same age. We met just under a year ago on Christmas, when I traveled to Leeds to celebrate the successful acquisition of the sacred lands with Mireille. We spent a little more than an hour together, in which time he gave his blessing to his mother's support of my unusual project. It was all too brief, yet it instantly felt like we were siblings. And I was so grateful to have this extraordinary man as a newfound brother: highly sensitive, loving, generous, spirited—like his mother, yet different—who recognized me as the sister he'd always wanted and never had, a man who accepted my work unconditionally. Now our mother is dead. Both Ray and I are left bewildered and devastated, like two orphaned lion cubs, looking up to the stars and questioning the meaning of existence.

Mireille departed on December 12.

Over the last few weeks, I sat by her bedside, holding her hand, and she was clearer and more resolute than ever. She made lists of any and all unfinished matters that needed attention. But she refused any treatment, traditional or alternative.

"I've done what I came to do," she told me, radiant and silver-haired, propped up on a comfortable chair with big cushions, preparing for her final adventure.

"Don't cry for me, darling daughter," she said, observing my irrepressible sadness. "I need you to help me to be brave."

She ensured she was surrounded by photographs of Marah, Letaba, Regeus, and Zihra, and then in the last days, when she went to the hospital, she insisted that the photographs of her radiant brood go with her, her lion family she'd helped rescue from the hunter's bullet.

Her dying words to me were: "We'll never be parted. Now go, open those gates. I'll be with you!"

As Ray and I walk slowly together down the river sand toward the baobab, heads bowed, Daphne and the others start a chant of aching lament in the African tradition. And my heart weeps rivers.

CHAPTER 32

First Steps in Wonderland

February 13, 2006. 7:00 a.m. Mireille left us just over two months earlier, and I've been mourning her death ever since, a dense black period of grief and loss and ineffable sadness. Jason tried to comfort me many times with words of encouragement, but what is there to say? Only that Mireille would have wanted the White Lion plan to go on.

This morning, sitting under the baobab tree at dawn, I start to register the landscape around me for the first time. The last of the festive season in the bushveld is fading. Christmas came and went, and I barely noticed. Unlike the northern hemisphere of white Christmases, here in Timbavati, December through February is the height of summer.

I look around me. Defying the drought, the trees seem to be making every effort to decorate themselves in their Sunday best, dangling with long-forgotten Christmas decorations, faded flowers and blooms on desperately dry branches. I see that the sickle bush, so named because of its cruel sickle thorns, has transformed magically into bright yellow and pink pompoms, and the cluster-leaf terminalia tree is spangled with four-sided star ornaments, once a brilliant burgundy, now bleached in the summer sun. Normally this time of year in Timbavati is an enchanted time, a festive, sunny season, but over the past two months the bleakness in my heart wiped out the days, one after the other, and I simply couldn't see what there was to celebrate.

The fact that Christmas was Marah's sacred birthday made the occasion all the more painful for me. I should have given orders for her release on December 25th—it was her birthright, no less—but I didn't feel brave or strong enough to face the consequences: the total onslaught from neighbors; the legal battles to prevent seizure and confiscation of the lions; the media hype; even the best wishes of our increasing circle of supporters. I simply wasn't ready.

These past few weeks after Mireille's passing, I could barely function, weighed down by a leaden heaviness, mourning the totally unexpected, cruel loss of my newfound godmother, while lamenting Marah's continued incarceration—neither of which tragedies were within my power to put right.

Yet all the while, all around me, operations of the White Lion project continued. Jason never let up. I was vaguely aware of the teams laying bales of lucerne and pellets of Boskos for the starving animals, a concentrated mix of indigenous leaves and grasses, all over the lands, particularly at water points. Timbavati had summer rainfall, but this year the rains simply didn't fall. And with the searing heat, we suffered even greater animal casualties. All around me, I've seen death and destruction. A wasteland waiting for rains that won't come.

As for all the practicalities in our project, I was incapable of assisting. Instead, I spent night after night alone at the baobab tree, where Mireille's ashes were scattered, sleeping out under the stars, tuning in to the land and the lions, my destiny and theirs. Knowing that one day, after grieving my loss long enough, I would be able to proceed with what Mireille wanted most: freedom.

Mireille had a very dear friend, Dorothy Shields, who, appropriately, had had a star named after Mireille—a star positioned at the foot of the Southern Cross. Looking up at her star on my many endless nights alone, I had cause to remember the belief of the indigenous people that the White Lions are starbeings, and that Timbavati itself means "the place where starlions came down." This time-honored founding belief—from Ancient Egypt in the north of Africa to the Bushman and Tsonga people in the south, those people so beloved of Mireille—that truly great people, whether kings, queens, or high priestesses, became lions in death and returned to the stars, took on even greater meaning for me now.

Many nights I lay awake all night under the stars, watching the Mireille star shine bright beneath the Southern Cross and feeling the presence of Queen Maria too. Somehow, it seemed these two great matriarchs were working together from the ancestral realms. I felt Maria's unfailing courage and Mireille's unconditional generosity of spirit even stronger than before. Their means of effecting positive change on Earth seemed even more powerful from those realms than their achievements in physical form.

Dreams are the means by which my shaman teacher often sent messages to me from the ancestral world, but over the past year of operating this project on the ground, I've been so fraught with decision-making and practical measures that I tend to drop into an exhausted coma at night without allowing these messages to come through.

Sleeping out beneath the wise branches of this ancient tree of life, under the cosmic skies, lying directly on Mother Earth's warm, nurturing body, with only a mat beneath me and a blanket for cover, changed everything. The meaningless irregularities of human law have come into alignment with a divine plan. When Mireille died so suddenly, I began doubting the success of my project and fearing failure. But last night, in meditation, an imperative from ancestral wisdom came flowing into my consciousness with the clarity of a mountain stream, direct from its source: *Delay no longer. Human wrangling and human agendas cannot hamper the future of Nature's most sacred animal. Gather your strength. Enough grief. Time for action.*

Finally, the time for action has come. In the tranquility of early morning, a duo of woodland kingfishers herald the onset of day. After another of my all-night vigils at the baobab, Jason has arrived to collect me. He spent last night monitoring the lions on his own.

Although I didn't sleep at all, at last I feel whole again and deeply at peace with the universe.

Nothing and no one will stop me now. The electric fences are up and running; the barricade is complete; the pipeline is laid; the collars are fixed; the telemetry is operational. All preparations are in place, and I'm prepared too. It's time.

"You ready, Jase?"

"Absolutely. You?"

"Finally. Yes. I'm ready."

We arrive at Base Camp, and I walk into the kitchen, feeling like I'm treading on air. The dogs are bounding around me. I'm so excited! It's utterly liberating knowing we are about take action at long last!

Jason is clear and focused, radioing the team to gather in fifteen minutes for a meeting.

As Jason walks into the office, Xhosa, Thomas, and two foreign volunteers who joined us recently look up expectantly from their breakfast, as if they can smell change in the air.

"Thomas—arrange for the collection of a wildebeest carcass," Jason instructs. "Xhosa—double-check those *boma* keys."

"Wait for it!" Xhosa declares, staring directly at me. I smile and give him the nod.

"Put on your crash helmets, everybody!" I announce. "As God-mum would say: tomorrow we're gonna burn rubber!"

"Yes! I knew it!" Xhosa is bouncing up and down in his chair, still holding his porridge spoon in one hand.

"Correct. We release the lions at dawn," Jason announces. "We've talked through procedure many times. Now it's for real. No margin for error."

"Phew. About time!" I hear Thomas's laconic remark as I stroll out of the kitchen; then he calls after me, "But still no permit—sure it's not a rash step?"

I keep walking. I'm in the office, closing my files, one after the other, and moving them from the desk to the bookshelf. The permit application file, the letters to authorities, the legal letters file. The canned-hunting file is also open on the desk. I shut that too. Since the canned-hunting "storm-out" of the government forum meeting four months ago, the situation has drastically worsened. The minister's pronouncements were bold at the time but have fizzled since. The facts speak for themselves. Sanctuaries and reintroduction programs are still being denied permits, while permission is freely granted to hold lions in cages, circuses, and captive-breeding camps for commercial-hunting purposes. Big money brags loudest. No sooner did the minister make his bold declaration than he retracted his draft policy and backpedaled fast—with the canned-hunting consortiums after him, baying for blood. As a former hunter himself, he is viewed as a traitor, and they want to bring him down. So he is running scared, and in his wake all national and provincial legislation has been stalled and shelved. Meanwhile, it is big business as usual for the canned-hunting industry—only bigger and even worse.

Appallingly, the status quo is the same. But everything in our world is about to change. Marah and her family will finally be free!

IT'S 4:00 P.M. EVERYONE IS EXCITED and exhausted simultaneously. Outside, there's a build-up of dense cumulus clouds, and inside there's a build-up of intensity—almost to the breaking point. We've spent the whole day finalizing last details and going through protocols yet another time. Who's responsible for making the drop of the carcass; who monitors the lions while the carcass is put out; who drives the vehicle for the drop-off; who drives the monitoring vehicle; who opens the gate; who monitors the lions while the gate is being opened; who carries radios; who carries keys. We've considered every conceivable "what if" scenario. What if the lions panic and charge out of the *boma,* heading for the perimeter fences? What if, in all their excitement, they actually break out of the external perimeter fence and we have to track them and dart them before they are shot and killed as "problem animals"? What if they are too frightened to leave the *boma* at all? What if they split up, and then we can't find the two who aren't wearing radio collars? Jason has an intimate understanding of lion behavior in general, so he has a pretty good guess how the sequence is likely to pan out. But we both know that Nature invariably breaks the textbook rules, so we are allowing for unexpected twists and turns.

At day's end, doing the final checklist, I think of Mireille and how she and her Swiss notebook would have risen to this occasion, cross-checking, and ticking off lists. Ah, Godmum!

There's also the question of who will chaperone the camera crew. Having each tense moment recorded and then, very possibly, exposed to the world adds immense additional tension to the event. If it were up to Jason and me, we'd prefer to live the moment out of the public eye. But knowing what I do about Marah's mission to help save humanity, it would be selfish and deeply wrong to keep the Queen of Lions all to myself.

Under normal circumstances, the film crew who started making the documentary a year back would have covered this story as well. However, over the intervening period since they filmed here, we have been disappointed by their lack of thoroughness and background research. In fact, we were shocked to realize the production was putting dangerous misinformation into the public domain—which, wittingly or unwittingly, supported the canned-hunting industry. Finally, I made the difficult decision of dissociating from this production entirely. Their final product subsequently went on to the international circuit, then thankfully was withdrawn due to public outcry at its factual inaccuracies and misplaced support of the canned-hunting industry. But they resurrected the documentary again, having removed the canned-hunting promotional sections and left in interviews with "authorities" expounding the view that White Lions would never survive in the wild. I reflected on the ego of these so-called experts, pontificating without evidence and without giving Nature a chance. Unfortunately, this convenient argument has since been taken up by the canned-hunting industry to justify keeping White Lions in cages. With all the other challenges facing Marah, I've watched how the man-made pressures and vested interests keep mounting against her on all fronts. So now, as I take this giant step to allow her a chance to prove herself, despite all the obstacles humans have placed in her way, I pray she will succeed in the wild, against all odds.

A National Geographic crew have filmed Marah's story over the past few months, impressing us with their meticulous wildlife filmmaking methods and respectful approach to the cats and their territorial space. All things considered, it is important that this film crew should have the rights to cover this historic moment. So Jason has gotten the message to them that we are planning the release tomorrow, and two cameramen have joined us this evening for the final dry run. They'll be spending the night in our temporary accommodation, in tents beside the Tsau River.

All prepped and raring to go, our whole team has finally dispersed, and I am finally preparing for bed.

Beaming from ear to ear, Xhosa pops his head out of the bathroom, toothbrush in hand, echoing Godmum's words, "Parachutes inflated, team! Weeee! Here we go—gonna be quite a rush! Get your beauty sleep, everyone. Tomorrow's on—come hell or high water!"

Something in my bones tells me that Xhosa has just given us a weather forecast.

It's 3:00 a.m. The team's gathered around the kitchen table again, drenched with rainwater.

"Wish you hadn't said that, X!" I comment in a mock scolding voice. "Now all hell's broken loose, and high waters are everywhere!"

"And that's before we've even gotten close to opening the gates," Jason adds, shaking his head.

"Sorry, Linda; sorry, Jason!' Xhosa responds, his dreadlocks bedraggled.

We've gathered in the kitchen without lights, only a flickering candle. The storm must have taken down trees and electric lines. There's lightning flashing on all horizons, and the downpour is intensifying. On the one hand, everyone's utterly relieved the endless drought has finally broken! Rain at long last! But water is pouring through the ceiling in numerous places all over the house, and one leak is actually streaming in just above the kitchen table itself.

"Can I at least get a bucket to catch the rain?" Xhosa offers.

"Every bucket, pot, and pan's already in use—all over the house," I say. "Take a candle, and look for yourself!"

There's no point trying to sleep either—our double bed is totally soaked.

It's a dimly lit morning. Now 6:00 a.m. on our intended day of release. I venture out into the mud bath just beyond our kitchen door to check the rain gauge. Over 140 milliliters of torrential rain fell overnight, flooding our ramshackle farmhouse. An urgent message is crackling over the radio from Nelson, warning us that the floodwater took down perimeter fences at river outlets. The Tsau River has burst its banks. Tree trunks thundering down the flooded ravines have upended load-bearing poles embedded in concrete, washing away areas of fence line. Now Nelias's voice is on the radio, informing us the bridge he built nearly fifty years ago for the previous owners, spanning the dry river canyon, has been washed away.

These are unforeseen circumstances, and we immediately have to revise our plan for releasing the pride. Instead, a massive clean-up operation is about to commence. All hands available must assist in reerecting the electrics on the fences, patching the roads, and restoring the infrastructure.

It's Valentine's Day, but the mood is serious and hyperfocused.

Worried that the lions themselves may now be roaming free in the deluge, we urgently need to secure our perimeters. That's Jason's emergency mission. He immediately heads off with his team to temporarily stave up the flattened sections of external fence line. As he pulls out, he instructs Thomas to proceed on foot and join up with Nelson at the flooded river, in order to contact the film crew and inform them of the entirely new game plan. With the electricity down, our radios have run out of charge, which means there's no way of contacting the crew in their camp by the river. There's even the unimaginable possibility that the cameramen have been washed away in the flood! Thomas will check on them urgently, and all being well, his next step will be to rescue the water pump from being washed away at the highwater mark.

My Wellies are up to the ankles in mud, and I am about to climb into the Land Rover in order to head out to the lions and make sure all is well in their *boma.* Mine was the last radio message before our radio power failed, so I am relieved to see Nelias waiting for me en route, as instructed. He'll be able to assist me with the lions, in case of a crisis.

Driving in low range through roads of thick mud, I take care to follow the central route without any detours, as Jason advised. With the dry riverbeds now flooded, many roads are impassable. Most secondary roads I cross en route are rushing like rivers, churning with ruddy topsoil. Sitting beside me with a solemn expression, Nelias is comparing the deluge with his memory of the fifty-year floodline; only, he says, this flood was higher.

I engage the diff lock. With the wheels spinning, I'm just able to traverse a newly gouged trench across our path. Months ago in the midst of the drought, our bush squad started to prepare for the rainy season, laying two-meter-thick gabions under the earth's surface below the fenceline at the river outlets: large submerged "cages" of wire mesh, filled with rocks to ensure they remain immovable in times of flooding. Crossing one of these submerged gabions now, I am relieved to see that our structure has held under the torrent.

Nelias and I are finally at the lions' *boma*, where we see at a glance that both the north and south poles of Marah's camp have blown down. The dense netting we hung as a feeding screen acted as a sail in the blustering overnight winds, pulling the poles out of their foundations. But we are also relieved to see that all of the cats are huddled together in the middle of their fenced area, looking radiant and newly washed down, staring out at us like beacons—perfectly safe and sound. With the weak morning sun shining through, droplets of rain shimmer like multicolored diamonds in their snow-white fur. No problem there!

Not knowing whether the perimeter of our reserve is secured yet, however, it's vital to contain the big cats safely in their *boma*. Jason's original design created two *bomas* joined by a central fence, so I need to get the family into the western *boma* in order for Nelias to restore their fencing poles without incident. I drop Nelias at the central point, where he picks up a heavy metal chain, preparing to tug the central sliding gate closed, as soon as Marah and her cubs follow me through. With this strategy in mind, I drive along the border of their western *boma,* calling to them. Sure enough, the curious cats come bounding over to my vehicle, giving Nelias just the opportunity he needs to close them safely into the western *boma* with a forceful tug of the sliding gate. He then sets about restoring the poles to their vertical position, and I assist him in fixing them in place temporarily with rocks. Unusually, the curious lions don't come to investigate; instead they're frolicking in the interior. After more than eight months of drought, they are clearly celebrating the rains, however destructive these torrents have apparently been to our carefully laid plans.

I need to get back to assess the emergency salvage operations. Driving along slowly, I look out over the sodden landscape. I don't quite yet comprehend why Nature has been so uncooperative. Naturally, the release will have to be postponed until further risk assessment.

Feeling the clay churning up beneath my wheels, I put my foot down on the fuel, carving deeper and deeper into the earth, then lose control as the chassis starts to slip, slide, and finally tilt over into a deep groove. Exasperated, I realize I've gotten us totally stuck! Climbing out, I can see at a glance that the vehicle is so deeply stuck in the mud that it's pointless even trying to dig us out with the spade Jason has secured to the rear door. Instead, Nelias and I have to abandon the Land Rover and begin our long trudge back to camp.

Mud-spattered and still somewhat shamefaced for having gotten our primary vehicle stuck in the mud, I finally arrive back at camp. Cibi and Sam come careering through the wet pools outside the kitchen to meet and greet Nelias and me. I enter the kitchen and see all parties accounted for. I feel ashamed but quickly learn, in fact, that all the other vehicles—the film crew's truck, Jason's other Land Rover, and the tractor—are stuck as well.

We are going to have to call in outside help to get us out of our situation.

Sitting down, exhausted, with a mug of coffee, I know the only solution to get out of the mire is to redefine the parameters completely. The old order simply won't hold. A new world order has to be born. So it strikes me that on one level, the floods are a devastating setback. Our plans have been thwarted yet again. Or so it seems. However, on another level, I am beginning to view this natural occurrence as a positive event, opening the gateway for the lions' freedom.

Having studied signs from Nature through Maria Khosa's inspiring lessons, I appreciate the symbolic meaning behind the floods. The old bridges are gone. The man-made fences have been taken down by Nature. Floodwaters have passed through the Sacred Lands, cleansing everything in their path. All signs indicate that Mother Nature herself has opened The Way for her beloved children of light.

APRIL 8, 2006. EASTER FRIDAY. 9:00 A.M. It's taken just over six weeks to salvage and restore the flood damage. A massive task. But we're back on track. Today, we're finally ready to open the *boma* gates and free the lions. I believed I was ready before, but now I know I have Mother Nature on my side. Everything has changed since the floods. This time, nothing and no one will stop us.

I've pulled the Land Rover in close to the front entrance of the *boma,* alongside the film crew's vehicle, which is optimally positioned for a perfect view of the gates. Jason has provided the lions with a kudu carcass to keep them preoccupied at the far corner of the *boma,* and he's monitoring their activities from the pickup truck.

Around me, the habitat has transformed into lush green foliage, dense with ground cover, unrecognizable from the wasteland that existed before. The savanna is verdant, with the trees full-canopied, and thick grasses have grown through the bleached skeletons, concealing the ravages of the long drought.

We didn't intentionally plan the significance of this date—Easter Friday—we simply found that we were ready and nothing would delay us further. I still don't have the final permit to sanction the step I'm about to take, but I no longer care. I don't need permission to support Mother Nature and protect her sacred White Lions.

"All on track my side," Jason's voice comes over the radio, loud and clear, cool and professional. "Countdown," he instructs.

"Okay, heading for the gates—now," I respond, tremulously pushing open the Land Rover door and climbing out. "Ten, nine, eight, seven, six, five, four . . ." I say into the radio as I walk toward the gates.

Proceeding step by step, undetected by the lions in the far *boma*, I approach the gates, key in hand. My heart's pounding with love and pride, and I don't even attempt to stop the tears streaming down my face. I can feel Mireille's loving presence with me, as if she's here, as always, holding my hand. And Maria, and Ingwavuma.

A few meters away, the cameras are beginning to roll.

"Tell us how you're feeling," a voice instructs through a loudspeaker.

I agreed to Reuters International joining National Geographic for this epic event. I've also allowed my dear friend, Brad Laughlin, to cover the story for personal records, so that we might share this moment with friends and supporters. Brad and Leslie have spent much of the last six weeks with me, generously assisting in every possible way. Today, in order to minimize impact on the lions, the agreement was that all three cameramen cram into one vehicle, together with their equipment. Everyone was very obliging. I've reached the gates now, and I momentarily turn my head to observe them, squeezed into the Nat-Geo army-style Land Cruiser with slots to hold lenses, and no elbow room. It's hot out here in the sun. It must be a roasting oven in there!

"This is the moment I've been waiting for—for five years . . ." I respond.

Turning my full attention on the *boma* gates again, I place the key in the Yale lock, my hand trembling, and I step back. Both *boma* gates swing wide open.

I get back behind the wheel of the Land Rover and wait breathlessly. I'm totally on edge with excitement and anticipation, every nerve ending is wired into the lions' next steps. Once the first White Lion paw places its imprint into freedom on this fateful day, a whole new chapter will begin!

Leslie is sitting expectantly beside me in the passenger seat. A spiritual teacher, she's dedicated many years of her life to refining her metaphysical abilities, and over the lead-up to today's event, Leslie and I often had sat quietly together with the lions, communicating and receiving their telepathic answers. We communicated with them about the challenges they'll face once they're released into their extended natural habitat, focusing our communications on Marah and reminding her of the urgent need to master her hunting techniques, and the dangers she may encounter at the fence lines. We also explained telepathically that these borders are only temporary, and that, as soon as humanly possible, we'll be attempting to expand our natural territories and reclaim more land.

Now, with the gates standing open for the first time, Leslie and I quietly tune in to Marah, conveying what she may expect once she leaves the safety of the *boma*.

"Zihra heading in your direction!" Jason's voice crackles through the radio, unable to mask his own excitement.

From my position, Zihra's been out of sight until now, but I suddenly catch sight of her sleek, lynx-like figure through the binoculars, emerging from the farthest corner of the *boma*, behind the lush grass. She's spotted the open gate! Now she's pussyfooting her way toward the exit, tentatively, casting a backward glance over her shoulder for her mother. The boys are following her, cautiously, heads bobbing up and down with curiosity, and floppy paws lifted high with each step as they follow their sister's lead through the long grass. Through the binoculars I can see their expressions and swishing tails show pure excitement!

Only Marah's holding back. I don't doubt she knows exactly what's taking place today, so the pressure on her must be absolutely immense. But what's she thinking? Is she having doubts? She needs sanction from no one, so why's she waiting?

By definition, a leader doesn't follow. A true leader takes the first step into the unknown, without guarantees, without official mandate, without road maps to follow—only her heart and inner knowledge of fairness and justice. There are no guarantees. Knowing full well the weight of responsibility in charting the first steps into the unknown, a leader takes these steps regardless. She doesn't wait for human consciousness to be approving or condoning; she takes consciousness with her as she courageously breaks new ground on behalf of humanity. That's the nature of leadership.

I look deep into the distant reaches of the *boma* through my binoculars, searching for my adored lioness. She's entirely out of sight, but Jason on the far side reports by radio that she's making no sign of wanting to leave her captive quarters. He says she has one paw on the kudu carcass, her head facing forward, poised in a classic sphinx position.

Meanwhile, Zihra's continuing her intrepid mission toward the open gate, her brothers following her lead! Zihra doesn't know fear. She's all bright-eyed and swishy-tailed. By contrast, her mother is intimately familiar with the darkness that lies in the heart of humanity; it's the cross Marah has to bear.

Putting myself in Marah's position, a shadow suddenly crosses my own vision. Are there dangers beyond these gates, known to the Queen, which I can't even comprehend? I shudder and focus on the positive. She's divinely appointed and divinely protected. The Queen will choose her own timing.

For her innocent cubs, the Big Moment has arrived! They've actually stepped beyond the threshold, out into their new world! Zihra first, then Letaba, then, a little behind, Regeus. They're about to saunter down the grassy path toward a mapane thicket, but realizing their mother isn't following, all three turn around and head back for her.

They resist entering the *boma* again and instead circle outside the enclosure and walk down the full length of the northern border to find her.

In the far distance, I can just see them peering in at their mother.

They must be making low guttural sounds of encouragement,

because I hear Jason's voice explaining through the radio: "Cubs calling. . . . Marah's returned to the carcass. . . . Doesn't look like there's much left to eat, but she's hanging on to it anyway."

From the moment Marah steps out of the confinement of the *boma,* she'll be expected to provide not only for herself, but also for her fast-growing offspring. These are some of the practical challenges that have worried Jason all along.

Without ever having interacted with the wild, without any natural training from her own mother (from whom she was forcibly removed at birth), how can Marah possibly reclaim the laws of the bushveld?

My heart's aching for her. I feel what she herself must be experiencing, acutely. Just knowing a few of the challenges, I would be hanging onto that carcass for dear life too!

"She's looking up now," Jason's voice comes through the radio, "and she's moving in the direction of the cubs."

In the far distance, I pick out the gracious figure of Marah for the first time, her royal head raised above the high grass. Her eyes are fixed on the open gate, then beyond the gate, to the film crew's vehicle with its lenses aimed at her.

Taking another look at the filming vehicle—from Marah's perspective—I have no difficulty understanding her reticence. All I see are the long-lens high-definition TV cameras pointing out of the camera portals, like a row of machine guns. In an unlikely flash of comparison, I suddenly have a vision of Princess Diana, and how the paparazzi hounded this royal, never more than in those last moments of freedom. This morning, it seemed rather unsympathetic of me to enforce the restriction on all three cameramen in one cramped vehicle roasting in the sun, like a can of sardines. However, watching and experiencing Marah's hesitation, I'm now regretting that I allowed camera crews at all.

These are all highly professional and dedicated cameramen, and sensitive to the issues. So I radio them now and ask them to pull the vehicle back a distance away from the gate, to give the Lion Queen her space. I know they'll do this willingly, and I watch the vehicle start up and pull back behind an apple leaf tree.

Even so, Marah still holds back. Jason reports she's returned to the carcass and is gnawing the last unfinished scraps. I can imagine the trepidation she's feeling, and both Leslie and I concentrate on giving her encouragement, telepathically.

In response, we both receive the same telepathic message: "What if I fail to hunt in the wild?"

"Don't expect miracles overnight," I try to convey my answer to Marah. "Jason and I are here at all times. All you have to do is to indicate to us whenever you need assistance, and we'll gladly leave a carcass under a tree for you."

"And if I fail? The world's watching me."

"You won't fail, Queen Marah," I respond. "Every step you take is a success—we know you're restoring order to chaos."

These are strange words of response that come to me, but I know them to be true.

The hunting is, after all, just a formality in returning Marah to her natural condition. We must not forget that the Lion Queen will make this epic transition back to her natural world in her own unique way and on her own terms.

She's back in sight now through my binoculars, and I'm relieved to see her whole disposition looks calmer. Finally, she summons her composure. Serenely, she walks straight out of her captive enclosure with her head held high, a queen to the very last, looking neither left nor right, but straight as a laser. Watching her from outside, the cubs are literally leaping for joy! She steps out over the threshold, and they follow, one by one, bounding after their royal mother into the dense bushveld.

I allow myself the deepest sigh of relief.

A new era has begun: Dawn of the White Lions!

Hennie Hoffman

LINDA TUCKER grew up in South Africa during Apartheid and attended the universities of Cape Town and Cambridge. In 2002, she founded the Global White Lion Protection Trust, a nonprofit community conservation organization that works not only to protect the white lions, but also to conserve the knowledge of the Tsonga and Sepedi cultures, which celebrate the white lion as a sacred living heritage. She has been a guest speaker at multiple international conservation congresses, and her work has been featured in documentaries produced by National Geographic and CBS. She lives in Tsau White Lion Heartland, a protected wilderness area neighboring the Timbavati Private Nature Reserve, with her partner, lion ecologist Jason Turner, and the white lion prides they have reintroduced to their ancestral lands.